NOLO® Products & Services

➡ Books & Software

Get in-depth information. Nolo publishes hundreds of great books and software programs for consumers and business owners. They're all available in print or as downloads at Nolo.com.

➡ Legal Encyclopedia

Free at Nolo.com. Here are more than 1,400 free articles and answers to common questions about everyday legal issues including wills, bankruptcy, small business formation, divorce, patents, employment and much more.

➡ Plain-English Legal Dictionary

Free at Nolo.com. Stumped by jargon? Look it up in America's most up-to-date source for definitions of legal terms.

➡ Online Legal Documents

Create documents at your computer. Go online to make a will or living trust, form an LLC or corporation or obtain a trademark or provisional patent at Nolo.com. For simpler matters, download one of our hundreds of high-quality legal forms, including bills of sale, promissory notes, nondisclosure agreements and many more.

➡ Lawyer Directory

Find an attorney at Nolo.com. Nolo's unique lawyer directory provides in-depth profiles of lawyers all over America. From fees and experience to legal philosophy, education and special expertise, you'll find all the information you need to pick a lawyer who's a good fit.

➡ Free Legal Updates

Keep up to date. Check for free updates at Nolo.com. Under "Products," find this book and click "Legal Updates." You can also sign up for our free e-newsletters at Nolo.com/newsletters/index.html.

NOLO®   The Trusted Name
(but don't take our word for it)

"*In Nolo you can trust.*"
THE NEW YORK TIMES

"*Nolo is always there in a jam as the nation's premier publisher of do-it-yourself legal books.*"
NEWSWEEK

"*Nolo publications…guide people simply through the how, when, where and why of the law.*"
THE WASHINGTON POST

"*[Nolo's]…material is developed by experienced attorneys who have a knack for making complicated material accessible.*"
LIBRARY JOURNAL

"*When it comes to self-help legal stuff, nobody does a better job than Nolo…*"
USA TODAY

"*The most prominent U.S. publisher of self-help legal aids.*"
TIME MAGAZINE

"*Nolo is a pioneer in both consumer and business self-help books and software.*"
LOS ANGELES TIMES

18th edition

California Tenants' Rights

by Attorneys Janet Portman & David Brown

Eighteenth Edition	MARCH 2010
Editors	JANET PORTMAN
Book Design	TERRI HEARSH
Cover Design	SUSAN PUTNEY
Proofreading	JIM BRUCE
Index	ELLEN SHERRON
Printing	DELTA PRINTING SOLUTIONS, INC.

Portman, Janet.
   California tenants' rights / Janet Portman & David Brown. -- 18th ed.
      p. cm.
   Includes index.
   ISBN-13: 978-1-4133-0936-2 (pbk.)
   ISBN-10: 1-4133-0936-4 (pbk.)
   1. Landlord and tenant--California--Popular works. I. Brown, David. II. Title.
   KFC145.P67 2010
   346.79404'34--dc22
                              2008041609

Please note

We believe accurate, plain-English legal information should help you solve many of
your own legal problems. But this text is not a substitute for personalized advice
from a knowledgeable lawyer. If you want the help of a trained professional—and
we'll always point out situations in which we think that's a good idea—consult an
attorney licensed to practice in your state.

Acknowledgments

California Tenants' Rights is one of Nolo's earliest books, first published in 1972. Since then, it has helped countless California renters learn and assert their rights. We wish to acknowledge the contributions of its original authors, Jake Warner, Nolo's founder; Myron Moskovitz and Ed Sherman, coauthors; and the many editors and updaters who worked on the book over the years.

Table of Contents

California Tenants' Rights: Your Legal Companion

What do you do when your landlord refuses to fix the leaky roof, reneges on a promised parking space, or threatens you with eviction? You might be merely annoyed by the discomfort or inconvenience, or intimidated by the fear of losing your home, but in any case you're probably unsure of your rights under the law.

This book is the answer. California tenants enjoy some of the most innovative and thoughtful landlord-tenant protections in the country, but to take advantage of them, you need to know what they are. Here you'll learn the bottom line on your rights as a renter, including privacy, adequate notice of rent increases and terminations, repairs, fair housing, anti-retaliation protection, and more.

You'll learn about your responsibilities, too. For example, if your landlord won't perform important repairs, you have the right to withhold rent payments—but only if you're current on the rent. If you don't understand your legal responsibilities, you might lose out on the legal remedies at your disposal.

The second half of this book is devoted to eviction defense, which will help you if you've been handed a termination notice and have to decide—quickly—what to do next. Should you fight the eviction or just move out? It's not always an easy decision, and there's always emotion involved.

Even if you win, the toll on your time, energy, and wallet will be significant. And winning is never a sure thing, even if you're sure you have a solid legal defense and can prove it. All bets are off once you turn your fate over to a judge or jury. If you lose, you'll have an eviction on your record, which may make it very hard to rent another place to live. It's not illegal for landlords to flatly refuse to rent to people who have ever been evicted, and many do just that.

If you do decide to fight the eviction, we'll guide you through the court process and show you where to get the official forms, how to fill them out, and where to file them. Having represented countless tenants in court, we'll share with you the benefit of our experience, from where to stand to what to say—and not say.

If you live in one of the California cities (there are about 15) that offer tenants the benefits of rent control or eviction defense ordinances, you're lucky—you have greater rights than people who rent elsewhere in the Golden State. For example, many rent control ordinances require landlords to pay interest on security deposits, though state law does not. You'll find helpful summaries of these local laws, along with information on how to find the ordinances themselves online (they change frequently) and how to contact the agencies in charge of enforcing them.

Armed with the information in this book, you can confidently negotiate with your landlord when you sign a lease or rental agreement, knowing what's what in the way of permissible lease terms. Later, as your tenancy continues, you'll know what you can legally expect from the landlord—and how to enforce your rights if you need to.

Good luck and good landlords!

Guide to Abbreviations
Used in This Book

We use these standard abbreviations throughout this book for important statutes and court cases covering tenants' rights.

California Codes

B&P	Business and Professions
CC	Civil
CCP	Civil Procedure
UHC	Uniform Housing Code
H&S	Health and Safety
CCR	California Code of Regulations

Federal Laws

U.S.C.	United States Code
C.F.R.	Code of Federal Regulations

Cases

Cal.App.	California Court of Appeal
Cal.Rptr.	California Court of Appeal and California Supreme Court
Cal.	California Supreme Court
N.J. Spr.	New Jersey Superior Court Reports
A. or A.2d	Atlantic Reporter
S.E. or S.E.2d	South Eastern Reporter
F. Supp.	United States District Court
F.2d	United States Court of Appeal
U.S.	United States Supreme Court

Opinions

Ops. Cal. Atty. Gen.	California Attorney General Opinions

Looking for a Place and Renting It

Looking for a house or apartment to rent is often a frustrating and time-consuming task. Since it is human nature to become harried and frazzled under pressure, many mistakes are made at this stage that later turn out to be costly, both in time and money. Try to stay cool.

Get Organized

Before you start looking for a place, decide:
- how much you can afford to pay
- what your space and living needs are
- how long you plan on staying, and
- what sort of area you want to live in.

Be realistic both as to your budget and as to what is available, and set definite guidelines in advance. If you can't find a place that meets your guidelines, don't change them without taking time to think the matter over carefully. Some of the worst and most costly mistakes are made by people who sign a lease or put down a deposit at the end of a long, frustrating day only to realize later that the place is unsuitable.

It is extremely important that you keep good records. As part of your getting organized, get a large manila envelope or file folder in which to keep all papers having to do with your rental transaction. Misplacing and losing papers (deposit agreements, leases, rent receipts, and so on) is a common mistake that should be avoided. Your landlord is in business and has probably learned how not to make such basic mistakes, so you should do the same. Set up a safe place in which to save your papers, receipts, canceled checks, and anything else that you think might possibly be important at a later time.

If you have trouble finding a place, you may get help from a "homefinding service." Some do a good job of trying to help people find a place to rent, but some are sloppy, and a few are actually crooked. For example, several homefinding services have been caught running ads about imaginary apartments in good locations at low rents, only to tell people who show up, "We just rented that one, but here's another one"—at a higher rent—"you will really like." Another problem is that companies often sell rental lists that are so outdated that most or all of the apartments have been rented. In other words, do a little investigating (for example, talk to some other home-seekers or check with the Better Business Bureau) before you pay anyone to help you find a home. If you feel an apartment locator service has seriously misrepresented its service, ask for your money back and file a complaint with the Consumer Fraud Division of your local district attorney's office.

Make a list of your housing needs and priorities before you start looking for a place to rent. Here are examples of items to consider when choosing an apartment or other rental:

Price Range: Jot down how much you can afford to spend on rent, including utilities.

Location: If you know what city or neighborhood you want to live in, list it. If you want to live close to a skiing, hiking, or surfing site, note that also. Be as specific as possible about where you want to live.

Rooms and Interior Features: Note the number, sizes, and types of rooms you want. List the number of bedrooms and bathrooms, as well as their specific features. For example, if you must have two bathrooms, specify whether you need two full bathrooms or one full and one half. List any other rooms you'd like, such as a separate dining room, a family room, a finished basement, a separate home office, or a space for your washer and dryer. Be as detailed as possible about your housing needs. If sunny rooms, air conditioning, a modern kitchen, and lots of storage are important, include them on your list. You might also be concerned about noisy neighbors. Ask the landlord or manager if there have been complaints about the neighbors.

Security: Depending on the crime rate in the area you are looking at, you may want to rent in a building with a front gate security system. This type of system allows you to screen visitors at the front gate to the building before they actually get to the front door of your residence.

Pets: If you own a pet, you will want to find out whether the landlord allows pets.

Yard and Exterior Features: If you like to garden or need a yard for your dog, put this on your list along with details on the size or type of yard.

Parking: Parking can be a critical consideration if you are planning to live in a city. Write down how many motor vehicles you have and what type of parking you will need, such as garage parking or easy street parking with no restrictions. The crime and vandalism rate in your area will also determine what kind of parking you want.

Neighborhood Features: This category covers a lot and should be considered carefully. Neighborhood features you may be concerned about include low crime rates; walking distance to book stores, shops, or parks; low-traffic streets; lots of families with small children; quiet neighborhoods; limited access communities; or senior citizen housing. If you have or plan to have school-age children, the proximity to and the quality of local schools will be very important considerations.

Work or School Commute: Consider the maximum times and distances you are willing to travel to and from work or school by car or public transit. If you want to walk or bike to work or school, note that here. If you want to commute by public transit, check out the nearest bus or train stops and lines.

Learn About Rental Agreements

Before you start looking for a place, you should know a little about rental agreements. First—the most important rule—don't sign any papers until you understand what's in them, or you may regret it later!

Landlords rent their properties using one of these methods:

- a written lease
- a written rental agreement, or
- an oral lease or rental agreement.

An oral lease or rental agreement is made without anything being written down—you just talk over what the deal is and agree to it. The other two, the written lease and the written rental agreement, have all the terms you agree to written down on a paper, which you and the landlord sign. Let's look at each in some detail.

Oral Agreements

It is perfectly legal to make a deal orally—that is, without writing anything down, and without signatures—as long as it covers a year or less. (If the oral agreement is for over a year, it is not enforceable by a court after the first year.) The landlord agrees to let you move in, and you agree to pay a certain amount of rent on some schedule, like weekly, every other week, or every month.

The oral agreement has some advantages: It is relatively informal, and you aren't subjected to the long list of terms and rules contained in most written leases and rental contracts. However, if you want the clarity of having everything written down, you will probably want your deal in writing.

Oral agreements are legal and enforceable for up to one year. But even short of a year, as time goes by and circumstances change, people's memories can change, too. Then, if something goes wrong, both sides end up in front of a judge who has to decide whose recollection of the agreement to believe. For this reason, even if you make an oral agreement, it is wise to get some of the landlord's promises in writing. For example, if your landlord promises to make specific repairs, allow you to have a pet, or do anything else that you want to make sure the landlord remembers, write it down and have the landlord date and sign it.

Written Leases and Rental Agreements

The written lease and rental agreement are basically the same except for one important difference. The lease fixes all the terms of the agreement so that no changes can be made for a given period of time—

most commonly, one year. If you rent under a lease, your rent cannot be raised until the lease runs out, nor can you be told to move unless you break the terms of the lease. You, too, are expected to perform your obligations under the lease (including rent payments) until it runs out.

The written rental agreement—often called a "month-to-month" agreement—has everything written down, just like the lease, but the time period of your tenancy is indefinite. The agreement self-renews every month until you or the landlord terminate it. This means that you can move out or your landlord can raise your rent or order you to move out on 30 days' notice (sometimes 60). However, if your landlord raises the rent more than 10% of the lowest rent charged within the previous 12 months, the landlord must give you 60 days' notice. And if you're renting under a government-subsidized program, you're entitled to 90 days' notice before the landlord can terminate your tenancy. See "Rent Increase Notices" in Chapter 3 for a full explanation of these rules. Also, in certain communities that have rent control laws, landlords must show "just cause" to evict. (See Chapter 3 for a list of cities with just cause eviction provisions and Chapter 14 for details on termination.)

Except for these very important differences, leases and written rental agreements are so much alike that they are sometimes hard to tell apart. Both of them cover the basic terms of rental (names, addresses, amount of rent and date due, deposits, and so on), and both of them tend to have a lot of other fine-print provisions to protect the landlord.

Be careful! Since they look so much alike, some forms can look like a lease, and sound like a lease, and even cover a year's period, but if they contain a provision that rent can be raised or that the agreement can be terminated on 30 days' notice (or 60 days for tenants who have been in the rental for a year or more; 90 days for subsidized tenancies), then they are really only written rental agreements.

Read it carefully! It is crucial that you read the entire lease or rental agreement and understand it before you sign it. If the main document refers to another document such as "house rules," make sure you read a copy of these, too. If there is any part of the written document that you don't understand, get advice—but not from the people who want you to sign it. If you want your rights protected, you will have to see to it yourself.

Legally, a written agreement can be typed or written down in longhand on any kind of paper, in any words, so long as the terms are legible. However, as a practical matter, nearly all landlords use standard printed forms that they buy in stationery stores or get from landlord associations. These forms have been prepared by lawyers or real estate associations, and they are usually as favorable as possible to the landlord. These forms need not look like death certificates, nor read like acts of Congress, but such is often the case. Some of the worst ones include clauses requiring you to waive your privacy, accept shorter-than-normal notice periods for rent increases and termination, accept responsibility for fixing things that should be handled by your landlord, and generally leave you in a very vulnerable position. We discuss the common provisions and tell you some things to watch out for below.

If the lease offered to you by the prospective landlord is not satisfactory, it is legal and simple to change it if both parties can agree on the changes. All you do is cross out unwanted portions, write in desired changes, and have all parties who are going to sign the document initial the changes. Make sure that you sign the lease at the same time as the landlord, and that you get a copy then and there. This assures both sides that no changes can be made after only one party has signed.

If a lease or month-to-month rental agreement is negotiated primarily in Spanish, Chinese, Tagalog, Vietnamese, or Korean, then the landlord must give the tenant a written translation of the lease or rental agreement before it is signed. The only exception is if the tenant provides his or her own interpreter, who can fluently read and write English and the foreign language, and who is not a minor. (CC § 1632.)

RESOURCE

Nolo publishes California-specific lease and rental agreement forms. These are fair to both landlord and tenant. If your landlord doesn't have a written rental agreement, or proposes using a substandard one, offer Nolo's instead. Go to www.nolo.com and search for "The California Landlord's Law Book: Rights and Responsibilities," by David Brown, Ralph Warner, and Janet Portman. The rental documents are available as tear outs and on the book's CD-ROM.

Typical Provisions in Leases and Rental Agreements

Your lease or rental agreement may be as short as one page or longer than ten. It may be typed or handwritten, easy to understand, or full of legalese. Most landlords use preprinted forms they buy in stationery stores, order from a landlords' association, or find in a software program.

Most leases and rental agreements contain "the usual suspects" of rental provisions or clauses. You'll often see them as numbered paragraphs. Unfortunately, the provisions are often dressed up in fancy legal language or buried in gargantuan sentences. This section offers plain meanings for the most common terms you'll find in a lease.

Names and Addresses of Landlord and Tenants

The tenant may be referred to as the "lessee" and the landlord as the "lessor." They may also be called the "parties" to the agreement. If a property manager or company is authorized to receive notices and legal papers on the landlord's behalf, you should also see that name and address.

Learning the Name of the Owner

In the past, some owners have instructed their managers not to tell the tenants who they were or where they could be located, so the tenant could not "bother" them. State law tries to solve this problem. It provides that:

- The rental agreement must state the name and address of both the manager and the owner (or person authorized by him to receive notices, demands, and lawsuits against the owner). This information must be kept current, with the tenant being informed of all changes, or,
- Instead of putting this information in each rental agreement, the owner may choose to post notices containing the same information in the building. A notice must be posted in at least two easy-to-see places (including all elevators). (CC §§ 1962 and 1962.5.)

If the owner fails to follow this law, then the person who rented the dwelling for the owner automatically becomes his agent for receiving notices, demands, and lawsuits.

Landlords typically want all adults who will live in the premises, including both members of a couple, to sign the lease or rental agreement. Chapter 12 provides complete details on the legal responsibilities of tenants and cotenants and related issues such as adding a new roommate. "Families With Children and Overcrowding" in Chapter 4, discusses occupancy limits that may restrict who lives in the rental unit.

Rental Property Address and Details

The property address is often called "the premises." Your lease or rental agreement may also include details on any furnishings, parking space, storage areas, or other extras that come with the rental property.

Term of the Tenancy

The term is the length of the rental. The document should include the beginning date and whether it's a month-to-month tenancy or a lease. If it's a lease, the ending date should also be specified. Leases often have a term of one year. The important differences between leases and rental agreements are discussed above. Chapter 14 explains how tenancies end.

Rent

Leases and rental agreements usually specify the amount of rent due each month, when and where it's due, acceptable forms of payment, and late fees. Chapter 3 covers rent rules in detail.

Deposits and Fees

Expect to see details on the dollar amount of a security deposit and/or last month's rent. Chapter 13 explains state laws that govern the use and return of security deposits and why it's important to know your landlord's cleaning and maintenance requirements.

Utilities

The landlord should state who pays for what utilities. Normally, landlords pay for garbage and sometimes for water, if there is a yard. Tenants usually pay for other services, such as phone, gas, and electricity. If tenants will share gas or electric meters (where, for example, a tenant's meter also services a common area, or where one meter measures more than one rental's use), the rental document must disclose this, and how charges will be allocated. (CC § 1940.9.)

Condition of the Rental Unit

Most leases and rental agreements include a clause in which you agree that the premises are in habitable (livable) condition and you promise to alert the landlord to any defective or dangerous condition. Chapters 6 and 7 covers tenants'

important rights and responsibilities regarding repair and maintenance.

Inspect Before You Sign

Always inspect the rental unit before you sign a lease or rental agreement. Think (and look) carefully before signing off on a clause that states that the rental is in fine shape. Look for damage, dirt, mildew, pest or rodent problems, and obvious wear and tear. Write down (be as specific as possible) both serious problems, such as a broken heater or leaking roof, and minor flaws such as a stained kitchen counter, dirty drapes, or faded paint. Back up your written statement with photographs.

As much as possible, try to get your landlord to fix problems before you move in. Write down any agreement in a letter of understanding as described in "Get It In Writing," below.

Keeping tabs on the condition of the rental at move-in is an excellent way to protect yourself when it comes time to move out and get your security deposit returned. Without good proof of the condition of the premises at the start of the tenancy, your landlord may keep all or part of your deposit, claiming you left the place filthy or damaged it—for example, stained the rug, cracked the bathroom mirror, or left behind a broken garbage disposal. Your initial inspection (and photos) will establish that the problems existed at the start of the tenancy and are not your fault. Chapter 13 discusses how to avoid disputes over security deposits at move-out time.

Tenant's Repair and Maintenance Responsibilities

A carefully written lease or rental agreement will include a statement that makes you responsible for keeping the rental premises clean and in good condition and obligates you to reimburse the landlord for the cost of repairing damage caused by your abuse or neglect. Some agreements go further and spell out specific tenant responsibilities, such as fixing clogged drains or broken windows. Many leases and rental agreements also tell you what you can't do in the way of repairs—such as painting walls or adding built-in bookshelves without the landlord's permission. Chapter 6 covers important tenant rights and responsibilities regarding repairs and maintenance, and your options if your landlord fails to provide habitable housing.

When and How Landlords May Enter Your Rental Unit

California law specifies when landlords may legally enter rented premises—for example, to deal with an emergency or make repairs—and the amount of notice required. Some landlords include this information in the lease or rental agreement. Others are ignorant of these laws and write entry provisions that are illegal. Chapter 5 covers the landlord's right to enter rental property and tenant privacy rights.

Extended Absences

Some leases and rental agreements require you to notify the landlord in advance if you will be away from the premises for a certain number of consecutive days (often seven or more). Such clauses may give the landlord the right to enter the rental unit during your absence to maintain the property as necessary and to inspect for damage and needed repairs. You'll most often see this type of clause if you live in a cold-weather place where, in case of extremely cold temperatures, landlords want to drain the pipes to guard against breakage.

Limits on Your Behavior

Most form leases and rental agreements contain a clause forbidding you from using the premises or adjacent areas, such as the sidewalk in front of the building, in such a way as to violate any law or ordinance, including laws prohibiting the use, possession, or sale of illegal drugs. These clauses also prohibit you from intentionally damaging the property or creating a nuisance by annoying or disturbing other tenants or nearby residents—for example, by continuously making loud noise. Leases and rental agreements may prohibit smoking, in individual units as well as in common areas.

Restrictions on Number of Occupants

Most landlords will set a limit to the number of people who can live in each rental unit. Landlords are not free to set unreasonably low figures (for example, two people for a two-bedroom flat) in order to maintain a "quiet atmosphere" or to reduce wear and tear. State law requires landlords to allow two persons per bedroom plus one more, unless the landlord can point to legitimate business reasons that justify a lower number (this is difficult to do).

Restrictions on Use of the Property

Landlords may throw in all kinds of language limiting your use of the rental property and who may stay there. These may be minor (for example, no plants on wood floors or bikes in the hallway) or quite annoying. These may be in a separate set of rules and regulations or individual clauses. Basically, your landlords can set any kind of restriction they want, as long as it's not discriminatory or retaliatory or otherwise violates state law. Some common restrictions involving pets, home businesses, sublets, and guests are discussed below.

No Pets

Your landlord has the right to prohibit all pets, or to restrict the types allowed—for example, forbidding dogs or cats, but allowing birds. However, a landlord may not prohibit "service" or "comfort" animals used by physically or mentally disabled people, as provided by the fair housing laws. Many landlords spell out pet rules—for example, that the tenants will keep the yard free of all animal waste or that dogs will always be on leash.

No Home Businesses

Landlords may prohibit you from running a business from your home, by including a clause specifying that the premises are "for residential purposes only." The concern here is generally about increased traffic and liability exposure if one of your customers or business associates is hurt on the premises. Obviously, working at home on your computer is not likely to bother your landlord, and may not even be noticed.

If you want to run a day care operation in your rented home, your landlord cannot flatly prohibit it. (H & S § 1597.40.) You must be licensed, and part of that process will involve an on-site inspection, to determine whether the physical space comports with minimum requirements under state law. (2001 California Building Code, California Code of Regulations, Title 24, Part 2, Volume 1.)

No Assignments or Sublets Without Landlord Permission

Most careful landlords will not let you turn your rental over to another tenant (called "assignment"), let someone live there for a limited time while you're away (called a "sublet"), or let you rent an extra bedroom to another occupant, with you as the "landlord" (also called a sublet), without their written consent.

Limits on Guest Stays

It's common for landlords to limit overnight guests, such as allowing a guest for no more than ten days in any six-month period, with written approval required for longer stays. Landlords do this to keep long-term guests from gaining the status of full-fledged tenants who have not been screened or approved and who have not signed the lease or rental agreement.

Megan's Law Database

Every written lease or rental agreement must include a specific paragraph that tells tenants about the statewide database containing the names of registered sexual offenders. Members of the public may view the state's Department of Justice website to see whether a certain individual is on the list (www.meganslaw.ca.gov).

Disclosures Required by Law

In addition to disclosures described above, California requires landlords to make the following disclosures, either in the rental document or elsewhere:

- **Location near a former military base.** Landlords must tell you if the property is within a mile of an abandoned or closed military base in which ammunition or explosives were stored. (CC § 1940.7.)
- **Periodic and other pest control.** Landlords who have periodic pest control must inform tenants about the frequency of treatments. (CC § 1940.8.)
- **Intentions to demolish the rental.** If the landlord has applied for a demolition permit, it must inform tenants. (CC § 1940.6(a)(1)(D).)
- **Lead paint.** All landlords must give tenants the federal form, "Disclosure of Information on Lead-Based Paint or Lead-Based Paint Hazards," and inform tenants of the known presence of lead paint.
- **Mold.** Landlords who know of the presence of mold in a rental must inform tenants. (H & S § 26147.)

Attorney Fees and Court Costs in a Lawsuit

Many leases and rental agreements specify who will pay the costs of a lawsuit if you go to court over the meaning or implementation of a part of your rental agreement or lease—for example, a dispute about rent or security deposits. These clauses do not apply to legal disputes that arise independently of the lease or rental agreement—for example, lawsuits over alleged discrimination. By law in California, judges will apply these clauses "both ways," even when they're not written that way. In other words, a clause that specifies that a losing tenant will pay a winning landlord's fees and costs (but doesn't say that a winning tenant will get paid by the landlord) will work the other way too if the tenant wins. (CC § 1717.)

Grounds for Termination of Tenancy

You'll often see a general clause stating that any violation of the lease or rental agreement by you, or by your guests, is grounds for terminating the tenancy according to the procedures established by state or local laws.

Lease Terms: What to Watch Out For

Some leases and rental agreements contain provisions that are illegal and therefore unenforceable. When it comes to these provisions, think about whether to use your bargaining power by trying to get the landlord to scratch them out. You may want to mention that these provisions are illegal, in order to show the landlord how one-sided the agreement is, and then ask the landlord to eliminate or change other (enforceable) provisions.

Provision That the Landlord Is Not Responsible for Damage and Injuries

This provision says that if the landlord is negligent in maintaining the place and you, your family or guests are injured, or your property is damaged (for example, if someone falls down broken stairs), the landlord is not responsible for paying for your losses. This is called an "exculpatory" provision. Under state law, such a provision is invalid. (CC § 1953.)

Provision Making Tenant Responsible for Repairs

This provision requires you, the tenant, repair or maintain the premises. This provision does not relieve the landlord of the legal obligation to see that the place complies with the housing codes and the duty to maintain a fit and habitable rental.

Provision Waiving Your Self-Help Repair Rights

California tenants have the right, in certain circumstances, to make necessary repairs and deduct the cost from the rent; and to withhold rent until the landlord accomplishes the repair (these remedies, known as "repair and deduct," and "rent withholding," are explained in detail in Chapter 6). A lease provision that purports to waive these rights will not be enforced by a judge.

Waiver of Right to Legal Notice

This provision says the landlord can sue to evict you or can raise the rent or change the terms of the lease without giving notice (such as a three-day notice to pay your rent or vacate) required by law. It is not valid. (CC § 1953.)

Provision Setting Notice Period

This provision sets the amount of time the landlord must give you before a notice of termination or rent raise or change in terms becomes operative. If there is no such provision, and you are a month-to-month tenant, the law requires that the landlord give you at least 30 days' notice. (However, see "Rent Increase Notices" in Chapter 3 for exceptions.)

Right to Inspect

Many forms have a provision that gives the landlord the right to come into your place to inspect it, or for other purposes. Under state law, the landlord's right to enter the dwelling is limited to certain reasons, and any attempt to add to these reasons in the lease or rental agreement is void. (CC § 1954.) We discuss your rights to privacy in detail in Chapter 5.

Right of Reentry Provision

This provision permits the landlord to come in and throw you out if you don't pay the rent, without giving you legal notice or going to court. It is not valid. (CC § 1953.)

Waiver of Jury Trial

One variation on this provision says that you waive your right to a trial by jury in any eviction lawsuit brought by the landlord. It is not valid. (CC § 1953.) Similarly, a lease clause in which the tenant agrees that any lawsuit concerning the lease or its implementation will be tried before a judge without a jury is void. (*Grafton Partners LP v. Superior Court (PricewaterhouseCoopers LLP)*, 36 Cal. 4th 944 (2005).)

Keep in mind that you and the landlord may still decide, once litigation has begun, that you will submit the case to a judge and not a jury. But an advance waiver of the right to a jury trial is not a legal option in California. Also, you and the landlord may decide in the rental agreement that future disputes will be submitted to mediation, binding arbitration, or a referee appointed by the court. (*Woodside Homes of California, Inc. v. Superior Court (Kimberly Wheeler)*, 142 Cal. App.4th 99 (2006).)

Waiver of Right to Appeal

This provision prevents you from appealing a court decision in any eviction lawsuit. It is not valid. (CC § 1953.)

Treble Damages

This provision says that if the landlord sues to evict you and wins, he may get not just the actual damages he has suffered (usually unpaid rent), but three times as much. A court will not enforce a clause like this.

Landlord's Attorney Fees

This provision says that if the landlord has to sue to evict you or collect rent and wins, you will pay the landlord's attorney fees. This can amount to hundreds, or even thousands, of dollars. This provision is valid, and the landlord usually cannot get attorney fees unless the lease or rental

agreement has such a provision. Therefore, you may want to ask that it be scratched out. If it stays and you lose your job or your income is otherwise cut off and you can't pay the rent, you risk getting a judgment against you for attorney fees in addition to back rent.

However, you should understand that whenever there is an attorney's fee provision in a lease or written rental agreement, the law says that the attorney's fee provision entitles you to collect your attorney fees from the landlord if you win the lawsuit (in legalese, if you are the "prevailing party"), even if the provision does not say this. (CC § 1717.) For this reason, some tenants actually prefer to have an attorney fees clause—even a seemingly one-sided one—in their written agreement, feeling that if their landlord seriously violates a provision of the agreement and they have to sue, they want to be able to collect their attorney fees.

If the case is dismissed or settles, the law considers that there is no "prevailing party," in which case a one-sided attorney fee clause will not apply both ways. Say, for example, your landlord files an unlawful detainer action against you for non-payment of rent and then dismisses the case when you come up with the rent. You may think that you "won" the case (after all, you were not evicted), but you won't be entitled to attorney fees from your landlord, and you will have to pay his lawyer's bill. When you consider how many cases settle before trial, the comfort of the two-way attorney fees law seems rather lukewarm, and it is something to keep in mind when negotiating your lease.

Late Charges

This provision requires the tenant to pay a "late charge" if the rent is paid late. The charge may be set as a percentage of the rent (such as 4%), a flat charge (such as $10), or a flat charge per day (such as $5 each day the rent is late). (See "Late Charges" in Chapter 3.) This provision will probably survive a court challenge if the amount is a reasonable estimate of the amount the lateness of your payment will cost the landlord—that is, the administrative cost of processing the late payment and the loss of interest on your rent. However, if the charge is higher than this, in an effort to "terrorize" you into paying your rent on time, the charge is probably a "penalty" provision, which is invalid. If the late charge seems suspiciously high to you (for example, a $30 charge on a $300 rent payment late by a few days), ask the landlord to justify it or lower it.

Restrictions on Occupants and Guests

Restrictions on the number of occupants and the length of time guests may stay are common in leases and rental agreements. These are valid so long as they are not arbitrary. The landlord has legitimate interests in seeing that the number of occupants does not get so high that there would be excessive wear on the rental, common areas, and facilities. The landlord also has a legitimate interest in ensuring that new occupants and guests will not be obnoxious people who might disturb other tenants or wreck the place.

These restrictions may not, however, be based on the age, sex, or gender of the occupant or guest. A provision forbidding any overnight guests of the opposite sex of the tenant, for example, is illegal. (CC § 51. See also *Atkisson v. Kern County Housing Authority,* 59 Cal.App.3d 89 (1976).) So would a provision saying, "No overnight guests under 12 years of age." (CC § 51. See also *Marina Point, Ltd. v. Wolfson,* 30 Cal.3d 721 (1982) and "Families With Children and Overcrowding" in Chapter 4.)

Some agreements require the tenant to give the landlord prior notice of overnight guests, or to obtain the landlord's prior consent. These provisions are probably valid, though a provision regarding consent would probably be read to mean that the landlord could not arbitrarily withhold consent. These provisions can be annoying, however, as they allow the landlord to nose into the tenant's private affairs. You might ask the landlord to write in something like, "This restriction shall apply only to overnight guests who stay more than five nights in any 30-day period."

Family Day Care Homes

Under state law (H&S § 1597.40), a landlord may not forbid a tenant's use of rental premises as a licensed family day care home. If you obtain a state license to run a family day care home, you may do so legally—regardless of whether your lease or rental agreement prohibits the operation of a business on the premises or limits the number of occupants. Local zoning and occupancy limits also don't apply to a state-licensed family day care home. If you want to run a family day care home, you must notify your landlord in writing of your intent, after having first obtained a state license, 30 days in advance of starting the child care operation.

Requiring the Tenant to Give Notice on a Specific Day

Some landlords want month-to-month tenants to give tenancy termination notices on a specific day of the month, typically the last day. Under this scheme, a termination notice delivered on any other day won't take effect until the last day of the month, which means that a tenant who gives a 30-day notice on, say, the tenth, will in effect be giving 50 days' notice (because the landlord won't recognize it until the 30th of that month). The tenant can, of course, vacate at any time, but the landlord will argue that it is entitled to rent for the entire 50-day period. Typically, the landlord will deduct the unpaid rent from the security deposit.

No California statute or case directly addresses whether requiring notice on a specific day of the month is legal. We think that it is unlikely that a court would uphold such a requirement, especially if the rule applies to tenants only (that is, where *the landlord* remains free to deliver a 30-day notice at any time, and the 30 days begins as of the day of his delivery). Even when the limitation applies to both parties however, its legality is iffy, because the provision has the effect of modifying the landlord's proper use of the security deposit (C.C. § 1950.5), which is unenforceable. In addition, the notice statute currently does not address whether the landlord can modify the 30- and 60-day rules in this manner. (C.C. §1946.1.) This statute replaced the older C.C. § 1946, which *did* allow landlords to shorten the notice period to as little as seven days; by implication, the new law's omission of this short-notice option means that the Legislature intended that no variations on the rules would be allowed. Though it may be convenient for landlords to deal with tenant turnover on the day rent is due and avoid having to pro-rate rent (and though the prospect of requiring that rent be paid over an extended period is attractive), we think that requiring notice to be delivered only on the date rent is due would not be upheld in court.

Opening Landlords' Doors to Pets

Project Open Door, a San Francisco Society for the Prevention of Cruelty to Animals (SPCA) program, offers pet-owning tenants helpful materials on how to negotiate with a landlord. The SPCA also offers landlords:

- checklists to help screen pet-owning tenants
- model policies for tenants with dogs or cats
- model agreements to add to standard leases and rental agreements, and
- free mediation if landlords and tenants have problems after moving in.

For more information, contact the San Francisco SPCA at 2500 16th Street, San Francisco, CA 94103, 415-554-3000.

Provision Restricting Water-Filled Furniture

If the building where you rent was built after 1973, it is not legal for a landlord to ban water-filled furniture. A landlord may, however, require you to have $100,000 of liability insurance to cover potential damage and meet other requirements specified by law. (Chapter 15 discusses renter's insurance.) For property built before 1973, a landlord may legally refuse to allow waterbeds. (CC § 1940.5.)

Liquidated Damages Provision

Occasionally, a lease includes a "liquidated damages" clause. Such a clause says that if you move out before the lease expires, you are supposed to pay the landlord a certain amount of money (damages) for the losses caused by your early departure. Usually, landlords set the amount of liquidated damages at several hundred dollars, or announce that you will forfeit your entire security deposit.

If you think that sounds unfair, you're right. As is discussed in Chapter 12, if you move out before your lease expires, you are legally responsible to pay the landlord only for the actual losses you cause. The landlord is legally obligated to minimize those losses by trying to find a new tenant to replace you as soon as possible. Why should the landlord, who didn't lose any money when you moved out, get a windfall?

Courts don't look kindly on liquidated damages, either. If the amount of liquidated damages far exceeds the landlord's actual damages, a judge will probably rule that you don't have to pay them. Of course, it takes time and trouble to go to court to get your money (the security deposit) back, so it's better to get a clause like this crossed out of the lease before you sign it.

Cash Rent

Your lease or rental agreement may not demand that you pay the rent in cash. (CC § 1947.3.) Landlords may demand cash rent only after you've given them a check that bounces, or a money order or cashier's check whose issuer has been told to stop payment. Even then, the demand for cash rent may last only three months.

The "Crime Free Lease Addendum"

Your lease or rental agreement may include a lengthy attachment called a "Crime Free Lease

Addendum." If you and the landlord sign this attachment, it becomes part of your lease (alternately, the landlord may include it as a clause in the rental document itself). It's important that you understand the meaning and consequences of this type of lease clause.

Developed by the police department of Mesa, Arizona, this addendum prohibits the use of the premises for any illegal activity, including the use, storage, and selling of illegal drugs; gang activity; prostitution; illegal weapons use; or any breach of the lease or rental agreement that jeopardizes the health and safety of other tenants or the landlord. It warns the tenant that a single instance of any of these prohibited acts will be grounds for the termination of the lease and eventual eviction, and tells you that a criminal conviction for an offense is not necessary (the landlord or a judge need only be convinced by a preponderance of the evidence that you have violated the clause's terms). The addendum has been copied by landlords in many states, including California.

On the one hand, most law-abiding tenants will have no problem abiding by these terms, and will be happy to be doing business with a landlord who takes the responsibilities regarding tenants' safety so seriously. And, indeed, many of the prohibitions in the clause simply repeat existing state law. For example, your landlord will be on solid ground if the landlord terminates your tenancy after learning that you sell or use illegal drugs—with or without this clause. So what's there to be wary of?

Unfortunately, some innocent tenants may be snared in this clause's broad net. Be aware that some landlords have interpreted the "crime free" requirement so as to place responsibility on a tenant for illegal activity that the tenant did not intend, did not know about, or had no opportunity to control. For example, suppose your babysitter uses drugs while you're away, and you can prove that you had no reason to suspect that this illegal activity would occur. Should you still lose your tenancy? We don't think so, but some landlords would point to the language of this clause and say

yes. We suggest that you see an attorney if you find yourself in this position.

If your lease or rental agreement includes a crime free clause, try to get the landlord to include language providing that only your *intentional* or *knowing* violation of its terms will be grounds for termination. For example, below is the portion of the Mesa addendum that deals with a tenant's violation (presumably, your California landlord will be savvy enough to substitute the correct California citations for the ones used by Arizona landlords). We suggest adding the language that appears in brackets:

"[KNOWING AND INTENTIONAL] VIOLATION OF THE ABOVE PROVISIONS SHALL BE A MATERIAL AND IRREPARABLE VIOLATION OF THE LEASE AND GOOD CAUSE FOR IMMEDIATE TERMINATION OF TENANCY. A single [knowing and intentional] violation of any of the provisions of this added addendum shall be deemed a serious violation, and a material and irreparable noncompliance. It is understood that a [knowing and intentional] single violation shall be good cause for immediate termination of the lease under A.R.S. 33-1377, as provided in A.R.S. 33-1368. Unless otherwise provided by law, proof of violation shall not require a criminal conviction, but shall be by a preponderance of the evidence."

Which Is Better, a Lease or a Month-to-Month Rental Agreement?

If you have a lease for a substantial term, like a year or more, you are assured that the landlord cannot end your tenancy or raise the rent so long as you pay your rent on time and meet your other obligations under the lease and the law. This kind of security is extremely valuable where housing is hard to find and rents are rising, which, as you know all too well, often describes the rental market.

If your unit is covered by a local rent control and eviction control ordinance, your need for the protection that a lease provides is lessened. Nevertheless, such ordinances do allow some rent increases, and they usually allow the landlord to evict in order to move himself or a relative into the place. A lease will normally protect you against these dangers.

Of course, if you expect to be moving in a very short time, you may prefer a month-to-month rental agreement, so that you can leave simply by giving 30 days' notice. But don't be too sure that a month-to-month tenancy is what you want. If you're in a tight rental market, it is usually not difficult to "break" a lease if you have to. We discuss this possibility in Chapter 12. Basically, the rule is that if you have a lease and move out before the term is up, the landlord can sue you for the rent until the lease runs out, but must make a reasonable effort to find another tenant. Once a new tenant moves in, your responsibility for the rent ends.

If you prefer a lease, but are worried about some specific event that might force you to leave the area, consider simply providing for that event in the lease. If your boss might transfer you to Phoenix, put a provision in your lease saying, "Tenant may terminate this lease upon 30 days' written notice, provided that, with such notice, Tenant also gives Landlord a copy of a note from Tenant's employer saying that Tenant is being transferred to a location out of the city."

The written rental agreement is often preferred by landlords. It gives them the right to raise the rent as often as they wish (unless there is a local rent regulation ordinance) and to get rid of tenants that they don't like. In most cases, from a tenant's point of view, the written rental agreement does not have the advantages of a lease.

Fees and Deposits

Almost every landlord requires the tenant to give a substantial security deposit, sometimes including "last month's rent." The laws concerning how much can be charged and when deposits must be returned are discussed in Chapter 13. Here we will discuss some other fees and deposits that are occasionally required.

Holding Deposit

Sometimes, making a deal with a landlord requires some type of cash deposit, then and there, to ensure you don't change your mind and back out of the deal. If you give the landlord the cash, sometimes as much as a month's rent, the landlord will "hold" the place for you until you bring your first month's rent and any deposits or fees you agreed on, or pending the result of a credit check. This is called a "holding" or "bond" deposit.

If you give a landlord a holding deposit and later decide not to take the place, you probably will be unable to get your whole deposit back. Therefore, be sure you really want the place before giving this kind of deposit. The law is very unclear as to what portion of a holding deposit a landlord can keep if a would-be tenant changes his mind about renting the property or doesn't come up with the remaining rent and deposit money. The basic rule is that a landlord can keep an amount that bears a "reasonable" relation to the landlord's costs—for example, for more advertising and for pro-rated rent during the time the property was held vacant. A landlord who keeps a larger amount is said to be imposing an unlawful penalty. Whatever you and the landlord agree on, such as your right to get half of the holding deposit back if you decide not to take the place within a certain number of days, be sure you get it in writing.

Also, be sure you and the landlord understand what will happen to the deposit when you take the place. Usually it will be applied to the first month's rent. To make this clear, have the landlord give you a receipt for the deposit, and write on the receipt what will happen to the deposit when you come back with the rent.

Finder's Fees

Some landlords—especially in cities with rent control—try to collect high "finder's fees" just for renting the place to the tenant.

It works like this: When a prospective tenant applies to a landlord or management company, the tenant is told to either (1) pay a finder's fee directly to the landlord or management company to qualify to get a particular unit, or (2) go to an apartment locator service and pay a finder's fee. In some situations, the locator service will have been set up primarily to collect the fee and isn't really in the business of locating apartments.

In a rent control city, this sort of fee is probably a sneaky way to get a higher rent—illegally. To get the place, you may want to pay the fee. After you move in, however, try to get it back! You have a right to, as your payment of the fee was not really voluntary, and tenants generally cannot be required to waive their rights under a rent control law. Contact your local rent control board, city attorney, or district attorney's office (consumer fraud unit).

Even in a city without rent control, a finder's fee that goes to the landlord (or the landlord's agent) rather than to a true finder is probably still illegal. (*People v. Sangiacomo,* 129 Cal.App.3d 364 (1982).) This issue is covered by state law, which allows fees and deposits to be used only to remedy tenant defaults in payment of rent, cleaning the premises, and paying for damage to the premises. (CC § 1950.5.) The landlord who simply pockets the finder's fee is probably violating this statute, and you can sue in small claims court to get it back.

Credit-Check and Screening Fees

Landlords often charge a fee to check the credit and background of prospective tenants. But state law limits credit-check or application fees and specifies what landlords must do when accepting these types of screening fees from prospective tenants. Under CC § 1950.6, landlords can charge only "actual out-of-pocket" costs of obtaining a credit or similar tenant "screening" report, plus "the reasonable value of time spent" obtaining a credit report or checking personal references and background information on a prospective tenant.

The maximum screening fee a landlord can charge is set by law. This figure (at least $37.57) may be adjusted upward annually by the landlord based on the Consumer Price Index. (CC § 1950.6.) To determine the current allowable charge, go to the Consumer Price Index website at www.bls.gov/cpi and search for the article, "How to Use the Consumer Price Index for Escalation."

Upon an applicant's request, a landlord must provide a copy of any consumer credit report that the landlord obtained on the individual. CC § 1950.6 also requires that the landlord give or mail applicants a receipt itemizing their credit-check and screening fees. If a landlord ends up spending less (for the credit report and time) than the fee charged the applicant, the landlord must refund the difference. (This may be the entire screening fee if the landlord never got a credit report or checked references on an applicant.)

Finally, landlords cannot charge any screening or credit-check fee if they don't have a vacancy and are simply putting someone on a waiting list (unless the applicant agrees to this in writing).

To avoid disputes over credit-check fees and the amount of time a landlord takes to check your credit and background, it is wise to sign a brief agreement with a landlord, such as the one shown below.

Landlord-Tenant Agreement Regarding Tenant's Credit Information

Credit Information

Tenant authorizes Landlord to verify all credit information for the purpose of renting the premises at _____

_____ .

Landlord shall not release such information for any other purpose without the express written approval of the Tenant.

If Landlord does not agree to sign lease within _____ days of receiving a deposit from Tenant for the purpose of reserving the premises, the total application fee of $_____ shall be refunded to Tenant, less the amount actually spent to verify credit or background information.

Tenant may withdraw from the agreement and receive a refund of the total application fee (less an amount used to verify credit information) up until such time as Landlord signs the lease.

_____
Landlord

_____
Tenant

Rental Applications and Credit Reports

You may be required to fill out a written rental application by the landlord or manager. The application will likely ask you for information regarding your employment, income, and credit, and may ask you for some references. Make sure that all of your references are people who know you well and who have positive impressions of you. Enthusiastic employment references are a good choice.

The most important part of the rental application is the credit check. If you have a poor credit record, be armed with information about yourself, showing that you will pay your rent despite what your credit record shows.

If the landlord or manager checks your credit, you should be aware that the check will probably result in an "inquiry" in your credit record. An inquiry is an indication in your credit record that someone has asked for your credit record. Many inquiries within a short period of time may raise doubt about your creditworthiness later—a creditor may think you were shopping around and looking to borrow a lot. You may need to explain that the inquiries were from landlords, and you were merely shopping and bargaining for the best rental.

Several companies, called tenant-screening agencies, collect and sell credit and other information about tenants—for example, if they pay their rent on time or if they've ever been evicted. These reports go way beyond the information contained in a credit report. There is no public access, however, to unlawful detainer lawsuit records within the first 60 days of the filing of the complaint (newspapers, however, can petition the court for an exception to this rule on a case-by-case basis). (21 CCP § 1161.2(a).) And if you won an eviction lawsuit against you, the record of that lawsuit will be sealed 60 days after the judgment (applies to judgments in your favor entered on or after January 1, 2004). (CCP § 1161.2(e).) (Unfortunately, it is probably unrealistic to expect that a record that's disseminated to various online databases can ever be truly "sealed," however.) If asked to, these companies also will gather and sell "investigative reports" about a person's character, general reputation, personal characteristics, or mode of living.

Many landlords routinely request screening and credit reports on prospective tenants from these agencies. If a landlord does not rent, or charges higher rent, to someone because of negative information in a credit or screening report, the landlord must so notify the tenant and give the person the name and address of the agency that reported the negative information. The landlord must also tell applicants that they have a right to obtain a copy of his file from the agency that reported the negative information, as long as they request the file within 60 days. (CC § 1785.20.) Landlords must also tell you that the credit reporting agency did not make the rejection decision and cannot explain it; and that if you dispute the information in the report, you can provide a consumer statement for your file that sets forth your position.

Almost all background or investigative checks are considered "investigative consumer reports" under the federal Fair Credit Reporting Act. (15 U.S.C. §§ 1681 and following.) A landlord who requests a background check on a prospective tenant must:

- tell the applicant within three days of requesting the report that the report may be made; and that it will concern the applicant's character, reputation, personal characteristics, and criminal history, and
- tell the applicant that more information about the nature and scope of the report will be provided upon written request. The landlord must provide this added information within five days of being asked by the applicant.

Free Credit Report

If you'd like to see a copy of your credit report, it's simple and cheap. The Federal Trade Commission (FTC) approved a rule that allows consumers to receive a free copy of their credit report every 12 months. Go to www.annualcreditreport.com.

How Landlords Must Handle Your Credit Information

Landlords must take steps to safeguard and eventually destroy credit reports and any information they have that's derived from these reports. This "Disposal Rule" comes from the Federal Trade Commission (FTC), which issues rules that implement the Fair and Accurate Credit Transaction Act (the "FACT Act"). The rule applies to all businesses, even one-person landlords. You might want to ask your prospective landlord whether he or she follows the practices described below.

Safe Retention

Landlords should keep these reports in a secure location, in order to minimize the chance that someone will use the information for illegal purposes, including identity theft. Good practices include storing these reports, and any other documents that include information taken from them, in a locked cabinet. Only known and trusted people should have access, and only on a need-to-know basis. Reports stored on a computer or PDA (such as a BlackBerry), or information derived from them, must also be kept secure (use a closely guarded password).

Destroying Unneeded Reports Routinely

The FACT Act requires landlords to dispose of credit reports and any information taken from them when they no longer need them. Landlords may think they need these reports long after they've rejected or accepted an applicant—the reports may be essential in refuting a fair employment or housing claim. Under federal law, such claims must be filed within two years of the claimed discrimination, but some states set longer periods. Landlords whose states gives plaintiffs extra time to sue may keep the records at least two years and longer.

Landlords should destroy old records using an effective destruction method. The Disposal Rule requires landlords to choose a level of document destruction that is reasonable in the context of their business. For example, a landlord with a few rentals would do just fine with an inexpensive shredder, but a multiproperty owner might want to contract with a shredding service. Computer files must also be erased, by deleting not only the directory, but the text as well.

Remedies When Landlords Willfully Disregard the Disposal Rule

The Disposal Rule comes with teeth for those who willfully disregard it—landlords who know about the law and how to comply, but deliberately refuse to do so. You can sue for your actual damages (say, the cost of covering a portion of a credit card's unauthorized use), or damages per violation of between $100 and $1,000, plus your attorney fees and costs of suit, plus punitive damages. The FTC and state counterparts can also enforce the FACT Act and impose fines.

How to Check a Place Over

If you see a place that you think you will like, take a walk around the neighborhood. Check out stores, schools, and bus stops. Walk around the building you are interested in renting and try to meet some of the neighbors. (If you can, talk to the tenants who are moving out.) Ask them how they have gotten along with the landlord. Make sure that you can feel at home in all respects. Take an especially close look at the condition of the unit you may rent. Look for dirt and damage, and carefully check all doors, windows, screens, stoves, furnaces, hot water heaters, and any other appliances. Make lists of any defects you find—later you can negotiate with the landlord for improvements and repairs. At the very least, be sure to get the landlord to sign an acknowledgment of the existing conditions, so she can't blame you later for causing them. The best way to do this is by completing the Landlord-Tenant Checklist discussed below.

A Checklist of Things to Inspect

Here is a checklist of things you should look for when inspecting a place. All requirements mentioned are contained in the State Housing Law. (See Chapter 6.) While checking some items on this list may seem obvious almost to the point of being simple-minded, the unhappy truth is that many people do not check a rental unit thoroughly before moving in and have all sorts of trouble getting repairs made later. So please slow down and look carefully (and then look again) before you sign on the dotted line.

Check the STRUCTURE (Floors, Walls, Ceiling, Foundation)

The structure of the place must be weatherproof, waterproof, and rodent proof.

"Weatherproof" means there must be no holes, cracks, or broken plaster. Check to see if all the walls are flush (that they meet directly, with no space in between). See if any floorboards are warped. Does wall plaster fall off when you touch it?

"Waterproof" means no water should leak in. If you see dark round spots on the ceilings or dark streaks on the walls, rain water might have been leaking through.

"Rodent proof" means no cracks and holes that rats and mice could use.

Check the PLUMBING

The landlord must provide a plumbing system connected to your community's water system and also to its sewage system (unless you have a septic system).

All plumbing must be in good condition, free of rust and leaks. Sometimes the condition of the plumbing is hard to discover, but there are several tests you can run to see if there might be problems.

Flush the toilet. Does it take too long to flush? Does it leak on the floor? Is the water discolored? If so, the pipes may be rusty or unclean.

If the water is connected, fill a sink with hot and cold water. Turn the faucets on all the way, and listen for vibrating or knocking sounds in the pipes. See if the water in the sink is discolored. Drain the sink, and see if it takes too long for the water to run out.

Check the BATHROOM

The State Housing Law requires that every apartment and house have at least one working toilet, wash basin, and bathtub (or shower) in it. The toilet and bathtub (or shower) must be in a room that gives privacy to the occupant and is ventilated. All of these facilities must be installed and maintained in a safe and sanitary condition.

Check the KITCHEN

The State Housing Law requires that every apartment and house have a kitchen. The kitchen must have a kitchen sink, which cannot be made of wood or other absorbent material.

Check the HOT WATER

The landlord must see that you have both hot and cold running water (although he can require you to pay the water and gas bills). "Hot" water means a temperature of not less than 110 degrees F.

Check the HEAT

The landlord must provide adequate heating facilities. Unvented fuel-burning heaters are not permitted.

Check the LIGHT AND VENTILATION

All rooms you live in must have natural light through windows or skylights, which must have an area not less than one-tenth of the floor area of the room, with a minimum of ten square feet.

Hallways and stairs in the building must be lighted at all times.

Check for Signs of INSECTS, VERMIN, AND RODENTS

The landlord must provide facilities that prevent insect and rodent infestation and, if there is infestation, provide for extermination services.

These pests can be hard to notice. Remember, however, that they are very shy and stay out of sight. Therefore, if you see any fresh signs of them, they are probably very numerous and will bother you later on. Also, these pests travel from house to house. If your neighbors have them, they will probably get to you.

Check for rodent trails and excrement. Rats and mice travel the same path day after day and leave a gray coloring along the floor and baseboards. Look at the kitchen carefully, for rodents go there for food supplies. Check in closets and cupboards and behind appliances for cockroaches.

Check for possible breeding grounds for pests, such as nearby stagnant water or garages and basements with piles of litter or old couches.

Check the WIRING AND ELECTRICITY

Loose or exposed wiring can be dangerous, leading to shock or fires. The landlord must provide safe and proper wiring.

If electrical power is available in the area, the place must be connected to it. Every room you live in must have at least two outlets (or one outlet and one light fixture). Every bathroom must have at least one light fixture.

Check for FIRE SAFETY

The landlord must provide safe exits leading to a street or hallway. Hallways, stairways, and exits must be free from litter. State law requires landlords to provide information on emergency procedures in case of fire to tenants in multistory rental properties. (H&S § 13220.) Storage rooms, garages, and basements must not contain combustible materials. State law requires that all multiple-unit dwellings offered for rental be equipped with smoke detectors. (H&S § 13113.7.)

Check for Adequate TRASH AND GARBAGE RECEPTACLES

The landlord must provide adequate garbage and trash storage and removal facilities. Garbage cans must have tight-fitting covers.

Check the General CLEANLINESS OF THE AREA

Landlords must keep those parts of the building that they control (hallways, stairs, yards, basement, driveway, and so on) in a clean, sanitary, and safe condition.

Check the LOCKS

Landlords must install deadbolts on swinging main entry doors, common area doors, and gates and certain windows. See Chapter 11 for details. (CC § 1941.3.)

Check for EARTHQUAKE SAFETY

A building's earthquake resistance is a very impor-tant consideration in deciding where you want to rent, yet few people even think about it. Because the law does not provide specific protection for tenants living in unsafe buildings, you must be a wise shopper and ask specific questions about the building and its surroundings.

How Safe Is the Land Under the Building?

Proximity to a major fault is not the only factor you should consider when scoping out a place to rent. Be aware that:

- An unstable hillside is susceptible to land-slides if an earthquake hits. The danger depends on the soil condition—rock is better than unconsolidated dirt. Flat, solid ground is best.
- The worst place for a building is on landfill. Fill is common along many California bays and rivers, including San Francisco Bay. In a quake with a lot of vigorous shaking, older fill and bay mud may liquefy.

- Don't rent a place that is downstream from a dam. Some dams could fail (leak or even break) in an extremely strong earthquake.

How Safe Is the Building Itself?

Ask the building's manager or owner these questions:

- Does the building have a steel or wood frame? Is it built from steel-reinforced concrete, or is it a concrete shear-wall building that is not irregularly shaped or does not have a "soft story"? These are usually safe buildings. Pay particular attention to buildings that have a ground-level garage. Solid shear walls that normally support that portion of the building during an earthquake are often removed to make way for garage doors or windows. The result is a building that is more likely to collapse onto that first floor in a major earthquake. Ask the manager or owner whether the walls of the garage (especially the front and back walls) have been strengthened with plywood sheathing. If they haven't been strengthened, know that you are taking a risk when you rent there.
- Is the building bolted to the foundation? If not, it can be shaken off of its foundation and severely damaged.
- Does the building have a lateral bracing system? If not, it will not be able to withstand the lateral forces of an earthquake.
- Is there plywood sheathing built around sliding glass doors, bay windows, or picture windows to decrease the risk of breakage?
- Does the building have a tile roof? Tile roofs are very heavy and may collapse during an earthquake. However, if the building is in a high-risk area for wildfires, tile roofs are highly recommended because they are fire-resistant.
- Are all water heaters properly strapped and fitted with a flexible gas supply line, so that they can't fall over and cause a fire or

explosion triggered from a gas leak? State law requires existing water heaters to be braced, anchored, or strapped. (H&S §§ 19210-19217.)

- Where is the main gas shut-off, so that you may shut the gas off during an emergency? If the main gas line to the building is not shut off after a major earthquake, there is a high risk of fire or explosions due to leaking gas.

- Does the manager or owner have an earthquake preparedness plan to ensure that all tenants know how to safely exit the building and how to shut off any utilities if necessary?

CAUTION

Beware of brick! Unreinforced brick buildings have the worst record in terms of durability during an earthquake. Some buildings are not made of brick, but have a brick or stone veneer attached to the outside walls for aesthetic purposes. This veneer may be nice to look at, but unreinforced veneer is very susceptible to earthquake damage. Your building may not collapse in a major earthquake because it has a brick veneer, but anyone standing next to the building during an earthquake may be injured by bricks or stones falling off of the building.

RESOURCE

For more information on earthquake safety, check the State Government listings in your phone book for the nearest Earthquake Preparedness Project.

What If the Place Does Not Meet the Above Standards?

If the place has serious problems, you should probably not rent it if you can possibly avoid it. A landlord who would even show you such a place probably won't or can't make the needed repairs. If the landlord promises to fix it up, be careful. First, ask other tenants how good the landlord is at keeping promises. Second, make him put his

promises in writing and sign it, as illustrated in "Get All Promises in Writing," below. Be sure he also puts down dates on which certain repairs will be completed. Also, get him to write down that you will not have to pay your rent if he fails to meet the completion dates. If he doesn't want to agree to these things, he probably isn't taking his obligation to repair very seriously.

If you like the place but it has a few problems, simply ask the landlord to promise to make the necessary repairs. You might point out that he is required to make such repairs before renting, under the State Housing Law, but you will rent the place and let him repair it later, if he makes his promise (with dates) in writing and signs it.

How to Bargain for the Best Deal

Once you decide that you might like to rent a particular place, then negotiate the terms of the rental with the landlord or manager. Often you will be presented with a "take it or leave it" proposition, where the landlord is not open to making changes. Many times, however, landlords will be open to reasonable changes. Whether it be the rent that you are trying to change, or particular terms in the contract, it never hurts to try.

In your first negotiation, it is good to remember that landlords who are impressed with you will be more likely to want you as a tenant. Take a moment to consider what sort of folks you would like to rent to if you were a landlord. Certainly, a good first impression can be made on the application form. Most landlords ask you to fill out an application listing your jobs, bank, cars, income, and references. It is a good idea to make up your own form in advance, much as you would write a job resume, and photocopy your application. If you don't get the first place, it will be available to submit when you apply for other units.

How good a deal you can get from a landlord depends on how badly you are needed. If there are very few places available at the asking rent and a lot of people are looking, the landlord may tell you to take the deal (rent, security deposit, and form lease) or forget the whole thing. Even an attempt to bargain may make the landlord reluctant to rent to you.

If you are in an area where there are lots of places for rent and not too many people looking (say a university area in the spring), you will have more bargaining power. The landlord wants to rent the place soon (to get the rent) and may be afraid of losing you to another landlord.

If you can, try to talk to the last tenant who lived in the place. That person might give you some very valuable information on how to deal with the landlord, what is wrong with the place, and generally what it is like to live there. Other tenants or neighbors in the area might also be helpful on this.

The more you look like a responsible tenant, the more bargaining power you will have. Every landlord wants responsible tenants who will pay rent regularly, not mess up the place, and not complain about anything. The more you appear to be this way, the better the deal you will get. The landlord won't rent to you at all unless he trusts you, and if he trusts you, he may be willing to give you things you ask for in order to keep you.

If you have any bargaining power, try to use it. Even if the rent is fair and the landlord won't budge on that, there are other concessions you might get if you ask. The landlord may have a better refrigerator in storage, or be willing to eliminate some lease provisions you don't like, or do some other things mentioned in this book.

Get All Promises in Writing

Your future relationship with your landlord may be very pleasant. Hope for the best and try to be open, honest, and friendly. However, at the same time, take sensible steps for your own self protection, just in case things take a nasty turn.

It often happens that a tenant moves into an apartment that has not been properly cleaned, or that needs painting or repairs. The landlord may say that the tenant can deduct money from the rent in exchange for cleaning, painting, or repairs. Whatever promises the landlord makes, you should be aware that it is very common for this sort of vague, oral agreement to lead to misunderstanding, bitterness, and financial loss. The time to protect yourself is at the beginning. This may be your only chance to do so.

If you plan to attach cupboards, shelves, bookcases, air conditioners, room dividers, or anything at all to the premises, you should get something in writing from the landlord permitting you to install such things, and (if you plan it) to remove them later. By law, anything that is nailed, screwed, or bolted to the premises becomes the property of the landlord. (CCP § 13; Government Code § 6700 et seq.) If you remove the object when you leave, your landlord will have the right to compensation for any damage to the premises, and may also be able to recover the value of the object removed, unless there is a written agreement to the contrary. In addition, most landlords are sensitive to having the premises altered without their consent and may get quite irritated if they discover changes after they have been made.

If a landlord promises to clean, paint, build a deck, install a fence, or reimburse you for material and work, or if there are any other kinds of promises you want to depend upon, get them in writing and include a date for completing the work. Asking for a promise in writing need not cause you tension or embarrassment. Just tell the landlord, politely, that you have made a simple list of what has been agreed to, and you want to go over it for clarification. If the landlord agrees that the list is accurate, include a line saying that this list is made a part of the written lease or rental agreement, and have the landlord date and sign it. There should be two copies, one for the landlord and one for your own file. (See "Sample Addendum to Lease or Rental Agreement," below.)

Sample Addendum to Lease or Rental Agreement

January 1, 20xx

Landlord Smith Realty and Tenant Patricia Parker make the following agreement, which is hereby added to the lease (or rental agreement) they entered into on _____ , 20xx:

1. Patricia Parker agrees to buy paint and painting supplies not to exceed a cost of $120 and to paint apartment #4 at 1500 Acorn Street, Cloverdale, California, on or before February 1, 20xx and to forward all receipts for painting supplies and paint to Smith Realty.

2. Smith Realty agrees to reduce the payment due February 1, 20xx by $150 in consideration for the painting to be done by Patricia Parker and in addition to allow Patricia Parker to deduct the actual cost of paint and painting supplies (not to exceed $120) from the rent payment due February 1, 20xx.

3. The premises are being rented with the following defects:

   a. dent in oven door

   b. gouge over fireplace in wall

   These defects will be fixed by Smith Realty by
   _____ , 20____ .

_____
Smith Realty Company

_____
Patricia Parker By: B. C. Smith

The use of written contracts is standard among businesspeople and among friends when they are in a business relationship. The purpose of such writings is to remind people of what they once agreed to do. If the landlord balks at putting things in writing, be very careful in all future dealings.

If the landlord won't paint, clean, or make repairs, be sure to list the faults as particularly and completely as you can, and get the landlord to sign and date the list. Otherwise, when you move out the landlord may claim that you caused the damage and refuse to refund all, or a part, of your deposit.

If the landlord doesn't want to sign your list, get a few of the most responsible of your friends to take a look at it and write a simple dated note of what they saw. And, if possible, have a friend take photographs of all defects. After the photographs are developed, the person taking them should identify each photo on the back by location, date, and signature. All notes and pictures should go into your file with your other records.

The Landlord-Tenant Checklist

Another good self-protection device for both landlord and tenant involves taking an inventory of the condition of the premises at the time you move in, when the landlord conducts the pre-move-out inspections, and then again when you move out. This means no more than making a brief written record of the condition of each room and having it signed by you and your landlord. Not only does the inventory give both of you an accurate record of the condition of the unit, but the act of making it provides a framework for communication and the resolution of potential disputes about security deposits when you move out. (See "Avoiding Deposit Problems" in Chapter 13.) We include a sample landlord-tenant checklist below.

When filling out your checklist, mark "OK" in the space next to items that are in satisfactory condition. Make a note—as specific as possible—next to items that are not working or are in bad or filthy condition. Thus, you might state next to the "Stove and Refrigerator" listing: "generally good, but crack in freezer door." Be sure to note things like worn rugs, chipped enamel, holes in screens, dirty cabinets, and so on.

Landlord/Tenant Checklist
General Condition of Rental Unit and Premises

1234 Fell Street
Street Address

Apt. 5
Unit Number

San Francisco
City

	Condition on Arrival	Condition on Initial Move-Out Inspection	Condition on Departure	Actual or Estimated Cost of Cleaning, Repair/Replacement
Living Room				
Floors & Floor Coverings	OK			
Drapes & Window Coverings	OK			
Walls & Ceilings	OK			
Light Fixtures	OK			
Windows, Screens, & Doors	back door scratched			
Front Door & Locks	OK			
Smoke Detector	OK			
Fireplace	N/A			
Other				
Kitchen				
Floors & Floor Coverings	cigarette burn hole (1)			
Walls & Ceilings	OK			
Light Fixtures	OK			
Cabinets	OK			
Counters	discolored			
Stove/Oven	OK			
Refrigerator	OK			
Dishwasher	OK			
Garbage Disposal	N/A			
Sink & Plumbing	OK			
Smoke Detector	OK			
Other				

	Condition on Arrival	Condition on Initial Move-Out Inspection	Condition on Departure	Actual or Estimated Cost of Cleaning, Repair/Replacement
Dining Room				
Floors & Floor Coverings	OK			
Walls & Ceilings	crack in ceiling			
Light Fixtures	OK			
Windows, Screens, & Doors	OK			
Smoke Detector				
Other				
Bathroom				
Floors & Floor Coverings	OK			
Walls & Ceilings	OK			
Windows, Screens, & Doors	OK			
Light Fixtures	OK			
Bathtub/Shower	tub chipped			
Sinks & Counters	OK			
Toilet	OK			
Other				
Other				
Bedroom				
Floors & Floor Coverings	OK			
Windows, Screens, & Doors	OK			
Walls & Ceilings	OK			
Light Fixtures	dented			
Smoke Detector	OK			
Other				
Other				
Other				

	Condition on Arrival	Condition on Initial Move-Out Inspection	Condition on Departure	Actual or Estimated Cost of Cleaning, Repair/Replacement
Other Areas				
Heating System	OK			
Air Conditioning	N/A			
Lawn/Garden	N/A			
Stairs & Hallway	N/A			
Patio, Terrace, Deck, etc.	N/A			
Basement	OK			
Parking Area	OK			
Other				
Other				
Other				
Other				
Other				

☑ Tenants acknowledge that all smoke detectors and fire extinguishers were tested in their presence and found to be in working order, and that the testing procedure was explained to them. Tenants agree to test all detectors at least once a month and to report any problems to Landlord/Manager in writing. Tenants agree to replace all smoke detector batteries as necessary.

Notes:

Furnished Property

	Condition on Arrival	Condition on Initial Move-Out Inspection	Condition on Departure	Actual or Estimated Cost of Cleaning, Repair/Replacement
Living Room				
Coffee Table	two scratches on top			
End Tables	N/A			
Lamps	OK			
Chairs	OK			
Sofa	OK			
Other				
Other				
Kitchen				
Broiler Pan	N/A			
Ice Trays	OK			
Other				
Other				
Dining Area				
Chairs	OK			
Stools	N/A			
Table	leg bent slightly			
Other				
Other				
Bathroom				
Mirrors	OK			
Shower Curtain	OK			
Hamper	N/A			
Other				

	Condition on Arrival	Condition on Initial Move-Out Inspection	Condition on Departure	Actual or Estimated Cost of Cleaning, Repair/Replacement
Bedroom				
Beds (single)	OK			
Beds (double)	N/A			
Chairs	OK			
Chests	N/A			
Dressing Tables	OK			
Lamps	OK			
Mirrors	OK			
Night Tables	N/A			
Other	N/A			
Other Area				
Bookcases				
Desks				
Pictures	hallway picture frame chipped			
Other				
Other				

Use this space to provide any additional explanation:

Landlord/Tenant Checklist completed on moving in on ___ May 1 ___ , 20 _XX_ .

Ina Eppler   and   _Chloe Gustafson_

Landlord/Manager   Tenant

                                                                   Tenant

                                                                   Tenant

Landlord/Tenant Checklist completed at Initial Move-Out Inspection on ___ , 20 ___ .

_____   and

Landlord/Manager   Tenant

                                                                   Tenant

                                                                   Tenant

Landlord/Tenant Checklist completed on moving out on ___ , 20 ___ .

_____   and

Landlord/Manager   Tenant

                                                                   Tenant

                                                                   Tenant

Cosigning Leases

Some landlords require a cosigner on leases and rental agreements as a condition of renting. Normally, they ask the cosigner to sign the lease or rental agreement, or a separate contract pledging to pay for any rent or damage losses that the tenants fail to pay.

Many cosigner clauses are not enforceable in court, because they are so vague that they don't qualify as contracts. Also, if a landlord and tenant change the terms of their rental agreement—or even renew it—without the signed approval of the cosigner, the cosigner is no longer responsible. (CC § 2819; *Wexler v. McLucas,* 48 Cal.App.3d Supp. 9 (1975).) If a landlord sues a tenant for eviction, and for money damages (back rent), the cosigner can't be sued as part of the same suit. The cosigner must be sued separately either in a regular civil lawsuit or in small claims court.

Know Your Manager

Many medium-to-large apartment complexes have managers. (State law requires a resident manager in any multiunit property of 16 units or more. (CCR Title 25, § 42.) Some owners use management corporations, who specialize in managing lots of rental units and who get paid a percentage (usually between 5% and 10%) of the rental income. Such companies tend to be sticklers for rules and procedures, but are usually less emotionally involved than owners, and are often more rational at arriving at businesslike compromises. Often, however, the owner will simply give a resident free or reduced rent to look after the property on a part-time basis. This can be either good or bad as far as you are concerned, depending on the personality of the manager and whether the manager has any real authority to take care of problems. Just as there are all sorts of landlords, there is an equal variety of managers.

In dealing with a manager on a day-to-day basis, not only is it important to notice who he is and how best to deal with him, it is also important to notice his relationship to the owner. Remember, the owner and the manager may have very different interests. Some owners, for example, may want the property to yield a maximum amount of profit with a minimal amount of trouble, while others may be investing for long-term real property appreciation and be willing to be reasonably generous to tenants in the meantime (these owners realize that low tenant turnover is the key to making money). Similarly, some managers might want to do as little work as possible for their free rent, while others, especially those who are in the business, may want to do a bang-up job in hopes that word will spread and they will get other jobs.

A landlord is legally responsible for the quality of the job done (or not done) by the manager or management company. Should you be in a situation in which the premises are not being kept clean or in good repair, or if the manager is obnoxious or invading your privacy, you will probably want to deal directly with the owner if possible. In any case, where communications are sticky or broken down, you should send duplicate copies of letters and other communications to the owner as well as to the manager.

Sharing a Home

Lots of unmarried people rent a place together. Whether it involves sharing a bed or not, sharing a home can have all sorts of legal ramifications. Of course, there are the legalities when it comes to dealing with the landlord, but sometimes the legal rules governing the relationship between the roommates are of even more importance.

The Legal Obligations of Roommates to the Landlord

If two people—let's call them James and Helen—enter into a lease or rental agreement (written or oral), they are each on the hook to the landlord for all rent and all damages to the apartment—except "normal wear and tear." It makes no difference who—or whose friends—caused the damage, or who left without paying the rent. Let's look at several common situations.

EXAMPLE 1: James and Helen both sign a written rental agreement providing for a total monthly rent of $1,500 for a flat. They agree between them to pay one-half each. After three months, James refuses to pay his half of the rent (or moves out with no notice to Helen and the landlord). In either situation, Helen is legally obligated to pay all the rent, as far as the landlord is concerned. James, of course, is equally liable, but if he is unreachable or out of work, the landlord will almost surely come after Helen for the whole amount. Since James and Helen have rented under a month-to-month written rental agreement, Helen can cut her losses by giving the landlord a 30-day written notice of intention to move. She can do this even if James is lying around the place, refusing to pay or get out.

If Helen ends up paying the landlord more than her agreed share of the rent, she has a right to recover from James. If payment is not made voluntarily, Helen can sue James in small claims court.

RESOURCE

See *Everybody's Guide to Small Claims Court*, by Ralph Warner (Nolo), for more information on how to use small claims court.

EXAMPLE 2: The same fact situation as Example 1, except that this time there is a lease for one year. Again, both partners are independently liable for the whole rent. If one refuses to pay, the other is still liable, unless a third person can be found to take over the lease, in which case both partners are off the hook from the day that a new tenant takes over. As we discuss in Chapter 12, because of the housing shortage in most parts of the state, it is often easy for a tenant to get out of a lease at little or no cost, simply by finding an acceptable new tenant and steering him or her to the landlord. A newspaper ad will usually do it. The landlord has an obligation to limit his damages (called "mitigation of damages" in legal lingo) by renting to a suitable new tenant as soon as possible. Should the landlord fail to do this, he loses the legal right to collect damages from the original tenants.

Having a Friend Move In

Perhaps just as common as two or more people renting a home together is for one person to move into a place already rented and occupied by another. This is often simple and smooth when the landlord is cooperative, but can involve some tricky legal questions if the landlord raises objections.

In some situations, where the landlord is not in the area or is not likely to make waves, it may be sensible to simply have the second person move in and worry about the consequences later. But is this legal? Is a tenant required to tell the landlord when a second person moves in? It depends on the lease or rental agreement. If no mention is made as to the number of persons allowed in the apartment,

Sample Agreement Between Roommates

Agreement

Helen Mattson and James Kennedy, upon renting an apartment at 1500 Redwood Street, #4, Philo, California, agree as follows:

1. Helen and James are each obligated to pay one-half of the rent and one-half of the utilities, including the basic monthly telephone charge. Each person will keep track of and pay for his or her long distance calls. Rent shall be paid on the first of each month, utilities within ten days of the day the bill is received.

2. If either Helen or James wants to move out, the one moving will give the other person 30 days' notice and will pay his/her share of the rent for the entire 30-day period even if he/she moves out sooner. If both Helen and James wish to move, they will be jointly responsible for giving the landlord 30 days' notice.

3. No third persons will be invited to stay in the apartment without the mutual agreement of both Helen and James.

4. If both Helen and James want to keep the apartment but one or the other or both no longer wish to live together, they will have a third party flip a coin to see who gets to stay. The loser will move out within 30 days and will pay all of his/her obligations for rent, utilities, and any damage to the apartment.

[*Here is an alternative for number 4.*]

4. If both Helen and James want to keep the apartment but no longer wish to live together, the apartment will be retained by the person who needs it most. Need will be determined by taking into consideration the relative financial condition of each party, proximity to work, the needs of minor children, if any, and [*list any other factors important to you*]. If Helen and James can't decide this issue by themselves or with the help of a mutually agreed-upon mediator, the determination will be made by a third party (the arbitrator). If it is not possible for Helen and James to agree on an arbitrator, the arbitrator will be chosen by [*fill in name*]. The arbitrator will be paid by the person who gets to keep the apartment. The determination will be made within ten days after either party informs the other that he or she wishes to separate, and after the arbitrator has listened to each person present his or her case. The arbitration award will be conclusive on the parties, and will be prepared in such a way that a formal judgment can be entered thereon in any court having jurisdiction over the dispute if either party so desires. After the determination is made, the person who is to leave will have an additional ten days to do so. The person who leaves is obligated for all rent, utilities, and any damage costs for 30 days from the day of the original determination to separate.

_____   _____
Date   Helen Mattson

_____   _____
Date   James Kennedy

use your own discretion and knowledge of your landlord. Some don't care, but most probably do. We suspect that as a general rule, even in the absence of a lease or rental agreement provision dealing with the area, moving someone in without the consent of a landlord is not the most sensible thing to do. The landlord will probably figure out what is going on before long and may resent your sneakiness more than he resents your roommate. We advise you to read the lease or rental agreement to see how many people are allowed to live on the premises and if there are any restrictions on additional people. Sometimes additional people will be allowed for a slight increase in rent. (If you live in a rent control area, your local ordinance may restrict how much rent can be increased in this situation.) Many landlords will not care whether you are married, living together, or just friends, but will expect to collect more money if more people live in their rental unit.

CAUTION
Under state law, a written rental agreement may be terminated on 30 days' notice (60 days if the tenant has lived there for one year or more, and 90 days for government-subsidized tenancies) without the necessity of the landlord giving a reason. Thus, a landlord who wants to get rid of you can normally do so without too much trouble if you don't have a lease. So it pays to be reasonable when moving roommates in and out.

The Legal Relationship Between the Person Moving In and the Landlord

If Helen moves into James's apartment without being added to the rental agreement or lease, what is the relationship between Helen and James's landlord? Is Helen obligated to pay rent if James fails to pay? What if James moves out, but Helen wants to remain? If James ruins the paint or breaks the furniture, does Helen have any obligation to pay for the damage?

Because she has not entered into a contract with the landlord, Helen has no legal obligations to him regarding the rent, nor does she have an agreement with him regarding her right to live in the apartment. Helen's only possible legal obligation is to James. Of course, if Helen damages the property, she is liable just as a visitor, a trespasser, or a thief who caused damage would be liable. If James leaves, Helen has no right to take over his lease without the landlord's consent.

Helen can, of course, enter into a lease or rental agreement contract with the landlord (or join James'), which would give her the rights and responsibilities of a tenant. This can be done by:

Sample Letter When a New Roommate Moves In

1500 Redwood Street #4
Philo, California
June 27, 20xx

Smith Realty
10 Ocean Street
Elk, California

I live at the above address, and regularly pay rent to your office.

As of July 1, 20xx, there will be a second person living in my apartment. As set forth in my lease, I enclose the increased rent due, which now comes to a total of $800. I will continue to make payments in this amount as long as two people occupy the apartment.

Should you wish to sign a new lease specifically to cover two people, please let me know. My friend, Helen Mattson, is regularly employed and has an excellent credit rating.

Very truly yours,

James Kennedy

James Kennedy

- signing a new lease or rental agreement, which specifically includes both James and Helen as tenants.
- making an oral rental agreement with the landlord. Be careful of this one, as an oral agreement can consist of no more than a conversation between Helen and the landlord in which she says she will pay the rent and keep the place clean, and the landlord says okay. There may be some legal question as to whether an oral agreement between Helen and the landlord is enforceable if there is still a written lease or rental agreement between the landlord and James that doesn't include Helen, but it is our experience that most judges would bend over backwards to give Helen the rights and responsibilities of a tenant if she seemed to be exercising them and the landlord has accepted her presence (especially her rent).
- the actual payment of rent by Helen and its acceptance by the landlord, especially if it is done on a fairly regular basis. As in the preceding paragraph, this would set up a month-to-month tenancy between Helen and the landlord and would mean that either could end the tenancy by giving the other proper written notice of intention to end it.

Should the situation ever arise that James wants to move out and Helen remain, it is important that the legal relationships be clarified. James should give the landlord a written notice of what he intends to do at least 30 days before he leaves. If he does this, he is off the hook completely in a written or oral rental agreement situation. If a lease is involved and James is leaving before it runs out, Helen will be left having to pay the rent on her own, but since James has broken the lease, the landlord could terminate Helen's lease, too. As long as Helen is a reasonably solvent and nondestructive

person, the landlord would suffer no loss by accepting her as a tenant to fill out the rest of the lease.

RENT CONTROL

If Helen has attained the status of a tenant, the landlord will probably not be able to raise the rent after James leaves, except as otherwise permitted by the local rent control ordinance. If, on the other hand, Helen has not become a tenant, she will be considered a "new tenant," and, if she became a tenant after January 1, 1996, the rent can be raised as much as the landlord wants when the original tenant moves out.

Sample Letter When One Tenant Moves Out and the Other Remains (Lease)

1500 Redwood Street #4
Philo, California
June 27, 20xx

Smith Realty
10 Ocean Street
Elk, California

I live at the above address under a lease that expires on October 30, 20xx. A change in my job makes it necessary that I leave the last day of February. As you know, for the last six months my friend, Helen Mattson, has been sharing this apartment. Helen wishes to remain and enter into a new lease with you for the remainder of the original lease term. She is employed, has a stable income, and will, of course, continue to be a responsible tenant.

We will soon be contacting your office to work out the details of the transfer. If you have any concerns about this proposal, please give us a call.

Very truly yours,

James Kennedy
James Kennedy

Sample Letter When One Tenant Moves Out and the Other Remains (Rental Agreement)

1500 Redwood Street #4
Philo, California

June 27, 20xx

Smith Realty
10 Ocean Street
Elk, California

I live at the above address and regularly pay rent to your office. On July 31, 20xx, I will be moving out. As you know, my friend, Helen Mattson, also resides here. She wishes to remain and will continue to pay rent to your office on the first of each month.

Very truly yours,

James Kennedy

James Kennedy

The Legal Relationship Between the Person Moving In and the Person Already There

Alas, it often happens that a relationship that is all sunshine and roses at the start becomes unhappy over time. When feelings change, memories blur as to promises made in happier times, and the nicest people become paranoid and nasty. Suddenly, questions such as, "Whose apartment is this, anyway?" may turn into serious disputes. We suggest that when feelings are relaxed (preferably at the time that the living arrangement is set up), both people make a little note as to their mutual understandings, either as part of a comprehensive living together arrangement or in a separate agreement (see the "Sample Agreement Between Roommates," above). If this is done in good faith, as an aid to the all-too-fallible human memory, it need not be a negative experience.

If you get into a serious dispute with your friend involving your shared home and have no agreements to fall back on, you will have to do the best you can to muddle through to a fair solution. Here are a few ideas to guide your thinking:

- If only one of you has signed the agreement with the landlord and that person pays all the rent, then that person probably should have the first claim on the apartment, especially if that person occupied the apartment first. The other should be given a reasonable period of time to find another place, especially if he or she has been contributing to the rent and/or has been living in the home for any considerable period of time.

- If you both signed a lease or rental agreement and/or both regularly pay rent to the landlord, your rights to the apartment are probably legally equal, even if one of you got there first. Try to talk out your situation, letting the person stay who genuinely needs the place the most. Some people find it helpful to set up an informal mediation proceeding with a third person helping the parties arrive at their own solution. If this doesn't work, you may wish to locate a neutral third-party arbitrator to hear the facts and make a decision. If you do this, make sure that the arbitrator is not a close friend, as the person who loses is likely to have hard feelings. Lean over backwards to be fair about adjusting money details concerning such things as last month's rent and damage deposits. Allow the person moving out a reasonable period of time to find another place. *We have found that the best compromises are made when both people feel that they have gone more than half way.*

- Each person has the right to his or her belongings. This is true even if they are behind in their share of the rent. Never lock up the other person's property.

- It is a bad idea to deny a person access to his or her home except in extreme circumstances.

If you are thinking of locking out a roommate, you should also be ready to sign a formal police complaint or go to court and get a restraining order under California's Domestic Violence Prevention Act. (CCP § 541.) You can get more information about this procedure from your County Clerk's office. In many instances, locking out a person is not legal and you can be sued for damages.

RESOURCE

A number of California cities and counties have free or low-cost landlord-tenant mediation and arbitration services. In addition, the nonprofit Community Board program offers excellent mediation services in many San Francisco neighborhoods.

Guests

What about overnight guests—particularly those who stay over often? What relationship, if any, do these people have with the landlord? More important, is the landlord entitled to any legal recourse if you have a "regular" guest? The answer to this question often depends on what it says in a lease or written rental agreement or written tenant rules authorized by one of these documents. (See Chapter 1.) Many restrict the right to have overnight guests to a certain number of days per year, and require registration if a guest will stay more than a few days. While these sorts of lease provisions aren't often strictly enforced, they are legal and, in the case of persistent or serious violations, can be grounds for a landlord evicting a tenant who has a lease. Even in rent control areas that require just cause for eviction, a tenant who violates guest rules may be evicted, but under the terms of many ordinances, the tenant must first be given a written notice to correct the violation—that is, to follow the "guest" provision of the lease or written rental agreement.

Absent a specific lease or rental agreement provision dealing with the area, there is no precise line between guests and roommates. A person may be a frequent overnight visitor—four or five times a week—but still qualify as a guest in the landlord's mind, whereas a roommate may be in residence only a couple of days a week, as is common with flight attendants. A person's status as guest might be considerably enhanced by showing that the guest maintains a separate residence, complete with furniture and mailing address. However, to the landlord who sees the person on the premises more than the actual tenant, this might not prove persuasive.

Where the landlord is seeking to evict on the basis of a lease provision that prohibits occupancy of more than a certain number of people, the landlord must (absent a provision limiting the number of days a guest can stay in the premises) prove that the extra occupant is in fact a resident. However, as we mentioned earlier in this chapter, in all but rent control cities, the landlord can evict for no reason at all if you have no lease. Accordingly, unless you live in an area covered by a just cause for eviction rent control ordinance (see Chapter 14) or have a lease, it might be a good idea to clarify your guest's status with your landlord at the outset instead of leaving things to his imagination.

All About Rent

Today most tenants pay 35% or more of their incomes on rent—sometimes many thousands of dollars a month. This money obviously means a lot to you, so you should understand your rights regarding when to pay, how much to pay, and whether the landlord can increase the rent. Rent is also very important to the landlord, because it often goes immediately to the lender or mortgage holder. And nonpayment of rent is taken very seriously by the courts.

When Is Rent Due?

Under state law, rent is due at the end of the term of the tenancy—for example, at the end of the month, in a month-to-month tenancy—unless the lease or rental agreement provides otherwise. (CC § 1947.) Almost every lease and rental agreement (whether written or oral) provides otherwise, however. Most require payment at the beginning of the term. Thus, rent for use of the place in March would be due on March 1.

If the rent due date falls on a weekend or holiday, your rent is still due on that date, unless your lease or rental agreement specifies otherwise (many landlords will give you until the next business day). (*Gans v. Smull*, 111 Cal.App.4th 985 (2003).)

If you fail to pay your rent on the date it is due, the landlord may not throw you out or sue to evict you the next day. The landlord must first serve you with a written notice demanding that you pay the rent or get out in three days. If the third day falls on a Saturday, Sunday, or holiday, you get until the next business day to pay the rent. (CC § 11, CCP § 12A.) Only after that day can the landlord file a lawsuit to evict you. (See Chapter 14 for details on three-day notices.)

Late Charges

A fairly common landlord practice is to charge a fee to tenants who are late with their rent.

Some cities with rent control ordinances regulate the amount of late fee charges. Check any rent control ordinance applicable to your properties. Most California cities and unincorporated areas, however, do not regulate what you can be charged for late fees.

Unfortunately, some landlords try to charge excessive late fees. This is not legal. Late charges must be reasonably related to the amount of money it costs the landlord to deal with your lateness. Rental agreements and lease clauses that provide for unreasonably high late charges are not enforceable. (*Orozco v. Casimiro*, 212 Cal.App.4th Supp. 7 (2004).) Moreover, a landlord's late fee is not likely to survive a legal challenge unless the lease or rental agreement includes language like this: "Because landlord and tenant agree that actual damages for late rent payments are very difficult or impossible to determine, landlord and tenant agree to the following stated late charge as liquidated damages."

While there are no statutory guidelines as to how much a landlord can reasonably charge as a late fee, here are some guidelines that will help you decide if the amount is excessive:

- A reasonable late charge might be a flat charge of no more than $20 to $40, depending on the amount of rent. It is common for a landlord to give a tenant a grace period of from one to five days, but there is no law that requires this. A late charge that is out of proportion to the rent (say $75 for being one day late with rent on a $450 per month apartment) would probably not be upheld in court.
- If your landlord imposes a late charge that increases with each additional day of lateness, it should be moderate and have an upper limit. For example, $10 for the first day rent is late, plus $5 for each additional day, with a maximum late charge of 4% to 6% of the rental amount, might be acceptable to a judge, unless the property carries a high rent, in which case somewhat higher amounts might be allowed.

Some landlords try to disguise excessive late charges as a "discount" for early payment of rent. One landlord we know concluded he couldn't get away with charging a $50 late charge on a late $425 rent payment, so instead he designed a rental agreement calling for a rent of $475 with a $50 discount if the rent was not more than three days late. Ingenious as this sounds, it is unlikely to stand up in court, unless the discount for timely payments is very modest. This is because the effect of giving a relatively large discount is the same as charging an excessive late fee, and a judge is likely to see it as such and throw it out.

Partial Rent Payments

On occasion, you may be short of money to pay your full rent on time. The best way to deal with this is to discuss the problem with your landlord and try to get the landlord to accept a partial payment. Except in the unusual situation where your lease or rental agreement gives you the right to make partial payments, the landlord is under no obligation to accept part of the rent on the due date along with your promise to catch up later.

Unfortunately, there is normally nothing to stop the landlord from accepting a partial rent payment on one day and serving you with a three-day notice to pay the rest of the rent or quit the next. However, if you can get your landlord to specifically agree in writing that you can have a longer time to pay, the landlord is bound by this agreement. Here is a sample.

Sample Agreement for Partial Rent Payments

John Lewis, Landlord, and Betty Wong, Tenant, agree as follows:

1. That Betty Wong has paid one-half of her $500 rent for Apartment #2 at 11 Billy St., Fair Oaks, CA, on March 1, 20xx, which is the date the rent for the month of March is due.

2. That John Lewis agrees to accept all the remainder of the rent on or before March 15, 20xx and to hold off on any legal proceeding to evict Betty Wong until after that date.

March 1, 200x	John Lewis
Date	John Lewis, Landlord

March 1, 200x	Betty Wong
Date	Betty Wong, Tenant

Rent Increases

Rent may not be increased during a fixed-term lease unless the lease allows it. If you rent month to month, the landlord can increase your rent with a properly delivered 30- or 60-day notice (see below).

If you live in public housing or "Section 8" housing, in most cases the rent may not be increased to an amount more than 30% of your income (after certain deductions are taken). A rent increase is invalid if you live in an area covered by rent control and it exceeds the amount allowed by the rent control ordinance. We discuss rent control below.

A rent increase is invalid if the landlord imposed it in order to retaliate against you because you exercised some legal right, such as complaining about the condition of the building or organizing a tenants' union. See Chapter 6 and Chapter 14 for more on retaliation.

A rent increase is invalid if the landlord imposed it in order to discriminate against you on the basis of race, sex, children, or any other prohibited reason mentioned in Chapter 4.

Other than these restrictions, there is nothing in state law to prevent the landlord from doubling or even tripling the rent. Again, you are legally protected against such acts only if you are lucky enough to live in a city or county that has a local rent control ordinance.

Rent Increase Notices

Most of the time, a landlord may raise the rent on a month-to-month tenancy by "serving" a written notice on the tenant saying that the rent will be increased in 30 days (or more). (If the tenant has a *lease,* no rent increase is appropriate until the lease ends.) Local rent control laws, of course, limit the increase to the amount set by the rent control board.

30-Day or 60-Day Notice?

In certain situations, you're entitled to 60, not 30, days' notice when the landlord wants to raise the rent. If the total of all the rent increases over the past 12 months (including the current raise) is equal to or less than 10% of the lowest rent charged to you during that time, 30 days' notice will suffice. But if the total increase is more than 10% of any monthly rent charged during the previous year, you are entitled to a 60-day notice. Follow these steps to know which notice period applies to the rent increase you've received.

Step 1. Calculate when the new rent will take effect under a 30-day notice. For now, assume a 30-day period is all that's needed. Determine when the new rent will kick in by looking at your rent increase notice (see the discussion below for information on how your landlord must deliver the notice).

Step 2. Check your rent rate history. Count back 12 months from the effective date of the increase (you got that date in Step 1, above). Look at the rent you were charged for each of those 12 months, and choose the lowest rent.

Step 3. Calculate 10% of the lowest rent charged. Multiply the lowest rent charged (you identified that figure in Step 2) times 0.1 to get your "10% Figure."

Step 4. Calculate the Total Rent Increase over the past 12 months. If the current increase is the only increase during the previous 12 months, the answer is simple—the increase is the one you're facing now. But if your landlord has increased the rent previously during these months, add up all of the increases plus the current one to get the Total Rent Increase.

Step 5. Compare the 10% Figure from Step 3 with the Total Rent Increase in Step 4. If the Total Rent Increase is the same as or lower than your 10% Figure, you know that you'll need to come up with that new rent in 30 days—in other words, the landlord's 30-day notice is sufficient. But if the total is higher, your landlord should have used a 60-day notice.

It's important to understand what happens if your landlord gives you a 30-day notice when a 60-day notice is what's called for. We think that the notice is defective—it's as if the landlord never gave you notice at all, so you do not have to pay the added rent. Nor do you have to pay the added rent in 60 days—it's not up to you to add the needed time to a defective notice. The landlord will have to start over and give you a new notice with the proper, 60-day period specified.

Effect of Sale of Premises on Tenant's Rights

If your landlord sells the house or apartment building where you rent, your rights as a tenant remain the same. If you have a month-to-month agreement, the new landlord must give you 30 days' notice in order to raise your rent (60 days in some situations), change other terms of your tenancy, or have you move out (60 days if you've lived there two or more years). There may be further restrictions in communities with rent control laws requiring the landlord to show "just cause" to evict. (See Chapter 3 for the law on rent increases and details on rent control, and Chapter 14 for information on evictions.)

If you have a lease, the new landlord cannot evict you (unless you break the terms of the lease) or change the terms of your agreement until the lease runs out. (Landlord bankruptcy is an exception to this. See the note below.) For example, the new landlord cannot make you give away your dog if your lease does not prohibit pets.

The examples below illustrate how to calculate the 10% figure. As you'll see, the tricky situations arise when landlords raise the rent frequently within any 12-month period.

RENT CONTROL

Rent Control. Normally, increases in rent control situations will be well below the 10% threshold, because the local rent board regulates them yearly (and no board is likely to approve an increase that high!). However, if your landlord has banked prior increases or has permission to impose a capital expenditures increase, the total may well exceed 10% of the lowest rent charged in the previous 12 months. In those situations, the landlord would have to use a 60-day notice.

EXAMPLE 1: Len rents a house to Tom for $1,000 a month. Len wants to raise the rent $100, to $1,100, effective February 1. Tom looks back at how much rent he has been charged for the 12 months preceding Feb. 1. The rent was $1,000 for each of those months. Tom does the math and figures out that 10% of $1,000 is $100. Since the increase isn't *more* than 10% of the lowest rent charged in the 12 months preceding the February 1 target date, Len can properly use a 30-day notice. Assuming Len has served the notice correctly, Tom must pay the new rent on February 1.

EXAMPLE 2: Sally decided to raise Spencer's rent from $650 to $750. On May 1, she gave him a 30-day notice. Spencer knew that he would be entitled to 60 days' notice if the increase (combined with any others he'd had over the past 12 months) was over 10% of the lowest rent charged during those 12 months. Sally didn't know the law.

Spencer's rent had been a steady $650 from June 1 of the preceding year to now. He knew that any increase over $65 (that's 10% of $650) required a 60-day notice. He reasoned that Sally's notice was simply ineffective, and when June 1 arrived, he gave Sally a rent check for $650.

Sally looked at the amount and demanded the new rent, then listened incredulously as Spencer explained the law. She argued that he should just "tack on" 30 days to her notice, making the rent increase effective July 1. Spencer refused, and Sally wisely decided to start over by delivering a proper 60-day notice on June 1. Spencer won't have to pay the new rent until August 1—if Sally had done it right from the start, the increase would have kicked in on July 1.

How Rent Increase Notices Must Be Served

Questions often arise over the way landlords must tell you about a rent increase which is understandable because the law has changed. Until January 1, 2001, landlords had to serve you personally or, if that wasn't possible, serve a responsible member of your household (followed by mailing a copy to you); this is called "substituted service." As a last resort, a landlord could post the increase on the door (and mail a copy also).

Now, however, landlords can serve a rent increase notice by ordinary first-class mail addressed to you at the premises—without having to try to serve you personally first. Of course, a landlord can still serve a rent increase by personal service or substituted service, explained above.

If you receive a notice by mail instead of personal delivery to you or your sub, you're entitled to an additional five days' notice of the rent increase. This means getting 35 days' notice for a 10%-or-less increase and 65 days' notice for an over-10% increase. (CC § 827(b)(1)(B)(2) & (3); CCP § 1013.)

Be very sure to understand that if your landlord wants to change other terms of the tenancy besides the rent, such as the amount of the security deposit or a pets rule, the landlord must use personal or substituted service. *Mail service is available only for rent changes.*

Responding to Improper Notice

If your landlord has delivered the bad news in the wrong way—using a 30-day notice when a 60-day was required, or failing to add time for mailed notices—you have a choice. You can stand on your rights and refuse to pay—hoping that this will buy you some time while the landlord goes back to square one and does it right. However, there is always the chance that the landlord will refuse to be educated and will terminate your tenancy for non-payment of rent, precipitating an eviction lawsuit.

Think long and hard whether it's worth it to go to court and prove your point in this arena. Even if you win, you'll spend time and money proving your point. Especially if the amount of the increase is in keeping with market rents and you have a good relationship with the landlord, you may want to simply pay the increase and not question the way in which you were served the notice.

Rent Control and Eviction Protection

Rent control is a local phenomenon, established either through the initiative process or by the act of a city council or a county board of supervisors. State law regulates some specifics of the various rent control ordinances. The Costa-Hawkins Rental Housing Act restricts cities' power to impose rent control on single-family homes and condominium units, and also requires cities to allow landlords to raise rents after certain types of vacancies occur. (CC § 1954.50-1954.53.)

Some form of rent regulation now exists in 17 California communities, including Los Angeles, San Diego, San Jose, and San Francisco. Two cities—Glendale and San Diego—have just cause eviction protections, but do not regulate rents. Richmond and Ridgecrest are similar, but their eviction protections apply only to rental properties that have been foreclosed.

Cities With Rent Control and Eviction Protection Ordinances

Berkeley	Palm Springs
Beverly Hills	Richmond**
Campbell* (mediation only)	Ridgecrest**
East Palo Alto	San Francisco
Fremont* (mediation only)	San Diego
Glendale	San Jose*
Hayward	Santa Monica
Los Angeles	Thousand Oaks
Los Gatos*	West Hollywood
Oakland	

* Rent control cities without just cause eviction protection

** Eviction protection in foreclosed properties only

Rent control ordinances generally control more than how much rent a landlord may charge. Many cities' ordinances also govern how and under what circumstances a landlord may terminate a tenancy, even one from month to month, by requiring the landlord to have "just cause" to evict. Many cities, most notably Los Angeles, require landlords to register their properties with a local rent control agency.

Before we describe how rent control works, a few words of caution:

- Cities change their rent control laws frequently, and court decisions and voter referenda affect them. You should read the material here only to get a broad idea of rent control. It is absolutely necessary that you also contact your city or county to find out whether rent control presently exists and, if it does, to get a copy of current ordinances and any regulations interpreting it. "Rent Control Laws," below, gives you all the necessary contact information.
- State law requires local rent control agencies in cities that require registration of rents

to provide, upon request of the landlord or tenant, a certificate setting out the permissible rent for a particular unit. (CC § 1947.8.) The landlord or tenant may appeal the rent determination to the rent control agency within 15 days. If no appeal is filed, the rent determination is binding on the agency. If an appeal is filed, the agency must provide a written decision in 60 days.

- No two rent control ordinances are exactly alike. Some cities have elected or appointed boards that have the power to adjust rents; others allow a certain percentage increase each year as part of their ordinances. Some cities have enlightened ordinances with just cause for eviction provisions that require landlords to give and prove valid reasons for terminating month-to-month tenancies. All cities, however, are subject to "vacancy decontrol," which means that when a tenant moves out voluntarily (or is asked to leave for a just cause), the unit can be rerented at the market rate.

In order to summarize how each ordinance works, we have prepared a Rent Control Chart at the end of the chapter that outlines the major points of each ordinance. Here are brief explanations of key terms we use in the chart and the discussion below.

Exceptions: No city's rent control ordinance covers all rental housing within the city. San Francisco, for example, exempts all rental units built after June 1979, whereas Los Angeles exempts those built after October 1978.

Administration: Most rent control ordinances are administered by rent control boards whose members are appointed by the mayor, city council, or board of supervisors (the boards are elected in Santa Monica and Berkeley). The formal name, address, and phone number of the board is in the Rent Control Chart.

Registration: The cities of Berkeley, East Palo Alto, Los Angeles, Palm Springs, Santa Monica, Thousand Oaks, and West Hollywood all require the owners of rent controlled properties to register the properties with the agency that administers the rent control ordinance. This allows the rent board to keep track of the city's rental units, as well as to obtain operating funds from the registration fees.

These cities forbid landlords who fail to register their properties from raising rent. In fact, cities may require a landlord to refund past rent increases if the increases were made during a period in which the landlord failed to register property. However, the courts have ruled that it is unconstitutional for rent control ordinances requiring registration to allow tenants to withhold rents just because the property isn't registered. (*Floystrup v. Berkeley Rent Stabilization Board,* 219 Cal.App.3d 1309 (1990).)

Some cities, including Berkeley and Santa Monica, impose administrative penalties (fines) on landlords who fail to register property. However, both of these types of penalties are now limited by state law in cases where the landlord's failure to register was not in bad faith and was quickly corrected (that is, the landlord registered the property) in response to a notice from the city. (CC § 1947.7.) To make things easier for landlords who make honest mistakes, state law requires cities to allow landlords any rent increases, which would have been allowed had the property been registered, to be phased in over future years if the following conditions are met:

- The landlord's original failure to register the property was unintentional and not in bad faith.
- The landlord has since registered the property as required by the city and paid all back registration fees.
- The landlord has paid back to the tenant any rents collected in excess of the lawful rate during the time the property wasn't properly registered.

Some rent control ordinances require, as part of the registration process, that the landlord provide the name and address of current tenants. Additional information concerning a tenant may be requested. Under state law, rent control agencies are directed to treat this information as confidential. (CC § 1947.7.)

Rent Formula and Individual Adjustments: Each city has a slightly different mechanism for allowing rent increases. All cities allow periodic (usually yearly) across-the-board increases. The amount of the increase may be set by the rent control board, or the ordinance may allow periodic increases of either a fixed percentage or a percentage tied to a local or national consumer price index. In most cities, landlords (and sometimes tenants) may petition the board for higher (or lower) rents based on certain criteria.

By state law, landlords can raise rents to any level after a tenant voluntarily vacates or is evicted for nonpayment of rent. (CC § 1954.53(d).) However, once the property is rerented, a city's rent control ordinance will once again apply and will limit rent increases for the new tenants in that residence. The only exception is where the ordinance provides that the property is no longer subject to rent control, as is the case in Hayward, Palm Springs, and Thousand Oaks.

Capital Expenditures: In most rent control situations, landlords may ask their rent boards for permission to raise rents above the yearly allotment if they can prove that they have had to spend significant amounts on capital improvements to the property. "Capital improvements" means work that adds significant value to the property, appreciably prolongs its useful life, or adapts it to new uses. It is major work done to the structure of the building, such as replacing the roof, redoing the wiring, repairing a foundation, and seismic upgrading. Capital improvements do not include routine repair and maintenance.

Unfortunately, it's often difficult to know for sure whether a particular piece of work will qualify as a capital improvement. Rent control boards across the state do not consistently use the same criteria when evaluating a landlord's request. But some cases are pretty clear—we know of an Oakland landlord who gave his tenants bottles of champagne to thank them for their patience while construction was done on their building—and then argued to the rent board that his capital expenditures included not only the cost of the construction work, but also the cost of the champagne!

Eviction Protection (Just Cause for Eviction): Unfortunately, some unscrupulous landlords have sought to evict tenants solely in order to create a new vacancy and set a higher rent. In other words, in order to charge more rent, which can be done only with a new tenancy, the landlord evicts the current tenant, often for little or no reason beyond the desire for more rent. To guard against such abuse, some rent control ordinances require the landlord to show "just cause" for eviction. A just cause eviction provision requires landlords to give (and prove in court, if necessary) a valid reason for terminating a month-to-month tenancy. The most common reason for just cause eviction is tenant failure to pay rent on time. What constitutes just cause to evict is discussed below.

Cities That Require Just Cause for Eviction

Berkeley	Richmond*
Beverly Hills	Ridgecrest*
East Palo Alto	San Diego (tenancies of 2+)
Glendale	San Francisco
Hayward	Santa Monica
Los Angeles	Thousand Oaks
Oakland	West Hollywood
Palm Springs	

** Applies to foreclosed properties only.

Note: San Jose and Los Gatos do not have just cause eviction. Their ordinances, however, penalize a landlord who tries to evict a tenant in retaliation. The tenant has the burden of proving that the landlord's motive was retaliatory. See Chapter 14 for details on retaliatory evictions.

General Types of Rent Control Laws

As noted above, although no two cities' rent control laws are identical, they can be broadly categorized into three types. Obviously, this sort of gross classification isn't perfect, but it should help you place your city in the scheme of things.

Weak Rent Control

Let's start with the Bay Area cities of San Jose, Oakland, Hayward, and Los Gatos, all of which have weak rent control ordinances. Although the rent control ordinances of these areas set forth a certain formula (usually fairly generous to landlords, in the 5%-8% range) by which rents can be increased each year, it is possible for a landlord to raise the rent above this figure and still stay within the law. This is because each of these cities' ordinances require a tenant whose rent is increased above the formula level to petition the board within a certain period (usually 30 days) and protest the increase. If you do not protest the increase within the time allowed, the increase is effective, even though it is higher than the formula increase allowed. If the increase is protested, a hearing is held, at which the board decides if the entire increase should be allowed.

In addition, except in Hayward and Oakland, the rent control ordinances in these cities do not require the landlord to show just cause for eviction. Just cause means that your landlord may not terminate your tenancy (or refuse to renew a lease) for any reason other than one that is allowed by the ordinance, such as nonpayment of rent, intentional damage to the rental, or the presence of unauthorized occupants. Other common just cause reasons include the desire of the landlord to move himself or close family members into the rental, (called an "owner move-in" eviction) or the landlord's decision to get out of the rental business altogether or to convert the building to condominiums.

Finally, none of the ordinances in these cities require landlords to register their units with the board, and only Oakland's applies to single-family homes (but only for tenancies that began prior to January 1, 1996).

Moderate-to-Strict Rent Control

Unlike the practice in cities with mild rent control, landlords in cities with moderate-to-strict rent control bear the burden of petitioning the rent board for an above-formula rent increase and of justifying the need for such an increase based on certain cost factors listed in the ordinance, such as increased taxes or capital improvements. These cities also require the landlord to show a good reason ("just cause") to evict a tenant.

The rent control laws of Los Angeles, San Francisco, Beverly Hills, Palm Springs, and Thousand Oaks have traditionally been considered "moderate," while the rent control laws of Berkeley, East Palo Alto, Santa Monica, and West Hollywood have been considered "strict." Landlords in strict rent control cities must register their properties with the rent control board. Berkeley and Santa Monica also allow tenants to petition for lower rents based on a landlord's failure to maintain or repair rental property.

Landlords may not, however, raise rents (even after a voluntary vacancy or eviction for cause) where they have been cited for serious health, safety, fire, or building code violations that they have failed to remedy for six months preceding the vacancy. (CC § 1954.53 (f).)

In cities with moderate and strict rent control, which require the landlord to petition the board before increasing the rent over a certain amount, a landlord can't circumvent the ordinance by having the tenant agree to an illegal rent. Even if a tenant agrees in writing to pay a higher rent and pays it, the tenant can sue to get the illegal rent back. (*Nettles v. Van de Lande*, 207 Cal.App.3d Supp. 6 (1988).) This cannot happen, however, in weak rent control cities that require the tenant to object to a rent increase if he or she wants to stop it from going into effect.

Decreases in Services as Illegal Rent Increases

If for some reason you're not getting all the use out of your apartment that you were promised when you moved in, the rent board may determine that you've been given an illegal rent increase. In one San Francisco case, elderly tenants successfully argued that their services had been decreased when the landlord moved their garbage cans up a flight of stairs.

Rent Mediation Laws

In a few cities where city councils have felt tenant pressure, but not enough pressure to enact rent control ordinances, so-called voluntary rent "guidelines," or landlord-tenant "mediation" services, have been adopted. The chief beneficiaries of these dubious standards and procedures seem to be the landlords, since voluntary programs have no power to stop rent increases. On rare occasions, however, voluntary mediation or guidelines may work, particularly with smaller landlords who are trying to be fair. If your city or county isn't on the rent control list, check to see if it has a voluntary program.

Just Cause Protection in San Diego and Glendale

Two non-rent-control California cities—San Diego and Glendale—require a landlord in certain cases to have "just cause" to terminate a tenancy, even one from month-to-month. In the termination notice, the landlord must state which reason justifies the termination. See "Rent Control Laws" at the end of this chapter for details.

Rent Control Board Hearings

Almost all cities with rent control provide for a hearing procedure to deal with certain types of complaints and requests for rent adjustments. In cities with weak rent control, a tenant's protest of a rent increase higher than that allowed by the applicable rent increase formula will result in a hearing at which the landlord must justify the increase. In other rent control cities, the landlord must request a hearing in order to increase rent above the formula amount. Finally, a few cities—such as Santa Monica and Berkeley—allow tenants to initiate hearings to decrease rents on the basis of the landlord's alleged neglect or lack of maintenance on the property.

In the first two types of hearings, whether initiated by a tenant who protests a rent increase over the formula amount in a weak rent control city, or by a landlord in a city that requires landlords to first obtain permission before exceeding the formula increase, the landlord must demonstrate at the hearing that a rent increase higher than that normally allowed is needed in order to obtain a fair return on the owner's investment. This most often means establishing that taxes, maintenance costs, utility charges, or other business expenses, as well as the amortized cost of any capital improvements, make it difficult to obtain a fair return on one's investment, given the existing level of rent.

Initiating the Hearing

A hearing is normally initiated by the filing of a petition or application with the rent board. In describing this process, let's assume that a landlord is filing a petition in a strict or moderate rent control city that requires landlords to obtain permission before raising rents above the formula increase allowed. You, the tenant, wish to protest the increase. Remember, this process is approximately reversed in weak rent control cities, which require the tenant to protest such an increase.

In some cities, including Los Angeles and San Francisco, a landlord can file two types of petitions seeking an above-formula rent increase. If a landlord seeks an increase on account of recent capital improvements the landlord has made, the landlord will file a "petition for certification" of such improvements. If the owner seeks a rent increase on other grounds, the landlord files a "petition for arbitration."

Preparing for the Hearing

As a general rule, you will greatly increase your chances of prevailing if you appear at the hearing fully prepared. The hearing officer will be much better disposed to listen to your concerns if you are thoroughly familiar with the issues and make your presentation in an organized way.

As part of planning your preparation, first obtain a copy of the ordinance and any applicable regulations for the area in which your property is located. Then determine which factors the hearing officer must weigh in considering whether to give the landlord an upward individual adjustment from the formula increase. Your job is to show that the increase being requested is either not justified at all, or too high. To do this you will need to carefully review the landlord's claimed expenses and compare them to what is allowed under the ordinance.

You should also be prepared to produce a witness who is familiar with any items that you think might be contested. If for some reason your witness cannot appear in person, you may present a sworn written statement or "declaration" from that person. The statement should be as specific as possible. At the end, the words "I declare under penalty of perjury under the laws of California that the foregoing is true and correct" should appear, followed by the date and the person's signature.

Before the date set for your hearing, go and watch someone else's. (Most cities' hearings are open to the public, and even if they are sometimes closed, you can almost always arrange to attend as an observer if you call ahead.) Seeing another hearing may even make the difference between winning and losing at yours. This is because both your confidence and your capabilities will grow as you understand what the hearing officers are interested in and how they conduct the hearing. By watching a hearing, you will learn that while they are relatively informal, all follow some procedural rules. It is a great help to know what these are so you can swim with the current, not against it.

You are permitted to have an attorney or any other person, such as an employee or volunteer from a local tenants' rights group, represent you at a rent adjustment hearing. (Many landlords are represented at such hearings by their apartment managers or management companies.) Hiring someone to speak for you is probably not necessary. If you do a careful job in preparing your case, you will probably do as well alone as with a lawyer or other representative. One good alternative is for a group of tenants similarly situated to chip in and consult with an attorney or someone else thoroughly familiar with rent board hearings to discuss strategy. After the lawyer provides you with advice and information, you can handle the hearing yourself.

The Actual Hearing

Once you've prepared for the hearing, it's time to make your case. Here's how to be most effective.

Before the Hearing Begins

Arrive at the hearing room at least a few minutes before it is set to begin. Check in with the clerk or other official. Ask to see the file that contains the papers relevant to the application (either yours or the landlord's, depending on the type of ordinance). Review this material to see if there are any comments by office workers, rent board investigators, your landlord, or other tenants. Read the comments very closely, and prepare to answer questions from the hearing officer on any of these points.

As you sit in the hearing room, you will probably see a long table, with the hearing officer seated at the head. In a few cities, the hearing is held before several members of the rent board, and they may sit more formally on a dais or raised platform. In any event, you, the landlord, your representatives (if any), and any witnesses will be asked to sit at a table or come to the front of the room. A clerk or other employee may make summary notes of testimony given at the hearing. Or, in some cities, hearings are tape recorded. If, under the procedure followed in your city, no record is kept, you have the right to have the proceedings transcribed or tape recorded, though at your own expense.

The Hearing Officer's Role

The hearing officer (who may be a city employee or volunteer mediator or arbitrator) or chairperson of the rent board will introduce herself or himself and the other people in the room. If you have witnesses, tell the hearing officer. The hearing officer, or sometimes an employee of the rent board, will usually summarize the issues involved in the hearing. At some point, you will be sworn to tell the truth; it is perjury to lie at the hearing. When these preliminaries are complete, you and your landlord will have an opportunity to present your cases.

Many hearing officers, rent board employees, and members of rent boards tend to be sympathetic to tenants. This is not the same thing as saying that they will bend over backwards to help you. Like most judges (who on balance are probably more sympathetic to landlords), most make an honest effort to follow the law. In other words, your job is to work to make your legal position as unassailable as possible.

A rent adjustment hearing is not like a court hearing. There are no formal rules of evidence. Hearing officers will usually allow you to bring in any information that may be important, though in a court of law it might not be admissible. Relax and just be yourself.

Making Your Case

Present your points clearly, but in a nonargumentative way. Sometimes an outline on a 3" x 5" card will help you to focus. Don't get carried away with unnecessary details. You probably won't be given much time, so be prepared and get to the point quickly. The hearing officer may ask you questions to help you explain your position. Make sure you present all documentary evidence and witnesses necessary to back up your case. Later, the hearing officer will give the landlord or her representative a chance to present her case and to ask you questions. Answer the questions quietly. It is always counterproductive to get into an argument. Even if you feel the landlord is lying or misleading, don't interrupt. You will be given time later to rebut the testimony. Direct all your argument to the hearing officer, not to the landlord or her representative.

When your witnesses are given the opportunity to testify, the normal procedure is simply to let them have their say. You may ask questions if the witness forgets something important, but remember, this is not a court and you don't want to come on like a lawyer. Very likely, the hearing officer will also ask your witnesses questions. The landlord has the right to ask the witnesses questions as well.

In rare instances, you may get a hearing officer or rent board chairperson who dominates the hearing or seems to be hostile to you, or perhaps to tenants in general. If so, you will want to stand up for your rights, without needlessly confronting the hearing officer. Obviously, this can be tricky, but if you know your legal rights and put them forth in a polite but direct way, you should do fine. If you feel that the hearing officer is simply not listening to you, politely insist on your right to complete your statement and question your witnesses.

Just before the hearing ends, the hearing officer should ask if you have any final comments to make. Don't repeat what you have already said, but make sure all your points have been covered and heard.

At the end of the hearing, the hearing officer will usually tell you when you can expect the decision. A written decision will usually be mailed to you within a few days or weeks of the hearing. Some cities, however, do not issue written decisions; the hearing officer just announces the decision at the end of the hearing.

The Decision

Depending on the city and the hearing procedure, you may or may not end up with a written decision and an explanation of why it was so decided.

In most cities, if a landlord's application for an increase was heard by a hearing officer, you have the right to appeal to the full rent board if the increase is allowed and you still feel it is improper. Your landlord has this same right if you prevail. If you make an appeal, you must file within a certain time and state your reason for the appeal. You may or may not have the opportunity to appear in person before the rent board.

The rent board will probably take the findings of the hearing officer at face value and limit its role to deciding whether the hearing officer applied the law to these facts correctly. On the other hand, the rent boards of some cities (including Los Angeles) will allow the entire hearing to be held again. (This is sometimes called a "de novo" hearing.) In addition, the board will not usually consider any facts you raise in your statement that you could have brought up at the earlier hearing, but didn't. If you discover a new piece of information after the original hearing, however, the board might consider it.

If it's your landlord who is appealing and you are satisfied with the earlier decision, you will want to emphasize the thoroughness and integrity of the earlier procedure and be ready to present detailed information only if it seems to be needed.

The rent board will generally have more discretion to make a decision than does a single hearing officer. If your case is unique, the board may consider the implications of establishing a new legal rule or interpretation.

If you again lose your decision before the board, or if your city permits only one hearing in the first place, you may be able to take your case to court, if you are convinced that the rent board or hearing board failed to follow either the law or their own procedures. However, if the hearing officer or board has broad discretion to decide issues such as the one you presented, you are unlikely to get the decision overturned in court. Speak to an attorney about this as soon as possible, as there is a time limit (usually 30 days) for filing an appeal. To appeal a rent board decision, you must have a transcript of the hearing to give to the court.

What to Do If the Landlord Violates Rent Control Rules

Take the following steps if you suspect your landlord has in any way violated your city's rent control rules.

- Get a copy of your local ordinance—and any regulation interpreting it—and make sure you are right. You may want to call the local rent board to confirm that what the landlord is doing violates the law. Contact any local tenants' rights organization and get the benefit of its advice.
- If you think your landlord may have made a good faith mistake, try to work the problems out informally.
- If that doesn't work, file a formal complaint with your city rent board.
- If the landlord's conduct is extreme, talk to a lawyer. You may have a valid suit based on the intentional infliction of emotional distress, on invasion of privacy, or on some other grounds, including those provided in the ordinance itself.

Rent Control Laws

The following pages summarize the major features of California's local rent control laws. However, for more specifics and any recent changes not reflected in this book, it is absolutely essential that you obtain a copy of your local ordinance and any regulations interpreting it from the address listed after "Administration."

Finding Municipal Codes and Rent Control Ordinances Online

If you live in a city that has rent control, you should get a current copy of the city's rent control law. You can usually get a paper copy from the administrative agency that oversees the workings of the ordinance. It's quicker, however, to read the material online. Most cities have posted their ordinances, as you will see from the list below. Use the Rent Control Chart, which provides detailed, city-by-city analyses, as a guide to your own reading of the law. Keep in mind that ordinances often change and their meaning evolves as rent boards issue regulations and make decisions.

Berkeley

www.ci.berkeley.ca.us

Click "Municipal Codes & Zoning Ordinance" to get to the Municipal Code. For rent control provisions, see Municipal Code Chapter 13.76. The Rent Stabilization Board itself is at www.ci.berkeley.ca.us/rent.

Beverly Hills

www.ci.beverly-hills.ca.us
www.beverlyhills.org

Go to the "shortcuts" pull-down menu and choose "Municipal Code" on the next page. For rent control provisions, see Title 4, Chapters 5 and 6, of the Municipal Code.

Campbell

www.ci.campbell.ca.us

Click "City Clerk," and choose "Municipal Code" on the next page. For rent control provisions, see Title 6, Chapter 6.09, of the Municipal Code.

East Palo Alto

www.ci.east-palo-alto.ca.us

Go to the "Browse by Topic" pull-down menu and choose Municipal Code under "City Hall and Government." Then press the "Go" button.

Fremont

www.ci.fremont.ca.us

In the "Departments" and "List of Departments" pull-down menu, click "City Clerk's Office." On the next page, click "Fremont Municipal Code."

Glendale

www.ci.glendale.ca.us/gmc/index/asp

Choose Title 9, then click 9.30, Just Cause and Retaliatory Eviction (Glendale Municipal Code §§ 9.30.010 through 9.30.100).

Hayward

www.ci.hayward.ca.us

For Municipal Code, click "Municipal Code—Fees." Then click "Hayward Municipal Code." However, the Rent Control Ordinance is not part of the Municipal Code and not available online.

Los Angeles

www.ci.la.ca.us
www.lacity.org

To get to the Los Angeles Municipal Code from the official city website, click on the "City Charter, Rules & Codes" box at the left. On the next page, click on "Municipal Codes." On the next page, choose "Municipal Code." Rent control provisions are in Chapter XV.

Los Gatos

www.town.los-gatos.ca.us

Move your cursor to "Government" at left, and then move the cursor to "Town Codes," and click that. Rent control provisions are in Chapter 14, Article VIII.

Oakland

www.ci.oakland.ca.us

Click the "Municipal Code" pull-down menu and then click "Rent Ordinance." Click "Go." Rent control provisions are in Title 8, Chapter 8.22.

Palm Springs

www.ci.palm-springs.ca.us

Under "Departments," click "City Clerk." Scroll down to "Municipal/Zoning Ordinance Code." Rent control provisions are in Title 4, Chapter 4.02 and following.

Richmond

www.ci.richmond.ca.us

Choose "Municipal Code" on the homepage, then choose Article VII (Businesses), Chapter 7.105.

San Diego

www.sandiego.gov

Choose City Hall, then select the Municipal Code link. Select Chapter 9, Article 8, Division 7 (San Diego Municipal Code §§ 98.0701 through 98.0760).

San Francisco

www.ci.sf.ca.us/rentbd
www.sfgov.org/site/rentboard_index.asp

The second site is the best place to get rent control ordinance provisions and regulations, maintained by the rent board (click "Ordinances and Rules"). For the entire collection of city codes, go to the City's main website at www.ci.sf.ca.us. Click on "Municipal Codes" under "City Resources," which is below an "Explore" heading. This page also includes the Administrative Code, including the Chapter 37 rent control provisions.

San Jose

www.ci.san-jose.ca.us
www.sanjose.ca.gov

Click "Municipal Code" (under "Local Government") at right.

Santa Monica

www.ci.santa-monica.ca.us/rentcontrol

This city's rent control laws are in the City Charter, not in the Municipal Code. Click "Charter Amendment and Regulations." The Rent Control Board maintains the site listed here. If you want to see the Municipal Code as well, go to the official city site at www.ci.santa-monica.ca.us or santa-monica.org/home/index.asp, and choose "Municipal Code" under the Quick Index pull-down menu.

Thousand Oaks

www.ci.thousand-oaks.ca.us

This city's rent control ordinances (755-NS [7/1980], 956-NS [3/1987], and 1284-NS [5/1997]), were never made a part of the Municipal Code, and thus cannot be found in the online Municipal Code. If you'd like to look at the Municipal Code anyway, go to the official city site above. Then click "Common Questions," then up to "City Hall," then choose "Municipal Code" from the pull-down menu.

West Hollywood

www.ci.west-hollywood.ca.us
www.weho.org

To get to the Municipal Code from this city's official site, click "Municipal Code" under "City Hall."

California Imposes Statewide Limitations on Cities' Rent Control Ordinances

State law significantly limits local rent control laws in the 14 California cities that have them. (CC §§ 1954.50–53.) The law has three major components.

No rent control for single-family residences.

As of January 1, 1999, tenancies that began on or after January 1, 1996 in single-family residences

and condominiums will no longer be subject to rent control. Only tenants who have continuously occupied the premises since before January 1, 1996 may enjoy the benefits of rent control past January 1, 1999. This includes not only tenants with leases signed before January 1, 1996, but also those tenants who have rented the same unit on a month-to-month basis, starting prior to January 1, 1996. (CC § 1954.52(a)(3).)

No rent control for new residences.

This law also prohibits any rent control on new residences, defined as those that have certificates of occupancy issued after January 31, 1995.

For more details on this state law, contact the local agency that administers rent control in your area. (CC § 1954.52(a)(1), (2).)

"Vacancy decontrol" for apartments.

This change affects Berkeley, East Palo Alto, Santa Monica, and West Hollywood, the only cities that formerly did not let landlords raise the rent when a tenant moves out and another comes in.

Effective January 1, 1999, landlords may raise the rent on multifamily housing units in any rent-controlled city if the prior tenant left voluntarily or was evicted for nonpayment of rent. Once rerented at this new rent, however, the property is still subject to local rent control ordinances at the higher rent.

Landlords may not, however, raise rents after a voluntary vacancy if the landlord has been cited for serious health, safety, fire, or building code violations that have continued unabated for six months preceding the vacancy. (CC § 1954.53.)

Berkeley

Name of Ordinance: Rent Stabilization and Eviction for Good Cause Ordinance, City Charter Art. XVII, §§ 120-124, Berkeley Municipal Code Ch. 13.76, §§ 13.76.011-13.76.190.

Adoption Date: 6/3/80. Last amended 11/2005, by initiative.

Exceptions: Units constructed after 6/3/80, owner-occupied single-family residences, and duplexes. (§ 13.76.050.)

Rental units owned (or leased) by nonprofit organizations that (1) receive governmental funding and rent such units to low-income tenants, or (2) provide such units as part of substance abuse treatment.

Administration:

Rent Stabilization Board

2125 Milvia Street

Berkeley, CA 94704

510-644-6128

FAX: 510-644-7723

email: rent@ci.berkeley.ca.us

www.ci.berkeley.ca.us. (This is the general city site. Click on "Municipal Codes & Zoning Ord." to get to Municipal Code. For the rent board add /rent to the URL given above. The rent board's site, at the "Laws and Regs" icon, is the best way to get to rent control and eviction rules).

Registration: Required or landlords cannot raise rent. (The provision that a tenant can withhold rents if the landlord fails to register was ruled unconstitutional in *Floystrup v. Berkeley Rent Stablization Board* (1990) 219 Cal. App. 3d 1309.) Stiff penalties for noncooperation. (§ 13.76.080.)

Vacancy Decontrol: State law (CC § 1954.53) supersedes the ordinance. Upon voluntary vacancy or eviction for nonpayment of rent, rents may be increased to any level following such vacancies. Once property is rerented, it is subject to rent control based on the higher rent.

Just Cause: Required. (§ 13.76.130.) This requirement applies even if the property is exempt from other rent control requirements because it qualifies as new construction or government-owned/operated housing. Specific good cause to evict must be stated in both the notice and in any unlawful detainer complaint.

Other Features: The landlord's unlawful detainer complaint must allege compliance with both the implied warranty of habitability and the rent control ordinance, except for evictions for remodeling or demolition. If the remodeling, demolition, or moving in of the landlord or a relative on which the eviction was based doesn't occur within two months of the tenant's leaving, the tenant can sue the landlord to regain possession of property and recover actual damages (treble damages or $750 if the landlord's reason for the delay was willfully false). (§ 13.76.150.) Also, government-subsidized "Section 8" landlords must register their units and are subject to the yearly annual general adjustment if they raise rents above that set by the Housing Authority.

Berkeley Just Cause Evictions	
Reason Allowed for Just Cause Evictions	**Additional Local Notice Requirements and Limitations**
Nonpayment of rent.	Ordinary Three-Day Notice to Pay Rent or Quit is used.
Breach of lease provision.	Three-Day Notice to Perform Covenant or Quit is used. Provision must be "reasonable and legal and … been accepted by the tenant or made part of the rental agreement." If the provision was added after tenant moved in, landlord can evict for breach only if tenant was told in writing that she did not have to accept the new term. Tenant must be given "written notice to cease," which precludes an unconditional Three-Day Notice to Quit even if the breach is considered uncorrectable.
Willful causing or allowing of substantial damage to premises and refusal to both pay the reasonable cost of repair and cease causing damage, following written notice.	Even though damage is involved, an unconditional Three-Day Notice to Quit is not allowed. Only a three-day notice that gives the tenant the option of ceasing to cause damage and pay for repair is allowed.

Berkeley Just Cause Evictions (cont'd)

Reason Allowed for Just Cause Evictions	Additional Local Notice Requirements and Limitations
Tenant refuses to agree to rental agreement or lease on expiration of prior one, where new proposed agreement contains no new or unlawful terms.	This applies only if a lease or rental agreement expires of its own terms. No notice is required. However, tenant must have refused to sign a new one containing the same provisions; an improvised notice giving the tenant several days to sign the new agreement or leave is a good idea, even though not required by ordinance or state law.
Tenant continued to be so disorderly as to disturb other tenants, following written notice to cease, or is otherwise subject to eviction under CCP § 1161(4), for committing a nuisance, very seriously damaging the property, or subletting contrary to the lease or rental agreement, unless the landlord has unreasonably withheld consent to sublet where original tenant remains, property is not illegally overcrowded as a result of the subletting, and other requirements are met—see ordinance for details.	Although a warning notice should precede three-day notice based on disturbing neighbors, the three-day notice, according to CCP § 1161(4), may be an unconditional Three-Day Notice to Quit.
Tenant, after written notice to cease, continues to refuse landlord access to the property as required by CC § 1954.	If provision is in lease, use three-day notice giving tenant option of letting you in or moving. If not, and tenancy is month to month, use 30-day notice specifying reason, following written demand for access.
Tenant, after written notice to cease, continues to conduct illegal activity on the premises.	Although a warning notice should precede a three-day notice based on illegal activity, the three-day notice, according to CCP § 1161(4), may be an unconditional Three-Day Notice to Quit.

Berkeley Just Cause Evictions (cont'd)

Reason Allowed for Just Cause Evictions	Additional Local Notice Requirements and Limitations
Landlord wants to make substantial repairs to bring property into compliance with health codes, and repairs not possible while tenant remains.	Under state law, eviction for this reason is allowed only if rental agreement is month to month, not for a fixed term. Landlord must first obtain all permits required for the remodeling, must provide alternative housing for the tenant (at the same rent) if he owns other vacant units in city, and must give evicted tenant right of first refusal to rerent after remodeling is finished. (Tenant given alternate temporary housing may be evicted from it if he refuses to move into old unit after work is completed.)
Landlord wants to demolish property.	Landlord must first obtain city "removal permit." (Although ordinance requires "good faith" to demolish, a euphemism for not doing it because of rent control, the state Ellis Act severely limits cities from refusing demolition permits on this basis.)
Landlord wants to move in herself, lived there previously, and lease or rental agreement specifically allows for this.	Termination procedure must be in accordance with lease provision. Thirty days' written notice is required to terminate month-to-month tenancy unless agreement provides for lesser period as short as seven days.
Landlord wants to move self, spouse, parent, or child into property, and no comparable vacant unit exists in the property.	30-day notice terminating month-to-month tenancy for this reason must specify name and relationship of person moving in. (Month-to-month tenancies only.)
Landlord wants to go out of rental business under state Ellis Act.	The requirement that the landlord must give the tenant six months' notice and pay $4,500 in relocation fees to tenants of each unit was ruled illegal, as preempted by the state Ellis Act, in *Channing Properties v. City of Berkeley* (1992) 11 Cal. App. 4th 88, 14 Cal. Rptr. 2d 32.

Beverly Hills

Name of Ordinance: Rent Stabilization Ordinance, Beverly Hills Municipal Code, Title 4, Chapters 5 and 6, §§ 4-5.101 to 4-6.08.

Adoption Date: 4/27/79. Last amended 6/18/2004.

Exceptions: Units constructed after 10/20/78, units that rented for more than $600 on 5/31/78, single-family residences, rented condominium units. (§ 4-5.102.)

Administration:
Rent Information Office
455 N. Rexford Drive
Beverly Hills, CA 90210

310-285-1031

www.ci.beverly-hills.ca.us or www.beverlyhills.org. (General city site. No site for the rent control ordinance.)

Registration: Not required.

Vacancy Decontrol: Rents may be increased to any level on rerenting following eviction for nonpayment of rent, as well as for voluntary vacancies.

Once property is rerented, it is subject to rent control based on the higher rent.

Just Cause: Required for units other than those that rented for more than $600 on 5/31/78; for these units, a month-to-month tenancy may be terminated only on 60 days' notice, however. (§§ 4-5.501 to 4-5.513.)

Other Features: Though not required by the ordinance, termination notice should state specific reason for termination; this indicates compliance with ordinance, as alleged (item 13) in your unlawful detainer complaint. Landlord is required to pay tenant substantial relocation fee if evicting to move in self or relative, or to substantially remodel, demolish, or convert to condominiums. Tenant may sue landlord who uses moving-in of self or relative as a "pretext" for eviction, for three times the rent that would have been due for the period the tenant was out of possession.

Beverly Hills Just Cause Evictions

Reason Allowed for Just Cause Evictions	Additional Local Notice Requirements and Limitations
Nonpayment of rent.	Ordinary Three-Day Notice to Pay Rent or Quit is used.
Breach of lease provision, following written notice to correct problem.	Three-Day Notice to Cure Covenant or Quit is used. The tenant must be given "written notice to cease," which precludes an unconditional Three-Day Notice to Quit even if the breach is uncorrectable.
Commission of a legal nuisance (disturbing other residents) or damaging the property.	Unconditional Three-Day Notice to Quit may be used.
Tenant is using the property for illegal purpose. This specifically includes overcrowding as defined in ordinance based on number of bedrooms and square footage.	Unconditional Three-Day Notice to Quit may be used.
Tenant refuses, after written demand by landlord, to agree to new rental agreement or lease on expiration of prior one, where proposed agreement contains no new or unlawful terms.	This applies when a lease or rental agreement expires of its own terms. The ordinance requires the landlord to have made a written request for renewal or extension at least 30 days before the old one expired.
Tenant has refused the landlord reasonable access to the property as required by CC § 1954.	If access provision is in lease, use three-day notice giving tenant option of letting you in or moving. If not, and tenancy is month to month, use 30-day notice specifying reason, following written demand for access to property.
Fixed-term lease has expired, and person occupying property is subtenant not approved by landlord.	Eviction is allowed on this basis only if person living there is not original tenant or approved subtenant. If lease has not expired and contains no-subletting clause, use Three-Day Notice to Quit to evict for breach of lease.

Beverly Hills Just Cause Evictions (cont'd)	
Reason Allowed for Just Cause Evictions	**Additional Local Notice Requirements and Limitations**
Landlord wants to move self, parent, or child into property, and no comparable vacant unit exists in the property. In multiple-unit dwelling, landlord can evict only the most recently moved-in tenant for this reason.	Landlord must give tenant 90-day notice that states the name, relationship, and address of person to be moved in, and a copy of the notice must be sent to the City Clerk. Landlord must also pay tenant(s) a "relocation fee" of up to $2,500, depending on the length of tenancy and the size of unit. The fee must be paid when the tenant leaves, or tenant can sue landlord for three times the fee plus attorney's fees. (§ 11-7.05.) Landlord does not have to pay fee if tenant fails to leave at end of 90-day period or pays to relocate tenant to comparable housing elsewhere.
Landlord wants to substantially remodel property.	Landlord must first obtain removal permit from city. For substantial remodeling, tenant gets right of first refusal when work done. Landlord must give tenant one year's notice. Landlord must also pay tenant(s) a "relocation fee" of up to $2,500, depending on the length of tenancy and the size of unit. The fee must be paid when the tenant leaves, or tenant can sue landlord for three times the fee plus attorney's fees. Landlord does not have to pay fee if tenant fails to leave at end of 90-day period or pays to relocate tenant to comparable housing elsewhere. Notice, if not accompanied by fee, must inform tenant of its amount and that it is payable when the tenant vacates. The notice cannot be given until city approval of the project is obtained, and a copy of the notice must be sent to the City Clerk. Landlord must petition Board for permission and in some cases must provide replacement housing during remodeling.

Beverly Hills Just Cause Evictions (cont'd)	
Reason Allowed for Just Cause Evictions	**Additional Local Notice Requirements and Limitations**
Employment of resident manager has been terminated and the property is needed for occupancy by the new manager.	This type of eviction is not covered in this book because the question of what notice is required is extremely complicated, depending in part on the nature of the management agreement. You should seek legal advice.

Campbell

Name of Ordinance: Campbell Municipal Code, Title 6, Ch. 6.09, §§ 6.09.010 to 6.09.190.: **Adoption Date:** 1983. Last amended 12/98.

Exemption: Rental units on lots with three or fewer units. (§ 6.09.030(n).)

Administration:

Campbell Rental Dispute Program
Project Sentinel Mediation Services
1055 Sunnyvale-Saratoga Road, Suite 3
Sunnyvale, CA 94087

408-243-8585; and 888-331-3332

www.ci.campbell.ca.us. The general city site includes the Municipal Code. The site for the Rental Dispute Program is www.housing.org/campbell_rent_dispute_resolution.htm.

Registration: Not required.

Individual Adjustments: Tenants affected by an increase can contest it by filing a petition within 45 days after notice of increase or notice to quit, or 15 days from effective date of rent increase or notice to quit, whichever is later, or lose the right to object to the increase. Disputes raised by tenant petition are first subject to "conciliation," then mediation. If those fail, either party may file a written request for arbitration by city "Fact Finding Committee." Committee determines whether increase is "reasonable" by considering costs of capital improvements, repairs, maintenance and debt service, and past history of rent increases. However, the Committee's determination is not binding. (§§ 6.09.050-6.09.150.)

Vacancy Decontrol: No restriction on raises after vacancy.

Eviction: Ordinance does not require showing of just cause to evict, so three-day and 30-day notice requirements and unlawful detainer procedures are governed solely by state law.

Just Cause: Not required.

Other features: Rent increase notice must state: "Notice: Chapter 6.09 of the Campbell Municipal Code provides a conciliation and mediation procedure for property owners and tenants to communicate when there are disputes over rent increases. (Rent increases can include a significant reduction in housing services.) To use this nonbinding procedure, the tenants shall first make a reasonable, good faith effort to contact the property owner or the property owner's agent to resolve the rent increase dispute. If not resolved, the tenant may then file a petition within 45 calendar days of this notice or 15 calendar days following the effective day of the increase, whichever is later. There may be other tenants from your complex receiving a similar rent increase, in which case, the petitions will be combined. For more information you should contact the City's designated Agent at 408-243-8565. Petitioning for conciliation cannot guarantee a reduction in the rent increase."

Note. Because this ordinance does not provide for binding arbitration of any rent increase dispute, it is not truly a rent control ordinance. Compliance with any decision appears to be voluntary only.

East Palo Alto

Name of Ordinance: Rent Stabilization and Eviction for Good Cause Ordinance, Ordinance No. 076.

Adoption Date: 11/23/83. Last amended 4/88.

Exception: With respect to all aspects of the ordinance except just cause evictions, units constructed after 11/23/83, units owned by landlords owning four or fewer units in city, property rehabilitated in accordance with federal Internal Revenue Code § 174(k). (§ 5.) As noted, all landlords are subject to the ordinance's just cause eviction restrictions. (§ 14.05.050.A.2.)

Administration:
Rent Stabilization Board
2277 University Avenue
East Palo Alto, CA 94303

650-853-3114; and 650-853-3109

www.ci.east-palo-alto.ca.us. This is the general city site with access to the Municipal Code.

Registration: Required.

Vacancy Decontrol: State law (CC § 1954.53) supersedes the ordinance. Upon voluntary vacancy or eviction for nonpayment of rent, rents may be increased to any level following such vacancies. Once property is rerented, it is subject to rent control based on the higher rent.

Just Cause: Required (§ 13.A). This aspect of the ordinance applies even to new construction, which is otherwise exempt. Specific just cause to evict must be stated both in the notice and in any unlawful detainer complaint. (§ 13.B.)

Other Features: Landlord's complaint must allege compliance with both the implied warranty of habitability and the rent control ordinance, except for evictions for remodeling or demolition (§ 13.C). If remodeling, demolition, or moving self or a relative, on which eviction was based, doesn't occur within two months of the tenant's leaving, tenant can sue landlord to regain possession of property and recover actual damages (treble damages or $500 if reason willfully false). (§ 15.B.)

East Palo Alto's ordinance does not specifically allow eviction for illegal use of the premises, such as dealing drugs. Still, if the lease has a clause prohibiting illegal use of the premises, you can evict for breach of lease provision (see below). If there's no such lease provision, see an attorney about whether CCP § 1161(4)s, allowance of an eviction for illegal activity, may "preempt" the local ordinance.

East Palo Alto Just Cause Evictions	
Reason Allowed for Just Cause Evictions	**Additional Local Notice Requirements and Limitations**
Nonpayment of rent.	Ordinary Three-Day Notice to Pay Rent or Quit is used.
Breach of lease provision, following written notice to cease.	Three-Day Notice to Cure Covenant or Quit is used. Provision must be reasonable and legal and been accepted by the tenant or made part of the rental agreement. If the provision was added after the tenant first moved in, the landlord can evict for breach only if the tenant was told in writing that she didn't have to accept the new term. Ordinance forbids use of an unconditional notice.
Willful causing or allowing of substantial damage to premises and refusal to both pay the reasonable cost of repair and cease causing damage, following written notice.	Even though damage is involved an ordinary unconditional Three-Day Notice to Quit is not allowed. Only a three-day notice that gives the tenant the option of ceasing to cause damage and pay for the costs of repair, as demanded by the landlord, is allowed.
Tenant refuses to agree to rental agreement or lease on expiration of prior one, where new proposed agreement contains no new or unlawful terms.	This applies only when a lease or rental agreement expires of its own terms. No notice is required. However, an improvised notice giving the tenant several days to sign the new agreement or leave is a good idea.
Tenant continues to be so disorderly as to disturb other tenants, following written notice to cease.	Even if the tenant is committing a legal nuisance for which state law would allow use of a Three-Day Notice to Quit, ordinance requires that three-day notice be in conditional "cease or quit" form.

East Palo Alto Cause Evictions (cont'd)	
Reason Allowed for Just Cause Evictions	**Additional Local Notice Requirements and Limitations**
Tenant, after written notice to cease, continues to refuse the landlord access to the property as required by CC § 1954.	If provision is in lease, use three-day notice giving tenant option of letting you in or moving. If not, and tenancy is month to month, use 30-day notice specifying reason, following written demand for access to property.
Landlord wants to make substantial repairs to bring property into compliance with health codes, and repairs not possible while tenant remains.	Under state law, eviction for this reason is allowed only if rental agreement is month to month. Thirty-day notice giving specific reason must be used. Landlord must first obtain all permits required for the remodeling, must provide alternative housing for the tenant if he has other vacant units in city, and must give evicted tenant right of first refusal to rerent after remodeling is finished. (Tenant given alternate housing may be evicted from it if he refuses to move into old unit after work is completed. § 13.A.10.)
Landlord wants to demolish property.	Under state law, eviction for this reason is allowed only if rental agreement is month to month. Thirty-day notice giving specific reason must be used. Landlord must first obtain all permits required for the remodeling, must provide alternative housing for the tenant if he has other vacant units in city, and must give evicted tenant right of first refusal to rerent after remodeling is finished. (Tenant given alternate housing may be evicted from it if he refuses to move into old unit after work is completed. § 13.A.10.) (Although ordinance requires "good faith" to demolish, a euphemism for not doing it because of rent control, the state Ellis Act severely limits cities refusing demolition permits on this basis.)

East Palo Alto Cause Evictions (cont'd)

Reason Allowed for Just Cause Evictions	Additional Local Notice Requirements and Limitations
Landlord wants to move self, spouse, parent, grandparent, child, or grandchild into property.	Under state law, eviction for this reason is allowed only if rental agreement is month to month. Thirty-day notice giving specific reason must be used. Also, Thirty-day notice terminating month-to-month tenancy for this reason should specify name and relationship of person moving in.

Fremont

Name of Ordinance: City of Fremont Residential Rent Increase Dispute Resolution Ordinance (RRIDRO), Ordinance No. 2253, Fremont Municipal Code, Title III, Chapter 19, §§ 3-1900–3-1955.

Adoption Date: 7/22/97, last amended 5/8/2001.

Exception: None. Ordinance applies to "any housing unit offered for rent or lease in the city consisting of one or more units." (§ 3-1905.)

Administration:
East Bay Community Mediation
22227 Redwood Road
Castro Valley, CA 94546-7043

510-733-4940
FAX: 510-733-4944

www.ci.fremont.ca.us

Registration: Not required.

Rent Formula: No fixed formula; landlord must respond to Mediation Services within two business days and participate in good faith in conciliation, mediation, and/or fact-finding proceedings, or rent increase notice can be ruled void. (§§ 3-1925, 1930, 1935.) Also, only one rent increase is allowed in any 12-month period. (§§ 3-1910(d).)

Individual Adjustments: Tenants affected by an increase can contest it by contacting Mediation Services within 15 days. Disputes raised by tenant request are first subject to conciliation, then mediation. If those fail, either party may file a written request for determination of the dispute by a fact-finding panel. This panel determines if the increase is reasonable by considering costs of capital improvements, repairs, existing market rents, return on investment, and the Oakland/San Jose All Urban Consumer Price Index. Panel's decision is not binding, but if landlord fails to appear or fails to participate in good faith in conciliation, education, or fact-finding process, that "shall void the notice of rent increase for all purposes." (§§ 3-1925(g), 1930(e), 1935(l).)

Rent Increase Notice Requirements: 60 days' notice appears to be required for all rent increases, even those of 10% or less (§ 3-1915(c)). All tenants, on moving in, must be provided a notice informing them of the dispute resolution programs, and that they can receive a copy by calling City Office of Neighborhoods at 510-494-4500. All rent increase notices must show the name, address, and phone number of the responsible party [§ 3-1915(b)], and must also state the following in bold type:

> **NOTICE: You are encouraged to contact the owner or manager [list name] of your rental unit to discuss this rent increase. However, chapter 19 of Title III of the Fremont Municipal Code provides a procedure for conciliation, mediation, and fact finding for disputes over rent increases. To use the procedure and secure additional information about the city ordinance, you must contact Mediation Services at 510-733-4945 within fifteen days following receipt of this notice.**

If this language is not included, the notice is not valid. (§ 3-1915(a)(d).)

Vacancy Decontrol: No restriction on raises after vacancy.

Eviction: Ordinance does not require showing of just cause to evict, so three-day and 30-day notice requirements and unlawful detainer procedure are governed solely by state law.

Note: Because this ordinance does not provide for binding arbitration of any rent increase dispute, it is not a true rent control ordinance. Compliance with any decision appears to be voluntary, except that if a city mediator or fact finder rules the landlord has failed to appear or act in "good faith" in any conciliation, mediation, or fact-finding proceeding, the rent increase notice can be ruled invalid. In this respect, the ordinance could, under certain circumstances, act as a sort of mild rent control.

Glendale

Name of Ordinance: Not specified

Adoption Date: 2002, last amended 2004.

Exceptions: Leases of one year or more. (§ 9.30.032.)

Administration: None specified.

Registration: Not required.

Vacancy Decontrol: Not applicable (ordinance does not regulate rents)

Just Cause: Required. At the time landlord delivers a 30-, 60-, or 3-day notice, landlord must also provide the tenant with a written notice that recites the landlord's legal grounds for terminating the tenancy and tenant's right to relocation benefits, if applicable. (§ 9.30.040.)

Other Features: Tenants entitled to relocation fee of twice the fair market rent, plus $1,000, in certain instances. (§ 9.30.035.) In an eviction lawsuit brought by the landlord to recover possession of the rental, the tenant may raise as an affirmative defense the landlord's failure to abide by any provision of the ordinance. (§ 9.30.060.)

Glendale Just Cause Evictions

Reasons Allowed for Just Cause Evictions

Nonpayment of rent, breach of a "lawful obligation or covenant," nuisance, or illegal use of the premises or permitting any illegal use within 1,000 feet of the unit. "Illegal use" specifically includes all offenses involving illegal drugs, such as marijuana (without a doctor's prescription).

When an unauthorized subtenant not approved by the landlord is in possession at the end of a lease term.

When a tenant refuses to allow the landlord access "as permitted or required by the lease or by law."

When the landlord offers a lease renewal of at least one year, serves a notice on the tenant of the offer at least 90 days before the current lease expires, and the tenant fails to accept within 30 days.

When the landlord plans to demolish the unit or perform work on it that costs at least eight times the monthly rent, and the tenant's absence is necessary for the repairs; or when the landlord is removing the property from the rental market, or seeks to have a spouse, grandparent, brother, sister, in-law, child, or resident manager (if there is no alternate unit available) move into the unit. Under state law, these grounds may be used only if the tenancy is month-to-month, and 30 or 60 days' written notice is given. The landlord must pay the tenant relocation expenses of two months' rent for a comparable unit plus $1,000.

Hayward

Name of Ordinance: "Residential Rent Stabilization," most recent ordinance is No. 03-01 C.S.

Adoption Date: 9/13/83.

Last amended: 1/21/2003.

Exceptions: Units first occupied after 7/1/79, units owned by landlord owning four or fewer rental units in the city. (§ 2(l).)

Administration:
Rent Review Office
777 B Street, 4th Floor
Hayward, CA 94541

510-583-4454

www.ci.hayward.ca.us.

Provides no rent control information. Municipal Code is accessible, but the rent control ordinance is not part of Municipal Code. It can be accessed by going to the site noted above, choosing "Other Ordinances" after choosing "Codes, Ordinances, and Fees."

Registration: Not required.

Vacancy Decontrol: Rent controls are permanently removed from each rental unit after a voluntary vacancy followed by the expenditure by the landlord of $200 or more on improvements, and city certification of compliance with City Housing Code (Section 8).

Units still subject to controls (those for which there were no voluntary vacancies in preceding years) can be rerented for any rent amount, with property being subject to controls based on the higher rent.

Just Cause: Required. (§ 19(a).) This aspect of the ordinance applies even to voluntarily vacated property no longer subject to rent control. Specific good cause to evict must be stated in both the notice and in any unlawful detainer complaint. (§ 19(b).)

Special Features: Tenant may defend any eviction lawsuit on the basis of the landlord's failure to provide tenant with any of the information required under the ordinance. (§ 8(f).)

Hayward Just Cause Evictions	
Reason Allowed for Just Cause Evictions	**Additional Local Notice Requirements and Limitations**
Nonpayment of rent.	Ordinary Three-Day Notice to Pay Rent or Quit is used.
Willful causing or allowing of substantial damage to premises and refusal to both pay the reasonable cost of repair and cease causing damage, following written notice.	Even though damage is involved an ordinary unconditional Three-Day Notice to Quit is not allowed. Only a three-day notice that gives the tenant the option of ceasing to cause damage and pay for the costs of repair, as demanded by the landlord, is allowed.

Hayward Just Cause Evictions (cont'd)	
Reason Allowed for Just Cause Evictions	**Additional Local Notice Requirements and Limitations**
Breach of lease provision following written notice to cease.	Three-Day Notice to Cure Covenant or Quit is used. Provision must be reasonable and legal and have been accepted by the tenant or made part of the rental agreement. If the provision was added after the tenant first moved in, the landlord can evict for breach only if the tenant was told in writing that she didn't have to accept the new term. Notice must give the tenant the option of correcting the problem.
Tenant refuses to agree to rental agreement or lease on expiration of prior one, where new proposed agreement contains no new or unlawful terms.	This applies only when a lease or rental agreement expires of its own terms. No notice is required. However, an improvised notice giving the tenant several days to sign the new agreement or leave is a good idea.
Tenant continues to be so disorderly as to disturb other tenants, following written notice to cease.	Even if the tenant is committing a legal nuisance for which state law would allow use of a Three-Day Notice to Quit, ordinance requires that three-day notice be in conditional "cease or quit" form.
Tenant, after written notice to cease, continues to refuse the landlord access to the property as required by CC § 1954.	If provision is in lease, use three-day notice giving tenant option of letting you in or moving. If not, and tenancy is month to month, use 30-day notice specifying reason, following written demand for access to property.
Landlord wants to make substantial repairs to bring property into compliance with health codes, and repairs not possible while tenant remains.	Under state law, eviction for this reason is allowed only if rental agreement is month to month. Thirty-day notice giving specific reason must be used. Landlord must first obtain all permits required for the remodeling, and must give tenant notice giving him first chance to rerent after remodeling is finished. (No requirement for alternative housing.)

Hayward Just Cause Evictions (cont'd)

Reason Allowed for Just Cause Evictions	Additional Local Notice Requirements and Limitations
Landlord wants to demolish property.	Under state law, eviction for this reason is allowed only if rental agreement is month-to-month. Thirty-day notice giving specific reason must be used. Landlord must first obtain all necessary permits. (Although ordinance requires "good faith" to demolish, a euphemism for not doing it because of rent control, the state Ellis Act severely limits cities from refusing demolition permits on this basis.)
Landlord wants to move self, spouse, parent, child, stepchild, brother, or sister into property, and no comparable vacant unit exists in the property.	Under state law, eviction for this reason is allowed only if rental agreement is month-to-month. Thirty-day notice giving specific reason must be used. Landlord must first obtain all permits required for the remodeling, and must give tenant notice giving him first chance to rerent after remodeling is finished. (No requirement for alternative housing.) Thirty-day notice terminating month-to-month tenancy for this reason should specify name and relationship of person moving in.
Landlord wants to move in herself, and lease or rental agreement specifically allows this.	Termination procedure must be in accordance with lease provision. Thirty days' written notice is required to terminate month-to-month tenancy unless agreement provides for lesser period as short as seven days.
Tenant is using the property illegally.	Three-Day Notice to Quit is used.
Tenant continues, after written notice to cease, to violate reasonable and legal regulations applicable to all tenants generally, if tenant accepted regulations in writing in the lease or rental agreement, or otherwise.	If tenancy is not month to month and violation is very serious, use Three-Day Notice to Perform Covenant or Quit. If tenancy is month to month, use 30-day notice preceded by written warning.

Hayward Just Cause Evictions (cont'd)

Reason Allowed for Just Cause Evictions	Additional Local Notice Requirements and Limitations
Lawful termination of apartment manager's employment, where he or she was compensated with use of apartment.	This type of eviction is not covered in this book because the question of what notice is required is extremely complicated, depending in part on the nature of the management agreement. You should seek legal advice.

Los Angeles

Name of Ordinance: Rent Stabilization Ordinance, Los Angeles Municipal Code, Chapter XV, §§ 151.00–155.09.

Adoption Date: 4/21/79. Last amended 5/2005.

Exceptions: Units constructed (or substantially renovated with at least $10,000 in improvements) after 10/1/78, "luxury" units (defined as 0, 1, 2, 3, or 4+ bedroom units renting for at least $302, $420, $588, $756, or $823, respectively, as of 5/31/78), single-family residences, except where two or more houses are located on the same lot. (§ 151.02.G, M.)

Administration:

Los Angeles Housing Department
3550 Wilshire Boulevard, Suite 1500
Los Angeles, CA 90010

3415 S. Sepulveda Blvd., Suite 150
Los Angeles, CA 90034

6640 Van Nuys Boulevard
Van Nuys, CA 91405

690 Knox Street, Suite 125,
Torrance, CA 90502

For information regarding ordinance: call 800-994-4444 or 866-557-7368 (RENT).

www2.cityofla.org/LAHD for information on rent control and www.tenant.net/Other_Areas/Calif/losangel/index.html. For the L.A. Municipal Code, navigate the city's main website at www.ci.la.ca.us.

Registration: Required.

Vacancy Decontrol: Landlord may charge any rent after a tenant either vacates voluntarily or is evicted for nonpayment of rent or breach of a rental agreement provision, or to substantially remodel. (Controls remain if landlord evicts for any other reason, fails to remodel after evicting for that purpose, or terminates or fails to renew a subsidized housing lease with the city housing authority.) However, once the property is rerented, it is subject to rent control based on the higher rent. (§ 151.06.C.)

Just Cause: Required. (§ 151.09.) Every termination notice must state "the reasons for the termination with specific facts to permit a determination of the date, place, witnesses, and circumstances concerning the reason." (§ 151.09.C.1.) Tenant may not defend unlawful detainer action on the basis of lack of good cause or failure of the notice to state the reason if tenant has disobeyed a pretrial court order requiring him or her to deposit rent into court; see CCP § 1170.5 and *Green v. Superior Court,* 10 Cal.3d 616 (1974). (§ 151.09.E.) State law requires use of a 60-day termination notice of month-to-month tenancy, instead of a 30-day notice, for this city, if the tenant has occupied the premises for a year or more.

Other Features: Tenant may defend on the basis that the landlord failed to register the property in accordance with the ordinance. (§ 151.09.F.)

Los Angeles Just Cause Evictions

Reason Allowed for Just Cause Evictions	Additional Local Notice Requirements and Limitations
Nonpayment of rent.	Ordinary Three-Day Notice to Pay Rent or Quit is used.
Commission of a legal nuisance (disturbing other residents) or damaging the property.	Unconditional Three-Day Notice to Quit may be used.
Tenant is using the property for illegal purpose.	Unconditional Three-Day Notice to Quit may be used.

Los Angeles Just Cause Evictions (cont'd)

Reason Allowed for Just Cause Evictions	Additional Local Notice Requirements and Limitations
Breach of lease provision, following written notice to cease. (Landlord may not evict based on breach of no-pets clause added by notice of change of terms of tenancy, where no such clause existed at the outset of the tenancy. § 151.09.D.)	Three-Day Notice to Cure Covenant or Quit is used. The ordinance requires that the tenant be given "written notice to cease," which precludes an unconditional Three-Day Notice to Quit, even if the breach can be considered uncorrectable.
Tenant refuses to agree to rental agreement or lease on expiration of prior one, where new proposed agreement contains no new or unlawful terms.	This applies only when a lease or rental agreement expires of its own terms. No notice is required. However, an improvised notice giving the tenant several days to sign the new agreement or leave is a good idea, even though not required by ordinance or state law.
Landlord seeks to permanently remove the unit from the rental housing market.	Only month-to-month tenant can be evicted on this ground. Use 30-day notice specifying this reason.
Tenant, after written notice to cease, continues to refuse the landlord access to the property as required by CC § 1954.	If provision is in lease, use three-day notice giving tenant option of letting you in or moving. If not, and tenancy is month to month, use 30-day notice specifying reason, following previous written demand for access to property.
Landlord wants to move self, spouse, parent, child, or legally required resident manager into property. Landlord must pay relocation fee of $2,000-$2,500 to tenants except where moving legally required manager into property.	Only month-to-month tenant can be evicted on this ground. Landlord must serve tenant with copy of a form, the original of which must first be filed with the Community Development Department, that specifies the name and relationship of the person to be moving in.

Los Angeles Just Cause Evictions (cont'd)

Reason Allowed for Just Cause Evictions	Additional Local Notice Requirements and Limitations
Fixed-term lease has expired, and person occupying property is subtenant not approved by landlord.	Eviction on this basis is allowed only if person living there is not original tenant or approved subtenant. No notice is required. If lease has not expired and contains no-subletting clause, use Three-Day Notice to Quit to evict for breach of lease.
Landlord wants to: (1) demolish the unit, or (2) undertake "Primary Renovative Work," under a "Tenant Habitability Plan" filed with the Housing Department, and the tenant is "unreasonably interfering" with that plan; or (3) substantially renovate the rental unit, where the landlord has complied with all necessary notices and relocation requirements, and the tenant has refused to cooperate with the landlord's plans.	Only month-to-month tenant can be evicted on this ground. Use 30-day notice specifying this reason. Landlord must serve tenant with copy of a filed Community Development Department form describing the renovation work or demolition.

Los Gatos

Name of Ordinance: Los Gatos Rental Dispute Mediation and Arbitration Ordinance, Los Gatos Town Code, Chapter 14, Article VIII, §§ 14.80.010–14.80-315.

Adoption Date: 10/27/80. Last amended 3/2004.

Exceptions: Property on lots with two or fewer units, single-family residences, rented condominium units. (§ 14.80.020.)

Administration:
Project Sentinel—Mediation Services
1055 Sunnyvale-Saratoga Road, Suite 3
Sunnyvale, CA 94087

408-720-9888 and 888-331-3332

www.town.los-gatos.ca.us, official city website. Choose "Town Government," then "Town Codes." Rent control provisions are in Chapter 14, Article VIII. The site for the Rental Dispute Program is www.housing.org/los_gatos_rent_dispute_resolution.htm.

Registration: Not required. (However, a "regulatory fee" to pay for program is added to annual business license fee, when business license is required.)

Vacancy Decontrol: Landlord may charge any rent after a tenant vacates voluntarily or is evicted following Three-Day Notice for Nonpayment of Rent or other breach of the rental agreement. However, once the new rent for a vacated unit is established by the landlord and the property is rerented, it is subject to rent control based on the higher rent. (§ 14.80.310.)

Just Cause: Not required.

Other Features: Tenant faced with termination notice may invoke mediation/arbitration hearing procedure on eviction issue and stay landlord's eviction suit; if tenant wins mediation/arbitration hearing, eviction will be barred. (§ 14.80.205.)

Oakland

Name of Ordinance: "Ordinance Establishing a Residential Rent Arbitration Board," Oakland Municipal Code, Title 8, Ch. 8.22, §§ 8.22.010–8.22.200. See also Title 8, Ch. 8.22, §§ 8.22.300–8.22.480.

Adoption Date: 10/7/80. Last amended 10/2003.

Exceptions: Units constructed after 1/18/84, buildings "substantially rehabilitated" at cost of 50% of that of new construction, as determined by Chief Building Inspector. (§ 8.22.030.)

Administration:
Rent Adjustment Program
250 Frank H. Ogawa Plaza
Oakland, CA 94612

510-238-3721

FAX: 510-238-3691

www.ci.oakland.ca.us

www.oaklandnet.com

Choose the Municipal Code and go to Title 8, Chapter 8.22; or choose "Rent Ordinance"; and click "Go.

Registration: Not required.

Vacancy Decontrol: Landlord may charge any rent after a tenant vacates voluntarily or is evicted for nonpayment of rent. If tenant otherwise vacates involuntarily, landlord may not increase the rent for 24 months.

On eviction for reasons other than nonpayment of rent, ordinance allows increase of up to 12%, depending on rent increases over previous 12 months.

Once property is rerented, it is subject to rent control based on the higher rent.

Just Cause: Under a separate "Just Cause for Eviction" ordinance (Measure EE), enacted 11/5/2002, landlords may terminate a month-to-month rental agreement (or refuse to renew a lease) only when the tenant has failed to pay the rent (or has violated another important lease term), refused to enter into a written renewal of a rental agreement or lease, caused substantial damage, disturbed the peace and quiet of other tenants, engaged in illegal activities, or refused entry to the landlord when properly asked. Landlords may also terminate rental agreements or not renew leases when they want to live in the unit themselves (or intend it for a close family member), or to substantially renovate the unit. (See Municipal Code, Title 8, Ch. 22 §§ 8.22.300–8.22.480.)

Other Features: Rent increase notices must be in a form prescribed by Section 8.22.070(H)(1), which requires tenant be notified of right to petition rent board. All tenants, on moving in, must be provided a notice informing them of their rights under the ordinance. (§ 8.22.060.)

Landlord evicting to "rehabilitate" the property (presumably to obtain permanent exemption from controls) must obtain building permit before eviction.

Palm Springs

Name of Ordinance: "Rent Control," Palm Springs Municipal Code, Title 4, Chapters 4.02, 4.04, 4.08, §§ 4.02.010–4.08.190.

Adoption Date: 9/1/79. Last amended, by initiative, 12/94.

Exceptions: Units constructed after 4/1/79; owner-occupied single-family residences, duplexes, triplexes, and four-plexes; units where rent was $450 or more as of 9/1/79. (§§ 4.02.010, 4.02.030.)

Administration:

Rent Review Commission

3200 E. Tahquitz Canyon Way

Palm Springs, CA 92262

760-778-8465

www.ci.palm-springs.ca.us.

Registration: Required. (§ 4.02.080.)

Vacancy Decontrol: Rent controls are permanently removed after tenant voluntarily vacates or is evicted for cause.

Just Cause: Landlords must show just cause to evict for units subject to rent control. After voluntary vacancy or eviction for cause, just cause requirement does not apply anymore. (§ 4.08.060(j)(2).)

Palm Springs Just Cause Evictions	
Reason Allowed for Just Cause Evictions	**Additional Local Notice Requirements and Limitations**
Nonpayment of rent.	Ordinary Three-Day Notice to Pay Rent or Quit is used.
Breach of lease provision.	Three-Day Notice to Cure Covenant or Quit is used, or Three-Day Notice to Quit where breach cannot be cured, or improper subletting.

Palm Springs Just Cause Evictions (cont'd)

Reason Allowed for Just Cause Evictions	Additional Local Notice Requirements and Limitations
Creation or maintenance of a nuisance.	State law allows use of a Three-Day Notice to Quit.
Tenant is using the property illegally.	Three-Day Notice to Quit is used.
Landlord wants to move self, parent, child, grandparent, brother or sister, mother-in-law, father-in-law, son-in-law, or daughter-in-law into property.	Under state law, eviction for this reason is allowed only if rental agreement is month to month. Thirty-day notice giving specific reason must be used.

Richmond

Name of Ordinance: None specified

Adoption date: 6/2009.

Exceptions: Rental units owned or operated by any government agency or whose rent is subsidized by any government agency, including but not limited to Section 8 housing subsidies. Does not apply to a "purchaser for value," someone who is not employed by, affiliated with, or acting on behalf of an entity that acquires title to a rental unit following sale of the rental unit under the power of sale in a deed of trust or foreclosure, and who is not purchasing the property for the purpose of evading the protections of the ordinance. (§ 7.105.010.)

Adminstration: None specified.

Registration: Not required.

Vacancy Decontrol: Not applicable (ordinance does not regulate rents).

Just Cause: Required for bank-owned properties. At the time landlord delivers a 30-, 60-, or 3-day notice, landlord must also provide the tenant with a written notice that recites the landlord's legal grounds for terminating the tenancy. If relocation assistance is required, landlord must also serve tenant with a written notice describing tenant's right to relocation assistance. (§ 7.105.040.)

Other Features: Landlord may not retaliate against tenants who seek to assert their rights under this ordinance or under state or federal law, and tenants may raise such retaliation as a defense to an eviction lawsuit. Evidence of tenants' assertion of their rights within 180 days prior to the alleged retaliation creates a rebuttable presumption of retaliation. (§ 7.105.050.) Evicted tenants may be entitled to relocation assistance (twice the monthly rent, plus $1,000). (§7.105.030.)

Richmond Just Cause Evictions

Reasons Allowed for Just Cause Evictions

Failure to pay rent within seven days of receiving notice that rent is due.

Violation of a lease clause and failure to cure the violation (exempts failure to move out upon proper notice, and adding a dependent child to the tenancy).

Committing a nuisance or substantially interfering with the comfort, safety, or enjoyment of the landlord or other tenants.

Using the rental unit or common areas (or permitting them to be used) for illegal purposes.

Refusing to sign a written extension of a lease or rental agreement, within seven days of receiving it, that contains terms that are substantially the same as the prior rental agreement.

Refusal to grant access as permitted by law.

Possession of the rental unit by an unapproved subtenant.

Landlord seeks recovery of the rental for use by a resident manager or a qualified family member.

Landlord seeks to permanently remove the unit from rental housing, pursuant to state law; to demolish the unit; to perform work on the building that would make the unit uninhabitable for at least 30 days and that will cost not less than eight times the monthly rent.

To comply with a government order to empty the rental unit.

To comply with a contractual agreement or government regulation relating to the qualifications of tenancy with a government entity, when the tenant is no longer qualified.

San Diego

Name of Ordinance: "Tenants' Right to Know Regulations." San Diego Municipal Code §§ 98.0701 through 98.0760

Adoption date: 3/04, last amended 4/04.

Exceptions: Institutional facilities, such as schools; government owned or subsidized property subject to substantially similar or greater state or federal eviction controls; rentals to boarders in the landlord's principal residence, where landlord and tenant share facilities; hotel, motel, rooming house rentals that are not single room occupancy hotel rooms (as defined by San Diego Municipal Code Chapter 14, Article 3, Division 5); mobile homes; transient occupancies as defined by CC § 1940(b). Does not apply to tenants who have lived on the property less than two years. (§ 98.0725.)

Adminstration: None specified.

Registration: Not required.

Vacancy Decontrol: Not applicable (ordinance does not regulate rents).

Just Cause: Required. At the time landlord delivers a 30-, 60-, or 3-day notice, landlord must also provide the tenant with a written notice that recites the landlord's legal grounds for terminating the tenancy.

Other Features: In an eviction lawsuit brought by the landlord to recover possession of the rental, the tenant may raise as an affirmative defense the landlord's failure to abide by any provision of the ordinance.

San Diego Just Cause Evictions

Reasons Allowed for Just Cause Evictions

Refusal to give the landlord reasonable access to the rental unit for the purpose of making repairs or improvements, or for the purpose of inspection as permitted or required by the lease or by law, or for the purpose of showing the rental unit to a prospective purchaser or mortgagee.

San Diego Just Cause Evictions (cont'd)

Reason Allowed for Just Cause Evictions

Nonpayment of rent, violation of "a lawful and material obligation or covenant of the tenancy," commission of a nuisance, or illegal use of the premises.

Refusal "after written request of a landlord" to sign a lease renewal "for a further term of like duration with similar provisions."

To make necessary repairs or perform construction when removing the tenant is reasonably necessary to do the job, provided the landlord has obtained all necessary permits from the city.

When the landlord intends to withdraw all rental units in all buildings or structures on a parcel of land from the rental market, or when the landlord, a spouse, parent, grandparent, brother, sister, child, grandchild, or a resident manager plans to occupy the rental unit. These grounds may be used only if the tenancy is month to month (under state law, you're entitled to 60 days' written notice).

San Francisco

Name of Ordinance: Residential Rent Stabilization and Arbitration Ordinance, San Francisco Administrative Code, Chapter 37.

Adoption Date: 6/79. Last codified (conformed to current law) 6/30/2008.

Exceptions: Units constructed after 6/79; buildings over 50 years old and "substantially rehabilitated" since 6/79. (§ 37.2 (p).)

Administration:
Residential Rent Stabilization and Arbitration Board
25 Van Ness Avenue, Suite 320
San Francisco, CA 94102

415-252-4602
415-252-4600 (recorded info);
FAX 415-252-4699
"Fax-Back" Service (fax a question, they fax you an answer): 415-252-4660

www.ci.sf.ca.us/rentbd
www.sfgov.org/site/rentboard_index.htm.

Municipal Code/Administrative Code is available from the city official site, www.ci.sf.ca.us. Rent control laws (in superior format) and regulations are available from rent board site.

Registration: Not required.

Vacancy Decontrol: Landlord may charge any rent after a tenant vacates voluntarily or is evicted for cause. Once property is rerented for a year, it is subject to rent control based on the higher rent. (§ 37.3(a).)

Just Cause: Required. Every termination notice must state "the grounds under which possession is sought" and must advise the tenant that advice regarding the notice is available from the Board. (§ 37.9.)

Other Features: Tenant or Board may sue landlord, following either unsuccessful eviction attempt or successful eviction based on falsified reason, for treble damages and attorney's fees. (§ 37.9(e).) Landlord must file copy of tenancy termination notice (except Three-Day Notice to Pay Rent or Quit) with rent board within ten days after it is served on the tenant. (§ 37.9(c).) Must have just cause to remove certain housing services (such as parking and storage facilities) from a tenancy. (§ 37.2(r).)

San Francisco Just Cause Evictions

Reason Allowed for Just Cause Evictions	Additional Local Notice Requirements and Limitations
Nonpayment of rent.	Ordinary Three-Day Notice to Pay Rent or Quit is used.
Tenant "habitually pays the rent late or gives checks which are frequently returned ...."	This can only be used if tenancy is month to month, by using 30-day notice.
Breach of lease provision, following written notice to cease.	Three-Day Notice to Perform Covenant or Quit is used. Tenant must be given "written notice to cease," which precludes an unconditional Three-Day Notice to Quit, even if the breach is uncorrectable.

San Francisco Just Cause Evictions (cont'd)

Reason Allowed for Just Cause Evictions	Additional Local Notice Requirements and Limitations
Commission of a legal nuisance (disturbing other residents) or damaging the property.	Unconditional Three-Day Notice to Quit may be used.
Tenant is using the property for illegal purpose.	Unconditional Three-Day Notice to Quit may be used.
Tenant refuses, after written demand by landlord, to agree to new rental agreement or lease on expiration of prior one, where new proposed agreement contains no new or unlawful terms.	This applies only when a lease or rental agreement expires of its own terms. No notice is required. However, a written notice giving the tenant at least three days to sign the new agreement or leave should be served on the tenant with the proposed new lease or rental agreement.
Tenant, after written notice to cease, continues to refuse the landlord access to the property as required by CC § 1954.	If provision is in lease, use three-day notice giving tenant option of letting you in or moving. If not, and tenancy is month to month, use 30-day notice specifying reason, following written demand for access to property.
Landlord wants to rehabilitate the property or add capital improvements.	Allowed only if rental agreement is month to month. Ownership must have been previously registered with Board. Can't evict if rehab financed by city with "RAP" loans. If improvements are not "substantial rehabilitation" of building 50 or more years old, landlord must give tenant right of first refusal to reoccupy property when work is completed.
Fixed-term lease has expired, and person occupying property is subtenant not approved by landlord.	No notice is required. Ordinance allows eviction on this basis only if person living there is not original tenant or approved subtenant. (If lease has not expired and contains no-subletting clause, use Three-Day Notice to Quit to evict for breach of lease.)

San Francisco Just Cause Evictions (cont'd)

Reason Allowed for Just Cause Evictions	Additional Local Notice Requirements and Limitations
Landlord owning at least 25% interest (10% if bought before 2/91) wants to move self, parent, grandparent, child, grandchild, brother, sister, or spouse (including domestic partner) of any of the foregoing into the property. Note that spouses and domestic partners (those registered as such pursuant to the San Francisco Administrative Code Chapter 62.1 and 62.8) may aggregate their interests, but not tenants in common. Evictions for this reason are known as "owner move-in" evictions, or "OMI" evictions. They are the most contentious type of eviction and are often the subject of prolonged litigation. Before commencing an OMI eviction, you would be well advised to check the Ordinance and the Rent Board website, which is extremely helpful, for updates, details, and any added regulations.	Eviction for this reason is allowed only if rental agreement is month to month. Also, ownership must have been previously registered with Board. By popular vote in November 1998 (Proposition G), effective December 18, 1998, OMIs are not allowed as to: (1) Seniors 60 years of age or older who have lived in the rental for at least ten years; (2) Disabled or blind tenants who meet the Supplemental Security Income/ California State Supplemental Program (SSI/SSP) criteria for disability, as determined by the Program or any other method approved by the Rent Board, who have lived in the rental for at least ten years; and (3) Tenants with a "catastrophic illness" (as certified by the tenant's primary care physician) who have lived in the rental for at least five years. There are several restrictions to allowable OMIs. The landlord must live in the same building as the unit that is the subject of the OMI (unless the landlord owns only one unit in the building). Only one "owner move-in" eviction is allowed for a single building. The unit that is the subject of the first OMI becomes the designated OMI unit for that building for the future. Landlords may not do an OMI as to a particular unit if there is a comparable vacant unit in the building, and must cease eviction proceedings if a comparable unit becomes available prior to recovering possession. For buildings of three or more units built before 6/79, the landlord must obtain a conditional use permit from the city planning department.

San Francisco Just Cause Evictions (cont'd)

Reason Allowed for Just Cause Evictions	Additional Local Notice Requirements and Limitations
Landlord owning at least 25% ... (continued)	Certain tenants will be entitled to a $1,000 relocation benefit from the landlord. The landlord or other qualified relative who occupies the recovered unit must move in within three months and reside there continuously for 36 months
Landlord wants to demolish the unit.	Allowed only if rental agreement is month to month. Ownership must have been previously registered with Board. Landlord must obtain all necessary permits first.
Landlord wants to rehabilitate the property or add capital improvements.	Allowed only if rental agreement is month to month. Ownership must have been previously registered with Board. Can't evict if rehab financed by city with "RAP" loans. If improvements are not "substantial rehabilitation" of building 50 or more years old, landlord must give tenant right of first refusal to reoccupy property when work is completed.
Landlord wants to permanently remove property from the rental housing market.	Allowed only if rental agreement is month to month. Ownership must have been previously registered with Board. Although the ordinance requires that the landlord must pay relocation compensation of $1,500–$3,000, the Court of Appeal ruled in a case involving Berkeley's ordinance that this requirement was illegal, as preempted by the state Ellis Act. (See *Channing Properties v. City of Berkeley* (1992) 11 Cal. App. 4th 88, 14 Cal. Rptr. 2d 32.)

San Jose

Name of Ordinance: San Jose Rental Dispute Mediation and Arbitration Ordinance, San Jose Municipal Code, Title 17, Chapter 17.23, §§ 17.23.010-17.23.770.

Adoption Date: 7/7/79. Last amended 7/1/2003.

Exceptions: Units constructed after 9/7/79, single-family residences, duplexes, townhouses, and condominium units. (§ 17.23.150.)

Administration:

San Jose Rental Rights and Referrals Program
200 East Santa Clara Street
San Jose, CA 95113

408-975-4480

www.ci.san-jose.ca.us. This general city site provides no rent control information. The phone menu, however, at 408-975-4480, provides helpful information. Municipal Code is accessible. Rent control portions are in Title 17, Chapter 17.23. The Rental Rights and Referrals website is www.sjhousing.org/program/rentalrights.html.

Registration: Required.

Vacancy Decontrol: Landlord may charge any rent after a tenant vacates voluntarily or is evicted following Three-Day Notice to Pay Rent or Quit or other breach of the rental agreement. However, once the new rent for a vacated unit is established by the landlord and the property is rerented, it is subject to rent control based on the higher rent. (§ 17.23.190.)

Just Cause: Not required. Notice requirements and unlawful detainer procedures are governed solely by state law, except that 90 days' notice, rather than 60 days', is required to terminate a month-to-month-tenancy if the tenant has lived there a year or more. (§ 17.23.610A.) Sixty days' notice is also required if the tenant is served with an offer to arbitrate. (§ 17.23.615.)

Other: All tenants, on moving in, must be provided a notice informing of their rights under the ordinance. (§ 17.23.030.) Rent increase notices must notify tenant of right to petition, time limits, and the city rent program's address and phone number. (§ 17.23.270.)

In addition, ordinance requires that 90-day notice of termination be given to a tenant of month-to-month tenancy that's lasted over a year, or a 60-day notice if served with an offer to arbitrate. We believe this provision is invalid as superseded by recent state law allowing a 60-day notice without an offer to arbitrate.

Important: Copies of Notices to Vacate must be sent to the city. (§ 17.23.760.)

Santa Monica

Name of Ordinance: Rent Control Charter Amendment, City Charter Article XVIII, §§ 1800-1821.

Adoption Date: 4/10/79. Last amended 11/5/2002.

Exceptions: Units constructed after 4/10/79; owner-occupied single-family residences, duplexes, and triplexes; single-family dwellings not rented on 7/1/84. (Charter Amendment (C.A.) §§ 1801(c), 1815; Regulation (Reg.) §§ 2000 and following, 12000 and following.) However, rental units other than single-family dwellings not rented on 7/1/84 must be registered and the exemption applied for.

Administration:

Rent Control Board
1685 Main Street, Room 202
Santa Monica, CA 90401

310-458-8751

Email: rent_control@csanta-monica.org.

www.ci.santa-monica.ca.us/rentcontrol. This is an excellent site. Includes rent control laws in "Charter Amendment and Regulations"—both of which are not in the Municipal Code. See also www.tenant.net/Other_Areas/Calif/smonica/rentctrl.html.

Registration: Required. (C.A. §§ 1803(q), 1805(h).)

Vacancy Decontrol: State law (CC § 1954.53) supersedes the ordinance. Upon voluntary vacancy or eviction for nonpayment of rent, rents may be increased to any level following such vacancies. Once property is rerented, it is subject to rent control based on the higher rent.

Just Cause: Required. Specific good cause to evict must be stated in the termination notice. (Reg. § 9001.)

Other Features: Landlord's complaint must allege compliance with rent control ordinance. (C.A. § 1806.)

Santa Monica Just Cause Evictions	
Reason Allowed for Just Cause Evictions	**Additional Local Notice Requirements and Limitations**
Nonpayment of rent.	Ordinary Three-Day Notice to Pay Rent or Quit is used.
Breach of lease provision.	Three-Day Notice to Perform Covenant or Quit is used. Ordinance requires that the tenant has "failed to cure such violation," which precludes an unconditional Three-Day Notice to Quit, even if the breach is uncorrectable.
Tenant refuses to agree to rental agreement or lease on expiration of prior one, where new proposed agreement contains no new or unlawful terms.	This applies only when a lease or rental agreement expires of its own terms. No notice is required. However, an improvised notice giving the tenant several days to sign the new agreement or leave is a good idea.
Tenant is convicted of using the property for illegal purpose.	Three-Day Notice to Quit may be used, but only if tenant is actually convicted. This appears to mean that drug dealers can't be evicted unless first convicted. This provision may violate state law, which does not require a conviction. See CCP § 1161(4). If you wish to evict for illegal use without a conviction, try it based on a violation of a lease provision that forbids illegal use of the premises. Otherwise, see a lawyer about making the argument that this part of the ordinance is preempted by state law.

Santa Monica Just Cause Evictions (cont'd)	
Reason Allowed for Just Cause Evictions	**Additional Local Notice Requirements and Limitations**
Willful causing or allowing of substantial damage to premises, or commission of nuisance that interferes with comfort, safety, or enjoyment of the property, following written notice.	No requirement for alternative three-day notice giving tenant the option of correcting the problem. Three-Day Notice to Quit may be used.
Tenant, after written notice to cease, continues to refuse the landlord access to the property as required by CC § 1954.	If provision is in lease, use three-day notice giving tenant option of letting you in or moving. If not, and tenancy is month to month, use 30-day notice specifying reason, following written demand for access to property.
Fixed-term lease has expired, and person occupying property is subtenant not approved by landlord.	No notice is required. Eviction on this basis is allowed only if person living there is not original tenant or approved subtenant. (If lease has not expired and contains no-subletting clause, use Three-Day Notice to Quit to evict for breach of lease.)
Landlord wants to move self, parent, child, brother, sister, or spouse of foregoing into property.	Eviction for this reason is allowed only if rental agreement is month to month. Landlord must include on the termination notice the name of the current tenant, the rent charged, and the name, relationship, and address of person to be moving in. The notice must be filed with the Board within three days of service on the tenant. (Reg. § 9002(e).) The landlord must also offer any comparable vacant unit in the same building to the tenant and must allow the tenant to move back into the property if the relative does not occupy it within 30 days after the tenant moves out.

Santa Monica Just Cause Evictions (cont'd)

Reason Allowed for Just Cause Evictions	Additional Local Notice Requirements and Limitations
Landlord wants to demolish property, convert to condominiums, or otherwise remove property from rental market. (City's very strict ordinance has been modified by the state Ellis Act, which severely limits cities from refusing removal permits.)	Eviction for this reason allowed only if tenancy is month to month. Although the ordinance requires a landlord to pay a relocation fee of up to $4,000, the Court of Appeal ruled in a case involving Berkeley's ordinance that this requirement was illegal, as preempted by the state Ellis Act. (See *Channing Properties v. City of Berkeley* (1992) 11 Cal. App. 4th 88, 14 Cal. Rptr. 2d 32.) That ruling appears to apply only in cases where the landlord just wants to remove the property from the housing market.

Thousand Oaks

Name of Ordinance: Rent Stabilization Ordinance, Ordinance Nos. 755-NS, 956-NS, 1284-NS.

Adoption Date: 7/1/80. Last amended 5/20/97.

Exceptions: Rent control does not apply when tenant moved in after 1987, so only a few rentals are rent-controlled. Other exceptions include units constructed after 6/30/80; "luxury" units (defined as 0, 1, 2, 3, or 4+-bedroom units renting for at least $400, $500, $600, $750, or $900, respectively, as of 6/30/80); single-family residences, duplexes, triplexes, and four-plexes, except where five or more units are located on the same lot. (§ III.L of 956-NS.)

Administration:

Housing Redevelopment & Economic Division
2100 Thousand Oaks Boulevard,
Civic Arts Plaza, 2nd Floor, Suite B
Thousand Oaks, CA 91362

805-449-2393

www.ci-thousand-oaks.ca.us. This is the official city site, but it has no rent control information.

The Municipal Code is accessible, but rent control ordinances are not available online.

Registration: Required. (§ XIV.)

Vacancy Decontrol: Rent controls are permanently removed after tenant voluntarily vacates or is evicted for cause.

Just Cause: Required. (§ VIII.) Termination notice must state specific reason for termination.

Thousand Oaks Just Cause Evictions

Reason Allowed for Just Cause Evictions	Additional Local Notice Requirements and Limitations
Nonpayment of rent.	Ordinary Three-Day Notice to Pay Rent or Quit is used.
Breach of lease provision, following written notice to correct.	Three-Day Notice to Cure Covenant or Quit is used. Ordinance requires that the tenant be given "written notice to cease," which precludes an unconditional Three-Day Notice to Quit, even if the breach is uncorrectable.
Tenant is using the property for illegal purpose.	Ordinance allows use of unconditional Three-Day Notice to Quit.
Tenant continues to damage property or disturb other tenants, following written notice to cease.	Even if the tenant is causing nuisance or damage for which state law would allow use of a Three-Day Notice to Quit, ordinance requires that Three-Day notice be in alternative "cease or quit" form.
Tenant refuses, after written demand by landlord, to agree to new rental agreement or lease on expiration of prior one, where new proposed agreement contains no new or unlawful terms.	This applies only when a lease or rental agreement expires of its own terms. No notice is required. However, written notice giving the tenant at least three days to sign the new agreement or leave should be served on the tenant with the proposed new lease or rental agreement.
Tenant has refused the landlord access to the property as required by CC § 1954.	If provision is in lease, use Three-Day notice giving tenant option of letting you in or moving. If not, and tenancy is month to month, use 30-day notice specifying reason.

Thousand Oaks Just Cause Evictions (cont'd)	
Reason Allowed for Just Cause Evictions	**Additional Local Notice Requirements and Limitations**
Fixed-term lease has expired, and person occupying property is subtenant not approved by landlord.	No notice is required. Eviction on this basis is allowed only if person living there is not original tenant or approved subtenant. (If lease has not expired and contains no-subletting clause, use Three-Day Notice to Quit to evict for breach of lease.)
Landlord wants to substantially remodel, convert to condominiums, or demolish property.	Allowed under state law only if fixed-term tenancy has expired, or month-to-month tenancy is terminated by 30-day notice.
Landlord seeks to permanently remove the unit from the rental housing market.	Allowed under state law only if fixed-term tenancy has expired, or month-to-month tenancy is terminated by 30-day notice. (Although ordinance requires "good faith" to demolish, a euphemism for not doing it because of rent control, the state Ellis Act severely limits cities from refusing demolition permits on this basis.)

West Hollywood

Name of Ordinance: Rent Stabilization Ordinance, West Hollywood Municipal Code, Title 17, §§ 17.04.010-17.68.01, and Title 2, §§ 2.20.020-2.20.030.

Adoption Date: 6/27/85. Last amended 2009. Frequently amended; call for details.

Exceptions: Units constructed after 7/1/79 and units where owner has lived for two or more years ("just cause" eviction requirements do apply, however). However, many exemptions must be applied for in application for exemption (see below). (§ 17.24.010.)

Administration:

Department of Rent Stabilization and Housing
8300 Santa Monica Boulevard
West Hollywood, CA 90069

323-848-6450

www.ci.west-hollywood.ca.us or www.weho.org. Click "City Hall," then "Municipal Code."

Registration: Required. (§§ 17.28.010–17.28.050.)

Vacancy Decontrol: State law (CC § 1954.53) supersedes ordinance except where tenant evicted for reason other than nonpayment of rent.

On voluntary vacancy or eviction for nonpayment of rent, rents may be increased to any level on rerenting following such vacancies. (§ 17.40.020.)

On eviction for reasons other than nonpayment of rent, ordinance does not allow an increase.

Once property is rerented, it is subject to rent control based on the higher rent.

Just Cause: Required. (§ 17.52.010.) This aspect of the ordinance applies even to new construction, which is otherwise exempt from ordinance. Termination notice must state "with particularity the specific grounds" and recite the specific paragraph of ordinance under which eviction sought. State law requires use of a 60-day termination notice of month-to-month tenancy, instead of a 30-day notice, for this city, if the tenant has occupied the premises for a year or more.

Other Features: Copy of any unlawful detainer summons and complaint must be filed with Rent Stabilization Commission. Numerous procedural hurdles apply when evicting to move self or relative into property, and substantial relocation fee must be paid to tenant.

West Hollywood Just Cause Evictions

Reason Allowed for Just Cause Evictions	Additional Local Notice Requirements and Limitations
Nonpayment of rent.	Ordinary Three-Day Notice to Pay Rent or Quit is used.
The tenant's spouse, child, "domestic partner," parent, grandparent, brother, or sister can be evicted if the tenant has left, unless that person lived in the unit for at least a year and the tenant died or became incapacitated.	State law allows eviction for this reason by three-day notice only if the tenant's having moved the other person in was a violation of the lease or rental agreement. Thirty-day notice can be used if tenancy is month to month.
Commission of a legal nuisance (disturbing other residents) or damaging the property.	Unconditional Three-Day Notice to Quit may be used.
Tenant is using the property for illegal purpose.	Unconditional Three-Day Notice to Quit may be used.
Tenant refuses, after written demand by landlord, to agree to new rental agreement or lease on expiration of prior one, if new proposed agreement contains no new or unlawful terms.	This applies only when a lease or rental agreement expires of its own terms. No notice is required under state law. However, tenant must have refused to sign a new one containing the same provisions as the old one; a written notice giving the tenant at least three days to sign the new agreement or leave should be served on the tenant with the proposed new lease or rental agreement.
Tenant continues to refuse the landlord access to the property as required by CC § 1954.	If provision is in lease, use three-day notice giving tenant option of letting you in or moving. If not, and tenancy is month to month, use 30-day notice specifying reason.
Person occupying property is subtenant (other than persons mentioned in 2 and 3 above) not approved by landlord. (No requirement, as in other cities, for lease to have expired.)	Thirty-day notice may be used if tenancy is month to month. Otherwise, Three-Day Notice to Quit may be used if lease or rental agreement contains provision against subletting.

West Hollywood Just Cause Evictions (cont'd)

Reason Allowed for Just Cause Evictions	Additional Local Notice Requirements and Limitations
Failure to cure a lease or rental agreement violation within "a reasonable time" after receipt of written notice to cure it.	Three-Day Notice to Perform Covenant or Quit is used. Tenant must be given "a reasonable time" to correct the violation, which precludes an unconditional Three-Day Notice to Quit. Also, the tenant must have been "provided with a written statement of the respective covenants and obligations of both the landlord and tenant" before the violation. Giving the tenant a copy of the written lease or rental agreement should comply with this requirement. This ground does not apply if the total number of occupants permitted by the lease is exceeded by (1) one additional occupant, who is the "spouse, domestic partner, brother, sister, parent, grandparent or non-dependent child or grandchild" of the tenant; or (2) any number of children of the tenant (or of the tenant's spouse/domestic partner/head-of-household) brought into the household, whether by "birth, adoption, or change of legal custody," provided the total number of occupants does not exceed that permitted by local housing codes. Sec. 17.52.010(c),(d). Tenant(s) must give landlord written notice of new occupant's name and relationship to tenant.
Employment of resident manager, who began tenancy as such (not tenant who was "promoted" from regular tenant to manager) and who lived in manager's unit, has been terminated.	This type of eviction is not covered in this book because the question of what is required is extremely complicated, depending in part on the nature of the management agreement. You should seek legal advice.

West Hollywood Just Cause Evictions (cont'd)	
Reason Allowed for Just Cause Evictions	**Additional Local Notice Requirements and Limitations**
Employment of resident manager, who was a regular tenant before "promotion" to manager, has been terminated for cause.	Landlord must give tenant 60-day notice, give copy of notice to city, and pay tenant a relocation fee. There are other restrictions as well. This type of eviction can be extremely complicated; see a lawyer.
Landlord wants to move self, parent, grandparent, child, brother, or sister into property, and no comparable vacant unit exists in the property.	Tenant must be given 90-day notice that states the name, relationship, and address of person to be moved in, and a copy of the notice must be sent to the Rent Commission. Landlord must also pay tenant(s) of 15 months or more a "relocation fee" between $1,500 and $2,500 ($3,000 for senior citizen or handicapped person), depending on size of unit. Tenant is liable for repayment of the fee if he has not moved at the end of the 90-day period. Person moved in must live in property for at least one year, or bad faith is presumed and tenant may more easily sue landlord for wrongful eviction. Not allowed if tenant is certified by physician as terminally ill.
Landlord wants to move in, after returning from extended absence, and tenancy was under lease for specific fixed term.	No notice is required under state law when fixed-term lease expires, and ordinance doesn't seem to require notice, either. However, written letter stating intent not to renew, or clear statement in lease, is advisable.
Landlord wants to make substantial repairs to bring property into compliance with health codes, and repairs not possible while tenant remains.	Under state law, eviction for this reason is allowed only if rental agreement is month to month. Landlord must first obtain all permits required for remodeling. Thirty-day notice giving specific reason must be used.

West Hollywood Just Cause Evictions (cont'd)	
Reason Allowed for Just Cause Evictions	**Additional Local Notice Requirements and Limitations**
Landlord has taken title to single-family residence or condominium unit by foreclosure.	Tenant must be given 90-day notice that states the name, relationship, and address of person to be moved in, and a copy of the notice must be sent to the Rent Commission. Landlord must also pay tenant(s) of 15 months or more a "relocation fee" between $1,500 and $2,500 ($3,000 for senior citizen or handicapped person), depending on size of unit. Tenant is liable for repayment of the fee if he has not moved at the end of the 90-day period. Person moved in must live in property for at least one year, or bad faith is presumed and tenant may more easily sue landlord for wrongful eviction. Not allowed if tenant is certified by physician as terminally ill. (Vacancy decontrol provisions are not applicable if property is rerented following eviction.)

Westlake Village

This small city (population 10,000) has a rent control ordinance that applies to apartment complexes of five units or more (as well as to mobile home parks, whose specialized laws are not covered in this book). However, the city never had more than one apartment complex of this size, and that one was converted to condominiums. Since there is therefore now no property (other than mobile home parks) to which the ordinance applies, we don't explain the ordinance here.

Discrimination

There was a time when landlords could refuse to rent to just about anyone they didn't like. All sorts of groups—including African-Americans, Asians, Chicanos, women, unmarried couples, gays, families with children, and many more—were routinely subjected to discrimination. Fortunately, our state and federal legislatures have taken steps to end these abuses.

Today it is illegal for a landlord to refuse to rent to you or engage in any other kind of discrimination on the basis of your membership in any one of several "protected" groups. In addition, a refusal to rent to you that is not closely related to the legitimate business needs of the landlord may also be illegal. To put this more specifically, a combination of statutes and cases forbid discrimination on the following grounds:

- Race
- Religion
- Ethnic background and national origin
- Sex, sexual orientation, and gender identity
- Marital status
- Physical and mental disability
- Families with children (unless the rental units are specifically designated for older citizens, as is the case with retirement communities).

In addition, the California Supreme Court has held that state law forbids landlords from discriminating on the basis of one's personal characteristic or trait. (*Harris v. Capitol Growth Investors XIV*, 52 Cal.3d 1142 (1991).)

Forbidden Types of Discrimination

State law, and in some cases federal law, absolutely forbids discrimination on the following grounds, regardless of a landlord's claim of a legitimate business need:

Race: This is forbidden by California's Unruh Civil Rights Act (CC § 51-53), the Fair Employment and Housing Act (Government Code §§ 12955-12988), the U.S. Civil Rights Act of 1866 (42 U.S.C. § 1982—see *Jones v. Mayer Co.,* 329 U.S. 409 (1968)), and the Federal Fair Housing Act of 1968 (42 U.S.C. §§ 3601-3619).

Religion: This is forbidden by all the laws listed above, except the Civil Rights Act of 1866.

Ethnic Background and National Origin: Same as Religion, above.

Sex (including sexual harassment—see below): Same as Religion, above.

Marital Status (including discrimination against couples because they are unmarried): This is forbidden under California law by both the Unruh and Fair Employment and Housing Acts. (*Smith v. Fair Employment & Housing Commission,* 12 Cal.4th 1143, 51 Cal.Rptr.2d 700 (1996); *Hess v. Fair Employment and Housing Comm.* 138 Cal. App.3d 232 (1982); and *Atkisson v. Kern County Housing Authority,* 59 Cal.App.3d 89 (1976).)

Age: This is expressly forbidden by state law. (CC § 51.2.) In federal law, discrimination on the basis of age—including children and discrimination against the elderly, sometimes called "reverse discrimination"—is considered a part of discrimination on the basis of familial status.

Families With Children: Discrimination against families with children is forbidden by the federal Fair Housing Amendments Act of 1988 (42 U.S.C. § 3604.) and by the Unruh Civil Rights Act, except in housing reserved exclusively for senior citizens. (CC § 51.3 defines senior citizen housing as that reserved for persons 62 years of age or older, or a complex of 150 or more units (35 in non-metropolitan areas) for persons older than 55 years. Under federal law, housing for older persons is housing solely occupied by persons 62 or older, or housing intended for people over 55 that is, in fact, 80% occupied by people 55 or older (42 U.S.C. § 3607).) In addition, San Francisco, Berkeley, Los Angeles, Santa Monica, and Santa Clara County (unincorporated areas only) have local ordinances forbidding this sort of discrimination.

Disability: It is illegal for a landlord to refuse to rent to a person with a physical or mental handicap, or to offer different terms to disabled applicants. The landlord must permit the tenant to make reasonable modifications to the premises if necessary for the tenant to fully use the premises. When reasonable, the landlord may, however, require the tenant to restore the interior of the premises at the end of the tenancy. In addition, a landlord must rent to an otherwise qualified disabled person with a properly trained service or comfort animal, even if the landlord otherwise bans pets.

Sexual Orientation: This includes homosexuality. Discrimination on this basis is forbidden by the Unruh Civil Rights Act. (*Hubert v. Williams,* 133 Cal.App.3d Supp. 1 (1982).) In addition, a number of California cities specifically ban discrimination for this reason.

Gender Identity: Landlords may not discriminate against tenants who have changed, or are in the process of changing, their gender, through hormone treatment, surgery, or both. In practical terms, if a tenant's or applicant's dress and mannerisms don't match the landlord's expectations for someone with that person's stated gender identity, the landlord cannot refuse to rent (or otherwise discriminate) on that basis. (Government Code § 12920.)

Smoking: Discrimination against tenants who are smokers has not been directly tested in California courts. However, it's a good bet that a no-smoking policy for individual units, common areas, or even building-wide would withstand a smoker's challenge, especially in light of California's Air Resources Board decision to place second-hand smoke on its list of toxic pollutants. Indeed, California has a statewide law forbidding smoking in most workplaces and in restaurants (local restrictions may be even stricter). (Labor Code § 6404.5.) Interestingly, California courts have refused to give nonsmokers protection against discrimination (in a restaurant context). (*King v. Hofer,* 42 Cal.4th 678 (1996).) In view of these precedents, it's hard to imagine that smokers could attain protected status.

Animals: Although it is generally legal to refuse to rent to people with pets, it is illegal to do so in the case of service or comfort animals for the physically or mentally handicapped. (CC § 54.1(b)(5).) If you rent a condominium, your landlord would be on solid grounds to prohibit any pets, even though owners of condominiums may keep certain pets (regardless of what the homeowners' association has to say) under specified conditions per state law. (CC § 1360.5.)

Public Assistance: Discrimination against people on public assistance is forbidden by the Unruh Civil Rights Act. (59 Ops. Cal. Atty. Gen. 223 (1976).)

Immigration status: Landlords may not ask prospects or existing tenants about their immigration status (their right to be legally in the United States). (CC § 1940.3.) They may, however, ask a tenant whom they intend to pay as a resident manager to fill out IRS Form I-9, which will result in the landlord being shown identifying documents or visas that establish the tenant/manager's right to work in this country.

Other Unlawful Discrimination: After reading the above list outlining the types of discrimination forbidden by California and federal law, you may assume that it is legal for a landlord to discriminate for other reasons—say, because a person is a surfer. Or, because none of the civil rights laws specifically prohibits discrimination against men with beards or long hair, you might conclude that such discrimination is permissible. This is not true. Although federal civil rights laws have generally been interpreted by the courts to prohibit only those types of discrimination specifically covered by their terms (that is, discrimination based on "race, color, religion," and so on), California's Unruh Civil Rights Act has been construed by various California appellate courts to forbid all forms of "arbitrary" discrimination that bear no relationship to a landlord's legitimate business concerns. So, even though the Unruh Act contains only the words "sex, race, color, religion, ancestry, or national origin" to describe types of discrimination that are illegal, the courts have ruled that these categories are just examples of types of arbitrary and illegal discrimination. On this basis, the California Supreme Court has ruled that landlords can't discriminate against families with children, and has stated that discrimination on the basis of one's personal characteristic or trait is also illegal. (*Harris v. Capitol Growth Investors XIV,* 52 Cal.3d 1142 (1991).)

Although the most common forms of illegal discrimination in rental housing consist of refusing to rent to prospective tenants for an arbitrary reason or offering to rent to one person on tougher terms than are offered to others with no good reason for making the distinction, these aren't the only ways a landlord can be legally liable for unlawful discrimination. A landlord's termination of, or attempt to terminate, a tenancy for a discriminatory reason, or discrimination in providing services such as the use of pool or meeting room facilities or other common areas, is illegal and can provide the discriminated-against tenant with a defense to an eviction lawsuit as well as a basis for suing the landlord for damages. (See "What to Do About Discrimination," below.)

> **EXAMPLE 1:** Bill Lee rents apartments in his six-unit apartment building without regard to racial or other unlawful criteria. His tenants include an African-American family and a single Latin-American woman with children. When Constance Block buys the building from Bill, she immediately gives only these two tenants 30-day notices. Unless Constance can come up with a valid nondiscriminatory reason for evicting these tenants, they can fight the eviction on the basis of unlawful discrimination. They can also sue Constance for damages in state or federal court.

> **EXAMPLE 2:** Now, let's assume that Constance, having lost both the eviction lawsuits and the tenants' suits for damages against her, still tries to discriminate by adopting a less blatant strategy. One way she does this is by

adopting an inconsistent policy of responding to late rent payments. When her Caucasian tenants without children are late with the rent, she doesn't give them a three-day notice to pay rent or quit until after a five-day "grace period," while nonwhite tenants receive their three-day notices the day after the rent is due. In addition, when nonwhite tenants request repairs or raise other issues about the condition of the premises, the speed of Constance's response mimics a turtle's walk after waking from a snooze in the sun. These more subtle (or not so subtle, depending on the situation) means of discrimination are also illegal, and Constance's tenants have grounds to sue her, as well as to defend any eviction lawsuit she brings against them.

Legal Reasons to Discriminate

The fact that all forms of arbitrary discrimination in rental housing are illegal does not mean that every time you are turned down for an apartment, you are being discriminated against for an illegal reason. The landlord may have discriminated against you for a legal reason. What are legal reasons that justify a landlord in discriminating against a prospective tenant? There is no list set out in a statute, but if a landlord discriminates against prospective tenants because they have objective characteristics that would tend to make them poor tenants, the landlord is on solid legal ground. These characteristics include a bad credit history, credit references that don't check out, a past history of not paying rent or of using residential premises to run an illegal business (for example, drugs or prostitution), and anything else that honestly and directly relates to the quality of being a good tenant. A landlord can refuse to rent to a tenant, for example, on the basis of income, by requiring the tenant's income to be at least three times the amount of rent. (*Harris v. Capitol Growth Investors XIV,* 52 Cal.3d 1142 (1991).)

If a landlord relies on a credit report to take any action that negatively affects a tenant's (or prospective tenant's) interest, the tenant has a right to a copy of the report. (CC § 1787.2.)

Rentals to Single Boarders in Single-Family Homes

We have all seen advertisements like this, in newspapers and newsletters and on supermarket notice boards: "Widow seeks single, older Christian lady to share her home as a boarder ...." Based on what you know about illegal housing discrimination, you might be wondering how these advertisements escape prosecution. Isn't the ad above a perfect example of marital, age, religious, and sexual discrimination?

The answer is, yes. But the reality of the situation is that few spurned boarders, and certainly fewer government agencies, are interested in suing one-person landlords and forcing them to accept a housemate not of their choosing. And state housing law does, in any event, make housing preferences like the example above perfectly legal as long as there is:

- only one boarder, and
- the landlord has used no discriminatory advertising. (Government Code §§ 12955(c) & (d) and § 12927(c).)

The ban against discriminatory advertising means that the owner must not make any discriminatory notices, statements, or advertisements. However, how a one-person landlord would be able to communicate her preferences for her boarder without making any "notices, statements, or advertisements" is beyond our understanding.

Perhaps in response to the absurdity of the so-called "safe harbor" for the one-person landlord—she can have a discriminatory preference as long as she does not communicate it—the legislature amended the state Fair Employment and Housing Law to provide that advertisements for a boarder of a certain sex will not be considered a discriminatory act. (Government Code § 12927(2)(B).) In other words, the widow would be on solid ground if she mentions in a print or online ad only her desire for a female roommate, but her stated preferences for an older, single Christian would still, theoretically, constitute housing discrimination.

Occasional Rentals

Consider the owner who rents out his home while on a temporary job assignment in another state, or the family that occasionally takes an extended summer vacation and rents out their home. What about the teacher who rents out her home during every sabbatical—an occasional *but regular* rental situation? And how about the landlord who owns a vacation rental—one that the family uses regularly, but that is also regularly rented to weekenders and others on vacation? Are tenants who rent from these landlords entitled to the protection of the fair housing laws?

Unfortunately, the answers to these questions are not very clear. On the one hand, the Unruh Act applies only to "business establishments," which would seem to exclude the sporadic or one-time rental, but possibly not the infrequent-but-regular rental. However, the California Supreme Court has been mandated to apply Unruh "in the broadest sense reasonably possible," which might mean that tenants who rent in these situations would be covered by the fair housing laws. (*Burks v. Poppy Construction Company,* 57 Cal.2d 463, 20 Cal. Rptr. 609 (1962).) Moreover, the Fair Employment and Housing Act applies generally to "owners," and is not restricted to business establishments.

Small-scale landlords are subject to the fair housing laws. Regularly renting out a single apartment or house, or even half of an owner-occupied duplex, does constitute the operation of a business to which the Unruh Act applies. An owner-occupant of a duplex, triplex, or larger complex, is governed by civil rights laws in the renting of the other unit(s) in the building, even though he or she lives in one of the other units, because the owner-occupant is renting out property for use as a separate household, where kitchen or bathroom facilities aren't shared with the tenant. (See *Swann v. Burkett,* 209 Cal App.2d 685 (1962) and 58 Ops. Cal. Atty. Gen. 608 (1975).) The State Fair Employment and Housing Act also applies, but the federal Fair Housing Acts do not.

Families With Children and Overcrowding

The fact that discrimination against families with children is illegal does not mean a landlord must rent you a one-bedroom apartment if you have a family of five. In other words, it is legal to establish reasonable space-to-people ratios. But it is not legal to use "overcrowding" as a euphemism justifying discrimination because a family has children, if a landlord would rent to the same number of adults.

A few landlords, realizing they are no longer able to enforce a blanket policy of excluding children, try to adopt criteria that for all practical purposes forbid children, under the guise of preventing overcrowding. A common but illegal policy is to allow only one person per bedroom, with a married or living-together couple counting as one person. This standard would result in renting a two-bedroom unit to a husband and wife and their one child, but would allow a landlord to exclude a family with two children. One court has ruled against a landlord who did not permit more than four persons to occupy three-bedroom apartments. (*Zakaria v. Lincoln Property Co.,* 229 Cal.Rptr. 669 (1986).) Another court held that a rule precluding a two-child family from occupying a two-bedroom apartment violated a local ordinance similar to state law. (*Smith v. Ring Brothers Management Corp.,* 183 Cal.App.3d 649, 228 Cal.Rptr. 525 (1986).)

The Fair Employment and Housing Commission is the enforcement arm of the California Department of Fair Employment and Housing (DFEH). The DFEH (one of the places a tenant can complain about discrimination) will investigate a complaint for possible filing with the Commission based on a "two-plus-one" rule:

If a landlord's policy is more restrictive than two persons per bedroom plus one additional occupant, it is suspect. Thus, a tenant (or a group of them) may have a case if the landlord insists on two or fewer people in a one-bedroom unit, four or fewer in a two-bedroom unit, six or fewer in a three-bedroom unit, and so on. However, a landlord who draws the line at three people to a one-bedroom, five to a two-bedroom, and seven to a three-bedroom unit is probably within her rights.

The "two per bedroom plus one more" rule of thumb is not, however, absolute. A landlord may be able to justify a lower occupancy policy for a particular rental if he can point to "legitimate business reasons." This is hard to do—while the inability of the infrastructure to support more tenants (perhaps the septic system or plumbing has a limited capacity) may justify a lower occupancy policy, a landlord's desire to ensure a quiet, uncrowded environment for upscale older tenants will not. If your landlord's occupancy policy limits the number of tenants for any reason other than health, safety, and legitimate business needs, it may be illegal discrimination against families.

Look at the history of a landlord's rental policies. If the landlord used to disallow children before someone complained or sued about this, and only then adopted strict occupancy limits, it is likely that the landlord still intends to keep out children, and a court might well find the new policy illegal.

Often a child will be born after you have already resided in a place for some time. Is your landlord entitled to evict you if the birth of the new child would result in a seriously overcrowded situation? Legally, perhaps, especially if your lease or rental agreement makes it clear that the property can be occupied only by a set number of people, and the baby is one too many. However, if you face this situation and feel the landlord is in fact using the crowding issue as an excuse to get you out, carefully research the landlord's rental policies on other apartments. For example, if you find situations in which the landlord is allowing four adults to occupy a unit the same size as yours, and the landlord moves to evict you because the birth of your second child means your unit is now occupied by four people, you clearly have a good case.

Your landlord has the right, however, to insist on a reasonable increase in rent after a child is born if your lease or rental agreement specifically limits occupancy to a defined number of people—unless you're in a rent control city such as San Francisco, which prohibits landlords from charging extra rent for a newborn child.

How to Tell If a Landlord Is Discriminating

Occasionally apartment house managers—and even landlords themselves—will tell you that they will not rent to African-Americans, Spanish-surnamed people, Asians, and so on. This does not happen that often, because these people are learning that they can be penalized for discriminating.

Today, most landlords who wish to discriminate try to be subtle about it. When you phone to see if a place is still available, the landlord might say it has been filled if he hears a southern or Spanish accent. If he says it is vacant, then when you come to look at it he sees that you are African-American, he might say it has just been rented. Or, he might say he requires a large security deposit which he "forgot to put in the ad." Or he might say that the ad misprinted the rent, which is really much higher. Many variations on these themes can be played.

If you suspect that the landlord is discriminating against you, it is important that you do some things to check it out. For example, if you think the landlord is asking for a high rent or security deposit just to get rid of you, ask other tenants what they pay. The best way to check is to run a "test." Have someone who would not have trouble with discrimination (for example, a white male

without kids) revisit the place soon after you do and ask if it is available and, if so, on what terms. If the response is better, the landlord was probably discriminating against you. Be sure that your friend's references, type of job, and lifestyle are similar to yours, so the landlord cannot later say he took your friend and turned you down because of these differences.

What to Do About Discrimination

There are several legal approaches to the problems raised by discrimination. Regardless of what you do, if you really want to live in the place, you must act fast or the landlord will rent it to someone else before you can stop it.

Complain to the California Department of Fair Employment and Housing

The State of California Department of Fair Employment and Housing (DFEH) takes complaints on discrimination in rental housing. It has the power to order hefty damages for a tenant who has been discriminated against.

If you believe that you have been discriminated against, you can contact the office nearest you or call DFEH at 800-233-3212. You can also visit the DFEH online at www.dfeh.ca.gov, where you will also find phone numbers and addresses of regional offices. You will be asked to fill out a complaint form, and an investigator will be assigned to your case. You must file your complaint within 60 days of the date of the violation or the date when you first learned of the violation. The investigator will try to work the problem out through compromise and conciliation. If this fails, the Department may conduct hearings and maybe take the matter to court. You can also consult a private attorney and consider suing the discriminating landlord.

Complain to the U.S. Department of Housing and Urban Development

You can also lodge a complaint with the U.S. Department of Housing and Urban Development (HUD) if the discrimination is based on race, religion, national origin, sex, family status, or disability. This federal agency has most of the same powers as does the state but must give the state agency the opportunity (30 days) to act on the case first. The HUD equal opportunity office for California is located at 450 Golden Gate Ave., San Francisco, CA 94102, 415-436-6550.

You can also call HUD's housing discrimination hotline at 800-669-9777. HUD's power of investigation and sanctions are similar to those of the state. The experience of the authors has been that HUD is far more militant in going after discriminating landlords than is the state. However, the fact that HUD can't act until 30 days after the state has received the complaint reduces its efficiency a great deal.

Sue the Discriminating Landlord

You may also want to consider seeing a lawyer and suing the landlord. If you have been discriminated against because of sex, race, religion, physical disability, national origin, age, or familial status, you can sue in state or federal court. Discrimination claims on the basis of marital status and all "personal trait" discrimination claims can be brought only in state court. If you can prove your case, you will almost certainly be eligible to recover money damages.

Many, if not most, attorneys have had little experience with discrimination lawsuits. This is particularly true of lawsuits brought in federal court. Rather than try to find an attorney at random, you would be wise to check with an organization in your area dedicated to civil rights and fighting discrimination. They will undoubtedly be able to direct you to an experienced attorney.

Sexual Harassment by Landlords or Managers

Sexual harassment in housing covers a wide range of behavior—from a landlord's or manager's offensive sexual comments to physical encounters, even outright rape. A tenant who has been led to believe she must sleep with her landlord to have repairs made or to avoid eviction has been sexually harassed, as has a tenant whose manager enters her apartment without her permission and touches her against her will.

Sexual harassment by a landlord or manager is illegal under state and federal laws prohibiting discrimination on the basis of sex: California's Unruh Civil Rights Act, the Fair Employment and Housing Act, and the Federal Fair Housing Act of 1968. Harassment that involves a violation of a tenant's privacy rights is illegal under state law. (CC § 1954.)

It's against the law for a landlord or manager to retaliate against tenants for having exercised their rights to be free from sex discrimination, including sexual harassment. Retaliation includes increasing rent, giving a termination notice, or even threatening to do so. (See Chapter 14 for advice on defending yourself against retaliatory eviction.)

Here are some things you can do to stop sexual harassment and protect your rights as a tenant. These are also crucial steps to take if you later decide to take formal action against the harassment.

Document the Harassment

Write down what the landlord or manager said or did to you, and the place and dates of the incidents. Keep copies of any sexually explicit material or threatening letters the landlord or manager sent you. Note names of any witnesses and talk with other tenants to find out whether they have been harassed.

Tell the Harasser to Stop

As much as possible, deal directly with the harassment when it occurs—whether it's to reject repeated requests for a date or express your distaste for sexually explicit comments or physical contact.

Report the Incidents

If the apartment manager persists in sexually harassing you, or if you're uncomfortable speaking face to face, write the manager a letter spelling out what behavior you object to and why, and send a copy to the owner or property management firm. If the owner is the harasser, write the owner a letter demanding that these actions stop. If you feel the situation is serious or bound to escalate, say that you will take action against the harassment if it doesn't stop at once. Include a copy of the state and federal laws prohibiting discrimination on the basis of sex. If other tenants have been harassed,

ask them to send a joint letter. Keep copies of all correspondence.

Complain to a Fair Housing Agency

"What to Do About Discrimination," above, provides more information on how the Department of Fair Employment and Housing can help, although, as we note, there are limits to their assistance.

File a Lawsuit

If the harassment continues or if you're threatened with retaliatory eviction, but the state or federal housing agency fails to produce satisfactory results, consider filing a civil lawsuit. For example, if you have been physically harmed or threatened, consider filing an assault or battery action or a criminal complaint against the harasser.

The Obnoxious Landlord and Your Privacy

Section 1954 of the Civil Code establishes the circumstances under which a landlord can enter a tenant's home, and Section 1953(a)(1) provides that these circumstances cannot be expanded, or the tenant's privacy rights waived or modified, by any lease or rental agreement provision. The first thing to realize is that there are only five situations in which your landlord may legally enter rented premises while you are still in residence. They are:

1. to deal with an emergency
2. when you give permission for the landlord to enter
3. to make needed repairs (or assess the need for them)
4. to show the property to prospective new tenants or purchasers, and
5. when you give permission for an initial final inspection, after you've given notice that you're moving out (or your lease is about to end).

In most instances (emergencies and tenant permission excepted), a landlord can enter only during "normal business hours" and then only after "reasonable notice," presumed to be 24 hours. In addition, the landlord must give you written notice in many situations, as explained in "Written and Oral Notice," below.

Permissible Reasons to Enter

Because your right to privacy is so important, let's examine Section 1954 of the Civil Code carefully to make sure you thoroughly understand the details of how your right to privacy works.

Entry in Case of an Emergency

Under CC § 1954, your landlord or manager can enter the property without giving advance notice in order to respond to a true emergency that threatens injury or property damage if not corrected immediately. For example, a fire or a gas or serious water leak is a true emergency that, if not corrected, will result in damage, injury, or even loss of life. On the other hand, a landlord's urge to repair an important but non-life- or property-threatening defect, like a stopped-up drain, isn't a true emergency that allows entry without proper notice.

To facilitate a landlord's right of entry, the landlord and manager are entitled to have a key to the premises, including keys to any locks you may add.

Entry With the Permission of the Tenant

A landlord can always enter rental property, even without 24 hours' notice, if you so agree without pressure or coercion. For example, if your landlord (whom you feel is well motivated) has a maintenance problem that needs regular attending to—for example, a fussy heater or temperamental plumbing—you might want to work out a detailed agreement with the landlord allowing entry in specified circumstances.

Your landlord may also enter when you've given permission for an inspection or walk-through, at the end of your tenancy. This procedure is covered in "Landlord's Duty to Return Deposit" in Chapter 13.

Entry to Make Repairs

The law allows a landlord or repairperson, contractor, and so on to enter to make and assess the need for and cost of routine repairs or alterations. In this situation, however, the landlord must enter only during normal business hours and must first give reasonable notice. Customarily, "normal business hours" means 9 a.m. to 5 p.m., Monday through Friday, but no exact hours are specified in the statute. As we noted above, CC § 1954 contains a presumption that an advance notice of at least 24 hours is reasonable. However, you should understand that under the statute, the 24-hour notice period is presumed to be reasonable, but it is not absolutely required. If your landlord can establish a really good reason for it under the circumstances, giving a reasonable but shorter notice is legal.

> **EXAMPLE:** If your landlord arranges to have a repairperson inspect a wall heater at 2 p.m. on Tuesday, she should notify you on or before 2 p.m. on Monday. But if she can't reach you until 6 p.m.—for example, you can't be reached at home or at work—less than 24 hours' notice is probably okay. Of course, if you consent to your landlord's plan, the notice period is not a problem.

In some situations, the 24-hour notice period will not be a problem, as you will be delighted that your landlord is finally making needed repairs and will cooperate with reasonable entry requirements. However, there are definitely situations when a landlord will be totally unreasonable, as would be the case when a repairperson simply knocks at your door with no advance notice at an inconvenient time and asks to make a nonemergency repair. If this occurs, you have a legal right to deny entry.

Your landlord can't legally use the right to access your unit in order to harass you. Repeated inspections, even when 24-hour notice is given, might fall into this category. To fight back in this situation, see below.

If you have a waterbed, a landlord may "inspect the bedding installation upon completion (of installation) and periodically thereafter, to ensure its conformity" with the standards a landlord may impose. (CC § 1940.5(g).)

Entry to Show Property

Your landlord may enter your property to show it to prospective tenants (toward the end of a tenancy) and to prospective purchasers when the property is on the market, as long as the landlord complies with the "business hours" and "reasonable notice" provisions discussed below.

Unfortunately, problems often occur when an overeager real estate salesperson shows up on your doorstep without warning or calls on very short notice and asks to be let in to show the place to a possible buyer. In this situation, you are within your rights to say politely but firmly, "I'm busy right now—try again in a few days after we've set a time convenient for all of us." Naturally, this type of misunderstanding is not conducive to your peace of mind, especially if you fear that the landlord or real estate person may use a passkey to enter when you are not home.

There are several ways to deal with this situation:

- You can stand on your rights and notify your landlord to follow the law or you will sue for invasion of privacy (see "What to Do About a Landlord's Improper Entry," below).
- You can try to work out a compromise with your landlord by which you agree to allow the unit to be shown on shorter-than-24-hour notice in exchange for a reduction in the rent or other benefit. For example, you might agree in advance that two-hour notice is reasonable for up to eight house showings a month, in exchange for having your rent reduced $200 per month. This kind of tradeoff is perfectly logical—your rent pays for your right to treat your home like your castle, and any diminution of this right should be accompanied by a decrease in your rent.

CAUTION

Under no circumstances should you allow your landlord to place a key-holding "lock box" on the door. This is a metal box that attaches to the front door and contains the key to that door. It can be opened by a master key held by area real estate salespeople. Because a lock box allows a salesperson to enter in disregard of the 24-hour notice requirement, it should not be used—period.

Written and Oral Notice

Except in cases of emergency entry or when you have abandoned the premises or otherwise moved out, the landlord must give you written notice of any intent to enter, including the day and approximate time, and the purpose. (Because the statute specifies "the date" that the landlord intends to enter, landlords cannot legally give you a range of dates, as in "between June 4 and June 8." (CC §1954(d)(1).) The landlord may do this by delivering it personally to you, by leaving it with a responsible person at your home, or by leaving it on, under, or near the usual entry door. The landlord can also mail it to you, within six days of the planned entry.

Special rules apply when the landlord wants to enter to show your home to a prospective purchaser. If the landlord has advised you in writing of his intent to sell the premises within four months of his intended entry, and has told you that he or his real estate agent may be contacting you for the purpose of showing your rental, his oral notice (in person or by phone) will be sufficient. If delivered 24 hours before the intended entry, this oral notice will be presumed reasonable. The landlord or his agent must leave you a note that they were in your unit.

Finally, landlords and tenants can dispense with the written notice requirement if they agree that the landlord may enter without notice to make specified repairs or supply services, as long as their agreement is within one week of the landlord's subsequent entry. For example, on Sunday you and your landlord could agree that she'll fix your dishwasher by the end of the week, and you might agree that she won't need to give you written notice of the precise day and time. That's valid as long as the landlord does the work by the next Sunday. If she doesn't get to it, she'll need to give written notice as explained earlier. (CC § 1954(d)(3).)

What to Do About a Landlord's Improper Entry

Suppose now your landlord does violate your rights of privacy—what can you do about it?

As you have probably figured out by now, it is one thing to have a right, and quite another thing to get the benefits of it. This is especially true for tenants who do not have a lease and do not live in a city where a rent control ordinance requires just cause for eviction. In this situation, if you set about aggressively demanding your rights, you may end up with a notice to vacate—and while you might ultimately prevail by showing that the landlord has acted illegally in retaliation, you'll have expended a lot of time, energy, and money proving your point. It is also generally true that you can rarely accomplish good results with hard words. This doesn't mean that you shouldn't be firm or determined, but rather, try not to be offensive.

Here is a step-by-step approach that usually works in dealing with a landlord who is violating your right to privacy:

Step 1: Talk to the landlord (or manager) about your concerns in a friendly but firm way. If you come to an understanding, follow up with a note to confirm it.

Step 2: If this doesn't work, or if your landlord doesn't follow the agreement that you have worked out, it's time for a tougher letter. A sample letter is shown below.

Step 3: If, despite this letter, the invasions of your privacy continue, document them and either see a lawyer or take your landlord to small claims court.

One difficulty with a lawsuit against a landlord guilty of trespass is that it is hard to prove much in the way of money damages. Assuming you can prove the trespass occurred, the judge will probably readily agree that you have been wronged, but may award you very little money. Most likely, the judge will figure that you have not been harmed much by the fact that your landlord walked on your rug and opened and closed your door. However, if you can show a repeated pattern (and the fact that you asked the landlord to stop), or even one clear example of outrageous conduct, you may be able to get a substantial recovery. You can ask for up to $2,000 as a penalty, irrespective of other damages. (CC §§ 1940.2, 1942.5.) In this situation the landlord may be guilty of a number of "torts" (legal wrongdoings), including harassment (CCP § 527.6), breach of your implied covenant of quiet

Sample Letter When Landlord Violates Privacy

June 13, 20xx

Roper Real Estate Management Co.
11 Peach Street
San Diego, CA

Dear Mr. Roper:

Several times in the last two months, your employees have entered my apartment without my being home and without notifying me in advance. In no situation was there any emergency involved. This has caused me considerable anxiety and stress, to the point that my peaceful enjoyment of my tenancy has been seriously disrupted.

This letter is to formally notify you that I value my privacy highly and insist that my legal rights to that privacy, as guaranteed to me under Section 1954 of the Civil Code, be respected. Specifically, in nonemergency situations, I would like to have 24 hours' notice of your intent to enter my house.

I assume this notice will be sufficient to correct this matter. If you want to talk about this, please call me at 121-2121 between the hours of 9:00 a.m. and 5:00 p.m.

Yours truly,

Sally South

Sally South

enjoyment (your right to enjoy your home free from interference by your landlord) (*Guntert v. Stockton*, 55 Cal.App.3d 131 (1976)), intentional infliction of emotional distress, and negligent infliction of emotional distress.

In a suit by a tenant alleging that a landlord was guilty of the intentional infliction of emotional distress, you'll need to prove four things:

1. outrageous conduct on the part of the landlord;
2. intention to cause or reckless disregard of the probability of causing emotional distress;
3. severe emotional suffering; and
4. actual suffering or emotional distress. (*Newby v. Alto Riviera Apartments*, 60 Cal. App.3d 288 (1976).)

If your landlord or manager comes onto your property or into your home and harms you in any way, sexually harasses you, threatens you, or damages any of your property, see an attorney. You should also report the matter to the police. Some California police departments have taken the excellent step of setting up special landlord-tenant units. The officers and legal experts in these units have been given special training in landlord-tenant law and are often helpful in compromising disputes and setting straight a landlord who has taken illegal measures against a tenant.

Probably the time that a landlord is most likely to trespass is when the tenant has failed to pay rent. The landlord, faced with the necessity of paying a lot of money to legally get a tenant to move out, may resort to threats or even force. While it may be understandable that a landlord in this situation should be mad at the tenant, this is no justification for illegal acts. All threats, intimidation, and any physical attacks on the tenant should be reported to the police. Of course, it is illegal for the landlord to come on the property and do such things as take off windows and doors, turn off the utilities, or change the locks. If this is done, the tenant should see an attorney at once. Do not overreact when a landlord gets hostile. While a tenant has the right to take reasonable steps to protect himself, his family, and his possessions from harm, the steps must be reasonably related to the threat. The wisest thing to do, whenever you have good reason to fear that you or your property may be harmed, is to call the police.

You should know that a landlord's repeated abuse of a tenant's right to privacy gives a tenant under a lease a legal excuse to break it by moving out, without liability for further rent.

Other Types of Invasions of Privacy

Entering a tenant's home without the tenant's knowledge or consent isn't the only way a landlord can interfere with the tenant's privacy. Here are a few other commonly encountered situations, with advice on how to handle them.

Health, Safety, or Building Inspections

The law concerning when, how, and why your landlord can enter your rented home is, as you have seen, fairly short, simple, and tenant-friendly. But the rules are different when it comes to entry by state or local health, safety, or building inspectors.

Neighbor's Complaints to Government Inspectors

If inspectors have credible reasons to suspect that a tenant's rental unit violates housing codes or local standards—for example, a neighbor has complained about noxious smells coming from the tenant's home or about his 20 cats—they will usually knock on the tenant's door and ask permission to enter. Except in the case of genuine emergency, you have the right to say no.

But your refusal will buy you only a little time in most cases. Inspectors have ways to get around tenant refusals. A common first step (maybe even before the inspectors stop by the rental unit) is to ask your landlord to let them in. Many landlords will comply, although their legal authority to do so is questionable unless there is a genuine emergency.

If inspectors can't reach the landlord (or if the landlord won't cooperate), their next step will probably be to get a search warrant based on the information from the complaining neighbor.

To obtain a warrant, the inspectors must convince a judge that the source of their information—the neighbor—is reliable, and that there is a strong likelihood that public health or safety is at risk. Armed with a search warrant, inspectors have a clear right to insist on entry. If they believe that a tenant will refuse entry, they may bring along police officers, who have the right to do whatever it takes to overcome the tenant's objections.

Random Inspections

Fire, health, and other municipal inspectors sometimes randomly inspect apartment buildings even if they don't suspect noncompliance. These inspections are allowed under some local ordinances in California. To find out whether your city has a program of random building inspections, call your city manager or mayor's office.

You have the right to say no to a random building inspection. If you do so, the inspector will almost surely have a judge issue a search warrant, allowing the inspector to enter to check for fire or safety violations. Again, if there is any expectation that you may resist, a police officer will usually accompany the inspector.

An inspector who arrives when you are not home may ask your landlord to open the door on the spot, in violation of California state privacy laws. If the inspector has come with a warrant, the landlord can probably give consent, since even you, the tenant, couldn't prevent entry. But what if the inspector is there without a warrant? A cautious landlord will ask an inspector without a warrant to enter after they have given you reasonable notice (presumed to be 24 hours) under state law.

Inspection Fees

Many cities impose fees for inspections, on a per unit or building basis or a sliding scale based on the number of your landlord's holdings. Some fees are imposed only if violations are found. If your ordinance imposes fees regardless of violations, your landlord may pass the inspection cost on to the tenant in the form of a rent hike. It's not illegal to do this, and even in rent controlled cities, the cost of an inspection might justify a rent increase.

If your ordinance imposes a fee only when violations are found, your landlord should not pass the cost on to you if the noncompliance is not your fault. For example, if inspectors find that the owner failed to install state-mandated smoke alarms, the owner should pay for the inspection; but if you have allowed garbage to pile up in violation of city health laws, you should pay the inspector's bill.

The Cops

Even the police may not enter a tenant's rental unit unless they can show you or your landlord a recently issued search or arrest warrant, signed by a judge or magistrate. The police do not need a search warrant, however, if they need to enter to

- prevent or stop a catastrophe or a serious crime
- apprehend a fleeing criminal suspected of a serious offense, or
- prevent the imminent destruction of evidence of a serious crime.

Putting "For Sale" or "For Rent" Signs on the Property

Occasionally, friction is caused by landlords who put "For Sale" or "For Rent" signs on tenants' homes, such as a For Sale sign on the lawn of a rented single-family house. Although a landlord may otherwise be very conscientious about respecting your privacy when it comes to giving 24 hours' notice before showing property to prospective buyers or renters, putting a sale or rental sign on the property is a virtual invitation to prospective buyers or renters to disturb you with unwelcome inquiries. There is little law on the subject of your rights in this situation. However, it is our opinion that as you have rented the unit,

including the yard, the landlord has no right to trespass and erect a sign, and if your privacy is completely ruined by repeated inquiries, you may sue for invasion of privacy, just as if the landlord personally had made repeated illegal entries.

Keep in mind that in this age of computerized multiple-listing services, many real estate offices can, and commonly do, sell houses and all sorts of other real estate without ever placing a For Sale sign on the property, except perhaps during the hours when an open house is in progress. If a real estate office puts a sign advertising sale or rental in front of the property you rent, you should at least insist that it clearly indicate a telephone number to call and warn against disturbing the occupant in words like, "Inquire at 555-1357—Do Not Disturb Occupant." If this doesn't do the trick and informal conversations with the landlord do not result in removal of the sign, your best bet is to simply remove it yourself and return it to the landlord, or to write the landlord a firm letter explaining why your privacy is being invaded and asking that the sign be removed. If the violations of your privacy continue, document them and consider suing in small claims court. Of course, you will want to show the judge a copy of the letter.

Allowing Others to Enter the Premises

Except in the circumstances set out above in "Your Landlord's Right of Entry," your landlord has no right to enter your premises. It follows that the landlord also has no right to give others permission to enter. This includes allowing someone to enter who professes to have your permission. For example, landlords are often asked to open the door to people claiming to be the tenant's best friend or long-lost relative. Careful landlords will insist that these stories be backed up by clear permission from you, in writing or by phone at least. If your landlord has given in to an appealing story without checking with you first, he'll be liable if there is property loss or a physical assault.

Giving Information About You to Strangers

Your landlord may be approached by strangers, including creditors, banks, and perhaps even prospective landlords, to provide credit or other information about you. As with letting a stranger into your home, this may cause you considerable anxiety. Basically, your landlord has a legal right to give out normal business information about you as long as it's factual. However, if your landlord spreads false stories about you—for example, says you filed for bankruptcy when this isn't true—and you are damaged as a result (your credit rating is adversely affected or you don't get a job), you have grounds to sue the landlord.

In addition, if a landlord or a manager spreads other types of gossip about you (whether or not true), such as who stayed overnight in your apartment or that you drink too much, you may be in good shape to sue and obtain a substantial recovery, especially if the gossip damages you. This is because spreading this type of information usually has no legitimate purpose and is just plain malicious. If flagrant and damaging, this sort of gossip can be an invasion of privacy for which you may have a valid reason to sue.

Calling or Visiting You at Work

Should an apparent need arise for your landlord to call you at work (say when your Uncle Harry shows up and asks to be let into your apartment), try to be understanding when you take the call, no matter how inconvenient it may be. However, situations justifying a landlord calling you at work are fairly rare. If a landlord calls you to complain about late rent payments or other problems, politely say that you'll discuss it when you're at home. If this doesn't work, follow up with a brief note. If the landlord persists or tries to talk to your boss or other employees about the problem, your privacy is definitely being invaded. Consider going to small claims court or seeing a lawyer.

Unduly Restrictive Rules on Guests

A few landlords, overly concerned about their tenants moving new occupants into the property, go overboard in keeping tabs on the tenants' legitimate guests who stay overnight or for a few days. Often their leases, rental agreements, or rules and regulations will require you to "register" any overnight guest. While your landlord has a legitimate concern about persons who begin as "guests" becoming permanent unauthorized residents of the property (see Chapter 2), it is overkill to require you to inform your landlord of a guest whose stay is only for a day or two. As with other subjects we mention in this chapter, extreme behavior in this area—whether by an owner or a management employee—can be considered an invasion of privacy for which you may have a valid cause of action.

Major Repairs & Maintenance

Everywhere in California, you are legally entitled to rental property that meets basic structural, health, and safety standards and is in good repair. But suppose a landlord comes up short? When landlords fail to take care of important maintenance, you may have the legal right to use the "big sticks" in a tenant's arsenal—the rights to:

- withhold rent
- pay for repairs yourself and deduct the cost from the rent
- sue the landlord, or
- move out without notice.

This chapter describes your right to basic, important things, such as hot water, a floor that will not collapse under your feet, decent heat, and a roof that doesn't leak—in other words, your right to a safe and livable home. It also provides practical advice on how to get a reluctant landlord to perform needed repairs (and how to get them done yourself, using the big sticks mentioned above, if the landlord refuses). Less important maintenance and repair issues—such as unclogging kitchen drains or mowing the front lawn—are covered in the next chapter.

Your Basic Right to Livable Premises

All landlords are legally required to offer livable premises when they originally rent a unit, and to maintain it in that condition throughout the rental term. In legal terminology, this promise of fit housing has the lofty-sounding name "the implied warranty of habitability." The word "implied" means that by virtue of offering a residential rental, the landlord is automatically promising you a fit place to live—even if the landlord doesn't realize it.

Importantly, you have the right to a habitable rental even if you've willingly moved into a place that's clearly below habitability standards, or even if the lease or rental agreement you've signed states that the landlord doesn't have to provide a habitable unit. No California judge will accept these sleazy attempts to secure tenant "waivers," and none will uphold landlord "disclaimers."

So far, your right to a livable rental probably sounds rather imprecise. What does a "fit and habitable" rental really mean? Fortunately, in California the landlord's responsibility to provide habitable housing is quite specific. The sections below give you chapter and verse from state law, building codes, and court decisions. Taken together, they form an impressive list of entitlements for tenants.

Fit and Habitable: State Statutes

The major California law defining habitable housing is Civil Code § 1941.1 and § 1941.3. According to these laws, at a minimum every rental must have:

- effective waterproofing and weather protection of roof and exterior walls, including unbroken windows and doors
- plumbing or gas facilities that conformed to applicable law in effect at the time of installation, maintained in good working order
- a water supply approved under applicable law that is under the control of the tenant, capable of producing hot and cold running water, or a system that is under the control of the landlord, that produces hot and cold running water, furnished to appropriate fixtures, and connected to a sewage disposal system approved under applicable law
- heating facilities that conformed with applicable law at the time of installation, maintained in good working order
- electrical lighting, with wiring and electrical equipment that conformed with applicable law at the time of installation, maintained in good working order
- building, grounds, and appurtenances at the time of the commencement of the lease or

rental agreement, and all areas under control of the landlord, kept in every part clean, sanitary, and free from all accumulations of debris, filth, rubbish, garbage, rodents, and vermin

- an adequate number of appropriate receptacles for garbage and rubbish, in clean condition and good repair at the time of the commencement of the lease or rental agreement, with the landlord providing appropriate serviceable receptacles thereafter and being responsible for the clean condition and good repair of the receptacles under the landlord's control

- floors, stairways, and railings maintained in good repair

- deadbolt locks on certain doors and windows (see Chapter 11 for specifics), and

- No lead paint hazards (deteriorated lead-based paint, lead-contaminated dust or soil, or lead-based paint disturbed without containment). (CC §§ 1941.1 and 1941.3; H&S § 17920.10.)

State Housing Law

The State Housing Law, H&S § 17920.3, provides that the following problems render a rental unfit and substandard if they endanger you or the public:

1. Inadequate sanitation shall include, but not be limited to, the following:
   - Lack of, or improper water closet, lavatory, or bathtub or shower in a dwelling unit.
   - Lack of, or improper kitchen sink.
   - Lack of hot and cold running water to plumbing fixtures in a dwelling unit.
   - Lack of adequate heating.
   - Lack of, or improper operation of required ventilating equipment.
   - Lack of minimum amounts of natural light and ventilation required by this code.
   - Room and space dimensions less than required by this code.
   - Lack of required electrical lighting.
   - Dampness of habitable rooms.
   - Infestation of insects, vermin, or rodents as determined by the health officer.
   - General dilapidation or improper maintenance.
   - Lack of connection to required sewage disposal system.
   - Lack of adequate garbage and rubbish storage and removal facilities as determined by the health officer.

2. Structural hazards shall include, but not be limited to, the following:
   - Deteriorated or inadequate foundations.
   - Defective or deteriorated flooring or floor supports.
   - Flooring or floor supports of insufficient size to carry imposed loads with safety.
   - Members of walls, partitions, or other vertical supports that split, lean, list, or buckle due to defective material or deterioration.
   - Members of walls, partitions, or other vertical supports that are of insufficient size to carry imposed loads with safety.
   - Members of ceilings, roofs, ceilings and roof supports, or other horizontal members, that sag, split, or buckle due to defective material or deterioration.
   - Members of ceiling, roofs, ceiling and roof supports, or other horizontal members that are of insufficient size to carry imposed loads with safety.
   - Fireplaces or chimneys that list, bulge, or settle due to defective material or deterioration.
   - Fireplaces or chimneys that are of insufficient size or strength to carry imposed loads with safety.

3. Any nuisance.

State Housing Law (cont'd)

4. All wiring, except that which conformed with all applicable laws in effect at the time of installation if it is currently in good and safe condition and working properly.

5. All plumbing, except plumbing that conformed with all applicable laws in effect at the time of installation and has been maintained in good condition, or that may not have conformed with all applicable laws in effect at the time of installation but is currently in good and safe condition and working properly, and that is free of cross connections and siphonage between fixtures.

6. All mechanical equipment, including vents, except equipment that conformed to all applicable laws in effect at the time of installation and that has been maintained in good and safe condition, or that may not have conformed to all applicable laws in effect at the time of installation but is currently in good and safe condition and working properly.

7. Faulty weather protection, which shall include, but not be limited to, the following:
   • Deteriorated, crumbling, or loose plaster.
   • Deteriorated or ineffective waterproofing of exterior walls, roof, foundations, or floors, including broken windows or doors.
   • Defective or lack of weather protection for exterior wall coverings, including lack of paint, or weathering due to lack of paint or other approved protective covering.
   • Broken, rotted, split, or buckled exterior wall coverings or roof coverings.

8. Any building or portion thereof, device, apparatus, equipment, combustible waste, or vegetation that, in the opinion of the chief of the fire department or his deputy, is in such a condition as to cause a fire or explosion or provide a ready fuel to augment the spread and intensity of fire or explosion arising from any cause.

9. All materials of construction, except those that are specifically allowed or approved by this code, and that have been adequately maintained in good and safe condition.

10. Those premises on which an accumulation of weeds, vegetation, junk, dead organic matter, debris, garbage, offal, rodent harborages, stagnant water, combustible materials, and similar materials or conditions constitute fire, health, or safety hazards.

11. Any building or portion thereof that is determined to be an unsafe building due to inadequate maintenance, in accordance with the latest edition of the Uniform Building Code.

12. All buildings or portions thereof not provided with adequate exit facilities as required by this code, except those buildings or portions thereof whose exit facilities conformed with all applicable laws at the time of their construction and that have been adequately maintained and increased in relation to any increase in occupant load, alteration, or addition, or any change in occupancy.

    When an unsafe condition exists through lack of, or improper location of, exits, additional exits may be required to be installed.

13. All buildings or portions thereof that are not provided with the fire-resistive construction or fire-extinguishing systems or equipment required by this code, except those buildings or portions thereof that conformed with all applicable laws at the time of their construction and whose fire-resistive integrity and fire-extinguishing systems or equipment have been adequately maintained and improved in relation to any increase in occupant load, alteration, or addition, or any change in occupancy.

14. All buildings or portions thereof occupied for living, sleeping, cooking, or dining purposes that were not designed or intended to be used for those occupancies.

15. Inadequate structural resistance to horizontal forces. (H&S § 17920.3, irrelevant sections omitted.)

16. Finally, a building is substandard if the landlord has not complied with the requirements of the State Fire Marshal, who has the authority to set standards for structural fire safety and fire-resistant exits. (H&S § 13143.2.)

Fit and Habitable: No Risks to Health, Safety, or Property

The state statutes quoted above dictate the minimum condition for rental premises to qualify as fit and habitable. The law also approaches the issue from another angle, labeling a rental "substandard" if it has any problem in "State Housing Law," above, that "endangers the life, limb, health, property, safety, or welfare of the public or the occupants." (H&S §17920.3, also known as the State Housing Law.) As you read through the list, in "State Housing Law," remember that only when these conditions endanger life, limb, and so on, will they legally create a substandard, unfit rental.

What's a Nuisance?

The state housing law has a catchall provision that prohibits something called "nuisances." A nuisance is something that is dangerous to human life, detrimental to health, or morally offensive and obnoxious—for example, overcrowding a room with occupants, providing insufficient ventilation or illumination, inadequate sewage or plumbing facilities, permitting illegal activities, or allowing excessive noise or commotion, making it impossible to use or enjoy one's property. Drug use and dealing on the premises is also a legal nuisance. We advise you below on what to do when the nuisance is maintenance-related; Chapter 11 covers nuisances that are violations of the criminal law.

Fit and Habitable: Industry and Local Codes

Yet another source of law gives meaning to your right to a fit and habitable dwelling. The Uniform Housing Code, an industry code that is adopted by the state legislature and counties and cities (which may increase its requirements and protections), sets minimum standards. Many of them overlap

the standards in the State Housing Law, above, but some are unique. If you haven't yet seen the maintenance problem that's bedeviling you, read on. Each rental dwelling must have:

- A working toilet, wash basin, and bathtub or shower. The toilet and bathtub or shower must be in a room that is ventilated and allows for privacy.
- A kitchen with a sink, which cannot be made of an absorbent material such as wood.
- Natural lighting in every room through windows or skylights having an area of at least one-tenth of the room's floor area, with a minimum of 12 square feet (three square feet for bathroom windows). The windows in each room must be able to be opened at least halfway for ventilation, unless a fan provides for ventilation.
- Safe fire or emergency exits leading to a street or hallway. Stairs, hallways, and exits must be litter free. Storage areas, garages, and basements must be free of combustible materials.
- Every apartment building having 16 or more units must have a resident manager. (25 California Code of Regulations § 42.)

City or county building or housing codes are different from industry codes. They regulate structural aspects of buildings and usually set specific space and occupancy standards, such as the minimum size of sleeping rooms. They also establish minimum requirements for light and ventilation, sanitation and sewage disposal, heating, water supply (such as how hot the water must be), fire protection, and wiring (such as the number of electrical outlets per room). In addition, housing codes typically make property owners responsible for keeping hallways, lobbies, elevators, and the other parts of the premises the owner controls clean, sanitary, and safe.

Your local building or housing authority, and health or fire department, may have an informational booklet that describes the exact requirements your landlord must meet. In most urban areas, these local codes are more thorough than the state's general housing law—for example, some cities require landlords to install specific security items, such as peepholes, in exterior doors. However, local laws usually don't explain what you can do if your landlord fails to comply. To find out, you'll need to consult "How to Get Action From Your Landlord," below.

Exemptions for Older Buildings

When a new housing code is adopted, or an old one changed, it doesn't necessarily mean that all existing buildings are illegal because they are not "up to code." Especially when it comes to items that would involve major structural changes, lawmakers will often exempt older buildings by writing a "grandfather clause" into the code, exempting all buildings constructed before a certain date. Typically, however, a landlord who later undertakes major renovations or remodeling must comply with the new rules. If you suspect that major work is being planned or done without bringing the building up to code, contact your local housing department. If you fear landlord retaliation, do so anonymously, if possible. (Tenants' protections against retaliatory conduct are discussed in Chapter 14.)

Other new code requirements that are easy and inexpensive to make—for example, installing locks, peepholes, or smoke detectors—must be made regardless of the age of the building.

Fit and Habitable: Court Decisions

State legislators aren't the only ones who have weighed in on the subject of what constitutes fit housing. Judges, too, faced with cases in which tenants didn't pay the rent because they felt that the premises were unlivable, have often written decisions that gave tenants extended rights. In fact, the whole notion of an implied warranty of habitability came from a court case, not from the

legislature (that case was *Green v. Superior Court*, 10 Cal.3d 616 (1974)).

In evaluating whether a landlord is providing habitable housing, courts may also consider the weather, the terrain, and where the rental property is located. Features or services that might be considered nonessential extras in some parts of the country are legally viewed as absolutely necessary components of habitable housing in others. For example, in areas with severe winters, such as the Sierra, storm windows may be considered basic equipment.

Other Important Requirements

By now you have a pretty good idea of what your landlord must do (or refrain from doing) in order to live up to the duty to provide fit housing. Here are some other laws that, although important, don't fit within the "fit and habitable" category. This means that you can't use the remedies we discuss later in this chapter if your landlord fails to measure up (though you can take other steps, as explained in Chapter 7).

- Landlords are responsible for installing at least one telephone jack in their rental units, and for placing and maintaining inside phone wiring to that jack. (CC § 1941.4 and Public Utilities Code § 788.)
- Smoke detectors must be in all multiunit dwellings, from duplexes on up. Apartment complexes must also have smoke detectors in the common stairwells. (H&S § 13113.7)
- Landlords must install ground fault circuit interrupters for swimming pools and antisuction protections on wading pools, excepting single-family residence rentals. (H&S §§ 116049.1 & 116064.)

Finally, keep in mind that the meaning of the term "habitable housing" is not static, and court decisions are made in light of changes in living conditions and technology. For example, these days courts consider the prevalence of crime in urban areas when determining what constitutes habitable housing; and the presence of mold may make some dwellings unfit. Good locks, security personnel, exterior lighting, and secure common areas are now seen, in some cities, to be as important to tenants as are water and heat. (Chapter 11 discusses your rights to adequate security measures.)

Your Repair and Maintenance Responsibilities

You now know that you can expect your landlord to provide safe and habitable housing and adhere to norms of cleanliness and behavior under a variety of overlapping and specific legal rules. But your landlord isn't the only one with legal responsibilities. If you don't keep up your end of the bargain, at the least you can expect a deduction from your security deposit when you move out, for needed cleaning or repairs. Most importantly, you cannot use a "big stick" remedy in response to you landlord's failure to keep your rental fit and habitable if your own failings have "contributed substantially" to the habitability problem. (CC § 1941.2.) State housing law requires you to:

- Keep your rental as clean and sanitary as the condition of the premises permits. For example, if your kitchen has a rough, unfinished wooden floor that is hard to keep clean, you should not be expected to keep it shiny and spotless—but a tenant with a new tile floor would be expected to do a decent job. If you don't, and your landlord has to do a major clean up when you move out, expect a hefty deduction from your security deposit.

- Dispose all rubbish, garbage, and other waste in a clean and sanitary manner. For instance, if mice or ants invaded your kitchen because you forgot to take out the garbage before you left on a two-week vacation, you would be responsible for paying any necessary extermination costs.

- Properly use and operate all electrical, gas, and plumbing fixtures, and keep them as clean and sanitary as their condition permits. For example, bathtub caulking that has sprouted mold and mildew may render the tub unusable (or at least disgusting), but because proper cleaning could have prevented it, you are responsible. On the other hand, if the bathroom has no fan and the window has been painted shut, the bathroom will be hard to air out; resulting mildew might be your landlord's responsibility.

- Not permit anyone on the premises who, with your permission, willfully or wantonly destroys, defaces, damages, impairs, or removes any part of the structure or dwelling unit or the facilities or equipment—and of course, you yourself must not do any such thing.

- Occupy the premises as your home, using it only as it was designed or intended to be used for living, sleeping, cooking, or dining. For example, you can't use the dining room as a machine shop and then complain about the stains in the carpet.

What About Things You Break?

If you cause a serious habitability problem in your unit—for example, you carelessly break the sole toilet—you are responsible. A landlord who finds out about the problem can insist that you pay for the repair. Legally, you can't just decide to live without plumbing for a while to save money. If you drag your feet, the landlord can use your security deposit to pay for it, and if that isn't enough, sue you besides. Your landlord can't, however, charge you for problems caused by normal wear and tear—for example, a carpet that has worn out from use. (Chapter 13 discusses the difference between normal wear and tear and damage.)

Damage Caused by Criminals

If a burglar breaks into your home, smashing the cupboards and generally making a mess, who pays? Usually, the landlord pays for the repairs to the structure, as long as your carelessness (failing to lock a window, for example) didn't facilitate the intruder's entry. If you *were* careless, are you 100% liable for the damage? If your landlord sues you and a jury is asked to apportion the blame between you and the burglar, it's anyone's guess what figure they'll come up with.

Carelessness is not the only way you might be liable for a criminal's acts. For example, if you and your landlord agree that you will maintain the doors and windows in your single-family rental and you fail to do so, you may be held partially liable for the burglar's damage. And if the criminal happens to be someone whom you have let into the building, a jury will almost surely hold you responsible if they conclude that you knew or should have known that a criminal incident was likely.

Agreeing to Be Responsible for Repairs

You and your landlord may have agreed that you'll take on certain repair and maintenance responsibilities. Typically, tenants agree to do "routine maintenance" only. Unfortunately, landlords are rarely specific as to what that term means. And, as we've just explained, sometimes "routine" chores (such as replacing a thermostat) can be the difference between a fit rental and one that is legally uninhabitable. On the other hand, some expensive maintenance (such as a new paint job) has more to do with cosmetics than habitability. If you agree to do maintenance and repairs, it's important to understand the scope of your duties.

If you've taken on "routine" maintenance, chances are that you and the landlord expect you'll fix things that aren't overly expensive or complicated, and that don't involve getting into the building's structure or major heating or ventilation systems. For example, fixing a clogged toilet, replacing a front door lock, and replacing a cracked window in your apartment rental are routine tasks. Reroofing, rebuilding the lobby stairs, or replacing heating ductwork is not. If you've rented a single-family home, your responsibilities may be a bit larger, especially if you have proven yourself to have the skill, time, and inclination to take the jobs on.

Tenants who agree to perform maintenance may legally waive, or give up, their rights to repair and deduct (or withhold rent) for those specific repairs. (CC § 1942.1; see also *Knight v. Hallsthammar*, 29 Cal.3d 46 (1981).) This stands to reason—having secured a rent reduction (or payment) in exchange for your promise to attend to a type of repair, you shouldn't be able to turn around and demand that the landlord do the very job you said you'd do. This is the only situation in which waivers of your "big stick" remedies will stand up in court.

How to Get Action From Your Landlord: The Light Touch

Knowing that you have a legal right to habitable housing and getting it are, obviously, horses of very different colors. A lot depends on the attitude of your landlord—but some depends on your strategy, too. Here are some tips to maximize your chances of getting quick results, short of using the big sticks that we explain in the next section.

Put Repair Requests in Writing

By far the best approach is to put every repair and maintenance request in writing, keeping a copy for your files. You may want to call first, but be sure to follow up with a written request.

Written communications to your landlord are important because they:

- are far more likely to be taken seriously than face-to-face conversations or phone calls, because it's clear to the landlord you're keeping a record of your requests

- are less likely to be forgotten or misunderstood
- satisfy the legal requirement that you give your landlord a reasonable opportunity to fix a problem before you withhold rent or exercise other legal rights (see "What to Do If the Landlord Won't Make Repairs," below), and
- are evidence in case you ever need to prove that the serious problems with your rental were the subject of repeated repair requests.

In your request, be as specific as possible regarding the problem, its effect on you, what you want done, and when. For example, if the thermostat on your heater is always finicky and often doesn't function at all, explain that you have been without heat during the last two days during which the nighttime low was below freezing—don't simply say "the heater needs to be fixed." If the problem poses a health or safety threat, such as a broken front door lock or loose step, say so and ask for it to be fixed immediately. Competent landlords will respond extra quickly to genuinely dangerous, as opposed to merely inconvenient, situations. Finally, be sure to note the date of the request and how many requests, if any, have preceded this one.

If your landlord provides a repair request form, use it. If not, do your own. (See the sample shown below.) Always make a copy of your request and keep it in a safe place in your files.

TIP

In dangerous situations, you must take precautions, too. Once you're aware of a dangerous situation, you must take reasonable steps to avoid injury. Don't continue to use the outlet when you see sparks fly from the wall; don't park in the garage at night if the lights are burned out and there is a safer alternative. If you don't take reasonable care and are injured and sue the landlord, you can expect a judge or jury to hold the landlord only partially responsible. (See Chapter 9.)

Sample Request for Repair or Maintenance

To: Kay Sera, Landlord,
        Stately View Apartments

From: Will Tripp
        376 Seventh Avenue,
        Apartment No. 45,
        Appleville, CA

Re: Roof leak

Date: March 10, 20xx

As I mentioned to you on the phone yesterday, on March 9, 20xx I noticed dark stains on the ceilings of the upstairs bedroom and bath. These stains are moist and appear to be the result of the recent heavy rains. I would very much appreciate it if you would promptly look into the apparent roof leak. If the leak continues, my property may be damaged and two rooms may become unusable. Please call me so that I'll know when to expect you or a repairperson. You can reach me at work during the day (555-1234) or at home at night (555-4546).

Thank you very much for your attention to this problem. I expect to hear from you within the next few days, and expect that the situation will be corrected within a couple of weeks.

Yours truly,

Will Tripp
Will Tripp

Deliver Your Repair Request to the Landlord

If your landlord has an on-site office or a resident manager, deliver your repair request personally. If you mail it, consider sending it certified (return receipt requested), or use a delivery service (such as Federal Express) that will give you a receipt establishing delivery. If you fax your request, ask for a call (or a return fax) acknowledging receipt. Although taking steps to verify delivery will cost a little more, it has two major advantages over regular mail:

- It will get the landlord's attention and highlight the fact that you are serious about your request.
- The signed receipt is evidence that the landlord did, in fact, receive the letter. You may need this in the event that the landlord fails to make the repair and you decide to do it yourself or withhold rent. If a dispute arises as to your right to use a self-help measure, you'll be able to prove in court that you satisfied the legal requirement of notifying the landlord first.

If your first request doesn't produce results—or at least a call or note from the landlord telling you when repairs will be made—send another. Mention that this is the second (or third) time you have brought the matter to the landlord's attention. If the problem is getting worse, emphasize this fact. If you have low hopes for any response and are beginning to think of your next move (a self-help remedy, as described below), you might mention your intent to use such a remedy. And, of course, be sure to keep a record of all repair requests.

Keep Notes on All Conversations

Besides keeping a copy of every written repair request, keep a record of oral communications, too. If the landlord calls you in response to your repair request, make notes during the conversation or immediately afterward; write down the date and time that the conversation occurred and when you made your notes. These notes may come in handy to refresh your memory and help you reconstruct the history of your case. In most situations, if a dispute ends up in court, and you are unable to remember the details of the conversation, your notes can be introduced to fill the gap. Don't tape-record the phone call—it's illegal unless the other side agrees. (Penal Code § 632.)

You can keep track of other kinds of communications, too. If your dealings with your landlord are accomplished online, print out the message.

Put the Landlord's Promises in Writing

If you and your landlord agree on a plan of action, it's especially wise to write down your understanding of this agreement. Send a copy to the landlord, inviting him to reply if he thinks that you have missed or misstated anything. If he doesn't write back, the law presumes that he agreed with your version of the conversation. See the sample Letter of Understanding Regarding Repairs, below.

Sample Letter of Understanding Regarding Repairs

1234 Appian Way, #3
Beach City, CA 00000

September 3, 20xx

Ms. Iona Lott, Landlord
100 Civic Center Drive
Beach City, CA 00000

Dear Ms. Lott,

Thank you for calling me yesterday, September 2, 200X, regarding my request for repairs, dated August 27, 20xx. In that request, I told you that the hot water in my unit is very hot (123 degrees F. on my thermometer), even though the temperature gauge on the water heater is turned down as far as it can go. I am concerned that my young daughter may be injured by this scalding water, and am anxious that the temperature be lowered as soon as possible.

As I understand it, you agreed to have Ralph, your handyman, come check the problem on Saturday morning, September 6, between 9 and 10 a.m. Ralph will bring along a new thermostat should he need to replace the old one.

Please let me know if your recollection of our conversation and plans differs from mine.

Yours truly,

Howard Hillman

Howard Hillman

What to Do If the Landlord Won't Make Repairs

If your persistent and businesslike requests for repairs are ignored, you can take stronger measures. Your options include:

- calling state or local building or health inspectors
- withholding the rent
- repairing the problem (or having it repaired by a professional) and deducting the cost from your rent
- moving out, or
- paying the rent and then suing the landlord for the difference between the rent you paid and the value of the defective premises.

If the landlord hasn't fixed a serious problem that truly makes your rental unit uninhabitable—rats in the kitchen—you will want to take fast action. But before you use any of these big sticks, make sure that you can answer "Yes" to all of the questions in "Big Stick Prerequisites," below.

 TIP
Before doing repairs yourself, withholding rent, or using another "big stick," get proof of how bad the problem was. Take pictures of the problem or ask others to view the problem and write a description. Also consider asking an experienced and impartial contractor or repairperson to examine the situation and give you a written description of the problem and estimate for repair. Be sure the description is signed and dated.

Big Stick Prerequisites

Before you take drastic action, such as withholding the rent or moving out, be sure you can say "Yes" to each question below:

- **Is the problem serious, not just annoying, and does it imperil your health or safety?** Not every building code violation or annoying defect in your rental home (like your water heater's ability to reach only 107 degrees F, short of the code-specified 110 degrees) justifies use of a "big stick" against the landlord. In other words, be sure that this is a true habitability problem.
- **Did someone other than you or a guest cause the problem?** If you're at fault, you can't pursue the self-help options.
- **Did you tell the landlord about the problem and give him a reasonable opportunity to get it fixed?** The landlord has 30 days under state law or less if the circumstances warrant prompter attention.
- **At the end of your lease (or of the month, if you're renting month to month), are you willing to risk termination of your tenancy by an annoyed landlord?** Although your landlord may not legally retaliate against you by raising

the rent or terminating your tenancy, many landlords do so anyway. Your only recourse would be to refuse to move (or refuse to pay the higher rent), but that risks an eviction. Even if you prevail, it will involve a lot of time and effort. (Chapter 14 discusses retaliation.)
- **Are you willing to risk eviction if a judge decides that you shouldn't have used the big stick?** For example, if you withhold rent, the landlord may sue to evict you based on nonpayment of rent. Even if you're sure that your course of action was justified, a judge may decide otherwise. You'll have a second chance to pay the balance before being sued for eviction, but the experience will not be pleasant. And if you go through the eviction case and lose, a negative mark on your credit record may cause serious problems for future rentals, loans, and employment.
- **If you move out, can you find a comparable or better unit?** If the building is closed following deficiencies you've reported to inspectors, your landlord must help you with relocation expenses, but it will be a hassle to get the money (and to move). (H&S § 17980.7.)

Report Code Violations to Housing Inspectors

A local building, health, or fire department usually gets involved when a tenant complains (a change in ownership or owner financing may also trigger an inspection). The agency inspects the building and, if problems are found, issues a deficiency notice that requires the owner to remedy all violations. A landlord who fails to comply can face civil and criminal penalties—including not being able to evict a tenant of the property for nonpayment of rent. (H&S §§ 17997 to 17997.5.)

In some cases, a tenant's complaint about a single defect can snowball, with the result that several agencies require the landlord to make needed repairs. For example, say a tenant complains to the health department about a lack of heat. During its inspection, the health department observes an unsafe stove and an unventilated bathroom. The health department notifies the fire department about the stove and tells the building department about the bathroom, which results in inspections by both departments.

If you decide to complain to building, health, or fire inspectors, start with your local phone book and contact the appropriate local agency. You'll soon get routed to the inspections department.

Relocation Benefits

If you report a serious habitability problem to the housing, fire, or health inspectors, and you have to move while it's being remedied, you may get relocation benefits. (H&S § 17975 and following.) To be eligible, you (or your guest) cannot have caused or substantially contributed to the problem.

Withhold the Rent

If you conclude that your landlord has not met the responsibility of keeping your unit livable, you may be able to stop paying any rent to the landlord until the repairs are made. Before you can properly withhold the rent, be sure that you can say "Yes" to the questions in "Big Stick Prerequisites," above.

When you withhold rent, you simply stop paying rent until the landlord fixes the problem (at least two cities, however, have established escrow programs for tenants who withhold rent, as described in Step 1, below). The theory is that the landlord will be powerfully motivated to do the repair when the rent has stopped coming in. Once the rental is habitable, you begin paying rent. You will also owe the landlord a portion of the withheld rent, which reflects the value of the rental in its unfit condition (*see* "Paying the Landlord for the Value of the Unfit Rental," below, for methods of computing the proper amount).

CAUTION

Be sure you're ready to risk your tenancy. We can't say it enough times: Before withholding rent, be sure your ducks are in order and you are willing to risk an eviction lawsuit. If you can address the problem without incurring that risk (such as by suing in small claims court), you may be better off.

The Rent Withholding Steps

Here are the steps to follow when you've decided to withhold rent.

Step 1: Check for any local laws on rent withholding. State law does not require you to pay the rent into an escrow account (although it's a good idea, as explained below). But in at least two cities, Los Angeles and Sacramento, when landlords haven't complied with repairs ordered by building or health inspectors, the city can impose a rent escrow. Tenants pay rent directly to the city, which can authorize distributions for the purposes of repair only. Check your local ordinances to see if a rent escrow ordinance applies to you.

Step 2: Notify your landlord. Hopefully, you've followed our suggestions and sent written repair requests to your landlord. You may have already signaled your intent to withhold the rent if the problem isn't fixed. If you haven't yet, now's the time to give your landlord written notice of the problem and your intent to withhold rent. A sample letter is shown below. In your letter, refer to the California case (*Green v. Superior Court,* 10 Cal. 3d 616 (1974)) that allows withholding. Send the letter "return receipt requested."

Sample Letter Telling the Landlord You Intend to Withhold Rent

58 Coral Shores, #37
Shady Bay, CA 00000
407-555-5632

August 5, 20xx

Mr. Roy Hernandez
3200 Harbor Drive
Shady Bay, CA 12345

Dear Mr. Hernandez:

My family and I are your tenants at the above address. As you know, I called you on August 3, 20xx to report that the front porch has collapsed from dry rot at the top of the stairs, making it impossible to enter the flat except by climbing through a front window. You assured me that you would send a contractor the next day. No one came on August 4.

Under California Civil Code Section 1941.1, you are responsible for keeping the porch in good repair. California law gives tenants the right to withhold rent if your failure to make repairs renders the rental uninhabitable. (*Green v. Superior Court,* 10 Cal.3d. 616 (1974).) The absence of a front entrance makes our house unfit.

By hand-delivering this notice to you today, August 5, I am giving you reasonable notice as required by law. If the porch is not repaired by August 10, I will withhold rent until it is.

Yours truly,

Alicia Sanchez

Alicia Sanchez

Step 3: Collect evidence. In case your landlord tries to evict you for nonpayment of rent, you will want to prepare your defense from day one. You'll need to prove that the problem truly is serious and that you complied with the notice requirements of the rent withholding law. Of course, you'll want to keep copies of all correspondence with the landlord, plus photographs of the problem. Be sure to consider other ways (besides your own testimony) you can convince the judge that the problem was real and serious. For example, if your heater delivers a frigid blast, you'll want an estimate from a heating repairperson that corroborates the fact that the heater doesn't work.

In Superior Court, where evictions are handled, you cannot simply present a repairperson's written description of the problem (as you could in small claims court). For this reason, when choosing your repairperson/witness, pick someone whom you think will come to court to testify about the nature of the problem.

Step 4: Repeat your request for repairs. If the landlord hasn't responded satisfactorily to your first letter, give the landlord one last deadline—say, 48 hours or whatever period you feel is reasonable under the circumstances.

Step 5: Deposit your rent in escrow. Even if your city does not require this, we recommend that you deposit the withheld rent into an escrow account held by a neutral third party. This will dispel any suggestion that you are withholding rent simply in order to avoid paying it.

You can try asking a mediation service if it will establish an account for this purpose. Or, if you have an attorney, ask your lawyer to deposit the withheld rent in the lawyer's "trust account." You can also set up a separate bank account of your own and use it only for withheld rent. If you must pay for any of these services, you can ask the court to order the landlord to reimburse you if the landlord brings an eviction action (or you can deduct the cost of the escrow from the reduced rent you'll pay the landlord upon completion of the repairs, as explained below).

Your Landlord's Response

If a court or housing authority is holding your withheld rent, as in Los Angeles or Sacramento, your landlord cannot file an eviction action against you based on nonpayment of rent. The landlord can ask for release of some of the withheld rent to pay for repairs. While repairs are being made, you might be told to continue to pay the entire rent to the court or housing authority, or you may be directed to pay some rent to the landlord and the balance to the court or housing authority. When the dwelling is certified as fit by the local housing authorities or the court, any money in the account is returned to the landlord, minus court costs, inspection fees, and any money you get to keep (reflecting the lowered value of the rental while it was substandard).

Your landlord's response is likely to be quite different, however, when no housing authority is involved. If the landlord thinks your withholding is unjustified (or not done according to law, as would be the case if you failed to give the landlord a chance to repair the problem before you withheld the rent), the landlord will probably send you a three-day notice to pay rent or vacate, followed by a Summons and Complaint (an eviction lawsuit) if you do neither. In your Answer to the Complaint, you can raise the unfitness of the rental as an "affirmative defense" to the eviction suit. (Affirmative defenses to evictions are covered in Chapter 14.)

Paying the Landlord for the Value of the Unfit Rental

Many tenants make the unfortunate mistake of thinking that if they withhold the rent correctly, they won't have to pay anything for the months they endured an unfit rental. This is not so. Unless you've had to move out because of the repair problem, you owe the landlord the reasonable rental value of the rental in its unfit state. In legalese, this is a retroactive rent "abatement," or reduction.

You may get retroactive rent abatement through a court process (if the landlord has filed for eviction, but you've prevailed because the unit was unfit), or through negotiation with your landlord (when no court is involved). Here's how a judge will determine how much the landlord should compensate you for the inconvenience of having lived in a substandard rental unit. If a court is not involved, you can use this same system in negotiating with your landlord.

Market value. One-way to determine how much rent you owe for a substandard rental is to ask: What's the fair market value of the premises in that condition? For example, if an apartment with a broken heater normally rented for $1,200 per month but was worth only $600 without operable heating, the landlord would be entitled to only $600/month from the withheld rent. Of course, the difficulty with this approach—as with many things in law—is that it is staggeringly unrealistic. An apartment with no heat in winter has no market value, because no one would rent it. As you can see, how much a unit is worth in a defective condition is extremely hard to determine.

Percentage reduction. Another slightly more sensible approach is to start by asking what part of the unit is affected by the defect, and then to calculate the percentage of the rent attributable to that part. For example, if the roof leaked into the living room of your $900/month apartment, rendering the room unusable, you could reduce the rent by the percentage of the rent attributable to the living room. If the living room is the main living space and the other rooms are too small to live in comfortably, the percentage of loss would be much greater than it would be in more spacious apartments. Obviously, this approach is far from an exact science, too.

We recommend you use both methods to calculate the unit's reduced, real value. Sometimes, the calculations will be simple—for example, using the fair market value approach, if a broken air conditioner reduces your flat to an oven, its rental value can be determined by consulting ads for non-air-conditioned flats in your area. The percentage reduction method might, in some situations, yield a lower rental value. After you've used both methods, ask the judge to adopt the lower figure (or negotiate for that figure when dealing directly with your landlord) and to rule that the landlord is entitled only to that amount of rent per month, times the number of months that you endured the substandard conditions. The difference between the full rent and the realistic rent should go to you.

CAUTION

You must pay the retroactive, abated rent within five days of winning an eviction lawsuit. If you don't pay on time, the landlord will win and you'll be evicted. The lesson is clear: When withholding rent, keep it in a safe place (such as an escrow account) so that you can promptly pay the abated rent.

EXAMPLE: When Henry and Sue moved into their apartment, it was neat and well maintained. Soon after, the building was sold to an out-of-state owner, who hired an off-site manager to handle repairs and maintenance. Gradually, the premises began to deteriorate. At the beginning of May, 15 months into their two-year lease, Henry and Sue could count several violations of the building code, including the landlord's failure to maintain the common areas, remove the garbage promptly, and fix a broken water heater.

Henry and Sue sent numerous requests for repairs to their landlord over a two-month period, during which they gritted their teeth and put up with the situation. Finally they had enough and checked out their state's rent withholding law. They learned a tenant could pay rent into an escrow account set up by their local court. Henry and Sue went ahead and deposited their rent into this account.

In response, Henry and Sue's landlord filed an eviction lawsuit. In their defense, Henry and Sue pointed to the numerous code and habitability violations. The court agreed with the couple, did not allow the eviction, and ordered the following:

- During the time that they lived in these uninhabitable conditions, Henry and Sue were not required to pay full rent. Using the "market value" approach, the court decided that their defective rental was worth half its stated rent. Accordingly, since the landlord owed them a refund for portions of their rent for May and June, Henry and Sue would be paid this amount from the escrow account.
- The balance of the rent in the account would be released to the landlord (less the costs of the escrow and the tenants' attorney fees), but only when the building inspector certified to the court that the building was up to code and fit for human habitation.
- Henry and Sue could continue to pay 50% of the rent until needed repairs were made and certified by the building inspector.

Make Repairs and Deduct the Cost—"Repair and Deduct"

Another powerful legal remedy for getting major repairs accomplished is called "repair and deduct." (CC § 1941-1942.5.) It works like this: If you have tried and failed to get the landlord to fix a serious defect that renders your rental unfit, you can hire a repairperson to fix it (or buy a replacement part and do it yourself) and subtract the cost from the following month's rent. You can't spend more than one month's rent, and cannot use this remedy more than twice in any 12-month period. If the repair or replacement problem is the result of your failure to use the rental with ordinary care, or if it concerns a matter that you're responsible for (such as maintaining the unit in a clean and sanitary state), you cannot use this remedy.

When to Use Repair and Deduct

Repair and deduct's restrictions on how much you can spend (and how often) make the remedy a poor choice for tenants when it comes to expensive projects such as a major roof repair. Obviously, if you're limited to a twice-a-year expenditure of your monthly rent, you are not going to be able to pay for a $20,000 roof job. Sometimes, however, a number of tenants might pool their dollar limits to accomplish a costly repair. However, as we've explained, a major repair is one that remedies a habitability problem, regardless of its cost. There may be times when a relatively inexpensive job will turn an unfit rental into a habitable one. In these situations, if you're confident that you can competently choose a repairperson or replacement part, you will probably be better off using this remedy instead of withholding the rent. Here's why:

- **It's faster.** Because you'll be doing the work or supervising its completion, you can get going right away (after you've given the landlord time to do it himself, as explained below). With rent withholding, you'll have to wait for the landlord to do the work. Secondly,

- **When the job is not costly, it's less risky.** When you use this remedy, you will give your landlord a short rent check. The landlord can terminate your tenancy and file for eviction on that basis, if she feels you've used the remedy improperly. But she'll be less likely to do so if the check she gets is short by only a portion of the monthly rent, instead of not receiving any check at all, which happens with rent withholding.

The Repair and Deduct Steps

Follow these steps when deciding to use the repair and deduct remedy.

Step 1: Notify your landlord in writing of the problem and give him a reasonable time to fix it. If you've tried gentle persuasion, as suggested above, you've already taken this step. It doesn't hurt to write again, however, and signal your intention to invoke your right to repair and deduct. As ever, be sure to keep copies of your letters, and send them "return receipt" so that the landlord cannot claim later that he didn't receive them.

The big question here is: What's a "reasonable time" for the landlord to take action? Under the statute, 30 days is "presumed" reasonable. This means that if you wait 30 days, the landlord will have a hard time convincing a judge that your subsequent use of the remedy was too hasty. However, in some situations, a shorter time would also be reasonable, and you could act sooner than 30 days if circumstances warrant. For example, no heat in the midst of a cold spell requires a faster response than a finicky heater in the summer time; and a broken front door lock in an iffy neighborhood is worthy of immediate attention—in some situations, no more than a few hours would be a reasonable time to wait before handling the problem yourself.

Step 2: Collect evidence. In case your landlord tries to evict you for nonpayment of rent, you will want to prepare your defense from day one. See the same advice under Step 3 in "Withhold the Rent," above.

Step 3: Gather bids or collect pricing information. By choosing to use this remedy, you're doing the landlord's job for him. Put yourself in his shoes and approach the job as if the property belonged to you. While you don't have to hire the cheapest laborer or firm in the phone book, you do need to pay attention to cost. At the same time, the quality of the work needs to be in keeping with the standards that the landlord applies to the rest of the property. For example, if you're looking for a furnace repairperson, it might make sense to use an authorized repair shop if you know that the landlord consistently chooses "safe" repairmen. On the other hand, a handyman might be just fine if the landlord himself does the work (when he does it) or hires handymen himself.

Save your research or bids in a safe place. You may need them should the landlord challenge you on your choice and whether you made a good faith effort to secure the best deal.

Step 4: Attach copies of the bills, receipts, or invoices, plus evidence that you have paid them, to your next rent check, with a letter explaining why the rent is reduced. Do not reduce the rent until you have done the work and paid for it.

Sample Letter Telling the Landlord You Intend to Repair and Deduct

8976 Maple Avenue
Katyville, CA 12345
360-555-6543

January 14, 20xx

Hattie Connifer
200 Capitol Expressway, Suite 300
Katyville, CA 12345

Dear Ms. Connifer:

On January 10, I called your office and spoke to you about a major problem: I have no hot water. As I explained on the phone, on the evening of January 9 the water heater for my flat sprang a leak. Luckily, I was home and was able to divert the water to the outside with a hose, turn off the intake valve, and shut off the pilot.

At the end of our conversation on January 10, you assured me that you would send a repairperson to the flat the next day, January 11. As of today, no one has showed up, and I am enduring my fourth day of no hot water.

Under California law, I am entitled to remedy the problem and deduct the cost from my rent if you do not attend to the problem within 24 hours (California Civil Code §§ 1941–1942.5). I intend to do this if the heater is not replaced within 24 hours after you receive this letter, which I am personally delivering to your office.

Yours truly,

Wanda Wright

Wanda Wright

Move Out When Repairs Haven't Been Done

If your dwelling isn't habitable and hasn't been made so despite your complaints and repair requests, you also have the right to move out. This will discharge you from any further obligations under the rental agreement or lease. (CC § 1942(a).) This drastic measure is justified only when there are truly serious problems, such as the lack of essential services, or the presence of environmental health hazards such as lead paint dust. Chapter 10 explains your right to move out because of environmental toxins.

Your right to move out of a seriously unfit dwelling is borrowed directly from consumer protection laws. Just as the purchaser of a significantly defective car may return the car for a refund, you can consider the housing contract terminated and simply return the rental unit to the landlord if the housing is unlivable.

The law, of course, has a convoluted phrase to describe this simple concept. It's called "constructive eviction," which means that the landlord, by supplying unlivable housing, has for all practical purposes "evicted" you. Once you have been constructively evicted (that is, you have a valid reason to move out), you have no further responsibility for rent.

Before moving out, you must give the landlord notice of the problem and a reasonable opportunity to fix it. Refer to Steps 1 and 2 in "The Repair and Deduct Steps," above, for guidance on how to proceed.

If you move out permanently because of habitability problems, you may want to sue the landlord (in small claims court) to compensate you for out-of-pocket losses. For example, you may be able to recover moving expenses and the cost of a hotel for a few days until you find a new place. Also, if the conditions were substandard during prior months when you did pay the full rent, you may sue to be reimbursed for the difference between the value of the defective dwelling and the rent paid. In addition, if you are unable to find comparable housing for the same rent and end up paying more rent than you would have under the old lease, you may be able to recover the difference.

Move Out When the Premises Have Been Destroyed

If your home is totally damaged by natural disaster or any other reason beyond your control, which obviously renders it unlivable, you have the legal right to consider the lease or rental agreement at an end and to move out without responsibility for future rent. (CC § 1933(4).) You are not, however, entitled to reimbursement for rent payments you've already made. (*Pedro v. Potter*, 197 Cal. 751 (1926).)

TIP

If you have renter's insurance, file a claim. You may get help for resettlement costs and coverage for your lost or destroyed possessions. Coverage may not extend to destruction caused by floods or earthquakes. (Renter's insurance is covered in Chapter 15.)

Partial destruction, however, is another matter. If you must find another place to live because of partial damage to or destruction of the premises— no matter the cause—you and the landlord will face the question of whether to terminate the lease or rental agreement or just suspend it while repairs are made. Your course of action depends on whether your lease or rental agreement addresses this eventuality (if it doesn't, state law takes over).

Check Your Lease or Rental Agreement

First, check your lease or rental agreement for a clause covering what happens if the premises are partially damaged or destroyed. The rental document may give the landlord the right to terminate your rental or merely suspend it while repairs are made. If the landlord decides to keep the lease or rental agreement alive during repairs, you won't have to pay the landlord rent while you're

---

Stay or Go? Consider the Practicalities

You may find that the choice of whether to declare the tenancy at an end or to move out while repairs are made is up to you. Consider the following issues:

Terminate the lease or rental agreement. You'll want to terminate the rental if you can find new housing of comparable quality and cost. You won't have to live with the uncertainty of when you'll move back to the original dwelling, and it will save you the time and aggravation of an extra household move. And if your new housing comes with a lease, you may have to terminate the old one, since a lease won't allow you to move when you want.

If you decide to terminate the original lease or rental agreement, finalize the decision in writing. Have the landlord write "Terminated" on each page of your lease or rental agreement. Both of you should sign and date each page. Your landlord should refund your security deposit according to normal procedures. (See Chapter 13.)

Leave temporarily without terminating the lease. If your rental is a particularly great deal, the local market is very tight, or the repairs can be accomplished within a reasonable time, you'll want to hang on to your unit. If you are protected by rent control and you have lived in your rental for a significant period of time, you'll probably be loath to move. (Check your rent control ordinance for any special rules dealing with temporary move-outs.) Find a month-to-month rental while the original unit is repaired.

You and the landlord should add a page to the lease entitled "Suspension" that states that the landlord's and tenant's responsibilities have been suspended from a certain date until the day you move back in. Be sure to include the landlord's promise to notify you promptly as soon as the rental is ready. If the landlord will help you with relocation costs, note them. Both of you should sign and date this document.

living elsewhere, but you also won't get rental assistance from the landlord if your replacement housing is more expensive than your regular rent. Or, your landlord can declare the rental to be over (even if you'd rather move out temporarily). If you disagree with the landlord's call, all you can do is try to change the landlord's mind.

Default Rules for Partially Destroyed Rentals

Most rental agreements and leases do not include clauses that deal with the partial destruction of the property. If your rental documents are silent on the issue, the fate of your rental will depend on the application of the facts of your situation to state law, which provides that the lease or rental agreement will terminate if:

- the destruction is not the fault of the tenant
- the landlord had reason to believe, when the lease or rental agreement was signed, that the destroyed portion or aspect of the rental premises was a "material inducement" to the tenant (that is, a major reason why the tenant rented the premises), and
- the tenant gives notice to the landlord that he considers the lease to be over because of the destruction of an important aspect of the premises. (CC § 1932(2).)

EXAMPLE: Sandra wanted a rental with a large, fenced yard that would be a safe play area for her three small children. When she saw Alex's duplex, she was delighted at the spacious backyard and told him that it was the perfect answer to her needs. When he offered to show her another duplex that had no yard but a larger interior, she declined and told him that her most important requirement was the yard, and that she would make do with smaller rooms. Sandra signed a year's lease in late fall.

The weather that winter was exceptionally severe, and the rainstorms caused the hill behind Sandra's home to slide, burying the backyard in a foot of mud and crushing the fences. Although the house itself escaped damage, the yard was ruined. Sandra wrote to Alex to tell him that she considered the lease to be over, since the backyard, now unusable, was a major reason for her decision to rent. Sandra moved out and although she did not recover the balance of that month's rent, she was not responsible for any future rent. She got her entire security deposit back when Alex examined the house and determined that there was no damage beyond normal wear and tear.

Sue the Landlord

A consumer who purchases a product—be it a car, a hair dryer, or a steak dinner—is justified in expecting a minimum level of quality, and is entitled to compensation if the product is seriously flawed. The same goes for tenants. If your rental is not habitable, you can sue the landlord—whether or not you move out. You can use small claims court, which allows claims of up to $7,500.

Suing the landlord makes sense only if you can safely continue to live in your rental. For example, if the roof leaks only into the second bedroom, and you can move the kids into the living room for a while, you might want to stay and sue in order to avoid the hassle of moving, arranging for the repair yourself (repair and deduct), or figuring out the complications of rent withholding. But you wouldn't want to stay and sue if you are without heat in the winter or in danger of electrocution every time you use the kitchen stove.

What are the pros and cons of suing your landlord instead of using repair and deduct or rent withholding? On the positive side, if you lose your lawsuit you'll have lost some time and money, but you won't be evicted, as can happen with the unsuccessful use of repair and deduct or rent withholding. But suing isn't entirely risk-free, especially if you're a month-to-month tenant or nearing the end of a lease you would like to renew. Your annoyed landlord may simply decide to terminate or not renew. Although state antiretaliation laws theoretically protect you, asserting your rights will mean the threat of or the bringing of a lawsuit, a dreary prospect.

In your lawsuit, you ask the judge to rule that your unrepaired rental was not worth what you've paid for it. You want to be paid the difference between the monthly rent and the real value of the unit, times the number of months that you've lived with the substandard conditions. In short, you'll ask for a retroactive rent decrease—what we explained as a rent abatement above in "Withhold the Rent." In addition, you can sue your landlord for:

- lost or damaged property—for example, furniture ruined by water leaking through the roof

- compensation for personal injuries—including pain and suffering—caused by the defect (see Chapter 9), and

- your attorney fees and court costs if you had to hire a lawyer to sue the landlord (Chapter 17 discusses attorney fees).

You'll probably want to ask the court for an order directing the landlord to repair the defects, with rent reduced until they are fixed. Unfortunately, the judge will probably tell you that in small claims court, judges can only order the landlord to pay you for your losses. In practice, usually the money judgment gets the landlord's attention and repairs follow soon thereafter.

Minor Repairs & Maintenance

Ask a group of tenants which rental problem is most annoying, and chances are you'd hear, "Repairs!" Most wouldn't be referring to major problems that make a unit unlivable. What really bugs tenants are the day-to-day but nonetheless important problems: leaky faucets, malfunctioning appliances, security devices that don't work, worn carpets, noisy heaters, hot water heaters that produce a pathetic quantity of tepid water, and dozens of other frustrating breakdowns.

Unfortunately, if your landlord refuses to attend to minor repairs, you don't have much legal clout. You can't withhold rent, move out, or use most of the other "big stick" legal weapons discussed in Chapter 6. Even so, there are several proven strategies for getting results.

Minor Repairs: What Are They?

If a landlord balks at making repairs, your first step is to decide whether the problem is major (affecting the habitability of your rental unit) or minor. This distinction is necessary because you have different legal options depending on your conclusion.

Minor repair and maintenance includes:

- small plumbing jobs, like replacing washers and cleaning drains
- system upkeep, like changing heating filters
- structural upkeep, like replacing excessively worn flooring
- small repair jobs like fixing broken light fixtures or replacing the grout around bathtub tile, and
- routine repairs to and maintenance of common areas, such as pools, spas, and laundry rooms.

Don't assume that inexpensive repairs are always minor repairs. Sometimes an extremely important repair costs very little. For example, if the only thing between you and a heated apartment is the replacement of a $45 furnace part, the repair is "major" because an unheated dwelling is uninhabitable, even though the repair cost is insignificant. And because this is true, if the landlord didn't replace the furnace part promptly, you would probably be entitled to withhold rent or use one of the other "big stick" strategies discussed in Chapter 6. By contrast, replacing the living room carpet, which is worn but not a hazard, will be very expensive, but will be considered a minor repair if the consequence of not replacing it is less than an unfit dwelling.

Most often, minor repairs are the landlord's responsibility. But landlords are not required to keep the premises looking just like new—ordinary wear and tear does not have to be repaired during your tenancy. (When you move out, however, the cost of dealing with ordinary wear and tear will fall on the landlord and cannot come out of your security deposit.)

The Landlord's Responsibilities

Not every minor problem is your landlord's legal responsibility. If you or one of your guests caused it, carelessly or intentionally, you are responsible for repairing it—or, if your lease or rental agreement prohibits you from doing so, for paying the landlord to do it. But if you had nothing to do with the repair problem and it's not a cosmetic issue, chances go way up that your landlord is responsible, for one of the following reasons:

- A state or local building code requires that the landlord keep the damaged item (for example, a kitchen sink) in good repair.
- A lease or rental agreement provision or advertisement describes or lists particular items, such as hot tubs, trash compactors, and air conditioners. By implication, this makes the landlord responsible for maintaining or repairing them.
- The landlord made explicit promises when showing you the unit—for example, regarding the security or air-conditioning system.

Common Misconceptions About Routine Maintenance

Many tenants (and landlords) mistakenly think that every time a rental unit turns over, or a certain number of years have passed, the landlord must paint or clean drapes and carpets, or do some other kind of refurbishing. Unfortunately for tenants, the law almost never mandates cosmetic changes—even badly needed ones. Here are some common misconceptions:

Paint. California landlords are not required to repaint at specified times. Unless the paint creates a habitability problem—for example, it's so thick around a window that the window can't be opened, or flaking lead-based paint poses obvious health risks—the landlord can just let it go. (Lead-based paint creates so many potential problems that we discuss it separately in Chapter 10.)

Drapes and Carpets. So long as drapes and carpets are not so damp or full of mildew as to amount to a health hazard, and so long as carpets don't have dangerous holes that could cause someone to trip and fall, your landlord isn't legally required to replace them.

Windows. You're responsible for fixing (or paying to fix) a broken window that you or your guest intentionally or carelessly broke. If a burglar, vandal, or neighborhood child breaks a window, however, the landlord is usually legally responsible for the repair. Broken windows can sometimes be a habitability problem; see Chapter 6.

Rekeying. Unfortunately, landlords are not legally required to change the locks for new tenants. However, if you tell a landlord in writing that you are worried about renting a unit secured by locks for which previous tenants (and perhaps their friends) have keys, most landlords rekey the locks. (If the landlord knows of your concern but does not respond, and you are attacked or your place is burglarized by someone using an old key, the chances of the landlord being held liable in a lawsuit go way up. (See Chapter 13.) California landlords must, however, at least provide door and window locks. (CC § 1941.1). Chapter 11 gives you the details.

- The landlord has assumed the obligation to maintain a particular feature, such as a whirlpool bathtub, because the landlord has fixed or maintained it in the past.

Each of these reasons is discussed below. If you're not sure whether a minor repair or maintenance problem is the landlord's responsibility, scan the discussion to find out.

Building Codes

California state law (and some city ordinances) covers structural requirements, such as roofs, flooring, windows, and essential services such as hot water and heat. If your repair problem is also a violation of the building code, you may be facing a habitability problem, as discussed in Chapter 6. But building codes often cover other, less essential details as well. For example, state code requires a minimum number of electrical outlets per room. When a room has too few outlets, it's inconvenient, but probably not unsafe or unhealthy. Likewise, if a broken circuit breaker means that you have fewer working outlets, the consequence is probably not an unfit dwelling, but the landlord is still legally required to fix the problem.

Promises in the Lease or Rental Agreement

When it comes to legal responsibility for repairs, your own lease or rental agreement is often just as important (or more so) than building codes or state laws. If your written agreement describes or lists items such as drapes, washing machines, swimming pools, saunas, parking places, intercoms, or dishwashers, your landlord must provide them in decent repair. And the promise to provide them carries with it the implied promise to maintain them.

Promises in Ads

If an advertisement for your unit described or listed a feature, such as a cable TV hookup, that significantly affected your decision to move into the particular rental unit, you have the right to hold the landlord to these promises. Even if your written rental agreement says nothing about appliances, if the landlord's ad listed a dishwasher, clothes washer and dryer, garbage disposal, microwave oven, security gates, and Jacuzzi, you have a right to expect that all of them will be repaired by the landlord if they break through no fault of yours.

> **EXAMPLE:** Tina sees Joel's ad for an apartment, which says "heated swimming pool." After Tina moves in, Joel stops heating the pool regularly because his utility costs have risen. Joel has violated his promise to keep the pool heated.

The promise doesn't have to be in words.

> **EXAMPLE:** Tom's real estate agent showed him a glossy color photo of an available apartment, which featured a smiling resident using an intercom to welcome a guest. The apartment Tom rented did not have a working intercom, and he complained to the management, arguing that the advertisement implied that all units were so equipped. The landlord realized that he would have to fix the intercom.

Promises Made Before You Rented the Unit

It's a rare landlord or manager who refrains from even the slightest bit of puffing when showing a rental to a prospective tenant. You're quite likely to hear rosy plans for amenities or services that haven't yet materialized ("We plan to redo this kitchen—you'll love the snappy way that trash compactor will work!"). Whenever you hear promises like these, you would be wise to get them in writing, as part of (or attached to) your lease or rental agreement or, at the very least, in a prompt letter of understanding that cannot be repudiated later.

If this advice is coming to you now a bit late, and you don't in fact have anything in writing, don't give up hope. The oral promise is valid and enforceable—it's just a little harder to prove that it was made. If the promised trash compactor never appears, it's your word against the landlord's unless you have witnesses to the conversation. You'll be in a stronger position, proof-wise, if the promised feature is present in your unit but just doesn't work or breaks down after you move in, as explained just below.

> **EXAMPLE:** When Joel's rental agent shows Tom around the building, she goes out of her way to show off the laundry room, saying, "Here's the laundry room—we have two machines now, but will be adding two more soon." Tom rents the apartment. Two months go by and Joel still hasn't added the new machines. Joel has violated his promise to equip the laundry room with four machines.

Implied Promises

Suppose your rental agreement doesn't mention a garbage disposal, and neither does any ad you saw before moving in. And, in fairness, you can't remember your landlord ever pointing it out when showing you the unit. But there is a garbage disposal, and it was working when you moved in. Now the garbage disposal is broken and, despite repeated requests, your landlord hasn't fixed it. Do you have a legal leg to stand on in demanding that your landlord make this minor repair? Yes. Many courts will hold a landlord legally responsible for maintaining all significant aspects of your rental unit. If you rent a unit that *already has* certain features—light fixtures that work, doors that open and close smoothly, faucets that don't leak, tile that doesn't fall off the wall—many judges reason that the landlord has made an implied contract to keep them in workable order throughout your tenancy.

The flip side of this principle is that if you pay for a hamburger, the waiter doesn't have to deliver a steak. In other words, if your rental was shabby when you moved in, and the landlord never gave you reason to believe that it would be spruced up, you have no legal right to demand improvements—unless, of course, you can show health hazards or code violations. As when you buy secondhand goods "as is" for a low price, legally you are stuck with your deal. (But as you'll see, "Getting the Landlord to Make Minor Repairs," below, suggests some strategies—based on subtly showing your landlord the consequences of ignoring minor repairs—that may convince a reluctant landlord to take better care of business.)

Another factor that is evidence of an implied contract is the landlord's past conduct. A landlord who has consistently fixed or maintained a particular feature of your rental has made an implied obligation to continue doing so.

EXAMPLE: Tina's apartment has a built-in dishwasher. When she rented the apartment, neither the lease nor the landlord said anything about the dishwasher or who was responsible for repairing it. The dishwasher has broken down a few times and whenever Tina asked Joel to fix it, he did. By doing so, Joel has established a practice that he—not the tenant—is responsible for repairing the dishwasher.

TIP

Check your lease. Landlords who want to avoid responsibility for appliance repairs often insert clauses in their leases or rental agreements stating that the appliances are not maintained by the landlord.

TIP

Using the Landlord-Tenant Checklist at the start of your tenancy will give you a record of appliances and features—and their condition. If something needs repairs, you'll be able to use the Checklist as proof of its original condition. See Chapter 1 for instructions on using the checklist.

Agreeing to Do Maintenance

Leases and rental agreements usually include a general statement that you are responsible for keeping your rental unit clean, safe, and in good condition, and for reimbursing your landlord for the cost of repairing damage you cause, as explained at length in Chapter 6. Your lease or rental agreement will probably also say that you can't make alterations or repairs, such as painting the walls, installing bookcases, or fixing electrical problems, without your landlord's permission (see Chapter 8).

Landlords who are tired of maintenance and repair jobs may use the lease, rental agreement, or separate contract to give these responsibilities to a tenant. Especially if you rent a single-family home or duplex, you may be asked to agree to mow the lawn, trim the bushes, and do minor plumbing jobs and painting.

Commonly, a landlord proposes a rent reduction in exchange for some work. Or the landlord may offer other perks (a parking space, for example), or will offer an amenity if the tenant will perform the maintenance—for example, a hot tub in exchange for your promise to clean it.

Although usually legal, these arrangements often lead to dissatisfaction—typically, the landlord feels that the tenant has neglected certain tasks, or the tenant feels that there is too much work. If the dispute boils over, the landlord tries to evict the tenant.

When you take on repair duties, here's how to protect yourself and avoid disputes:

- **Sign an employment agreement separate from your rental agreement or lease.** This is especially important if you plan to do considerable work for your landlord on a continuing basis, such as keeping hallways, elevators, or a laundry room clean, or maintaining the landscaping. Tenants who are also building managers are in this position. Ask your landlord to pay you for your work, rather than give you a rent reduction. That way, if the landlord claims that the job is not done right, the worst that can happen is that you may be fired but your tenancy should not be affected. But if your maintenance duties are tied to a rent reduction and things go wrong, you and the landlord will have to amend the lease or rental agreement in order to reestablish the original rent. And if the maintenance jobs are spelled out in a lease clause, the landlord also has the option of terminating the lease on the grounds that your poor performance constitutes a breach of the lease. Be forewarned, however, that many landlords will not want to enter into an employer-employee relationship with you, because becoming an employer has its own set of complications.

- **Clearly write out your responsibilities and the landlord's expectations.** List your tasks and the frequency with which your landlord expects them to be done. Weekly tasks might include, for example, cleaning the laundry room, sweeping and wet mopping the lobby, and mowing the grass between April 1 and November 1.

- **Make sure the agreement is fair.** Ideally, your landlord will pay you a fair hourly rate. If your only choice is a rent reduction, make sure the trade-off is equitable. If you're getting only a $50 rent reduction for work that would cost the landlord $200 if done by a cleaning service, you're being ripped off.

- **Discuss problems with the landlord and try to work out a mutually satisfactory agreement.** If the landlord has complained about your work, maybe it's because the owner underestimated what's involved in cleaning the hallways and grounds. Your landlord may be willing to pay you more for better results or shorten your list of jobs. If not, cancel the arrangement.

Watch Out for Illegal Retaliation

Landlords who delegate some tasks are not relieved of all repair and maintenance responsibilities. For example, if you and your landlord agree that you will do gardening work in exchange for a rent reduction, and the landlord feels that you are not doing a proper job, the landlord cannot respond by shutting off your water.

CAUTION

Don't perform repairs involving hazardous materials. Any repair involving old paint or insulation (opening up a ceiling or wall cavity, for example) may expose you or others to dangerous levels of toxic materials. For example, sanding a surface for a seemingly innocuous paint job may actually create lead-based paint dust; the quick installation of a smoke alarm could involve disturbing an asbestos-filled ceiling. See Chapter 10 for more information on environmental hazards.

Getting the Landlord to Make Minor Repairs

By now you should have a pretty good idea as to whether your landlord is legally responsible for fixing the particular minor problem that is bedeviling you. Your next job is to get the landlord to do it. First, try to get the landlord to cooperate. If you can't, it may be time to take a confrontational approach.

Appealing to Your Landlord

Chances are you have already asked your landlord or manager to make repairs, only to be put off, ignored, or even told to forget it. Your next step is to write a formal demand letter—or, if you have already done it, a second one.

Before you pick up your pen or turn on your computer, take a minute to think about what words will most likely get action. Begin by remembering your landlord's overriding business concerns: to make money, avoid hassles with tenants, and stay out of legal hot water. A request that zeroes in on these issues will likely get the job done.

Special Concerns for Month-to-Month Tenants

If you have a month-to-month tenancy, your landlord can terminate your tenancy with just 30 days' notice (60 days if you've lived in the rental a year or more). That means you should think twice before trying one of the adversarial strategies discussed below—reporting your landlord for building code violations or suing in small claims court—over minor problems with your rental.

California's antiretaliation law may ultimately protect you from a termination notice delivered in retaliation. But if you have to defend an eviction lawsuit, you may end up wishing you'd never complained about that cracked tile. Remember, you can end your tenancy with 30 days' notice, so if you're really unhappy with your place, maybe you should look for another.

How to Write a Persuasive Repair Request

Whether this is your first or second formal demand letter, frame your repair request along one or more of the following lines, if possible:

- **It's a small problem now, but has the potential to be a very big deal.** A bathtub faucet that drips badly may be simply annoying now, but devastating later if the washer gives out while you're not home, flooding the tub and ruining the floor and downstairs neighbor's ceiling. When you ask that the faucet be repaired, point out the risk of letting things go.
- **There is a potential for injury.** Landlords hate to be sued. If a potential injury-causing problem is brought to their attention, it's

likely that their fear of lawsuits will overcome their lethargy, and you'll finally get results. Say, for instance, you have asked your landlord to repair the electrical outlet in your kitchen so that you can use your toaster. If you've received no response, try again with a different pitch: Point out that, on occasion, you have observed sparks flying from the wall, and a short in the wiring could cause an injury or fire.

- **There is a security problem that imperils your safety.** Landlords are increasingly aware that they can also be sued for criminal assaults against tenants if the premises aren't reasonably secure. (Chapter 11 discusses this topic in detail.) If you can figure out a way to emphasize the security risks of not fixing a problem—for example, a burned-out light bulb in the garage or a door that doesn't always latch properly—you may motivate the landlord to act promptly.
- **The problem affects other tenants.** If you can point to a disaster-waiting-to-happen that affects more than one tenant, you will greatly increase your chances of some action. For example, accumulated oil puddles in the garage threaten the safety of all tenants and guests, not just you. Faced with the possibility of a small army of potential plaintiffs, each accompanied by an eager attorney, even the most slothful landlord may spring into action.
- **You're willing to try to fix it, but may make the problem worse.** Finally, you might try offering to fix the problem yourself in a way that is likely to elicit a quick "No thanks, I'll call my contractor right away!" This is a bit risky, since your bluff might be called, but even the most dense landlord will think twice when you offer to make an electrical repair with a chisel and masking tape.

See the sample letter below for more ideas on writing a persuasive repair request.

Sample Letter Asking for Minor Repairs

90 Willow Run, Apartment 3A
Morgantown, California 00000

February 28, 20xx

Mr. Lee Sloan
37 Main Street, Suite 100
Morgantown, California 00000

Dear Mr. Sloan:

I would appreciate it if you could schedule an appointment with me to look at three problems in my apartment that have come up recently.

First, the kitchen sink is dripping, and it's getting worse. I'm concerned that a plate or dish towel might stop up the drain, leading to an overflow. At any rate, the water bill is yours, and I'm sure that you don't want to pay for wasted water.

I've also been having trouble opening the sliding doors on the bedroom closet. The track appears to be coming away from the wall, and the doors wobble and look like they might fall into the room when I open and close the closet.

Finally, it would really be great if you would give some thought to repainting the interior hallways. They looked clean when I moved in a year ago, but now are pretty grimy. I've spoken with the tenants in four of the other six units and they, too, would appreciate a return to your standards of old.

Thanks very much for thinking about my requests. I hope to hear from you soon.

Yours truly,
Chris Jensen
Chris Jensen

A written demand for repair or maintenance lets your landlord know that you are serious about the issue and are not content to just let it go. In addition, if your dispute ends up in small claims court, the demand letter can usually be introduced as evidence. Like this sample letter, your demand letter should:

- be neatly typed and use businesslike language.
- concisely and accurately state the important facts (this is important in case your letter ends up before a judge, who will need to be educated about the situation).
- be polite and nonpersonal. Obviously, a personal attack on your landlord may trigger an equally emotional response. Because you are appealing to the landlord's business interests, you want to encourage the landlord to evaluate the issue soberly, not out of anger.
- state exactly what you want—a new paint job, for example.

Always keep a copy of the letter for your files, and hand-deliver the letter or send it "return receipt requested."

Propose Mediation

If your demand letter does not produce results, consider involving the help of a local mediation center. Most community services handle lots of landlord and tenant problems, for free or at a very low cost. If they can coax the landlord to talk with you (and they're very good at doing that), you have a decent chance of ending up with an agreement. See Chapter 16 for more information on mediation.

Reporting Code Violations

If appealing to your landlord's business sensibilities doesn't work, other strategies are available to pry minor repairs out of your landlord.

If the problem you want fixed constitutes a code violation, such as inadequate electrical outlets or low water pressure, you should find an ally in the building or housing agency in charge of enforcing the code. (Chapter 6 explains how to find and what to expect from these local agencies.) Whether you'll get any action out of the agency will depend on the seriousness of the violation, the workload of the agency, and its ability to enforce its compliance orders. Because by definition your problem is minor, don't expect lots of help if code enforcement officials are already overworked.

Suing in Small Claims Court

If you can reasonably argue that you aren't getting what you paid for, you might decide to sue in small claims court. But before you do, write a second demand letter. Like the first letter (see the sample above), your second letter should describe the problems and alert the landlord to the negative consequences (to the landlord, not just to you) that may follow if repairs aren't made. In addition, state that you intend to sue if you don't get results. This may get the landlord's attention and save you a trip to the courthouse.

EXAMPLE: Chris Jensen wrote to her landlord on February 28, requesting repairs as shown in the sample letter above. She got no reply. Ten days later, she sent a second letter that summarized the first and concluded with this paragraph:

"If you are unable to attend to these repairs, I'll need to call in a handyman to repair the faucet and doors, and I will seek reimbursement from you in small claims court if necessary. As for the deterioration of the paint, I believe I am entitled to a reduction in rent, which I will also seek in small claims court. Of course, I sincerely hope that this will not be necessary."

If the second letter doesn't produce results, it's time to head for small claims court. You won't need a lawyer (in fact, in California you can't bring a lawyer to small claims court). Just go to the court and ask for the forms you need to sue someone. In small claims court, you can't get an order from the judge directing your landlord to paint, fix the dishwasher, or repair the intercom. You may, however, be compensated in dollars for living in a rental unit with repair problems. Here's how it works.

When you file your small claims court suit, you'll ask for an amount that reflects the difference between your rent and the value of the unit with repair problems. For example, if you're living with a broken air conditioner, and know that apartments without air conditioners rent for $50 less per month, use that figure (multiplied by the number of months or parts thereof that the unit's been broken) as your measure of damages. In court, your argument will be that you are not getting the benefit of what you're paying rent for—for example, a functioning dishwasher, presentable paint, or a working air conditioner.

You're more likely to succeed with this line of argument if you have a lease rather than a month-to-month agreement. If you have a long-term lease, you can argue that you are locked into a set rent for an extended period of time and should be compensated accordingly—that is, month after month, it appears that your landlord's inaction will mean that you'll receive less than what you are obligated to pay for. In contrast, a month-to-month tenant has no long-standing obligation; if you don't like the fact that the shower door now won't close, you can leave after giving relatively short notice, with no legal liability for future rent. A judge is likely to point this out and to tell you that, in effect, you agreed to the increasing shabbiness every month when you failed to send in a termination notice.

CAUTION

Don't stop paying rent. Although fairness dictates that if your rental unit is full of repair problems you ought to pay less rent, it's a mistake to pay your landlord less than the full monthly rent. Rent withholding, as discussed in Chapter 6, is legally appropriate only for major repairs. If you withhold even a portion of the rent because of a minor repair problem, you risk eviction for nonpayment of rent.

Your goal in small claims court is to convince the judge that these problems really make your rental unit worth less money. Use common sense—don't go running to court for small things. A small claims court judge is not going to adjust your rent because a little grout is missing from your bathroom tile. But if your dishwasher is broken, three faucets leak noisily, and the bathroom door won't close, your chances of winning go way up. You'll need to show the judge that:

- there are lots of minor defects, not just an isolated one, and
- you've given the landlord plenty of time and notice to fix the problems.

Be sure to bring evidence. Winning in small claims court depends more on what you drag into court with you than on what you say. Examples of key evidence include:

- copies of letters you've written asking for repairs
- your written notes on your landlord's response to your repair requests, including the number of times they were ignored or promised repairs didn't materialize
- witnesses—a family member, for example, who can describe the inoperable air conditioner
- photographs—your pictures of the cracked, flaking plaster, for example
- a copy of the local building or housing code, if the problem is covered there
- your lease or rental agreement, if it lists any of the items that need repair
- your lease or rental agreement, if it prohibits you from making repairs yourself
- a copy of the Landlord-Tenant Checklist, which you should have completed when you moved in and which is signed by you and the landlord, showing that the problem did not exist at the start of your tenancy, and
- ads, brochures, or For Rent signs describing features of your rental that are missing or malfunctioning.

EXAMPLE: Judy signed a one-year lease for a studio apartment at $750 a month. When she moved in, the place was in good shape. But six months into her tenancy, the condition of the apartment began to deteriorate. A water leak from the roof stained and buckled several areas of the hardwood floors; the kitchen cabinets, which were apparently badly made, warped, and would not shut; the dishwasher became so noisy the neighbor banged on the wall when it was in use; the soap dish fell off the bathroom wall; and the white entryway rug started to fall apart. Judy asked her landlord to attend to these problems and followed up with several written demand letters. Two months after her original request, Judy wrote a final demand letter.

When the landlord still did nothing, Judy filed suit in small claims court, asking the judge to award her damages (money) representing the difference between her rent and the value of the deteriorated apartment. After considering Judy's evidence, including copies of her demand letter, photographs of the defects, and the testimony of her neighbor, the judge agreed with Judy. The judge figured that the deteriorated apartment would have rented for $150 less a month, and ordered the landlord to pay Judy $450 to make up for the three months she had lived with the defects. Judy's landlord was quick to make repairs after learning this expensive lesson in court.

RESOURCE

Everybody's Guide to Small Claims Court in California, by Ralph Warner (Nolo), has all the details you need to file a small claims court lawsuit.

Making Minor Repairs Yourself

If you've concluded that a repair job isn't your landlord's responsibility, then it's in your lap. Before you head out to the hardware store, pause for a moment. You need to know, first, whether it makes sense from a practical point of view for you to do the repair or maintenance; and, second, whether it's legal.

Evaluating Your Skills and Time

Before you embark on a job, realistically assess its magnitude and your skills, tools, and time. Seemingly easy repairs often have hidden complexities. A simple job, like replacing the flexible hoses under the sink that connect the pipes to the faucet, may require special wrenches because of the cramped workspace. Do you have this equipment, or are you willing to purchase it? Time is also an issue: Are you willing to commit precious weekend or evening time to a plumbing project? Only an experienced, equipped handyperson (or one willing to consult a good do-it-yourself manual) should consider doing most home repairs.

You must also consider whether you are willing to take the risk of being held liable if one of your repair projects goes awry and results in property damage or, worse, someone's injury. Your landlord's insurance policy will not cover your misdeeds, and unless you have renter's insurance, you stand to lose a lot of money.

> **EXAMPLE:** Colin decided to replace a window that was broken by his daughter's basketball. He removed the shards of glass, fitted a new pane in place, and caulked the circumference. He did not, however, paint the caulk, and a year later it had cracked, allowing rainwater to seep onto the windowsill and down the wall. The landlord was furious when he realized that he would have to replace the sill and the drywall, simply because Colin had not done a workmanlike job. The cost of these repairs was taken out of Colin's security deposit.

Getting the Landlord's Permission

First, look at your lease or rental agreement. You may see a clause that forbids you from undertaking any "repairs, alterations, or improvements" without the landlord's consent. (Alterations and improvements are discussed in Chapter 8.) It may seem unfair, but such a clause is legal. And a "no repairs without consent" clause keeps the landlord in control of the property, while making you pay for it.

If your lease has a "no repairs" clause, you'll have to convince the landlord to give you permission. (See the sample letter below.) And even if you don't have such a clause, check with the landlord first, anyway. You won't need to do this if the repair or replacement is truly insignificant and nontechnical (or if it's unlikely to be noticed by the landlord), like replacing the entryway rug or installing mini-blinds where old ones used to be.

But for jobs that have the potential to get complicated, expensive, or have dire consequences if things go wrong, you'll want to have the official okay before proceeding. It may prevent your landlord from legally charging you if things go awry. Of course, a potential negative outcome may be the very reason your landlord will say "No way" and call for the bonded repairperson. But many landlords—if they trust you—will be happy to save themselves the time and trouble of lining up a worker, scheduling a time to be in your apartment, getting you to pay the bill, or deducting the expense from your security deposit and then getting you to bring the deposit up to its original level.

To protect yourself, put your repair proposal in writing, phrase it in a way that tells the landlord you'll proceed unless you hear to the contrary within a reasonable amount of time, and keep a copy for your records. That way, you have a record that your work was undertaken with the landlord's consent. A sample letter is shown below; notice how the tenant has communicated the problem, her experience with similar repairs, and a plan for repairing the item, all of which are designed to inspire the landlord's confidence.

Sample Letter Requesting Permission to Do a Minor Repair

890 Market Street, #3

Central City, California 00000

(214) 555-7890

January 4, 20xx

Jackson Montgomery

234 Fourth Street

Central City, California 00000

Dear Mr. Montgomery,

Last night, a fork accidentally fell into my garbage disposal, jamming the blades and causing the unit to stop. The disposal will have to be taken out and the blade assembly examined. The shear key, which prevents the engine from seizing, will need to be replaced.

I am familiar with the installation and maintenance of these appliances, having worked on one at my former residence. I have the tools to do the job. I'll proceed with this repair unless I hear from you to the contrary. Please leave me a note or call me before January 10 if you do not wish me to do the job. If I don't hear from you by then, I'll go ahead.

Yours truly,

Janet Green

Janet Green

Alterations & Satellite Dishes

Your lease or rental agreement probably includes a clause prohibiting you from making any alterations or improvements to your unit without the express, written consent of the landlord. (Often, your landlord will forbid you to undertake repairs, too. This issue is discussed in Chapter 1.) Landlords use these clauses—some of which contain a long list of prohibitions—so that tenants don't change the light fixtures, knock out a wall, install a built-in dishwasher, or even pound in a nail to hang a picture unless the landlord agrees first.

But what if you make one of these alterations or improvements without getting your landlord's permission—for example, you bolt a closet storage system to the wall? Unless you get the landlord's permission to remove the item, such improvements and additions become the landlord's property when you leave.

Discovering too late that you must leave behind what you thought of as a portable improvement can be a real blow. To help you avoid problems, this chapter explains:

- what types of improvements and alterations become the landlord's property
- what you can do, ahead of time, to forestall losing your property
- how to minimize your losses if your landlord insists that the improvement remain on the property, and
- special rules for cable TV access and satellite dishes.

Improvements That Become Part of the Property

Anything you attach to a building, fence, or deck or the ground itself belongs to the landlord, absent an agreement saying it's yours. (Lawyers call such items "fixtures.") This is a basic legal principle, and it's also spelled out in most leases and rental agreements. This means when you move out, the landlord is legally entitled to refuse your offer to remove the fixture and return the premises to its original state. In addition, many leases and rental agreements make it even clearer what types of improvements belong to the landlord. A typical clause looks something like this: "Any alterations, installations, or improvements, including shelving and attached floor coverings, will become the property of the owner and will remain with and as part of the rental premises at the end of the term."

In some cases, a landlord and departing tenant can't agree on who owns a particular piece of property, and the dispute ends up in court. Judges use a variety of legal rules to determine whether an object—an appliance, flooring, shelving, or plumbing—is something that you can take with you or is a permanent fixture belonging to your landlord. Here are some of the questions judges ask:

- **Did you get the landlord's permission?** If you never asked the landlord to install a closet organizer, or you did and got no for an answer, a judge is likely to rule for your landlord—particularly if your lease or rental agreement prohibits alterations or improvements.
- **Did you make any structural changes that affect the use or appearance of the property?** If so, chances are that the item will be deemed the landlord's, because removing it will often leave an unsightly area or alter the use of part of the property. For example, if you modify the kitchen counter to accommodate a built-in dishwasher but take the dishwasher with you, the landlord will have to install another dishwasher of the same dimensions or rebuild the space. The law doesn't impose this choice on landlords, nor does it force them to let you do the return-to-original work yourself.
- **Is the object firmly attached to the property?** In general, additions and improvements that are nailed, screwed, or cemented to the building are likely to be deemed "fixtures." For example, hollow-wall screws that anchor a bookcase might convert an otherwise free-standing unit belonging to the tenant to a fixture belonging to the landlord. Similarly, closet rods bolted to the wall become part of

the structure and would usually be counted as fixtures. On the other hand, shelving systems that are secured by isometric pressure (spring-loaded rods that press against the ceiling and floor) involve no actual attachment to the wall and for that reason are not likely to be classified as fixtures. Even if you have a very good reason for firmly attaching your addition—bolting a bookcase to the wall for earthquake protection, for example—you may still end up having to leave it behind.

- **What did you and the landlord intend?** Courts will look at statements made by you and the landlord to determine whether there was any understanding as to your right to remove an improvement. In some circumstances, courts will even infer an agreement from your actions—for instance, when your landlord stopped by and gave permission for you to install what you've described as a portable air conditioner, or helped you lift it into place. (Your chances of convincing the judge would be greatly enhanced if you had gotten permission in writing, as explained below in "Improving Your Rental Without Enriching Your Landlord.") By contrast, if you remove the landlord's light fixtures and, without the landlord's knowledge, install a custom-made fixture that could not be used in any other space, it is unlikely that you could convince a judge that you reasonably expected to take it with you at the end of your tenancy.

Improvements That Plug or Screw In

The act of plugging in an appliance doesn't make the appliance a part of the premises. The same is true for simple wiring or pipe attachments to join an appliance to an electrical or water source. For example, a refrigerator or free-standing stove remains the property of the tenant. Similarly, portable dishwashers that connect to the kitchen faucet by means of a coupling may be removed.

Improving Your Rental Without Enriching Your Landlord

Your best protection against losing an item you paid for is not to attach it to a wall in your unit. Fortunately, hundreds of items are on the market—bookcases, lighting systems, closet organizers, and even dishwashers—that you can take with you when you leave. To get some good ideas, visit a large hardware store, a home improvement center, or a business devoted to closet organization systems.

If you are determined to attach something to the wall or floor, talk to the landlord first. Try to get the landlord to agree to pay for the improvement or to let you remove it when you leave.

Decide beforehand which option you prefer. For example, because a custom-made track lighting system won't do you any good if you take it with you, find out whether the landlord will pay for it in the first place. On the other hand, if you want to take the fixture with you, impress upon the landlord your intent to carefully restore the property to its original condition. Keep in mind that if your restoration attempts are less than acceptable, the landlord will be justified in deducting from your security deposit the amount of money necessary to do the job right. And if the deposit is insufficient, the landlord can sue you in small claims court for the excess.

Approach your landlord as one business person dealing with another. If the improvement will remain and you seek reimbursement, point out that it will make the property more attractive. It might even justify a higher rent for the next tenant and thus pay for itself over the long run. Your landlord might agree to reduce your rent a little each month or simply reimburse you all at once.

If you and the landlord reach an understanding, put it in writing, using our Agreement Regarding Tenant Improvements to Rental Unit (there's a copy in the appendix). Carefully describe the project and materials, and state whether the landlord will reimburse you or allow you to take the improvement with you.

Agreement Regarding Tenant Alterations to Rental Unit

Lenny Lander _____ (Landlord)

and Tom Tenant _____ (Tenant)

agree as follows:

1. Tenant may make the following alterations to the rental unit at: ___54 Alta Way, Anytown, CA 94567___

_____

2. Tenant will accomplish the work described in Paragraph 1 by using the following materials and procedures: Lumen track lighting system, hard wired

_____ .

3. Tenant will do only the work outlined in Paragraph 1 using only the materials and procedures outlined in Paragraph 2.

4. The alterations carried out by Tenant (check either a or b):

   ☑ will become Landlord's property and are not to be removed by Tenant during or at the end of the tenancy

   ☐ will be considered Tenant's personal property, and as such may be removed by Tenant at any time up to the end of the tenancy. Tenant promises to return the premises to their original condition upon removing the improvement.

5. Landlord will reimburse Tenant only for the costs checked below:

   ☑ the cost of materials listed in Paragraph 2

   ☐ labor costs at the rate of $ _____ per hour for work done in a workmanlike manner acceptable to Landlord up to _____ hours.

6. After receiving appropriate documentation of the cost of materials and labor, Landlord shall make any payment called for under Paragraph 5 by:

   ☑ lump sum payment, within _____15_____ days of receiving documentation of costs, or

   ☐ by reducing Tenant's rent by $ _____ per month for the number of months necessary to cover the total amounts under the terms of this agreement.

7. If under Paragraph 4 of this contract the alterations are Tenant's personal property, Tenant must return the premises to their original condition upon removing the alterations. If Tenant fails to do this, Landlord will deduct the cost to restore the premises to their original condition from Tenant's security deposit. If the security deposit is insufficient to cover the costs of restoration, Landlord may take legal action, if necessary, to collect the balance.

8. If Tenant fails to remove an improvement that is his or her personal property on or before the end of the tenancy, it will be considered the property of Landlord, who may choose to keep the improvement (with no financial liability to Tenant), or remove it and charge Tenant for the costs of removal and restoration. Landlord may deduct any costs of removal and restoration from Tenant's security deposit. If the security deposit is insufficient to cover the costs of removal and restoration, Landlord may take legal action, if necessary, to collect the balance.

9. If Tenant removes an item that is Landlord's property, Tenant will owe Landlord the fair market value of the item removed plus any costs incurred by Landlord to restore the premises to their original condition.

10. If Landlord and Tenant are involved in any legal proceeding arising out of this agreement, the prevailing party shall recover reasonable attorney fees, court costs and any costs reasonably necessary to collect a judgment.

Lenny Lander _____   _January 4, 20xx_ _____
Signature of Landlord   Date

Tom Tenant _____   _January 4, 20xx_ _____
Signature of Tenant   Date

TIP

Save all receipts for materials and labor. Whether you will be reimbursed or will take the fixture with you when you leave, it is important to keep a good record of the amount of money you spent on the project. That way, there can be no dispute as to what you're owed if you are to be reimbursed. If the landlord changes his mind and doesn't let you remove the improvement at the end of your tenancy, you'll have receipts to back up your small claims lawsuit for the value of the addition.

Cable TV Access

Major changes in technology have expanded entertainment information services available from cable TV. You may be eager to take advantage of the offerings, but may not realize that doing so may involve the installation of a wire, cable, or other piece of hardware in the landlord's building. Chances are, however, that the landlord is well aware of this potential.

If you're lucky, the wonders of cable TV may already be in the rental property through coaxial cables that are strung along telephone poles or underground and into the building, with a single plug on the exterior of the structure and with branches to individual units. To sign up for service, you need only call the cable provider to activate the existing cable line to your unit. But what happens if the building does not have cable access now? And if the landlord has a contract with one provider, can you insist that he open his lines to another, competing provider?

Providing cable access is a bit more complicated than the situation you face when you ask to install a bookcase or paint a room. The federal government has something to say under the Federal Telecommunications Act of 1996 (47 U.S.C. §§ 151 and following). In this Act, Congress decreed that all Americans should have as much access as possible to information that comes through a cable or over the air on wireless transmissions. The Act makes it very difficult for state and local governments, zoning commissions, homeowners' associations, and landlords to impose restrictions that hamper a person's ability to take advantage of these new types of communications.

Previously Unwired Buildings

Fortunately, most residential rental properties are already wired for cable. In competitive urban markets especially, landlords have figured out that they'll have a hard time attracting tenants if they do not give them the option of paying for cable. However, in the event that the property does not have cable, your landlord is entitled to continue to resist modernity and say "No" to tenants who ask for access. If this is the response you get from your landlord, you may want to consider mounting a satellite dish. See "Satellite Dishes and Other Antennas," below, for rules governing these devices.

Buildings With Existing Contracts

Many multifamily buildings are already wired for cable. In the past, landlords have been able to secure attractive deals with the service providers, passing savings on to tenants. Many landlords signed "exclusive" contracts, whereby they promise the cable provider that they will not allow other providers into the building.

In October 2007, the Federal Communications Commission ruled that not only are exclusive contracts unenforceable, but exclusive clauses in existing contracts will not be enforced. This means that any exclusive clauses the landlord may now have in its contracts are unenforceable, and the landlord may not enter into any new ones. Landlords do *not*, however, have to let any cable company who asks into their building, nor do they have to allow access to a particular company when asked by tenants. If you would like cable service other than the one currently offered on the property, you'll need to convince your landlord that inviting that company into its property makes good marketing sense. For more information, see the FCC's "Small Entity Compliance Guide" (type this title into the search box at www.fcc.gov).

Satellite Dishes and Other Antennas

Wireless communications have the potential to reach more people with less hardware than any cable system. But there is one, essential piece of equipment: a satellite dish with wires connecting it to the television set or computer.

You may be familiar with the car-sized dishes often seen in backyards or on roofs of houses—the pink flamingo of the modern age. Recently, smaller and cheaper dishes, two feet or less in diameter, have shown up in appliance stores. Wires from the dishes can easily be run under a door or through an open window to a TV or computer. Tenants have attached these dishes to interior walls, roofs, windowsills, balconies, and railings. Landlords object, citing their unsightly looks and the potential for liability if one falls and injures someone.

Fortunately, the Federal Communications Commission (FCC) has provided considerable guidance on residential use of satellite dishes and antennas (Over-the-Air Reception Devices Rule, 47 C.F.R. § 1.4000, further explained in the FCC's Fact Sheet, "Over-the-Air Reception Devices Rule"). Basically, the FCC prohibits landlords from imposing restrictions that unreasonably impair your ability to install, maintain, or use a dish or other antenna that meets the criteria described below. Here's a brief overview of the FCC rule.

RESOURCE

For complete details on the FCC's rule on satellite dishes and other antennas, see www.fcc.gov/csb/facts/otard.html or call the FCC at 888-CALLFCC (toll free) or 202-418-7096. The FCC's rule was upheld in *Building Owners and Managers Assn. v. FCC*, 254 F.3d 89 (D.C. Cir.) (2001).

Devices Covered by the FCC Rule

The FCC's rule applies to video antennas, including direct-to-home satellite dishes that are less than one meter (39.37 inches) in diameter, TV antennas, and wireless cable antennas. These pieces of equipment receive video programming signals from direct broadcast satellites, wireless cable providers, and television broadcast stations. Antennas up to 18 inches in diameter that transmit as well as receive fixed wireless telecom signals (not just video) are also included.

There are, however, some exceptions. Antennas used for AM/FM radio, amateur ("ham"), and Citizen's Band ("CB") radio or Digital Audio Radio Services ("DARS") are excluded from the FCC's rule. Landlords may restrict the installation of these types of antennas in the same way that they can restrict any modification or alteration of rented space, as explained in the first section of this chapter.

Permissible Installation of Satellite Dishes and Antennas

You may place dishes or other antennas only in your own, exclusive rented space, such as inside the rental unit or on a balcony, terrace, deck, or patio. The device must be wholly within the rented space (if it overhangs the balcony, the landlord may prohibit that placement). Also, landlords may prohibit you from drilling through exterior walls, even if that wall is also part of your rented space.

The FCC rule specifies that you cannot place a reception device in common areas, such as roofs, hallways, walkways, or the exterior walls of the building. Exterior windows are no different from exterior walls—for this reason, placing a dish or antenna on a window by means of a series of suction cups is impermissible under the FCC rule (obviously, such an installation is also unsafe). Tenants who rent single-family homes, however, may install devices in the home itself or on patios, yards, gardens, or other similar areas.

Restrictions on Installation Techniques

Landlords are free to set restrictions on how the devices are installed, as long as the restrictions are not unreasonably expensive or are imposed for safety reasons or to preserve historic aspects of the structure. Landlords cannot insist that their maintenance personnel (or professional installers) do the work (but landlords may set reasonable guidelines as to how to install the devices, as explained below). Most importantly, if your landlord has not communicated an installation policy, you may go ahead and install the device without asking permission first (of course, do so in a safe manner). (*In re Frankfurt,* 16 FCC Rcd. 2875 (2001).)

Expense

Landlords may not impose a flat fee or charge you additional rent if you want to erect a dish or other antenna. On the other hand, the landlord may be able to insist on certain installation techniques that will add expense—as long as the cost isn't excessive and reception will not be impaired. Examples of acceptable expenses include:

- insisting that an antenna be painted green in order to blend into the landscaping, or
- requiring the use of a universal bracket that future tenants could use, saving wear and tear on the building.

TIP

Rules for mounting satellite dishes or other antennas shouldn't be more restrictive than those that apply to artwork, flags, clotheslines, or similar items. After all, attaching telecommunications items is no more intrusive or invasive than bolting a sundial to the porch, screwing a thermometer to the wall, or nailing a rain gauge to a railing. If your landlord's standards for telecommunications devices are much stricter than guidelines for other improvements or alterations, you may have a good argument that the landlord is violating the FCC rules. See "How to Handle Disputes," below, for information on how to respond to unreasonable landlord rules.

Safety Concerns

Landlords can insist that you place and install devices in a way that will minimize the chances of accidents and will not violate safety or fire codes. In fact, the FCC directs landlords to give tenants written notice of safety restrictions, so that tenants will know in advance how to comply. For example, it's not a good idea to place a satellite dish on a fire escape, near a power plant, or near a walkway where passers-by might accidentally hit their heads. Your landlord may also insist on proper installation techniques, such as those explained in the instructions that come with most devices.

Now, suppose that proper installation (attaching a dish to a wall) means that the landlord will have to eventually patch and paint a wall. Can the landlord use this as reason for preventing installation? No—unless there are legitimate reasons for prohibiting the installation, such as a safety concern. When you move out and remove the device, however, your landlord may charge you for the cost of repairing the attachment spot (such as replastering and repainting).

CAUTION

A savvy landlord will require tenants who install antennas or dishes to carry renter's insurance. If the device falls and injures someone, your policy will cover any claim. Whether requiring renter's insurance unreasonably increases the cost to you of receiving over-the-air signals has not been decided by the FCC or the courts.

Preserving the Building's Historical Integrity

Your landlord may argue that the historical integrity of the property will be compromised if an antenna or satellite dish is attached. This isn't an easy claim to make. A landlord can use this argument only if the property is included in (or eligible for) the National Register of Historic Places—the nation's official list of buildings, structures, objects, sites, and districts worthy of preservation for their significance in American history, architecture, archaeology, and culture. For more information on what's required to qualify for the Register and for a database of registered places, see www.cr.nps.gov.

Placement and Orientation of Antennas and Reception Devices

Tenants have the right to place an antenna where they'll receive an "acceptable quality" signal. As long as the tenant's chosen spot is within the exclusive rented space, not on an exterior wall or in a common area as discussed above, the landlord may not set rules on placement—for example, the landlord cannot require that an antenna be placed only in the rear of the rental property if this results in the tenant's receiving a "substantially degraded" signal or no signal at all.

Reception devices that need to maintain line-of-sight contact with a transmitter or view a satellite may not work if they're stuck behind a wall or below the roofline. In particular, a dish must be on a south-facing wall, since satellites are in the southern hemisphere. Faced with a reception problem, you may want to move the device to another location or mount it on a pole, so that it clears the obstructing roof or wall. Tenants who have no other workable exclusive space may want to mount their devices on a mast, in hopes of clearing the obstacle. Depending on the situation, you may have the right to do so. Here are the rules for masts.

- **Single-family rentals.** Tenants may erect a mast that's 12 feet or fewer above the roofline without asking permission first—and the landlord must allow it if the mast is installed in a safe manner. If the mast is taller than 12 feet, the landlord may require the tenant to obtain permission before erecting it—but

if the installation meets reasonable safety requirements, the landlord should allow its use.

- **Multifamily rentals.** Tenants may use a mast as long as it does not extend beyond their exclusive rented space. For example, in a two-story rental, a mast that is attached to the ground-floor patio and extends into the air space opposite your own second floor would be permissible. On the other hand, a mast attached to a top-story deck, which extends above the roofline or outward over the railing, would not be protected by the FCC's rule—a landlord could prohibit this installation because it extends beyond your exclusive rented space.

Supplying a Central Antenna or Satellite Dish for All Tenants

Faced with the prospect of many dishes and or other antennas adorning an otherwise clean set of balconies, some landlords have installed a central dish or other antenna for use by all.

Landlords may install a central antenna and restrict the use of individual antennas by tenants only if the central device provides:

- **Equal access.** You must be able to get the same programming or fixed wireless service that you could receive with your own antenna.
- **Equal quality.** The signal quality to and from your home via the central antenna must be as good as or better than what you could get using your own device.
- **Equal value.** The costs of using the central device must be the same as or less than the cost of installing, maintaining, and using an individual antenna.
- **Equal readiness.** Landlords can't prohibit individual devices if installation of a central antenna will unreasonably delay your ability to receive programming or fixed wireless services—for example, when the central antenna won't be available for months.

If a landlord has installed a central antenna after tenants have installed their own, the landlord may require removal of the individual antennas, as long as the central device meets the above requirements. Your landlord will have to pay you for the removal of your device and compensate you for the value of the antenna.

How to Handle Disputes About the Use and Placement of Satellite Dishes and Other Antennas

In spite of the FCC's attempts to clarify tenants' rights to reception and landlords' rights to control what happens on their property, there are many possibilities for disagreements. For example, what exactly is "acceptable" reception? If the landlord requires antennas to be painted, at what point is the expense considered "unreasonable?"

Ideally, your landlord will avoid disputes in the first place, by setting reasonable policies. But, if all else fails, here are some tips to help you resolve the problem with a minimum of fuss and expense.

Discussion, Mediation, and Help from the FCC

First, approach the problem the way you would any dispute—talk it out and try to reach an acceptable conclusion. Follow our advice in Chapter 17 for settling disputes on your own—for example, through negotiation or mediation. You'll find the information on the FCC website very helpful (www.fcc.gov/csb/facts/otard.html). Your direct broadcast satellite company, multichannel distribution service, TV broadcast station, or fixed wireless company may also be able to suggest alternatives that are safe and acceptable to both you and your landlord.

Get the FCC Involved

If your own attempts don't resolve the problem, you can call the FCC and ask for oral guidance. You may also formally ask the FCC for a written opinion, called a Declarary Ruling. For information on obtaining oral or written guidance from the FCC, follow the directions as shown on the FCC website at www.fcc.gov/csb/facts/otard.html. Fortunately for tenants, unless the landlord's objections concern safety or historic preservation, the landlord must allow the device to remain pending the FCC's ruling.

Go to Court

When all else fails, you can head for court. If the antenna or satellite dish hasn't been installed yet and you and the landlord are arguing about the reasonableness of the landlord's policies or your plans, you can ask a court to rule on who's right (just as you would when seeking the FCC's opinion). You'll have to go to superior court for a resolution of your dispute, where you'll ask for an order called a "Declaratory Judgment." Similarly, if the antenna or dish *has* been installed and the landlord wants a judge to order it removed, the landlord will have to go to superior court and ask for such an order. Unfortunately, the simpler option of small claims court will not usually be available in these situations, because most small courts handle only disputes that can be settled or decided with money, not requests about whether it's acceptable to do (or not do) a particular task.

Needless to say, being in superior court means that the case will be drawn-out and expensive. You could handle it yourself, but be forewarned—you'll need to be adept at arguing about First Amendment law and Congressional intent, and must be willing to spend long hours preparing your case. In the end, you may decide that it would have been cheaper to follow the Giants on cable TV.

RESOURCE

If you head into superior court, consult *Win Your Lawsuit: A Judge's Guide to Representing Yourself in California Superior Court,* by Judge Roderic Duncan (Nolo). This book will guide you through the process of filing and litigating a limited jurisdiction case (one that involves $25,000 or less).

Injuries on the Premises

If you have been injured on your landlord's property, you may have a good legal claim against your landlord. That doesn't mean you'll have to file a lawsuit—most valid claims against landlords are settled without trial. It may well be to your advantage to negotiate with the landlord's insurance adjuster or lawyer yourself, rather than to immediately hire a lawyer, who will typically take one-third of your recovery. If the landlord or insurer proves unreasonable, you can always hire a lawyer.

This chapter explains how to evaluate whether your landlord is liable for your injury, and what to do to maximize your chances of a just settlement or lawsuit verdict. Skip this chapter if you haven't been injured or aren't interested in learning about the issue.

What to Do If You're Injured

What is the best course of action to take if you're injured? If your injury is significant and costly—it has resulted in lost work, doctors' bills, and physical or emotional discomfort—and you think the landlord is at fault, you'll want to consider legal action. But don't go rushing off to the nearest personal injury lawyer just yet. Especially if your injury isn't very severe, you may be better off—at least initially —handling the claim yourself.

But if your injury is severe, see a lawyer right away. Injuries in this category include:

- a long-term or permanently disabling injury, such as the loss of a limb
- an injury that results in medical costs and lost income over $10,000, or
- heavy-duty toxic exposure, such as lead or pesticide poisoning.

This book can't cover all the ins and outs of pursuing a personal injury claim. Here, however, is an outline of the basic steps you should follow.

Get Immediate Medical Attention

The success of an accident claim often depends on what you do in the first hours and days after your injury. Although you may be in pain, angry, or even depressed, attention to these details immediately following the incident will pay off later.

It is essential to get prompt medical attention for your injury, even if you consider it to be of marginal help to your physical recovery. No insurance company, judge, or jury will take your word alone for the extent of your injury, pain and suffering. It may seem obvious to you that a sprained ankle caused immobility, swelling and pain, and made you miss a week's work. Nonetheless, you'll need the confirmation of a physician, and the professional opinion that you didn't suffer a mere soft tissue bruise, when it comes to convincing a skeptical insurance adjuster or jury of your injury's impact.

Moreover, if you intend to hold the landlord financially responsible for your injuries, the law expects you to take whatever steps are possible to lessen the extent of your injuries and speed your recovery. Oddly, the reason has little to do with concern for your physical well-being; rather, the law expects you to take reasonable steps to lessen the accident's financial impact on the landlord. In short, you'll need the verification of a doctor that you were a conscientious patient who did not prolong or ignore your injuries.

> **EXAMPLE:** May-Ling, a new tenant, slipped on a puddle of oil-slicked rainwater that habitually accumulated at the base of the garage stairs. She fell and badly twisted her back. Thinking that time would heal her wounds, she did not seek medical attention, though she did stay home from work for a week.
>
> She then filed a claim with the landlord's insurance company, seeking compensation for her pain and suffering and lost wages. The insurance adjuster questioned the severity of her injury and suggested that, had she consulted a doctor, she might have recovered sooner with the aid of muscle-relaxing medication. Unable to verify the extent of her

injury and having no way to effectively answer the claim that medical attention might have helped her, May-Ling settled her claim for a disappointing amount.

Write Everything Down

As soon as possible after the accident, jot down everything you can remember about how it happened. Include a complete list of everyone who was present and what they said. For example, suppose you tripped on a loose stair and the manager rushed over and blurted out, "I told Jim [the landlord] we should have replaced that last month!" Be sure to write this down and note the names of anyone who heard the manager say it.

Describe the precise nature of your injuries, including pain, anxiety, and loss of sleep. Make notes of every economic loss, such as lost wages, missed classes and events, and transportation and medical costs. If you have a conversation regarding the incident with anyone (the landlord, other tenants, an insurance adjuster, or medical personnel), make a written summary of the conversation.

Preserve Evidence

Claims are often won by the production of a persuasive piece of physical evidence: the worn or broken stair that caused the fall, the unattached throw rug that slipped when stepped on, the electrical outlet faceplate that showed burn marks from a short. Remember that physical evidence that is not preserved within a short time can be lost, modified by time or weather, repaired, or destroyed. For example, the landlord, not wanting more accidents, may quickly replace a loose stair that caused you to fall, and throw the old one away.

If preservation of the evidence would involve dismantling the landlord's property, you may have to settle for the next-best alternative, photographs or videos. Don't wait—make your record before repairs are made. Be sure to develop the film

immediately and have the date stamped on the disc or the back of the prints, or at least get a dated receipt. And to forestall challenges to the accuracy of your pictures (or a claim they were doctored), have someone else take them and be prepared to testify in court that they are a fair and accurate depiction of the scene. If you are experiencing pain, keep what's known as a "pain diary." Every day (and more often if appropriate), jot down how you feel, what you can and cannot do, and what medication you're taking to help yourself. This log may come in handy if you are asked to document your condition.

Contact Witnesses

Having an eyewitness can be an immeasurable help. Witnesses can corroborate your version of events and may even have seen important aspects of the situation that you missed. But you must act very quickly to find and preserve the observations and memories of those who could bolster your case—people's memories fade quickly, and strangers can be very hard to track down later.

 CAUTION

Don't tell witnesses not to talk to "the other side." Witnesses have no legal obligation to talk to you, although most will if they feel you have been wronged. Similarly, you have no authority to tell them not to talk to others. Moreover, trying to do so may come back to haunt you via a suggestion that you had something to hide. If a favorable witness tells an insurance adjuster a different story, you can expose the inconsistencies later in court.

If you find people who witnessed the incident, get their names, addresses, and as much information about what they saw as possible. Talk with them about what they saw and write it up. Ask them if they would be willing to review your summary for accuracy; if so, mail them a copy and ask them to correct it, sign it, and return it to you in the stamped envelope you have provided.

TIP

Don't overlook the witness who heard or saw another witness. It can often be important to have a witness who can describe what another witness said or did. For example, the manager who blurted out, "I told him we should have fixed that last month" will have every incentive to deny making that statement, since it pins knowledge of the defect on the property owner, his boss. If someone besides you also heard the manager say it, he'll have a tougher time disowning it. Get that person's name and statement.

Evaluate Your Case

Before you go making demands for money from your landlord or an insurance company, you need to know whether you have a legal leg to stand on. That's what most of the rest of this chapter explains. For now, remember that this evaluation step is critical and can't be skipped!

Notify the Landlord and the Insurance Carrier

Once you're convinced that you have a good case, write to the owner of the rental property, stating that you have been injured and need to deal with the owner's liability insurance carrier. You should have the owner's name and address on your lease or rental agreement (if you don't, send the letter to wherever you send the monthly rent). If you deal with a manager or management company, you should also notify them.

If a third party is involved, it won't hurt to notify them, too, if there is some basis for thinking that they may have been at least partially responsible. For example, a contractor or subcontractor may have created or contributed to the dangerous situation, or a repairperson may have done a faulty job, causing your injury.

A sample letter is shown below. If your case is substantial, you can expect that the owner will contact the insurer right away. On the other hand, a landlord who suspects that the claim is phony or trivial may hold off notifying the insurance company, fearing a rate increase or policy cancellation. You cannot force the landlord to refer the case or disclose the name of the insurer; all you can do is persevere until your persistence and the threat of a lawsuit become real enough for the landlord to call in the insurance company's help. (Or, your landlord may decide to settle with you without involving his carrier, which might be all right too, as explained below.)

Sample Letter to Landlord Regarding Tenant Injury

Alice Watson

37 Ninth Avenue North

South Fork, CA 00000

401-555-4567

February 28, 20xx

Fernando Diaz

3757 East Seventh Street

South Fork, CA 00000

Dear Mr. Diaz:

On February 25, 20xx, I was injured in a fall on the front steps of the duplex that I rent from you. The middle step splintered and collapsed as I walked down the stairs. Please refer this matter to the carrier of your business liability insurance and have them contact me at the above address.

Thank you for your cooperation.

Yours truly,

Alex Watson

Alex Watson

Negotiate, Mediate, or Sue

If you are successful at reaching the landlord's insurance carrier, chances are that you'll negotiate a settlement. You may choose mediation (in which a neutral third party helps both sides reach a settlement) if you feel that the insurance company is interested in settling the matter and will deal with you fairly. (If the result isn't adequate, you can always file a lawsuit.) But if the landlord stonewalls you, refusing to refer your claim to the insurance carrier or a lawyer, you may need to consider a lawsuit. Chapter 17 gives detailed information on negotiating with, mediating with, and suing your landlord if necessary. It also helps you decide whether to take your case to small claims court yourself, saving time and the expense of hiring a lawyer, or whether you are better off in a formal court with a lawyer.

CAUTION

Don't wait too long before filing suit. You must file your lawsuit within the time specified by California's "statute of limitations," which is two years from the date of injury for most injuries. However, choosing the proper statute of limitations can get tricky. On this point, you would be wise to consult a lawyer (you needn't hire the lawyer to handle the entire case, however).

RESOURCE

How to Win Your Personal Injury Claim, by Joseph L. Matthews (Nolo), explains personal injury cases and how to work out a fair settlement without going to court.

Everybody's Guide to Small Claims Court in California, by Ralph Warner (Nolo), provides great advice on small claims court, where you can sue for up to $7,500.

Represent Yourself in Court, by Paul Bergman and Sara J. Berman (Nolo), will help you prepare and present your case should you end up in court.

Is the Landlord Liable?

It isn't always easy to determine whether the landlord is legally responsible for an injury. Basically, your landlord may be liable for your injuries if those injuries resulted from:

- the landlord's unreasonably careless conduct
- the landlord's violation of a health or safety law
- the landlord's failure to make certain repairs
- the landlord's failure to keep the premises habitable, or
- the landlord's reckless or intentional acts.

And in rare instances, the landlord may be liable because courts or the legislature have decided that landlords are automatically liable for certain kinds of injuries, even though they haven't been careless.

Keep in mind that several of these legal theories may apply in your situation, and you (and your lawyer) can use all of them when pressing your claim. The more plausible reasons you can give for your landlord's liability, the better you will do when you negotiate with the landlord's insurance company.

So, hold onto your hat as you follow us into a short course on landlord liability. Trust us, we aren't asking you to wade through these issues without a reason. Unless you can evaluate your situation the way a lawyer (or jury) would, you won't know whether it's worth pursuing.

The Landlord Was Unreasonably Careless

Most personal injury claims against landlords charge that the landlord acted negligently—that is, acted carelessly, in a way that wasn't reasonable under the circumstances—and that the injury was caused by that carelessness.

Negligence is always determined in light of the unique facts of each situation. For example, it may be reasonable to put adequate lights in a dark, remote stairwell. If your landlord doesn't, and you're hurt because you couldn't see the steps and fell, your landlord's failure to install the lights might be negligence. On the other hand, extra lights in a lobby that's already well-lit might not be a reasonable expectation.

To determine whether or not your landlord was negligent and should be held responsible for your injury, you must answer six questions. The insurance adjuster will use these same questions to evaluate your claim, as will a lawyer (if you consult one). If your case looks strong, you'll probably be able to wrest a good settlement offer from the company. And if the insurance company isn't forthcoming, you'll be able to head to court confidently, where a judge or jury will use the same questions when deciding your case.

Evaluating Negligence Cases

If you think your landlord's carelessness caused your injury, you'll need answers to these questions before you can expect to recover damages:

- Did your landlord control the area where you were hurt or the thing that hurt you?
- How likely was it that an accident would occur?
- How difficult or expensive would it have been for the landlord to reduce the risk of injury?
- Was a serious injury likely to result from the problem?
- Did your landlord fail to take reasonable steps to prevent an accident?
- Did your landlord's failure to take reasonable steps to keep you safe cause your injury?

These questions are addressed in detail below.

Question 1: Did your landlord control the area where you were hurt or the thing that hurt you? The law will pin responsibility on your landlord only if he had the legal ability to maintain or fix the area or item that injured you. For example, the property owner normally has control over a stairway in a common area, and if its chronic disrepair causes a tenant to fall, the owner will likely be held liable. The owner also has control over the building's utility systems. If a malfunction causes injury (like boiling water in your sink because of a broken thermostat), he may likewise be held responsible. On the other hand, if you're hurt when your own bookcase falls on you, the landlord won't be held responsible, because he does not control how the bookcase is built, set up, or maintained.

Interestingly, the landlord may be held responsible for injuries that occur on property that he doesn't even own, as long as he makes use of it and takes no steps to fix problems or at least warn you of them. In one case, a tenant sued a landlord when the tenant tripped on a poorly maintained strip of land that actually belonged to the city, because the landlord knew that this adjacent land was regularly used by his tenants. (*Alcaraz v. Vece,* 14 Cal.4th. 1149 (1997).)

Question 2: How likely was it that an accident would occur? The landlord isn't responsible if the accident wasn't foreseeable. For example, common sense would tell anyone that loose handrails or stairs are likely to lead to accidents, but it would be unusual for injuries to result from peeling wallpaper or a thumbtack that's fallen from a bulletin board. If a freak accident does happen, chances are your landlord will not be held liable.

Question 3: How difficult or expensive would it have been for the landlord to reduce the risk of injury? The chances that your landlord will be held liable are greater if a reasonably priced response could have averted the accident. In other words, could something as simple as warning signs, a bright light, or caution tape have prevented people from tripping over an unexpected step leading to the patio, or would major structural remodeling have been necessary to reduce the likelihood of injury? But if there is a great risk of very serious injury, a landlord will be expected to spend money to avert it. For example, a high-rise deck with rotten support beams must be repaired, regardless of the cost, since there is a great risk of collapse and dreadful injuries to anyone on the deck. A landlord who knew about the condition of the deck and failed to repair it would surely be held liable if an accident did occur.

Question 4: Was a serious injury likely to result from the problem? The amount of time and money your landlord is expected to spend on making the premises safe will also depend on the seriousness of the probable injury if he fails to do so. For example, if the umbrella on a poolside table wouldn't open, no one would expect it to cause serious injury. If you're sunburned at the pool as a result, it's not likely that a judge would rule that your landlord had the duty of keeping you from getting burned. But if a major injury is the likely result of a dangerous situation—suppose the pool diving board was broken, making it likely you'd fall on the deck when using it—the owner is expected to take the situation more seriously and fix it faster.

The answers to these four questions should tell you (or an insurance adjuster or judge) whether or not there was a dangerous condition on the landlord's property that the landlord had a legal duty to deal with. Lawyers call this having a "duty of due care."

Let's look at how these first four questions would get answered in a few possible scenarios.

EXAMPLE 1: Mark broke his leg when he tripped on a loose step on the stairway from the lobby to the first floor. Since the step had been loose for several months, chances are the landlord's insurance company would settle a claim like this.

Mark's position is strong because of the answers to the four questions:

1. The landlord was legally responsible for (in control of) the condition of the common stairways.
2. It was highly foreseeable to any reasonable person that someone would slip on a loose step.
3. Securing the step would have been simple and inexpensive.
4. The probable result of leaving the step loose—falling and injuring oneself on the stairs—is a serious matter.

EXAMPLE 2: Lee slipped on a marble that had been dropped in the lobby by another tenant's child just a few minutes earlier. Lee twisted his ankle and lost two weeks' work. Lee will have a tough time establishing that his landlord had a duty to protect him from this injury. Here's what the questions turn up:

1. The landlord does have control over the public sidewalk.
2. The likelihood of injury from something a tenant drops is fairly low.
3. The burden on the landlord to eliminate all possible problems at all times by constantly inspecting or sweeping the lobby is unreasonable.
4. Finally, the seriousness of any likely injury resulting from not checking constantly is open to great debate.

EXAMPLE 3: James suffered a concussion when he hit his head on a dull-colored overhead beam in the apartment garage. When the injury occurred, he was standing on a stool, loading items onto the roof rack of his SUV. Did the landlord have a duty to take precautions in this situation? Probably not, but the answers to the four questions are not so easy.

1. The landlord exercises control over the garage, and certainly has a responsibility to reasonably protect tenants from harm there.
2. The likelihood of injury from a beam is fairly slim, since most people don't stand on stools in the garage, and those who do have the opportunity to see the beam and avoid it.
3. As to eliminating the condition that led to the injury, it's highly unlikely anyone would expect the landlord to rebuild the garage. But it's possible that a judge might think it reasonable to paint the beams a bright color and post warning signs, especially if lots of people put trucks and other large vehicles in the garage.

4. As to the seriousness of probable harm, injury from low beams is likely to be to the head, which is a serious matter.

In short, this situation is too close to call, but if an insurance adjuster or jury considered the case, they might decide that James was partially at fault (for not watching out for the beams) and reduce any award accordingly. (See "If You're at Fault, Too," below.)

If, based on these first four questions, you think the landlord had a legal duty to deal with a condition on the premises that posed a danger to you, keep going. You have two more questions to answer.

Question 5: Did your landlord fail to take reasonable steps to prevent an accident? The law won't expect your landlord to undertake Herculean measures to shield you from a condition that poses some risk. Instead, the landlord is required to take only reasonable steps. For example, if you've demonstrated that a stair was in a dangerous condition, you also need to show that the landlord's failure to fix it was unreasonable in the circumstances. Let's take the broken step that Mark (Example 1, above) tripped over. Obviously, leaving it broken for months is unreasonably careless—that is, negligent—under the circumstances.

But what if the step had torn loose only an hour earlier, when another tenant dragged a heavy footlocker up the staircase? Mark's landlord would probably concede that he had a duty to maintain the stairways, but would argue that the manager's daily sweeping and inspection of the stairs that same morning met that burden. In the absence of being notified of the problem, he would probably claim that his inspection routine met his duty of keeping the stairs safe. If a jury agreed, Mark would not be able to establish that the landlord acted unreasonably under the circumstances.

Question 6: Did your landlord's failure to take reasonable steps to keep you safe cause your injury? This last question establishes the crucial link between the landlord's negligence and your injury. Not every dangerous situation results in an accident. You'll have to prove that your injury was the result of the landlord's carelessness, and not some other reason. Sometimes this is self-evident: One minute you're fine, and the next minute you've slipped on a freshly waxed floor and have a broken arm. But it's not always so simple. For example, in the case of the loose stair, the landlord might be able to show that the tenant barely lost his balance because of the loose stair and that he had really injured his ankle during a touch football game he'd just played.

Here's a final example, applying all six questions to a tenant's injury.

EXAMPLE: Scotty's apartment complex had a pool bordered by a concrete deck. On his way to the pool, Scotty slipped and fell, breaking his arm. The concrete where he fell was slick because the landlord had cleaned the pool and spilled some of the cleaning solution earlier that morning. To assess his chances of collecting against his landlord for his injury, Scotty asked himself these questions:

1. Did the landlord control the pool area and the cleaning solution? Absolutely. The pool was part of a common area, and the landlord had done the cleaning.
2. Was an accident like Scotty's foreseeable? Certainly. It's likely that a barefoot person heading for the pool would slip on slick cement.
3. Could the landlord have eliminated the dangerous condition without much effort or money? Of course. All that was necessary was to hose down the deck.
4. How serious was the probable injury? Falling on cement presents a high likelihood of broken bones, a serious injury.

Having established that the landlord owed him a duty of care, Scotty considered the rest of his case.

1. Had his landlord also breached this duty? Yes; Scotty was sure a jury would conclude that leaving spilled cleaning solution on the deck was an unreasonable thing to do.

2. Did the spilled cleaning solution cause his fall? This one is easy, because several people saw the accident and others could describe Scotty's robust fitness before the fall. Scotty hadn't himself been careless (see "If You're at Fault, Too," below), so he decided he had a pretty good case.

Examples of Injuries From Landlord Negligence

Here are some examples of injuries for which tenants have recovered money damages due to the landlord's negligence:

- Tenant falls down a staircase due to a defective handrail.
- Tenant trips over a hole in the carpet on a common stairway not properly maintained by the landlord.
- Tenant injured and property damaged by fire resulting from an obviously defective heater or wiring.
- Tenant gets sick from pesticide sprayed in common areas and on exterior walls without advance notice.
- Tenant's child is scalded by water from a water heater with a broken thermostat.
- Tenant slips and falls on a puddle of oil-slicked rainwater in the garage.
- Tenant's guest injured when she slips on ultraslick floor wax applied by the landlord's cleaning service.
- Tenant receives electrical burns when attempting to insert the stove's damaged plug into the wall outlet.
- Tenant slips and falls on wet grass cuttings left on a common walkway.

The Landlord Violated a Health or Safety Law

The California legislature has enacted health and safety laws requiring smoke detectors, sprinklers, inside-release security bars on windows, childproof fences around swimming pools, and so on. To put real teeth behind these important laws, legislators (and sometimes the courts) have decided that if landlords don't take reasonable steps to comply with certain health or safety statutes, the law will consider them negligent. And if that negligence results in an injury, the landlord is liable for it. You don't need to prove that an accident was forseeable or likely to be serious, nor do you have to show that complying with the law would have been relatively inexpensive. The legal term for this rule is "negligence per se."

> **EXAMPLE:** State law specifies that all rental units must have smoke detectors, but there are none in your unit. A fire started at night while you were sleeping and you were injured. If you can show that had there been detectors, you would have become aware of the fire sooner and would have likely escaped without injury, you will not have to prove that the landlord was negligent. You'll have to prove only that the fire caused your injuries.

Bear in mind that landlords are expected only to take reasonable steps to comply with safety and health laws that fall within the negligence per se realm. For example, your landlord must supply smoke detectors. If the landlord has supplied one but you have disabled it, your landlord won't be held responsible if you are hurt by a fire that could have been stopped had you left the detector alone.

The landlord's violation of a health or safety law may also indirectly cause an injury. For example, if the landlord lets the furnace deteriorate in violation of local law, and you are injured trying to repair it, the landlord will probably be liable unless your repair efforts are extremely careless themselves.

EXAMPLE: The state housing code requires landlords to provide hot water. In the middle of the winter, your hot water heater has been broken for a week, despite your repeated complaints to the landlord. Finally, to give your sick child a hot bath, you carry pots of steaming water from the stove to the bathtub. Doing this, you spill the hot water and burn yourself seriously.

You sue the landlord for failure to provide hot water as required by state law. If the case goes to court, it will be up to the judge to decide whether the landlord's failure to provide hot water caused your injury. Since a judge could reasonably conclude that your response to the lack of hot water was a forseeable one, your landlord's insurance company might be willing to offer a fair settlement.

The Landlord Didn't Make Certain Repairs

For perfectly sensible reasons, many landlords do not want tenants to undertake even relatively simple tasks like painting, plastering, or unclogging a drain. Your lease or rental agreement may prohibit you from making any repairs or alterations without the owner's consent, or limit what you can do. (Chapter 8 discusses this.)

But in exchange for a landlord's reserving the right to make all these repairs, the law imposes a responsibility. If, after being told about a problem, the landlord doesn't maintain or repair something you aren't allowed to touch, and you are injured as a result, the landlord is probably liable. The legal reason is that the landlord breached the contract (the lease) by not making the repairs. (The landlord may be negligent as well; remember, there is nothing to stop you from presenting multiple reasons why the landlord should be held liable.)

EXAMPLE: The Rules and Regulations attached to Lori's lease state that management will inspect and clean the fan above her stove every six months. Jake, an affable but somewhat scatterbrained graduate student in charge of maintenance at the apartment complex, was supposed to do the fan checks. But deep into his studies and social life, Jake scheduled no inspections for a long time. Lori was injured when the accumulated grease in the fan filter caught fire.

Lori sued the landlord, alleging that his failure to live up to his contractual promise to clean the fan was the cause of her injuries. The jury agreed and awarded her a large sum.

Some other common examples might include:
- **Environmental hazards.** If your lease forbids repainting without the landlord's consent, the landlord is obligated to maintain the painted surfaces. If an old layer of lead paint begins to crack, deteriorate, and enter the air, the landlord will be liable for the health problems that follow. (Chapter 10 covers environmental health hazards such as lead-based paint.)
- **Security breaches.** Landlords typically forbid tenants from installing locks of their own. That means landlords may be liable if their failure to provide secure locks contributes to a crime. (See Chapter 11.)

The Landlord Didn't Keep the Premises Habitable

One of a landlord's basic responsibilities is to keep the rental property in a "habitable" condition.

Failure to maintain a habitable dwelling may make the landlord liable for injuries caused by the substandard conditions. For example, a tenant who is bitten by a rat in a vermin-infested building may argue that the owner's failure to maintain a rat-free building constituted a breach of duty to keep the place habitable, which in turn led to the injury. You must show that the landlord knew of the defect and had a reasonable amount of time to fix it.

This theory applies only when the defect is so serious that the rental unit is unfit for human habitation. For example, a large, jagged broken picture window would probably make the premises unfit for habitation, but a torn screen door obviously would not. The tenant who cut herself trying to cover the window with cardboard might sue under negligence and a violation of the implied warranty of habitability, while the tenant who injured herself trying to repair the screen would be limited to a theory of negligence.

EXAMPLE: Jose notified his landlord about the mice that he had seen several times in his kitchen. Despite Jose's repeated complaints, the landlord did nothing to eliminate the problem. When Jose reached into his cupboard for a box of cereal, a mouse bit him. Jose sued his landlord for the medical treatment he required, including extremely painful rabies shots. He alleged that the landlord's failure to eradicate the rodent problem constituted a breach of the implied warranty of habitability, and that this breach was responsible for his injury. The jury agreed and gave Jose a large monetary award.

The injury sustained by Jose in the example above could also justify a claim that the injury resulted from the landlord's negligence. And, if Jose's landlord had failed to take reasonable steps to comply with a state or local statute concerning rodent control, the landlord might automatically be considered negligent. Finally, the owner may also be liable if the lease forbade Jose from making repairs, such as repairing improper sewage connections or changing the way garbage was stored. As you can see, sometimes there are several legal theories that will fit the facts and support your claim for damages.

The Landlord Acted Recklessly

In the legal sense of the word, "recklessness" usually means extreme carelessness regarding an obvious defect or problem. A landlord who is aware of a long-existing and obviously dangerous defect but neglects to correct it may be guilty of recklessness, not just ordinary carelessness.

If your landlord or an employee acted recklessly, your monetary recovery could be significant. This is because a jury has the power to award not only actual damages (which include medical bills, loss of earnings, and pain and suffering) but also extra, "punitive" damages. (See "How Much Money You're Entitled To," below.) Punitive damages are almost never given in simple negligence cases, but are appropriate to punish recklessness and to send a sobering message to others who might behave similarly. But don't count your millions before you have them: In every situation, the line between ordinary negligence and recklessness is wherever the unpredictable jury thinks it should be. The size of the punitive award is likewise up to the jury, and can often be reduced later by a judge or appellate court.

The very unpredictability of punitive damage awards, however, can be to your advantage when negotiating with the landlord. The landlord may settle your claim rather than risk letting an indignant jury award you punitive damages.

EXAMPLE: The handrail along the stairs to the first floor of the apartment house Jack owned had been hanging loose for several months. Jack attempted to fix it two or three times by taping the supports to the wall. The tape did no good, however, and the railing was literally flapping in the breeze. One dark night when Hilda, one of Jack's tenants, reached for the railing, the entire thing came off in her hand, causing her to fall and break her hip.

Hilda sued Jack for her injuries. In her lawsuit, she pointed to the ridiculously ineffective measures that Jack had taken to deal with an obviously dangerous situation, and charged that he had acted with reckless disregard for the safety of his tenants. (Hilda also argued that Jack was negligent because of his unreasonable behavior and because he had violated a local ordinance regarding maintenance of handrails.) The jury agreed with Hilda and awarded her punitive damages.

The Landlord Intentionally Harmed You

Intentional injuries are rare but, unfortunately, they occur more often than you might guess. For example, if a landlord or manager struck and injured you during an argument, obviously that would be an intentional act for which the landlord would be liable.

Less obvious, but no less serious, are emotional or psychological injuries that can, in extreme circumstances, also be inflicted intentionally. Intentional infliction of emotional distress often arises in these situations:

- **Sexual harassment.** Repeated, disturbing attentions of a sexual nature that the harasser refuses to stop, which leave the victim fearful, humiliated, and upset, can form the basis for a claim of intentional harm.

  EXAMPLE: Rita's landlord Brad took advantage of every opportunity to make suggestive comments about her looks and social life. When she asked him to stop, he replied that he was "just looking out for her," and he stepped up his unwanted attentions. Rita finally had enough, broke the lease, and moved out. When Brad sued her for unpaid rent, she turned around and sued him for the emotional distress caused by his harassment. To his surprise, Brad was slapped with a multithousand-dollar judgment, including punitive damages.

- **Assault.** Threatening or menacing someone without actually touching them is an assault, which can be enormously frightening and lead to psychological damage.
- **Repeated invasions of privacy.** Deliberately invading a tenant's privacy—by unauthorized entries, for example—may cause extreme worry and distress. (Chapter 15 covers tenants' privacy rights.)

If You're at Fault, Too

If you sue your landlord for negligence, the landlord may turn right around and accuse you of negligence, too. And if you are partially to blame for your injury, the landlord's liability for your losses will be reduced accordingly.

Your Own Carelessness

If you are also guilty of unreasonable carelessness—for example, you were drunk and, as a result, didn't (or couldn't) watch your step when you tripped on a loose tread on a poorly maintained stairway—the landlord's liability will be proportionately reduced.

The legal principle is called "comparative negligence." Basically, this means that if you are partially at fault, you can collect only part of the value of your losses. For example, if a judge or jury ruled that you had suffered $10,000 in damages (such as medical costs or lost earnings) but that you were 20% at fault, you would recover only $8,000. If you're 99% at fault, you'll receive only 1% of your damages from your landlord.

Your Risk-Taking

Carelessness on your part is not the only way that your monetary recovery can be reduced. If you deliberately chose to act in a way that caused or worsened your injury, another doctrine may apply. Called "assumption of risk," it refers to a tenant who knows the danger of a certain action and decides to take the chance anyway.

EXAMPLE: In a hurry to get to work, you take a shortcut to the garage by cutting across an abandoned strip of pavement that you know has an uneven, broken surface. You disregard the sign posted by your landlord: "Danger: Use Front Walkway Only." If you trip and hurt your knee, you'll have a hard time pinning blame on your landlord, because you deliberately chose a dangerous route to the garage.

How Much Money You're Entitled To

If you were injured on your landlord's property and have convinced an insurance adjuster or jury that the landlord is responsible, at least in part, you can ask for monetary compensation, called "compensatory damages." Injured tenants can recover the money they have lost (wages) and spent (doctors' bills), plus compensation for physical pain and suffering, mental anguish, and lost opportunities.

Medical care and related expenses. You can recover for doctors' and physical therapists' bills, including future care. Even if your bills were covered by your own insurance company or medical plan, you can still sue for the amounts—but expect your insurance company to come after you, via a lien claim, if you recover anything in excess of your copayments or deductibles.

Missed work time. You can sue for lost wages and income while you were unable to work and undergoing treatment for your injuries. You can also recover for expected losses due to continuing care. The fact that you used sick or vacation pay to cover your time off from work is irrelevant. You are entitled to save this pay to use at your discretion at other times. In short, using up vacation or sick pay is considered the same as losing the pay itself.

Pain and other physical suffering. The type of injury you have suffered and its expected duration will affect the amount you can demand for pain and suffering. But insurance adjusters won't take your word for the level of discomfort you're experiencing. If you can show that your doctor has prescribed strong antipain medication, you'll have some objective corroboration of your distress. And the longer your recovery period, the greater your pain and suffering.

Permanent physical disability or disfigurement. If your injury has clear long-lasting or permanent effects—such as scars, back or joint stiffness, or a significant reduction in your mobility—the amount of your damages goes way up.

Loss of family, social, career, and educational experiences or opportunities. If you can demonstrate that the injury prevented you from advancing in your job or landing a better one, you can ask for compensation representing the lost income. Of course, it's hard to prove that missing a job interview resulted in income loss (after all, you didn't yet have the job). But the possibility that you might have moved ahead may be enough to convince the insurance company to sweeten their offer.

Emotional damages resulting from any of the above. Emotional pain—including stress, embarrassment, depression, and strains on family relationships—can be compensated. Like pain and suffering, however, it's hard to prove. If you have consulted a therapist, physician, or counselor, their evaluations of your reported symptoms can serve as proof of your problems. Be aware, however, that when you choose to sue for mental or emotional injuries, your doctor's notes and files regarding your symptoms and treatment will usually be made available to the other side.

In some cases, injured tenants can collect more than compensatory damages. A judge or jury may award punitive damages if it decides that the landlord acted outrageously, either intentionally or with extreme carelessness (recklessness). Punitive damages are punishments for this conduct.

Environmental Hazards

Because of some relatively recent changes in the law, landlords must now do more than provide housing that meets minimum health and safety standards. They are also expected to deal with some serious environmental health hazards. Simply put, laws now require landlords to take steps to ensure that you and your family aren't sickened by several common hazards, including lead, asbestos, and radon. Recently, the presence of mold has gotten the attention of landlords, tenants, and legislators.

This chapter explains landlords' obligations and offers some suggestions on how to spot problem areas, work with the landlord (or housing authorities), and take steps to protect yourself.

Asbestos

Exposure to asbestos has long been linked to an increased risk of cancer, particularly for workers in the asbestos manufacturing industry or in construction jobs involving the use of asbestos materials. More recently, the danger of asbestos in homes has also been recognized.

Homes built before the mid-1970s often contain asbestos insulation around heating systems, in ceilings, and in other areas. Until 1981, asbestos was also widely used in other building materials, such as vinyl flooring and tiles. Asbestos that is intact (or covered up) is generally not a problem, and the current wisdom is to leave it in place but monitor it for signs of deterioration. However, asbestos that has begun to break down and enter the air—for example, when it is disturbed during maintenance or renovation work—can become a significant health problem to people who breathe it.

OSHA Regulations

Until quite recently, landlords had no legal obligation to test for the presence of asbestos absent clear evidence that it was likely to be a health hazard. Now, owners of buildings constructed before 1981 must install warning labels, train staff, and notify people who work in areas that might contain asbestos. Unless the owner rules out the presence of asbestos by having a licensed inspector test the property, the law presumes that asbestos is present.

The U.S. Occupational Safety and Health Administration (OSHA) wrote these requirements to protect people who might be working in these buildings. But they are also a boon to tenants. In the process of complying with OSHA's requirements to inform and protect employees or outside contractors, your landlord will learn whether there is asbestos on the property and (based on its type and quantity) what must be done to protect the workers. But when landlords know about the presence of any dangerous defect on the rental property, regardless of the way they learned it, the law requires the landlord to take reasonable steps to make sure that tenants aren't harmed. In short, once the asbestos genie is out of the bottle, the landlord must take reasonable steps to protect your health or face the legal consequences.

Deteriorating Asbestos: An Obvious, Dangerous Defect

Problems with asbestos often arise when neither the landlord nor the tenant realizes that the material is embedded in ceilings and floors. Sometimes, however, the situation is not so subtle. Deteriorating asbestos that is open and obvious is a dangerous defect that your landlord must address pronto. It's no different from a broken front step or an inoperable front door lock. As the owner, the landlord is responsible for fixing conditions that could cause significant injury.

OSHA regulations cover two classes of materials: those that definitely contain asbestos (such as certain kinds of flooring and ceilings) and those that the law presumes contain asbestos. The second class is extremely inclusive, describing, among other things, any surfacing material that is "sprayed, troweled on, or otherwise applied." Under this definition, virtually every dwelling built before 1980 must be suspected of containing asbestos. Asbestos or asbestos-containing materials are typically found in or on:

- sprayed-on "cottage cheese" ceilings
- acoustic tile ceilings
- vinyl flooring, and
- insulation around heating and hot water pipes.

When the Landlord Must Test for Asbestos

Landlords are required to comply with OSHA's asbestos testing and protective rules when they undertake major remodeling or renovation jobs of pre-1981 buildings, as well as when they undertake lesser projects (such as the preparation of an asbestos-containing ceiling or wall for repainting). Even relatively noninvasive custodial work—such as stripping floor tiles containing asbestos—comes within the long reach of OSHA.

OSHA has concluded that post-1981 buildings are unlikely to contain asbestos, but if your post-1981 building does have asbestos (perhaps the builder or remodeler used recycled building materials), OSHA regulations cover it, too.

Protection From Asbestos

OSHA is very specific regarding the level of training, work techniques, and protective clothing for employees whose work involves disturbing asbestos. But they do not specifically address the measures that a landlord must take to protect tenants from exposure. However, the worker protection requirements give very useful clues as to what you can reasonably expect from your landlord in the way of tenant protections. In short, the more your landlord must do to protect workers, the more she must do to warn and protect tenants, too. If she doesn't and you are injured as a result, she risks being found liable. (See Chapter 9.)

- **Custodial work.** At the low end of the asbestos-disturbing spectrum, workers doing custodial work—for example, stripping the floor tiles in the lobby—must be trained (and supervised by a trained superior) in safe asbestos-handling techniques. Your landlord should warn all tenants that the work is planned, giving you an opportunity to avoid the area if you choose. The landlord should also make sure that tenants, their guests, and children don't come into contact with the debris. Conscientious landlords will use written notices to alert tenants, and place cones and caution tape around the area.

- **Major repairs or renovations.** If the landlord plans renovation or repair work for a pre-1981 building, the landlord must test for asbestos and provide more protection, including air monitoring, protective clothing, and medical surveillance of workers. You are entitled to appropriate warnings, and your landlord should minimize your exposure through fastidious work site procedures and isolation of dangerous materials.

EXAMPLE: Sally returned home to her apartment to find that workers were removing the ugly, stained ceiling tile in the lobby and hallways. She learned from the contractor that the project would last four days. Sally was concerned that her young sons, returning home from school in the afternoon and curious about the renovations, would hang around the halls and lobby or at least pass through them as they went in and out to play. Either way, Sally's sons would be exposed to the airborne fibers. Sally wrote a note to the landlord, explaining her concerns.

Sally's landlord recognized the reasonableness of her fears and the potential for injury. He spoke with the contractor, one who had been specially trained and licensed in asbestos removal, and arranged for the work to be done between the hours of 8 a.m. and 3 p.m. He insisted, and the contractor readily agreed, that the old tiles be removed and any asbestos-containing material covered at the end of each work day. Finally, the landlord hired two adults to monitor foot traffic in and around the renovation site, to ensure that no one lingered near the workers or came into contact with the removed materials.

How to Determine If Asbestos Is in Your Rental

You may learn of the presence of asbestos when your landlord tests in preparation for major renovations. Or, it might be obvious to you if, for example, the cottage cheese ceiling begins to slough off. Are there other ways to learn that asbestos is present?

You can't identify asbestos just by looking at it. Only someone trained in fiber identification using a special polarized light microscope can tell for sure. State-certified labs throughout California can identify asbestos in building materials. Contact a lab to find out how the sample should be collected and sent for testing. It's not an expensive test and should cost about $35 per sample. There's a list of labs on the Department of Health Services website at www.dhs.ca.gov (look for the Indoor Air Quality Program and choose asbestos).

Alerting and Motivating Your Landlord

Many landlords, unfortunately, have no idea about their duty to deal with the risks posed by asbestos. If you live in an older building and suspect that there is asbestos on the premises that is not being managed properly, alert your landlord and see to it that your health is protected. Here are some strategies.

When the asbestos is obvious but intact. Asbestos that is intact—for example, asbestos insulation that is covered with foil or wrapped with tape—probably does not pose a significant health risk

to you, since the fibers can't enter the air. It is important, however, that asbestos be monitored for signs of deterioration. For example, if the tape wrapping is tearing or falling away, it is no longer doing its job of containment. If you are worried about whether asbestos-containing materials in your home are dangerous, ask your landlord, in writing, to have the material inspected by a trained professional.

CAUTION
Never disturb asbestos-containing materials. Don't drill holes in walls or ceilings that contain asbestos, or sand asbestos tiles in preparation for a new coat of paint. First, you want to protect your health. Second, intentionally disturbing asbestos will almost certainly reduce, if not defeat, any legal claim you might have if your health is harmed by an asbestos-related problem. The law won't hold your landlord responsible for an injury that you deliberately courted, ignoring a risk you knew about.

When the asbestos is obvious and airborne. Take immediate action if asbestos in your living space has begun to break down or slough off. Asbestos that has begun to break down is extremely dangerous. If it is present in your living space in any significant amount, it makes your premises legally uninhabitable. (See Chapter 6 for your legal options, which may include withholding rent. Also, the text below discusses the option of moving out.) A sample letter from a tenant concerned about deteriorating asbestos is shown below.

TIP
Keep copies of all correspondence regarding asbestos or other environmental health hazards. If your landlord fails to take the right steps and you want to move out or seek other legal remedies, you'll need to be able to prove that you notified the landlord of the problem and waited a reasonable amount of time for a response.

Sample Letter Regarding Deteriorating Asbestos

37 Ninth Avenue North
Central City, California 00000
312-555-4567

February 28, 20xx

Margaret Mears
3757 East Seventh Street
Central City, California 00000

Dear Ms. Mears:

As you know, the ceilings in my apartment are sprayed-on acoustical plaster. I have begun to notice an excessive amount of fine, white dust in the apartment, and I believe it is the result of the breakdown of the asbestos fibers in the plaster. I am quite concerned about this, since inhaling asbestos can cause serious illness. Please contact me immediately so that you can take a look and arrange for a licensed inspector to examine the ceilings.

Yours truly,

Terry Lu

Terry Lu

When custodial or repair work is done improperly. When it comes to asbestos removal, the people who suffer most from a landlord's disregard of workplace safety are usually the workers themselves. But improper asbestos removal or disturbance is likely to affect you, too. Fortunately, there is something you can do about it. OSHA wants to hear about violations of workplace safety rules. You can reach OSHA by calling the phone number listed below in "Asbestos Resources." The California Department of Health Services is the state equivalent of OSHA, and you can contact it, too.

Move Out If Necessary

Sometimes it isn't possible to shield yourself from the effects of deteriorating asbestos, or even your landlord's major repairs or renovations involving asbestos. For example, if the acoustic ceilings in your apartment are being removed, it is unlikely (even if you and your landlord are prepared to take every precaution) that you can avoid inhaling some dangerous airborne fibers. In situations like this, especially if you or your family have health problems that make you especially vulnerable to the effects of asbestos, the best alternative might be to move out temporarily until the work is completed. (See Chapter 6 for a discussion of moving out because your rental is uninhabitable.) Since the responsibility to repair and maintain the structure is the landlord's, the cost of temporary shelter should be covered by the landlord as long as you can convincingly establish that remaining on the premises would constitute a significant health risk. See the sample letter below.

If you are able to give valid reasons why you should be temporarily absent while the asbestos removal work is done, and if you have a reasonable landlord who appreciates the potentially serious legal consequences of denying your reasonable request, chances are you'll be able to come to an agreement. (Don't ask to stay at the Ritz, however!)

But what if the landlord stubbornly refuses? Obviously, to protect your health, you'll want to move out anyway. And assuming the asbestos problems really are serious, you should stand a good chance of prevailing in a small claims court lawsuit for the cost of your temporary housing. Be sure to keep a copy of the letter you have sent (preferably by certified mail) to the landlord, a record of the landlord's refusal to pay for temporary accommodations, and all receipts for your expenses.

 TIP

Come to court prepared with asbestos-related information. If you go to small claims court, be prepared to explain the serious dangers of breathing asbestos fibers to the judge and why the landlord's work was so invasive that temporarily moving out was your only sensible alternative. See "Asbestos Resources," below. Also, see Chapter 17 for a discussion of small claims lawsuits.

Sample Letter Requesting Reimbursement for Temporary Housing

1289 Central Avenue, Apartment 8
Anytown, CA 00000
713-555-7890

June 13, 20xx

Mr. Frank Brown, Owner
Sunshine Properties
75 Main Street
Anytown, CA 00000

Dear Mr. Brown:

I have just received the notice you sent to all tenants on the first floor, alerting us to your plans to tear out the heating ducts and insulation during the week of July 6. The work will involve removing heating vents inside our apartment and removing the asbestos insulation through the openings. You estimate that the work will take two days for each apartment.

I do not think that it would be a good idea for me and my elderly mother to live in the apartment during this process. I am concerned that we will inhale airborne asbestos fibers that may cause difficulties in breathing. My mother suffers from chronic bronchitis and cannot risk exposure to anything that might worsen the condition. Dr. Jones, who treats my mother, would be happy to corroborate this fact.

I think that the best solution would be for us to move out while this work is being done. The nearby Best California Motel has reasonable rates and would be convenient to our jobs and transportation. Please contact me so that we might discuss this before the renovation work begins. You can call me at home at the above number most nights and weekends.

Yours truly,

Sharon Rock

Sharon Rock

cc: Dr. Jones

Asbestos Resources

For further information on asbestos rules, inspections, and control, contact the nearest office of the U.S. Occupational Safety and Health Administration (OSHA) or call 202-219-8148.

OSHA has also developed interactive computer software for property owners, called "Asbestos Advisor," designed to help identify asbestos and suggest ways to handle it. It may help you, or interested members of any tenants' association in your building, to determine whether asbestos is present and whether your landlord is managing it properly. The "Asbestos Advisor" is available free through the U.S. Department of Labor's electronic bulletin board, LaborNews, by telephoning 202-219-4784. You will also find it online at OSHA's website, www.osha.gov.

California has a state counterpart to the federal OSHA regulations (the law relevant to landlords is known as California's Asbestos Standards in General Industry (8 CCR § 5208)). Information on state enforcement is on the Department of Industrial Relations' website at www.dir.ca.gov/dosh/asbestos.html.

Instead of suing in small claims court, you may be tempted to utilize what the law calls a "repair and deduct" remedy (discussed in Chapter 7) by simply deducting the cost of replacement housing from your rent. It seems logical, but a judge might not allow it. Seizing upon this uncertainty, your landlord's response could be to terminate your tenancy and file for eviction for nonpayment of rent. If you lose, you will not only have to pay for the cost of the temporary housing, but face eviction from your rental as well. (In addition, you may be stuck with the landlord's attorney fees if there is an "attorney fees" clause in your lease. See "Printed Forms: What to Watch Out For" in Chapter 1.) It's far better to file a straightforward lawsuit asking for reimbursement, where the risk is simply losing the suit, not your home.

If your landlord refuses to cover temporary housing expenses, you might also want to consider moving out permanently. This option is most appropriate when the risk is great and the length of exposure relatively long. But to justify breaking the lease (and to avoid liability for future rent), you will have to be able to show that airborne asbestos really did make the premises uninhabitable. (See Chapter 6 for a full discussion of breaking the lease due to uninhabitability.) If the landlord is ripping out whole ceilings over a month's time, this argument will be strong. However, it will not amount to much if the landlord is drilling two small holes in the ceiling to install a smoke detector.

Court-Ordered Renovations

Local health authorities may sue a landlord who fails to repair code violations in a reasonable time. If a judge rules that the rental property's conditions "substantially endanger the health and safety of residents," and if your landlord must ask you to move in order to make repairs, state law dictates what happens:

- The landlord must provide you with comparable temporary housing nearby (you still pay your original rent to the landlord). If comparable housing isn't possible, the landlord pays the difference between the old rent and your new rent elsewhere, for up to four months.
- The landlord must pay your moving expenses, including packing and unpacking costs.
- The landlord insures your belongings in transit, or pays for the replacement value of property lost, stolen, or damaged in transit.
- The landlord pays your new utility connection charges.
- You must have the first offer to move back in when repairs are completed. (H&S § 17980.7.)

Lead

Exposure to lead-based paint and lead water pipes may lead to serious health problems, particularly in children. Brain damage, attention disorders, and hyperactivity have all been associated with lead poisoning. Studies show that the effects of lead poisoning are lifelong, affecting both personality and intelligence. In adults, the effects of lead poisoning can include nerve disorders, high blood pressure, reproductive disorders, and muscle and joint pain.

Lead Inspections

Although inspections are not required by state or federal law, landlords may voluntarily arrange for an inspection in order to certify on the disclosure form that the property is lead-free and exempt from federal regulations. (See list of exemptions, below.) Also, when a property owner takes out a loan or buys insurance, the bank or insurance company may require a lead inspection.

Professional lead inspectors don't always inspect every unit in large, multifamily properties. Instead, they inspect a sampling of the units and apply their conclusions to the property as a whole. Giving you the results and conclusions of a building-wide evaluation satisfies the law, even if your particular unit was not tested. If, however, your landlord has specific information regarding your unit that is inconsistent with the building-wide evaluation, he or she must disclose it to you.

For information on arranging a professional lead inspection or using a home testing kit, see "Dealing With Lead on Your Own," below.

Buildings constructed before 1978 are likely to contain some source of lead: lead-based paint, lead pipes, or lead-based solder used on copper pipes. In 1978, the federal government required the reduction of lead in house paint; lead pipes are generally found only in homes built before 1930, and lead-based solder in home plumbing systems was banned in 1988. Pre-1950 housing in poor and urban neighborhoods that has been allowed to deteriorate is by far the greatest source of lead-based paint poisonings.

Discovering (or being told by the landlord) that there is lead on the premises is not necessarily the end of a healthy and safe tenancy. "Getting the Landlord to Act," below, gives you advice on how to cope with a lead problem.

How Lead Poisoning Occurs

Lead-laden dust caused by the deterioration of exposed lead-based paint is the greatest source of lead poisoning. Falling on windowsills, walls, and floors, this dust makes its way into the human body when it is stirred up, becomes airborne, and is inhaled, or when it is transmitted directly from hand to mouth. Exterior lead-based house paint is also a potential problem because it can slough off walls directly into the soil and be tracked into the house.

Lead dust results from renovations or remodeling—including, unfortunately, those very projects undertaken to rid premises of the lead-based paint. Lead poisoning can also occur from drinking water that contains leached-out lead from lead pipes or from deteriorating lead solder used in copper pipes.

Children between the ages of 18 months and five years are the most likely to be poisoned by lead-based paint. Their poisoning is detected when they become ill or, increasingly, in routine examinations that check for elevated blood levels of lead.

Federal Protections

Unfortunately, neither federal nor state law require landlords to test for lead, nor do they require landlords to get rid of it if they know it's present. Still, the laws aimed at reducing lead poisoning do give some important benefits to tenants. At the least, if the landlord knows there are lead paint hazards on the premises, you're entitled to know that.

Rental Properties Exempt From Federal Regulations

- Housing for which a construction permit was obtained, or on which construction was started, after January 1, 1978. Older buildings that have been completely renovated since 1978 are *not* exempt, even if every painted surface was removed or replaced.
- Housing certified as lead-free by a state-accredited lead inspector. Lead-free means the absence of any lead paint—even paint that has been completely painted over and encapsulated.
- Lofts, efficiencies, studios, and other "zero-bedroom" units, including dormitory housing and rentals in sorority and fraternity houses. University-owned apartments and married student housing are not exempt.
- Short-term vacation rentals.
- A single room rented in a residential home.
- Housing designed for persons with disabilities (as explained in HUD's Fair Housing Accessibility Guidelines, 56 Code of Federal Regulations 9472, 3/6/91) *unless* any child less than six years old resides there or is expected to reside there.
- Retirement communities (housing designed for seniors, where one or more tenant is at least 62 years old) *unless* children under the age of six are present or expected to live there.

Disclosure

All property owners must inform tenants, before they sign or renew a lease or rental agreement, of any information they possess on lead paint hazard conditions on the property. They must disclose information on its presence in individual rental units, common areas, garages, tool sheds, other outbuildings, signs, fences, and play areas. If the property has been tested (testing must be done only by state-certified lead inspectors), a copy of the report, or a summary written by the inspector, must be shown to tenants.

With certain exceptions (listed below), every lease and rental agreement must include a disclosure page, even if the landlord has not tested. You can see the federally approved disclosure form "Disclosure of Information on Lead-Based Paint or Lead-Based Paint Hazards" by going to the Environmental Protection Agency's website, www.epa.gov.

If you were a tenant in your current home on December 6, 1996, your landlord must comply with these disclosure requirements according to whether you are a tenant with a lease or are renting month to month.

- **Tenants with leases.** Your landlord need not comply until your lease is up and you renew or stay on as a month-to-month tenant.
- **Month-to-month tenants.** Your landlord should have given you a disclosure statement when you wrote your first rent check dated after December 6, 1996 (September 6, 1996, if the landlord owns five or more units).

Information

The landlord must give all tenants the lead hazard information booklet "Protect Your Family From Lead in Your Home," written by the Environmental Protection Agency (EPA). If they choose, landlords may reproduce the booklet in a legal-size, 8½ x 14-inch format, and attach it to the lease. California's pamphlet, "Environmental Hazards: A Guide for Homeowners, Buyers, Landlords and Tenants," is a legally-approved substitute.

If your landlord has not given you a disclosure form or an EPA booklet, ask for them. If you get no results, notify the EPA. This will probably result in no more than a letter or call from the inspectors, since the EPA will usually not cite landlords unless their noncompliance with the laws is willful, widespread, and continuing. But a landlord who continues to ignore the law may be subject to the penalties described below.

Enforcement and Penalties

HUD and the EPA enforce renters' rights to know about the presence of lead-based paint by using "testers," as they do when looking for illegal discrimination (see Chapter 4). Posing as applicants, testers who get the rental will document whether landlords disclosed lead paint information when they signed the lease or rental agreement. Of course, individual complaints from tenants who have not received the required booklets can trigger an investigation, too.

Landlords who fail to distribute the required information booklet, or who do not give tenants the disclosure statement, may receive one or more of the following penalties:

- a notice of noncompliance, the mildest form of reprimand
- a civil penalty, which can include fines of up to $11,000 per violation for willful and continuing noncompliance
- an order to pay an injured tenant up to three times the tenant's actual damages, or
- a criminal fine of up to $11,000 per violation.

Government testers are also on the lookout for property owners who falsely claim that they have no knowledge of lead-based paint hazards on their property. Here's how it often comes up: A tenant complains to HUD if he becomes ill with lead poisoning after the landlord told him that she knew of no lead-based paint hazards on the premises. If HUD decides to investigate whether, in fact, the landlord knew about the hazard and failed to tell this tenant, their investigators get access to the landlord's records. They comb leasing, maintenance, and repair files—virtually the landlord's entire business records. If HUD finds evidence that the landlord knew (or had reason to know) of lead paint hazards, such as a contract from a painting firm that includes costs for lead paint removal or a loan document indicating the presence of lead paint, the landlord will be hard-pressed to explain why she's checked the box on the disclosure form stating that she has no reports or records regarding the presence of lead-based paint on the property. The tenant, in turn, will have good evidence to use in court.

RESOURCE

The Residential Lead-Based Paint Hazard Reduction Act was enacted in 1992 to reduce lead levels. It is commonly referred to as Title X [Ten] (42 U.S.C. § 4852d). The Environmental Protection Agency (EPA) has written regulations that explain how landlords should implement lead hazard reduction (24 Code of Federal Regulations Part 35 and 40 Code of Federal Regulations Part 745). California has enacted several statutes that target workplaces and schools, and focus on childhood poisoning prevention. For more information, see "Lead Hazard Resources," below.

Federal Rules Covering Renovations

When landlords renovate occupied rental units or common areas in buildings constructed before 1978, EPA regulations require that current tenants receive lead hazard information before the renovation work begins. (40 C.F.R. §§ 745.80-88.)

The obligation to distribute lead information rests with the "renovator." If the landlord hires an outside contractor to perform renovation work, the contractor is the renovator. But if the landlord, property manager, superintendent, or other employees perform the renovation work, the landlord is the renovator and is obliged to give you the required information.

The type of information that the renovator must give you depends on where the renovation is taking place. If the landlord is working on an occupied rental unit, resident tenants must get a copy of the EPA pamphlet "Protect Your Family From Lead in Your Home" (even if you already got one when you moved in). If common areas will be affected, the landlord must distribute a notice to every rental unit in the building.

What Qualifies as a Renovation?

According to EPA regulations, a "renovation" is any change to an occupied rental unit or common area of the building that disturbs painted surfaces. Here are some examples:

- removing or modifying a painted door, wall, baseboard, or ceiling
- scraping or sanding paint, or
- removing a large structure like a wall, partition, or window.

Not every renovation triggers the federal law, though. There are four big exceptions:

Emergency renovations. If a sudden or unexpected event, such as a fire or flood, requires emergency repairs to a rental unit or to the property's common areas, there's no need to distribute lead hazard information to tenants before work begins.

Minor repairs or maintenance. Minor work that affects two square feet or less of a painted surface is also exempt. Minor repairs include routine electrical and plumbing work, so long as no more than two square feet of the wall, ceiling, or other painted surface gets disturbed by the work.

Renovations in lead-free properties. If a licensed inspector has certified that the rental unit or building in which the renovation takes place contains no lead paint, the landlord isn't required to give out the required information.

Common area renovations in buildings with three or fewer units. Tenants in buildings with three or fewer units are not entitled to information about common area renovations.

If your landlord has repainted a rental unit in preparation for your arrival, this won't qualify as a "renovation" unless accompanied by sanding, scraping, or other surface preparation activities that may generate paint dust. Minor "spot" scraping or sanding can qualify for the "minor repairs and maintenance" exception if no more than two square feet of paint is disturbed on any surface to be painted. (EPA Interpretive Guidance, Part I, May 28, 1999.)

Receiving the EPA Pamphlet When Your Rental Is Renovated

Before starting a renovation to an occupied rental unit, the renovator must give the EPA pamphlet "Protect Your Family From Lead in Your Home" to at least one adult occupant of the unit being occupied, preferably the tenant. This is the same one you received (hopefully) when you signed your lease or rental agreement (see above). This requirement applies to all rental properties, including single-family homes and duplexes, unless the property has been certified lead-free by a licensed inspector.

Your landlord may mail or hand-deliver the pamphlet to you. If the landlord mails it, he must get a "certificate of mailing" from the post office dated at least seven days before the renovation work begins. If he hand-delivers it, you'll probably be asked to sign and date a receipt acknowledging that you received the pamphlet before renovation work began in the unit. You should get the pamphlet 60 days (or fewer) before the work begins (delivering the pamphlet more than 60 days in advance won't satisfy the landlord's obligations under the law).

Notice of Common Area Renovation

If the building has four or more units, the renovator —be it the landlord or his contractor— must notify tenants of all "affected units" about the renovation and tell them how to obtain a free copy of the EPA pamphlet "Protect Your Family From Lead in Your Home." (C.F.R. § 745.85(b)(2).) In most cases, common area renovations will affect all units in the property, meaning that all tenants must be notified about the renovation. But when renovating a "limited use common area" in a large apartment building, such as the 16th floor hallway but no others, the landlord need only notify those units serviced by, or in close proximity to, the limited use common area. The EPA defines large buildings as those having 50 or more units.

To comply, the renovator must deliver a notice to every affected unit describing the nature and location of the renovation work, its location, and the dates the renovator expects to begin and finish work. If the renovator can't provide specific dates, he may use terms like "on or about," "in early June," or "in late July" to describe expected starting and ending dates for the renovation. The notices must be delivered within 60 days before

work begins. The notices may be slipped under apartment doors or given to any adult occupant of the rental unit. Landlords may not mail the notices.

Penalties

Failing to give tenants the required information about renovation lead hazards can result in harsh penalties. Renovators who knowingly violate the regulations can get hit with a penalty of up to $27,500 per day for each violation. Willful violations can also result in imprisonment.

Recognizing Lead in Your Home

If your landlord has tested for lead and complied with federal disclosure requirements, you can skip this section. However, most landlords have not tested for lead. (This situation will surely change as banks and insurance companies begin to require testing as a prerequisite to loans and insurance coverage.) There are several clues as to whether there is lead in or around your home, and ways that you (or, ideally, your landlord) can find out for sure.

You will need to hire a licensed lead tester to get a precise assessment of the risk of lead in your home. Unfortunately, the cost is high—a few hundred dollars at least. If you (and possibly other tenants) choose to do an assessment, you'll be in a good position to lobby the landlord to do something about containing the risk. But even if you do not get a professional's opinion, but are fairly sure that lead is present in your home, you can still act prudently on your own to reduce the risk. (Sections below explain what you can do yourself and how to get the landlord to act.)

Paint

Your first step should be to determine the age of the building. If the landlord doesn't know or won't say, go to the local building permit office and ask to see the building's construction permit. If there is no permit on file, you'll have to estimate the structure's age.

As noted above, housing that was built before January 1, 1978, is almost certain to have lead-based paint. But buildings constructed later may have it, too, since the 1978 ban did not include a recall and lead-based paint remained on the shelves.

You can do your own test for lead. Home testing kits work like this: After swabbing a chemical solution over a painted surface, the swab will turn a certain color if lead is present. Kits are widely available at hardware and paint stores and are inexpensive, but unfortunately are unreliable about 30% of the time. For more reliable results, hire a professional tester who will use an X-ray gun to give an instant reading through all the layers of paint. A professional inspection will cost a few hundred dollars; if you can, share the cost with other tenants. (See "Lead Hazard Resources," below, for information on finding a HUD-approved contractor to test for lead.)

Lead Pipes

Pre-1930 construction generally used lead pipes. It's difficult to know for sure whether you have lead pipes until you examine the plumbing. When you look under the sink, you may be able to see the pipe coming out from the wall; if so, look for the tell-tale dark gray color. A plumber should be able to identify the pipes without difficulty.

Lead Solder

Lead solder was used to join sections of pipe as recently as 1988. You won't know whether it was used unless you can look at several soldered junctions; even then, you will probably need a plumber to tell you whether the solder was leaded or not.

Imported Vinyl Miniblinds

In 1996, the Consumer Product Safety Commission announced that miniblinds from China, Taiwan, Indonesia, and Mexico are likely to contain lead, which manufacturers add to stabilize the plastic. (American-made blinds may have also contained lead and are now made without lead, and should so state on the package.) As the surface vinyl deteriorates in the sun, lead dust enters the air. Even when landlords know that an apartment has leaded miniblinds, they don't have to tell tenants *unless* they know that the blinds have begun to deteriorate and produce lead dust. Be smart: Ask the landlord to replace old blinds now, before a problem occurs.

Soil

For decades, American cars ran on leaded gasoline —and the effects are still with us. Exhaust from lead-burning cars contains lead, which falls to the ground where it remains, relatively inert, for years. Neighborhoods adjacent to heavily traveled roadways have significant amounts of lead in the soil; the readings drop off dramatically as the distance from the roads diminishes. If you live near a busy freeway or throughway, assume the worst and take care of yourself. See "Getting the Landlord to Act," below, for suggestions on self-help.

Dealing With Lead on Your Own

You don't need to automatically reject, or move out of, a rental that contains lead. Remember, only deteriorating lead is the culprit.

If you do discover hazardous lead, an aggressive approach is often the best idea. If you live in older housing where lead is almost surely present and deteriorating, assume a worst-case scenario and adjust your housekeeping and hygiene habits accordingly. (Ideally, you'll want the landlord to eventually take more drastic measures, such as careful repainting, as discussed below.) Here's what the experts recommend that you do:

- Vacuum thoroughly and regularly, using a "HEPA" ("high energy particle arresting") vacuum that will filter out the fine lead dust. Ask your landlord to provide one.
- Even where a unit has been repainted, the old lead paint layer will eventually be reexposed if the surface gets a lot of wear, such as door and windowsill areas. Wash them with a

phosphate-based cleaner or a solution (like "Leadisolve") designed for lead pick-up.

> **CAUTION**
>
> **Don't disturb lead paint in buildings built before 1978.** Do not sand walls, windowsills, doors, or other surfaces—you'll risk releasing lead into the air (possibly even from paint several layers down), creating the very hazards you are attempting to avoid. Only painters who have been trained and equipped to capture and remove lead dust and chips should undertake renovations of this order. If you knowingly disturb lead and suffer an injury, it will be difficult to place legal responsibility on your landlord.

- If your unit has lead pipes or copper pipe with lead solder, draw water out of the pipes by letting the taps run for 30 seconds before using—even if you plan to boil it for tea. Don't use hot water for cooking. Better yet, use bottled water for drinking and cooking.
- If lead is in the soil outside, provide throw rugs at each entrance or ask folks to remove their shoes before entering.
- Consider covering lead-laced soil with sod or an impermeable material.
- If your household has young children (especially those who are still crawling), use extra care to clean floors, especially around windows. Wash children's toys and hands frequently, and clean pacifiers and bottles after they fall on the floor.
- Test your children for lead poisoning. Elevated blood levels in young children can be picked up in a simple blood test. Increasingly, the test is done as part of routine check-ups. If you live in a building that you suspect places your child at risk for lead poisoning, you need this information to protect your child. The Centers for Disease Control and Prevention recommend giving children a blood level test at age six months to one year. Do follow-up tests as needed.

> **CAUTION**
>
> **If a child's blood lead level is very high, move promptly and see a lawyer.** Evidence of lead poisoning will almost certainly entitle you to move out on the grounds of uninhabitability. (See "Move Out If Necessary," below.) You will definitely need expert legal assistance if you sue for damages.

Getting the Landlord to Act

Getting your landlord to hire a professional to test and assess the risk of lead poisoning may be a tall order—after all, no federal or state law requires it. And it may be next to impossible to get your landlord to paint over deteriorating lead paint. But even the most penurious, callous, or short-sighted landlord may respond to a threat to the bottom line.

Many landlords have learned (sometimes the hard way) that testing for lead and taking measures before tenants get sick is well worth the cost and time. Although landlords aren't liable for lead poisoning unless it can be shown that they knew that lead was present, these days it is increasingly difficult for landlords to plausibly argue that they were ignorant of this well-publicized issue. Lawsuits for lead poisoning can result in astronomical jury awards or settlements if the landlord is held responsible for the lifetime effects of an infant's brain damage. The cost of testing, risk assessment, and lead management pales in comparison.

> **TIP**
>
> **Educate your landlord.** If the landlord isn't aware of the potentially enormous liability for lead poisoning, try this tactic: Go to the websites mentioned below in "Lead Hazard Resources" and print the pages or pamphlets that explain the risks to landlord who ignore the writing (and the paint) on the wall.

Notify the Landlord of Problems

If you discover a lead hazard on the property, tell the landlord at once, in writing. A sample letter is shown below.

Sample Letter Regarding Lead Test Results

45 East Avenue North
Central City, CA 00000
816-555-7890

February 28, 20xx

Lester Levine
3757 East Seventh Street
Central City, CA 00000

Dear Mr. Levine:

We recently hired the environmental engineering firm of Checkit & Howe to test our duplex for the presence of lead-based paint. A report of their findings is enclosed. As you can see, there is indeed old, unstable lead paint on most of the windowsills and in the upstairs hall.

We are concerned about the effect that this deteriorating paint will have on the health of our children, aged three months and three years. At a minimum, we would like to discuss a safe and effective response to this problem. Please contact us as soon as possible so that we can arrange a meeting. We're home in the evenings and on weekends.

Yours truly,

Maynard G. and Zelda Krebs

Maynard G. and Zelda Krebs

Encl: Report of Checkit & Howe

Although the goal of your efforts is a safe place to live, not a successful lawsuit, don't lose sight of the fact that your landlord may avoid liability for lead injuries unless you can show that the landlord knew (or should have known) of lead hazards and failed to take reasonable steps to reduce them. In short, if you believe there is a lead risk on your property, you want to make it impossible for the landlord to plausibly deny knowing about it. If you use a kit to test your rental unit or its water supply and find the presence of lead, send the results (certified mail) to the landlord. If your child has elevated blood levels, do the same. Keep these receipts and any other evidence of the landlord's knowledge, such as notes of a conversation in which the landlord acknowledged the presence of pre-1978, chipping paint but refused to buy a HEPA vacuum.

Involve State, Local, or Federal Inspectors

Under state law and the ordinances of some cities (such as San Francisco), health inspectors have the power to inspect and order cleanups when a tenant complains to their enforcement agencies or reports a child's elevated blood level. (California H&S §§ 124160, 124165.) You can also report a lead problem to your local EPA office (for contact information, see "Lead Hazard Resources," below).

Consider a Lawsuit

Some lead-management measures, such as scrupulous housekeeping, are more time-consuming than expensive. However, money enters the picture when there's so much lead dust that containment is the only reasonable response—for example, sealing lead-based paint by covering it with a durable finish. If actual removal of the painted surfaces is necessary (perhaps the underlying structure is so deteriorated that it must be replaced), considerable expense is in the offing.

Forcing the landlord to deal with lead on the property will involve asking a judge to issue an order that directs that the work be accomplished in a certain way within a certain time. Lawsuits like this cannot be filed in small claims court. These lawsuits are typically complicated affairs that require lawyers. They can be very effective when a group of tenants sue together. See Chapter 17 for suggestions on finding and working with a lawyer.

If you spend time and money dealing with lead containment—using special detergents or vacuums, devoting extra time to fastidious housekeeping, putting up with the intrusion of contractors trying to deal with the lead problem—ask your landlord to reduce the rent accordingly. After all, these expenses are necessitated by the dilapidation of the property. If the landlord refuses and you have a lease requiring that you live in the unit for months or years, consider going to small claims court for an order reducing your rent, and ask that you be compensated for past labor and expenses, too. See Chapter 7 and *Everybody's Guide to Small Claims Court in California,* by Ralph Warner (Nolo), for help.

Lead Hazard Resources

Information on the evaluation and control of lead dust, disclosure forms, copies of the "Protect Your Family From Lead in Your Home" pamphlet, and lists of EPA-certified lead paint professionals may be obtained from the National Lead Information Center by calling 800-424-LEAD or checking the center's website at www.epa.gov/lead/nlic.htm. The EPA also provides pamphlets, documents, forms, and information on all lead-paint hazards and federal laws and regulations on its website, www.epa.gov/lead.

HUD issues a pamphlet entitled "Guidance on the Lead-Based Paint Disclosure Rule, Parts I and II," which may be obtained online from the HUD Lead Office website at www.hud.gov/lea/leahome.html.

HUD also maintains a "Lead Listing" of names, addresses, and phone numbers of trained lead paint contractors (for testing and abatement) in every state. Call 888-LEAD-LIST or access the list on the Web at www.leadlisting.org. For other HUD information on lead hazards, including a down-loadable pamphlet on how to safely remove lead hazards entitled "Lead Paint Safety, A Field Guide for Painting, Home Maintenance, and Renovation," visit www.hud.gov/lea.

California also provides information for tenants. Start with the Department of Health Services' website at www.dhs.ca.gov.

Move Out If Necessary

If the risk of lead poisoning is high and cannot be controlled, the smartest move may be moving out. Here are two scenarios that usually justify a move:

The rental is permeated with lead that you cannot effectively control. If lead constitutes a serious danger to your health—perhaps deteriorating paint has caused a serious lead dust problem, or old lead pipes have contaminated the water supply—you would be justified in breaking the lease and moving out on the grounds that your unit is legally uninhabitable. (See Chapter 6 for more on this topic.) To help counter any possible lawsuit by the landlord against you for future unpaid rent, be sure that you have your evidence in hand, such as a report from an EPA inspector or a state or local health inspector.

Renovations will create a lead problem. If the landlord plans repairs or renovations in an effort to contain a serious lead problem, you may be wise to leave the premises. Even meticulous cleanup procedures cannot eliminate the risk of inhaling lead dust created by renovation. California law requires the landlord to cover temporary housing expenses incurred when tenants must move out (see Chapter 6).

Radon

Radon is a naturally occurring radioactive gas that is associated with lung cancer. The U.S. Environmental Protection Agency (EPA) estimates that over one-quarter of American homes have unacceptably high levels of radon. Radon can enter and contaminate a house built on soil and rock containing uranium deposits. It can also enter through water from private wells drilled in uranium-rich soil.

Radon becomes a lethal health threat when it enters from the soil and is trapped in homes that are over-insulated or poorly ventilated. Radon is a smaller risk when it escapes from building materials that have incorporated uranium-filled rocks and soils (like certain types of composite tiles or bricks), or is released into the air from aerated household water that has passed through underground concentrations of uranium. Problems occur most frequently in areas where rocky soil is relatively rich in uranium and in climates where occupants keep their windows tightly shut to maintain heat in the winter and air conditioning in the summer. If you smoke and your house has high radon levels, your risk of developing lung cancer is especially high.

The California Department of Health Services is studying radon in homes in the Sierra region, where radon is potentially a problem, in the following counties: Alpine, Amador, Calaveras, El Dorado, Fresno, Inyo, Kings, Madera, Mariposa, Mono, Nevada, Placer, Tulare, and Tuolumne.

Fortunately, there are usually simple, inexpensive ways to measure and reduce radon levels in buildings. For example, good ventilation will disperse the gas in most situations. Solutions range from the obvious (open the windows) to the somewhat complex (use fans), but none of them involves tremendous expense.

There are no California or federal laws that require a private landlord to try to detect or get rid of radon. The radon problem has not become the subject of national laws requiring testing or even disclosure. But if you find radon in your rented property, there are still things you can do.

Finding Radon

Radon is invisible and odorless. To test the air in your house, you can buy a do-it-yourself kit (make sure it says "Meets EPA Requirements") or hire a professional. Testing takes at least three days, and sometimes months. Testers should have a certificate issued by the National Environmental Health Association (NEHA) or the National Radon Safety Board (NSRB). (California H&S § 106780.)

Testing for radon makes sense if you live in an area that is naturally rich in uranium soil and rock. If you live in the counties mentioned above, you know that the experts think your soil is more likely to have radon than other areas of California. If you're not in one of those counties, start with the public library and find out about your local geology. City planning departments, insurance brokers (who may have experience in dealing with radon-related claims), architects (who ought to understand the local geology), environmental engineers, and neighbors may be fruitful sources.

Solving Radon Problems

If radon is present in significant amounts, it needs to be blown out and kept out of the building.

Getting it out. Once radon has entered the house, it needs to be dispelled with fans and open windows. Because of the increased costs of heating and air conditioning, and the loss of security when windows are left open, these methods should be only temporary. The only good long-term solution is keeping radon out.

Keeping it out. Sealing cracks and other openings in the foundation is a basic radon reduction technique. Another method is soil suction—sucking the radon out of the soil before it enters the foundation or basement, and venting it into the air above the roof through a pipe. Increasing the air pressure within a house can also work, because radon enters houses when the air pressure inside is less than that of the surrounding soil. Equalizing the pressure in the basement or foundation reduces this pull.

The Landlord's Responsibility

Keeping radon out of your dwelling involves major expenditures and modifications to the building's structure. Obviously, this kind of work is your landlord's responsibility.

If your landlord is unaware of the radon issue, give the landlord a copy of the EPA booklet explaining it. (See "Radon Resources," below.) If you have grounds for concern—you notice radon detection devices in local stores, your neighborhood has several buildings that are vented for radon control or the geology of the area suggests the presence of uranium-rich soils—suggest that your landlord hire a testing firm. As always, if a group of tenants voices their concern, the landlord is more likely to pay attention than if you act alone. Obviously, if you perform a test, send the landlord a certified letter with a copy of the report.

Keep copies of letters and reports, and write a letter of understanding to the landlord summarizing any oral discussions of the issue. Meticulous business practices like these will impress your landlord with your seriousness and willingness to take legal action if necessary.

Move Out If Necessary

Unacceptably high levels of radon render a home unfit for habitation. If a certified tester has reached that conclusion, you have all that you need to demand that the landlord take prompt steps to remedy the problem. If the landlord fails to address it within a very short time, you can break your lease or month-to-month rental agreement and move out, citing a breach of the implied warranty of habitability (see Chapter 6). Your suspicion alone that radon is present (perhaps because your neighbor has a radon problem) will probably not protect you if the landlord sues you for unpaid rent.

It may be appropriate to move out temporarily if the landlord plans to install pumps or vents, which may take some time. See the discussion above that suggests strategies for recouping expenses of temporary housing.

Radon Resources

For information on the detection and removal of radon, contact the U.S. Environmental Protection Agency (EPA) Radon Hotline at 800-767-7236 or visit the EPA website (www.epa.gov/iaq/radon). You can also download a copy of the booklet "A Radon Guide for Tenants" and other publications, including "Consumer's Guide to Radon Reduction." California's Department of Health Services has lots of information—go to their website at www.dhs.ca.gov and type "radon" into the search box.

Carbon Monoxide

Carbon monoxide (CO) is a colorless, odorless, lethal gas. Unlike radon, whose deadly effects work over time, CO can build up and kill within a matter of hours. And, unlike any of the environmental hazards discussed so far, CO cannot be covered up or managed.

When CO is inhaled, it enters the bloodstream and replaces oxygen. Dizziness, nausea, confusion, and tiredness can result; high concentrations bring on unconsciousness, brain damage, and death. It is possible to be poisoned from CO while you sleep, without waking up.

Sources of Carbon Monoxide

Carbon monoxide is a byproduct of fuel combustion; electric appliances cannot produce it. Common home appliances, such as gas dryers, refrigerators, ranges, water heaters or space heaters, oil furnaces, fireplaces, charcoal grills, and wood stoves all produce CO. Automobiles and gas gardening equipment also produce CO. If appliances or fireplaces are not vented properly, CO can build up within a home and poison the occupants. In tight, "energy-efficient" apartments, indoor accumulations are especially dangerous. No state or federal agency has issued guidelines on permissible exposures.

CAUTION

If you smell gas, it's not CO. Carbon monoxide has no smell. Only a CO detector will alert you to its presence. To help identify leaking natural gas, utility companies add a smelly ingredient; when you "smell gas," you are smelling that additive. Because natural gas is so combustible, call the utility company or 911 immediately if you smell it.

Preventing Carbon Monoxide Problems

If your landlord has a regular maintenance program, it should prevent the common malfunctions that cause CO build-up. But even the most careful service program cannot rule out unexpected problems like the blocking of a chimney by a bird's nest or the sudden failure of a machine part.

Fortunately, relatively inexpensive devices, similar to smoke detectors, can monitor CO levels and sound an alarm if they get too high. If you purchase one, make sure it is UL-certified, and never rely on the detector as a replacement for regular, careful checking of the appliances in your home that produce CO.

CAUTION

If your CO detector sounds an alarm, leave immediately and do a household head count. Since one of the effects of CO poisoning is confusion and disorientation, get everyone out immediately—then check for signs of poisoning and call the fire department or 911.

Unlike smoke detectors, which are required by state law, CO detectors are not legally required. But that doesn't mean that you cannot persuade your landlord to install one. Detectors that are connected to the interior wiring of the house and backed up with emergency batteries are best. In a letter to your landlord, emphasize your concerns and the relative ease with which the landlord could put your mind at rest. A sample letter is set out below.

Responsibility for Carbon Monoxide

Most CO hazards are caused by a malfunctioning appliance or a clogged vent, flue, or chimney. It follows that the responsibility for preventing a CO buildup depends on who is responsible for the upkeep of the appliance.

Appliances. Appliances that are part of the rental, especially built-in units, are typically the responsibility of the landlord, although you are responsible for intentional or unreasonably careless damage. For example, if the pilot light on the gas stove that came with the rental is improperly calibrated and emits high amounts of CO, the landlord is responsible for fixing it. On the other hand, if you bring in a portable oil space heater that malfunctions, that is your responsibility.

Vents. Vents, chimneys, and flues are part of the structure, and the landlord typically handles their maintenance. In single-family houses, however, it is not unusual for landlord and tenant to agree to shift maintenance responsibility to the tenant.

If you have or suspect a CO problem that can be traced to the landlord's faulty maintenance, promptly request that the landlord fix it. If you are poisoned because your landlord failed to routinely maintain the appliances or to respond promptly to your repair request, the landlord will have a difficult time avoiding legal responsibility. (See Chapter 9.) To motivate your landlord to fix the CO-spewing gas dryer, it might be sufficient to subtly point out that failure to do so could cause a tragedy—and a lawsuit.

A sample letter bringing a CO problem to the landlord's attention is shown below. If you write such a letter, you would be smart to hand-deliver it to your landlord or manager, since the problem needs immediate attention. And in the meantime, don't use the appliance you suspect of causing the problem.

Carbon Monoxide Resources

The EPA website offers useful instructional material, including downloadable educational pamphlets, at www.epa.gov.iaq/co.html. Local natural gas utility companies often have consumer information brochures available to their customers. You can also contact the American Gas Association for consumer pamphlets on carbon monoxide. It can be reached by calling 202-824-7000 or visiting the association's website at www.aga.org.

Sample Letter Asking for CO Detector

34 Maple Avenue North, #3
Mountain Town, CA 00000
303-555-1234

February 14, 20xx

Cindy Cerene
1818 East Seventh Street
Mountain Town, CA 00000

Dear Ms. Cerene:

The kitchen in the apartment we rent from you has a gas stove and cook-top, which are about 15 years old, and there is a gas furnace in the hallway. These appliances appear to be working normally, but especially in the winter, when storm windows make the house airtight, I am concerned about the possible buildup of carbon monoxide. I would like to ask you to install a CO detector in the hallway near the bedrooms.

As you know, CO is a deadly gas that can kill within hours. We can't see it or smell it, and it could accumulate and poison us during the night. The only way to protect ourselves (besides your regular maintenance of these appliances) is with a detector. These devices are not very expensive, and can be easily installed. I would do it myself, except that our lease prevents me from undertaking alterations or improvements without your consent.

I hope that you'll give some thought to my request. Thanks very much for your consideration of this matter.

Yours truly,

Brian O'Rourke
Brian O'Rourke

Mold

Mold is the newest environmental hazard causing concern among renters. Across the country, tenants have won multimillion-dollar cases against landlords for significant health problems—such as rashes, chronic fatigue, nausea, cognitive losses, hemorrhaging, and asthma—allegedly caused by exposure to "toxic molds" in their building.

Mold is also among the most controversial of environmental hazards now in the news. There is considerable debate within the scientific and medical community about which molds, and what situations, pose serious health risks to people in their homes. Unlike lead, for example, where lead levels in blood can be accurately measured (and their effects scientifically predicted), mold is elusive. There is no debate, however, among some tenants who have suffered the consequences of living amidst (and inhaling) mold spores.

Where Mold Is Found

Mold comes in various colors and shapes. The villains—with names like stachybotrys, penicillium, aspergilus, paecilomyces, and fusarium—are black, white, green, or gray. Some are powdery, others shiny. Some molds look and smell disgusting; others are barely seen—hidden between walls, under floors and ceilings, or in less accessible spots such as basements and attics.

Mold often grows on water-soaked materials, such as wall paneling, paint, fabric, ceiling tiles, newspapers, or cardboard boxes. However, all that's really needed is an organic food source, water, and time. Throw in a little warmth and the organism will grow very quickly, sometimes spreading within 24 hours.

Humidity sets up prime growing conditions for mold. Buildings in naturally humid climates have experienced more mold problems than residences in drier climates. But mold can grow irrespective of the natural climate, as long as moisture is present. Here's how:

- Floods, leaking pipes, windows, or roofs may introduce moisture that will lead to mold growth in any structure—in fact, these are the leading causes of mold.
- Tightly sealed buildings (common with new construction) may trap mold-producing moisture inside.
- Overcrowding, poor ventilation, numerous over-watered houseplants, and poor housekeeping may also contribute to the spread of mold.

Unsightly as it may be, not all mold is harmful to your health—for example, the mold that grows on shower tiles is not dangerous. It takes an expert to know whether a particular mold is harmful or just annoying. Your first response to discovering mold shouldn't be to demand that the landlord call in the folks with the white suits and ventilators. Most of the time, proper cleanup and maintenance will remove mold. Better yet, focus on early detection and prevention of mold, as discussed below.

Laws on Mold Affecting Landlords

Unlike other environmental hazards such as lead, landlord responsibilities regarding mold have not been clearly spelled out in building codes, ordinances, statutes, and regulations. The main reason for the lack of standards is that the problem has only recently been acknowledged. California has been at the leading edge in trying to get a handle on the problem, as explained below.

Federal Law

No federal law sets permissible exposure limits or building tolerance standards for mold. As this book went to press, the House was considering The United States Toxic Mold Safety and Protection Act (HR 1269). This law would mandate comprehensive research into mold growth, create programs to educate the public about the dangers of toxic mold, and provide assistance to victims. In addition, the Act will generate guidelines

for preventing indoor mold growth, establish standards for removing mold when it does grow, provide grants for mold removal in public buildings, authorize tax credits for inspection and/or remediation of mold hazards, and create a national insurance program to protect homeowners from catastrophic losses. (You can follow the bill's progress online. Go to www.thomas.loc.gov and search for HR 1269.)

State Law

California is the first state to take steps toward establishing permissible mold standards. The Toxic Mold Protection Act of 2001 authorizes the state's Department of Health Services (DHS) to adopt, if feasible, permissible exposure levels (PELs) for indoor mold for sensitive populations, such as children and people with compromised immune systems or respiratory problems. If this is not feasible, the DHS may develop guidelines for determining when the presence of mold is a health threat. In addition, the California DHS will develop identification and remediation standards, which will guide contractors, owners, and landlords in how to inspect for mold and safely remove it. California's new law also requires landlords to disclose to current and prospective tenants the presence of any known or suspected mold. (H&S § 26100 and following.) (See the DHS website, given below in "Mold Resources.")

Local Law

San Francisco has added mold to its list of nuisances, thereby allowing tenants to sue landlords under private and public nuisance laws if they fail to clean up serious outbreaks (San Francisco Health Code § 581).

Landlord Liability for Tenant Exposure to Mold

With little law on the specific subject of mold, you'll have to rely on your landlord's general responsibility to maintain and repair rental property (the subject of Chapter 6) for guidance. The landlord's legal duty to provide and maintain habitable premises naturally extends to fixing leaking pipes, windows, and roofs—the causes of most mold. If the landlord doesn't take care of leaks and mold grows as a result, you may be able to hold the landlord responsible if you can convince a judge or jury that the mold has caused a health problem. Your position, legally, is really no different from what happens when the landlord fails to deal with any health or safety hazard on the property. For example, if the owner knows about (but fails to fix) a loose step, the owner will foot the bill if someone is injured as a result of tripping on the step.

The picture changes when mold grows as the result of your own behavior, such as keeping the apartment tightly shut, creating high humidity, and failing to maintain necessary cleanliness. Just as you don't want the landlord to police your lifestyle, you don't want him poking his head in to examine your housekeeping habits (indeed, privacy statutes prevent landlords from unannounced inspections, as explained in Chapter 15). When a tenant's own negligence is the sole cause of injury, the landlord is not liable.

Prevention—The Best Way to Avoid Mold Problems

A smart landlord's efforts should be directed squarely at preventing the conditions that lead to the growth of mold—and you should be the landlord's partner in this effort. This approach requires maintaining the structural integrity of the property (the roof, plumbing, and windows), which is the landlord's job. You, in turn, need to follow some practical steps and promptly report problems that need the landlord's attention.

The following steps are especially important if you live in a humid environment or have spotted mold problems in the past:

- **Check over the premises and note any mold problems; ask the landlord to fix them before you move in.** Fill out the Landlord-Tenant

Checklist form in the appendix and follow the advice on inspecting rental property at the start of a tenancy.

- **Understand the risks of poor housekeeping practices and recognize the factors that contribute to the growth of mold.** In particular, be sure you know how to:
  - ventilate the rental unit
  - avoid creating areas of standing water—for example, by emptying saucers under houseplants, and
  - clean vulnerable areas, such as bathrooms, with cleaning solutions that will discourage the growth of mold.

The EPA website, in "Mold Resources," below, includes lots of practical tips for discouraging the appearance of mold in residential settings.

- **Immediately report specific signs of mold, or conditions that may lead to mold, such as plumbing leaks and weatherproofing problems.**
- **Ask for all repairs and maintenance needed to clean up or reduce mold—for example:**
  - Request exhaust fans in rooms with high humidity (bathrooms, kitchens, and service porches), especially if window ventilation is poor in these areas.
  - Ask for dehumidifiers in chronically damp climates.
  - Reduce the amount of window condensation by using storm windows, if they're available.

These preventive steps will do more than decrease the chances that mold will begin to grow. If you have asked for them in writing and included the underlying reason for the request, you'll have good evidence to show a judge if a landlord refuses to step forward and your possessions are damaged or you are made ill by the persistence of the problem.

EXAMPLE: The closet in Jay's bedroom begins to sprout mold along the walls and ceiling. Jay asks his landlord, Sam, to address the problem (Jay suspects that the roof is leaking).

Sam refuses, and Jay begins to feel sick; his clothes and shoes are also ruined by the mold. When Jay sues Sam for the value of his ruined possessions, he shows the judge the written requests for repairs that Sam ignored. After showing the judge photos and an impressively moldy pair of shoes, Jay wins his case. He consults an attorney before pursuing a lawsuit based on his physical reactions to the mold.

How to Clean Up Mold

Although reports of mold sightings are alarming, the fact is that most mold is relatively harmless and easily dealt with. Most of the time, a weak bleach solution (one cup of bleach per gallon of water—do not use undiluted bleach) will remove mold from nonporous materials. You should follow these commonsense steps to clean up mold if the job is small. Use gloves and avoid exposing eyes and lungs to airborne mold dust (if you disturb mold and cause it to enter the air, use masks). Allow for frequent work breaks in areas with plenty of fresh air.

- Clean or remove all infested areas, such as a bathroom or closet wall. Begin work on a small patch and watch to see if you develop adverse health reactions, such as nausea or headaches. If so, stop and contact the landlord, who will need to call in the professionals.
- Don't try removing mold from fabrics such as towels, linens, drapes, carpets, and clothing—you'll have to dispose of these items.
- Contain the work space by using plastic sheeting and enclosing debris in plastic bags.

For more information, check out the sites noted in "Mold Resources," below.

CAUTION
People with respiratory problems, fragile health, or compromised immune systems should not participate in clean-up activities. If you have health concerns, ask for cleanup assistance. You may want to gently remind your landlord that it's a lot cheaper than responding to a lawsuit.

Testing for Toxicity

If you discover mold on the property, should you test it to determine the nature of the mold and its harmfulness? Most of the time, no. You and the landlord are much better off directing your efforts to speedy cleanup and replacement of damaged areas. Knowing the type of mold present and whether it produces toxins will not, in most cases, affect the appropriate method of cleanup.

Properly testing for mold is also extremely costly. Unlike detecting lead paint by using a swab kit, you cannot perform a reliable mold test yourself. (Over-the-counter kits, which cost around $30, provide questionable results.) A professional's basic investigation for a single-family home can cost $1,000 or more. And to further complicate matters, there are relatively few competent professionals in this new field. Unlike lead and asbestos inspectors, who must meet state requirements for training and competence, there are no state or federal certification programs for mold busters.

This said, it will be necessary to call in the testers if you contemplate suing the landlord. If you're suing for significant health impairment, you'll need a lawyer. In that event, the lawyer will test the mold as part of the "discovery" phase of the lawsuit—that period of time when each side gets to ask for and examine the other side's facts.

Insurance Coverage for Mold Damage

If your possessions have been ruined by mold and must be replaced, contact your renter's insurance agent immediately. Your renter's insurance may cover the cost of replacement. Do not expect the policy to cover the costs of medical bills, however—you'll need to turn to your own health insurance for that (or, you can sue the landlord).

Bedbugs

Bedbugs are wingless insects that are about one-quarter inch in length, oval but flattened from top to bottom. They're nearly white (after molting) and range to tan or deep brown or burnt orange (after they've sipped some blood, a dark red mass appears within the insect's body). They seek crevices and dark cracks, commonly hiding during the day and finding their hosts at night. Bedbugs nest in mattresses, bed frames, and adjacent furniture, though they can also infest an entire room or apartment. They easily spread from apartment to apartment via cracks in the walls, heating systems, and other openings.

Relatively scarce during the latter part of the 20th century, bedbug populations have resurged recently in Europe, North America, and Australia, possibly a result of the banning of effective but toxic pesticides such as DDT. Bedbugs do not carry disease-causing germs (perhaps their one saving feature). Their bites resemble those of a flea or mosquito. Bedbugs are expert stowaways, crawling into luggage, clothing, pillows, boxes, and furniture as these items are moved from an infested home or hotel to another location. Secondhand furniture is a common source of infestation.

Expert Help From Harvard

The Harvard School of Public Health has published the definitive guide to identifying and dealing with bedbugs. See their website, www.hsph.harvard.edu/bedbugs, for pictures, advice on eradication, and prevention. For even more detailed information, check out www.techletter.com, maintained by a pest management consulting firm (read their articles or order the comprehensive "Bed Bug Handbook: The Complete Guide to Bed Bugs and Their Control").

How to Deal With an Infestation

You'll learn that bedbugs have infested your home when you experience widespread, annoying bites that appear during the night. To minimize the outbreak and attempt to stop the spread of the pests to other rental units, your landlord must take the following steps immediately. You, too, must cooperate by cleaning and decluttering. If your landlord refuses to effectively deal with the infestation, you may have grounds to move out (because the rental has become uninhabitable). Understand that, unlike some other pest problems, dealing with bedbugs requires building-wide attention, which means that you must have your landlord's active involvement. Moreover, hiring an experienced exterminator is the only way to deal with a bedbug infestation. A can of Raid is not going to do the job.

Confirm the Infestation

First, you and the landlord must make sure that you're in fact dealing with bedbugs and not some other pest, such as fleas. Because several kinds of insects resemble bedbugs, you'll need to capture a critter or two and study them (see the advice from Harvard, mentioned above, on how to corral bedbugs). Go online to the sites mentioned above for more pictures of bedbugs than you ever wanted to see, and compare your samples. If it looks like a bedbug, call an experienced pest control operator, pronto. If you're not sure, submit your catch to a competent entomologist (insect specialist) for evaluation.

Map the Infestation, Using a Competent Exterminator

In a multiunit building, bedbugs can travel from one unit to another, leading to the nightmare of an entirely infested building. But chances are that one unit is the original source (and it will have the highest concentrations of bedbugs).

What Kills Bedbugs?

Although bedbugs are hard to kill using today's approved materials, exterminators have three ways to go after bedbugs:

- Insecticidal dusts, such as finely ground glass or silica, will scrape off the insects' waxy exterior and dry them out.
- Contact insecticides (such as chlorphenyl, available only to licensed pest control operators) kill the bugs when they come into contact with it.
- Insect growth regulators (IGR) interfere with the bugs' development and reproduction, and though quite effective, this takes a long time.

Pest control operators often use IGR in combination with other treatments. Most controllers will recommend multiple treatments, over a period of weeks, interspersed with near-fanatical vacuuming (to capture dead and weakened bugs). Anecdotal reports claim that even with repeated applications of pesticides, it's not possible to fully eradicate heavy infestations. Honest exterminators will not certify that a building is bedbug-free.

A competent exterminator can measure the concentration of bugs in the complaining tenant's unit, and also inspect and measure all adjoining units (on both sides and above and below the infested unit). Your landlord should give all tenants proper notice of the exterminator's inspection and explain what's involved (expect a competent exterminator to look closely into drawers, closets, and shelves). By "boxing" or "mapping" the source, you'll learn where the bedbug problem originated and whether and how far the problem has spread (this tells the landlord whether to treat adjoining units). Mapping the infestation (particularly if the exterminator does it more than once, over a period of time) may also help determine when a particular

unit became infested, which can help apportion financial responsibility for the extermination (see "Who Pays," below).

Declutter, Move Out, Exterminate, Vacuum—And Do It Again

Bedbugs thrive in clutter, which simply gives them more hiding places. Before you can effectively deal with the bugs, tenants in infested units must first remove clutter and neaten up (what to do with possibly infested items is covered below). You must remove all items from closets, shelves, and drawers; and wash all bedding and clothing (putting washed items in sealed plastic bags). You need to move out during treatment, and return when the exterminator gives the all clear. Most of the time, tenants can return the same day.

Bag the Bed

Bedbugs will always be found in an infested room's bed. The only way to rid a mattress of bedbugs is to enclose it in a bag that will prevent bugs from chewing their way out (they will eventually die inside). Use a bag guaranteed to trap bedbugs (some bags will simply deter allergens). See the articles from www.techletter.com, above, for more information on bed bags.

Upon return, you must thoroughly vacuum. Experienced exterminators will recommend a second and even a third treatment, with exhaustive cleaning and clutter-removing in between.

Infested items that can't be treated must be destroyed. Don't simply remove infested items and bring them back! Use extreme care when removing infested belongings and furniture. Bag them in plastic before carting them away—otherwise, you may inadvertently distribute the bugs to the rest of the building.

Exterminations and Relocation Costs: Who Pays?

In keeping with their obligation to provide fit and habitable housing, landlords must pay to exterminate pests that tenants have not introduced. Eradicating infestations caused by the tenant, however, can rightly be put on the tenant's tab. But determining who introduced the bedbugs is often very difficult.

Bedbugs in Multifamily Buildings

In a multiunit building, if the landlord approaches a bedbug problem by "boxing" the building as explained above, it may be able to identify the most infested rental unit. But identifying the source (or most infested) unit is not the same as proving that these tenants caused the problem. For example, suppose management traces the infestation to Unit 2, whose occupant moved into the building a few weeks ago. Serial mapping may show that adjoining Units 1 and 3 became infested after Unit 2 did, thereby suggesting that tenants in Units 1 and 3 were not responsible for their infestations. Suppose the tenant in the source unit (Unit 2) argues that the former occupants introduced the bedbug eggs that conveniently hatched after their departure. How will a landlord disprove this? Perhaps the landlord will discover that the new tenant came from a building that was also infested, but lacking this, the owner will have a hard time laying responsibility on the new resident. And even if the landlord did a thorough inspection of the unit before rerenting, there's no guarantee that they didn't miss some miniscule eggs. In short, because of the practical difficulty of identifying the tenant who introduced the bugs, the landlord often ends up footing the bill for extermination and relocation costs.

If mapping identifies a source unit that's occupied by a long-term resident, it will be similarly difficult to develop the facts needed to prove that this tenant introduced the bugs. How will the landlord learn about its tenants' habits, purchases, and travels, short of a full-blown lawsuit? And even if management

discovers, for example, that these tenants bought a secondhand couch recently, how will they prove it contained bedbugs? Or that bugs came home with them following their recent stay in a hotel, or travel abroad? The bottom line is that landlords usually end up footing the bill for cleaning up bedbugs in multiunit buildings.

Proper Cleaning and Housekeeping: Just Do Its

As you know from reading about your right to privacy, landlords must maintain a delicate balance between insisting that tenants take proper care of their property, and respecting their privacy. Landlords can require that rental units be kept in a sanitary condition, but they can't inspect every week to make sure their tenants' housekeeping efforts are adequate.

When it comes to effectively eliminating bedbugs, however, extreme housekeeping is needed. Most tenants are so grateful that their landlord is taking steps to deal with the bugs that they cooperate voluntarily. This is not the time to balk at inspections and regular treatments. Failure to cooperate will not only defeat the eradication efforts, it will destroy any chance you might have at compensation.

Bedbugs in Single-Family Rentals

Tenants of single-family rentals face a simpler picture when it comes to determining who's responsible for an infestation, because there's no issue of boxing the infestation and determining the source. If you are a long-term tenant who reports a problem, chances are it's a result of your activities; but tenants who have just moved in may argue that the former residents introduced the eggs.

Ruined Belongings: Who Pays?

In extreme cases, bedbugs infest every nook and cranny of a rental and its contents—books, clothes, furniture, appliances. One New York landlord reported getting a phone call from his tenant who discovered bedbugs and moved out with only the clothes on his back, leaving everything—everything—behind. This tenant sued the owner for the replacement cost of his belongings, claiming that the landlord's ineffective eradication methods left him no choice. Who pays?

Should this claim get before a judge, the answer would probably depend on the judge's view of the reasonableness of the landlord's response and the tenant's reaction. The more a landlord can show that it took immediate and effective steps to eliminate the problem, the better it would fare. As for the tenant's response, failure to cooperate with proper eradication plans will make it impossible to sue the landlord for the value of ruined belongings, even when the tenant was an innocent victim of another tenant's introduction of the pests.

Will Insurance Step Up for Bedbugs?

If you're facing a bedbug problem, you'll want to know whether your landlord's insurance policy or your own renter's policy will help you with the cost of replacing ruined belongings and related expenses. Here's the scoop:

Tenants' claims against the landlord's policy for lost or damaged belongings, medical expenses, and related moving and living expenses. Your landlord's commercial general liability policy will probably cover your claims here, up to the limits of the policy. You'll need to be able to show, however, that the cause of the problem was someone other than you.

Tenants' claims against their renters' insurance policies. If you have renters' insurance, you may get some help here. If you are at fault (you introduced the bugs), the liability portion of your policy should cover you, in the same way that it will cover you when you do other negligent things, such as failing to warn a guest about a wet floor, causing a slip and injury. If another tenant caused the infestation, you can still make a claim on your policy (your carrier may turn around and sue the responsible tenant, but that's their problem, not yours).

Breaking a Lease for a Bedbug Infested Rental

Most landlords will not tell prospective tenants about a past bedbug problem. Knowing that a bedbug can remain alive and dormant for over a year, and that eradication attempts are often not 100% effective, many prospects will never consider living in a unit that has experienced a bedbug problem, even when the landlord has done everything possible to deal with the bugs. Some landlords believe that disclosing a rental's bedbug past will make it unrentable, period.

Although disclosure is surely bad marketing, and no statute or court decision directs landlords to reveal a rental's bedbug history (unlike the situation with lead-based paint hazards, which they must disclose if they know them to be present), that's not the end of the matter. First, understand that if a prospect questions the landlord directly about a bedbug problem, especially if he makes it clear that this issue is of critical importance to him, the landlord must answer truthfully or risk the consequences:

Breaking the lease. A tenant who learns after the fact that the landlord hasn't answered truthfully will have legal grounds for breaking the lease and leaving without responsibility for future rent.

Increased chances of damages. In the event that the bug problem reappears and you sue over lost or damaged possessions, costs of moving and increased rent, and the psychological consequences of having lived with the bugs, your chances of recovering will be enhanced by the landlord's lack of candor. A competent lawyer will argue that the landlord's failure to disclose a potentially dangerous situation set the tenant up for misery that could have been avoided had the answers been truthful.

Now, suppose you don't question the landlord about a rental's bedbug history, the landlord remains silent, and a problem reappears. Will you have a strong case for breaking the lease without responsibility for future rent, or using the landlord's silence as a way to increase your chances of collecting damages? It's impossible to answer this in the abstract—like many legal questions, the answer will depend on the facts, such as how aggressively and thoroughly the landlord attempted to rid the property of bugs.

Finally, consider the bedbug problem that arises for the first time on this property, during your lease term. If the landlord's efforts to eradicate it are not successful, you will have a good case for arguing that the rental has become uninhabitable, thus giving you grounds to break the lease without future liability for rent (see Chapter 6 for a discussion of habitability).

Electromagnetic Fields

Electromagnetic fields (EMFs) are another one of the household "environmental hazards" that concern tenants.

Power lines, electrical wiring, and appliances emit low-level electric and magnetic fields. The intensity of both fields are thousands of times lower than the natural fields generated by the electrical activity of the human heart, brain, and muscles. The farther away you are from the source of these fields, the weaker their force.

The controversy surrounding EMFs concerns whether exposure to them increases a person's chances of getting certain cancers—specifically, childhood leukemia. Although some early research raised the possibility of a link, recent studies have discounted it. For example, a 1999 review by the U.S. National Institutes of Health concluded that the scientific evidence suggesting that EMF exposures pose any health risk was weak. The same conclusion was reached in 2001 by the U.K. National Radiation Protection Board. Interestingly, the scientific inquiry on the effects of EMFs has now shifted to the effects of cell phone reception and use. You probably have nothing to worry about regarding EMF exposure even if your rental sits under or near a set of power lines.

Since the landlord cannot insist that the power companies move their transmitters or block the emissions, the landlord is not responsible for EMFs or their effect—if any—on you. If you're worried, your only practical option is to move. If you have a month-to-month rental agreement or the lease is up, you can easily move on without legal repercussions. But what if you decide midlease that the EMFs are intolerable? Legally, you would be justified in breaking a lease or rental agreement only if the property presents a significant threat to your health or safety. (Breaking a lease when the property is unfit is explained at length in Chapter 6.) Given the professional debate regarding the danger from EMFs, it is unclear whether a court would decide that their presence makes the property unlivable.

The National Institute of Environmental Health Sciences has useful resources on EMFs. To find these, simply do a search on their website at www.niehs.nih.gov.

Crime on the Premises

Your landlord has some degree of legal responsibility to provide secure housing. This means the landlord must take reasonable steps to:

- protect tenants from would-be assailants, thieves, and other criminals
- protect tenants from the criminal acts of fellow tenants
- warn tenants about dangerous situations they are aware of but cannot eliminate, and
- protect the neighborhood from their tenants' illegal and noxious activities, such as drug dealing.

When landlords don't live up to this responsibility, they may be liable for any injuries or losses that befall you as a result. This chapter explores the security measures that you can legally expect from your landlord—and how to insist on them if your landlord doesn't do enough to safeguard tenants.

The Landlord's Basic Duty to Keep You Safe

State law requires landlords to take reasonable precautions to protect tenants from foreseeable harm. You can't expect your landlord to eliminate crime in your city or to provide an army of armed security. On the other hand, the landlord can't just turn over the keys, trusting to the local constable and fate to assure your safety.

State Laws

State and local building and housing codes are rich with specific rules designed to protect tenants. State law requires deadbolt locks on main exterior doors (except for sliding doors), common area doors, and gates and certain windows. (CC § 1941.3.) The law requires:

- deadbolt lock that is at least 13/16 inch long for each main entry door. A thumb-turn lock in place on July 1, 1998, will satisfy the requirement, but a 13/16th of an inch deadbolt must be installed when the landlord

repairs or replaces the lock. If there are other kinds of locking mechanisms used instead of a dead bolt, they must be inspected and approved by a state or local agency.

- Locks that comply with state or local fire and safety codes in existing doors or gates that connect common areas (such as lobbies, patios, and walkways) to rental units or to areas beyond the property (such as a main front door).
- Window locks on louvered and casement windows. Prefabricated windows with their own opening and locking mechanisms are exempt, as are those that are more than 12 feet above the ground. However, a window that is over 12 feet from the ground but less than six feet from a roof or any other platform must have a lock.

Local Ordinances

Many counties and cities have adopted housing codes designed to minimize the chances of a criminal incident on residential rental property—for example, by requiring peepholes. If your landlord does not comply with specific equipment requirements, you can complain to the agency in charge of enforcing the codes, often a local building or housing authority. (See below.)

If you are injured when a criminal takes advantage of your landlord's violation of a safety law—for example, an intruder enters your apartment building by way of a lock that's been broken for weeks—the landlord may be liable for your injuries.

RESOURCE

To get a copy of your local housing code or ordinance, call your city manager's or mayor's office, or look it up at your local public library. You may be able to get information from a local housing agency or local tenants' association. Many counties and cities have posted their ordinances online. Go to www.statelocalgov. net/state-ca.htm and search for your county or city.

The Landlord's General Responsibility

In addition to complying with local and state laws that require basic security measures, landlords have a general common law duty to act reasonably under the circumstances—or, expressed in legal jargon, to "act with due care." (See Chapter 10 on your landlord's duty to keep you safe from noncriminal harm.) For example, common areas must be kept clean and safe, so that they do not create a risk of accidents. When it comes to security, too, California judges have ruled that landlords must take reasonable precautions to protect tenants from foreseeable criminal assaults and property crimes.

The meaning of "reasonable precautions" depends on the situation. In general, if there have been prior incidents of crime on the landlord's property, and particularly if the landlord's lapse in security could have been remedied relatively easily, the chances that the landlord will be responsible for your injuries go way up. If you have been the victim of a crime on the premises—or are afraid you will be, sooner or later—ask yourself six questions to help you determine your landlord's responsibility.

Did your landlord control the area where the crime occurred?

Your landlord isn't expected to police the entire world. For example, a lobby, hallway, or other common area is an area of high landlord control. However, the landlord exerts no control over the sidewalk outside the front door.

How likely is it that a crime would occur?

Landlords are duty-bound to respond to the foreseeable, not the improbable. Have there been prior criminal incidents on the rental property? Elsewhere in the neighborhood? A landlord who knows that an offense is likely (because of a rash of break-ins or prior crime on the property) has a heightened legal responsibility to guard against future crime. But it's an open question whether a landlord's knowledge of crime in the neighborhood is enough to trigger more of a response.

How difficult or expensive would it have been for the landlord to reduce the risk of crime?

If relatively cheap or simple measures could significantly lower the risk of crime, it is likely that a court would find that your landlord had a duty to undertake them, especially in an area where criminal activity is high. For instance, would reasonably inexpensive new locks and better lighting discourage thieves? However, if the only solution to the problem is costly, such as structural remodeling or hiring a full-time doorman, a court would be less likely to impose these costs on your landlord unless the danger is very great.

How serious an injury was likely to result from the crime?

The consequences of a criminal incident (break-in, robbery, rape, or murder) may be horrific. There's really no debate over this.

Let's look at how these first four questions might be answered in three crime situations.

> **EXAMPLE 1:** Sam was accosted outside the entryway to his duplex by a stranger who was lurking in the tall, overgrown bushes in the front yard next to the sidewalk. There had been many previous assaults in the building. Both the bushes and the lack of exterior floodlights near the entryway prevented Sam from seeing his assailant until it was too late. If Sam filed a claim with the landlord's liability insurance company or sued the landlord, an adjuster or judge would probably conclude that the landlord was bound to take measures to protect Sam's safety, because:
>
> 1. The landlord controlled the common areas outside the duplex.
> 2. It was foreseeable that an assailant would lurk in the bushes and that another assault would occur.
> 3. The burden of trimming the shrubbery and installing lights was small in comparison to the risk of injury.

4. There are usually serious consequences from a criminal assault.

EXAMPLE 2: Caroline was assaulted in the house she rented by someone whom she let in, thinking that he was a gas company repairperson. There was a peephole in the front door, as required by local law, which she could have used had she asked to see proof of his identification. When Caroline sued her landlord, the judge tossed the case out. Her case collapsed on question 1: The landlord had no control over Caroline foolishly opening the door to someone whom she could have safely questioned (and excluded) from inside.

EXAMPLE 3: Max was assaulted and robbed in the open parking lot next to his apartment house when he came home from work late one night. The landlord knew that several muggings had recently been reported in the neighborhood, and he knew that his tenants parked there (he even mentioned the "free parking" when showing the rentals). Floodlights lighted the parking lot, but it was not fenced and gated. Here's how the four questions might be answered:

1. The landlord didn't own the lot, yet he knowingly benefited from his tenants' use of it. A judge might conclude that he had control, at least as far as warning tenants not to use the lot.
2. An assault seemed reasonably foreseeable in view of the recent nearby muggings.
3. However, the burden of totally eliminating the danger (fencing the lot) would have been very expensive.
4. The seriousness of the probable injury was great.

When Max sued, the case turned on whether the landlord's duty of care toward his tenants extended to their use of property that he did not own but benefited from. The judge has not announced his decision.

If, based on these first four questions, you think the landlord had a legal duty to deal with a condition on the premises that exposed you to the risk of crime, keep going. You have two more questions to answer.

Did your landlord fail to take reasonable steps to prevent a crime?

As ever, "reasonableness" is evaluated within the context of each situation. For example, returning to Sam (Example 1, above), the fact that the landlord let the bushes grow high and didn't replace the lights clearly was unreasonable. But suppose the landlord had cut the bushes back halfway and installed one light. Would that have been enough? It would be up to a jury to decide.

The greater the danger, the more a landlord must do. Past criminal activity on the premises increases your landlord's duty to keep you safe. "Reasonable precautions" in a crime-free neighborhood are not the same as those called for when three apartments in the landlord's building have been burglarized within the past month.

EXAMPLE: Allison rented an apartment in Manor Arms after being shown the building by the resident manager. Nothing was said about recent criminal activity in the building. A month after moving in, Allison was assaulted by a man who stopped her in the hallway, claiming to be a building inspector. Unbeknownst to Allison, similar assaults had occurred in the building in the past six months, and the manager even had a composite drawing of the suspect done by the local police. Allison's assailant was captured and proved to be the person responsible for the earlier crimes.

Allison sued the building owners after their insurance carrier refused to offer her a reasonable settlement. In her lawsuit, Allison claimed that the owners were negligent (unreasonably careless) in failing to warn her of the specific danger posed by the repeat assailant and in failing to beef up their security (such as hiring a guard service) after the first assault. The jury agreed and awarded Allison a large sum of money.

Landlords cannot eliminate all danger to tenants. In some situations, it may be enough to warn you. Just as caution tape and warning cones alert tenants to a freshly washed floor, you can expect your landlord to warn you about possible criminal problems by using:

- newsletters that remind tenants to be on the alert and use good sense
- letters that communicate specific information, such as a physical description of an assailant who has struck nearby, and
- signs that remind tenants to use the building's safety features, such as a notice posted in the lobby asking tenants to securely lock the front door behind them.

Did your landlord's failure to take reasonable steps to keep you safe contribute to the crime?

You must be able to connect the landlord's failure to provide reasonable security with the criminal incident. It is often very difficult for tenants to convince a jury that the landlord's failure to live up to his or her duty to keep you safe caused (or contributed to) the assault or burglary.

Think of it this way: If you fall because the rotten front step collapsed, you can usually trace the collapse directly to the landlord's failure to maintain the property. Now, suppose you can prove that the front door lock was broken (and had been for weeks) on the night you were assaulted. To hold the landlord liable, you have to be able to show that the assailant got into the building via that unlocked front door. This is where many lawsuits against landlords fall apart—the tenants can't connect the landlord's failure with the criminal's entry. And even if you can make a plausible case, you'll have to show that the landlord's lapse played a significant part in the ability of the criminal to commit the crime.

If a jury decides that the landlord didn't meet the duty to keep you safe, and that this failure facilitated the crime, it will typically split the responsibility for the crime between the landlord and the criminal. For example, jurors might decide that the landlord was 60% at fault and the criminal 40%. The landlord must compensate you accordingly. Not surprisingly, victims rarely collect the criminal's share.

In Sam's case (Example 1, above), he convinced the jury that, had the bushes been properly trimmed and the area well-lit, he could have seen the assailant or, more likely, the assailant wouldn't have chosen this exposed place to commit a crime. The jury found that the landlord was 70% at fault for Sam's injuries.

How Much Money You're Entitled To

To get financial compensation, you must show that you were harmed by the criminal incident. Tragically, this is often quite obvious, and the only issue that lawyers argue about is the worth, in dollars, of dreadful injuries. Compensation may also be awarded for mental anguish and continuing psychological effects of the encounter.

The Landlord's Promises

A landlord who promises specific security features—such as a doorman, security patrols, interior cameras, or an alarm system—must either provide them or be liable (at least partially) for any criminal act that they would have prevented. Remember, your lease is a contract, and if it includes a "24-hour security" promise or a commitment to have a doorman on duty at night, you have a right to expect it. Even a landlord's oral descriptions of security bind the landlord if they were a factor that led you to rent the unit. You can often also rely on statements about security in advertisements.

Your landlord won't be liable for failing to provide what was promised, however, unless this failure caused or contributed to the crime. Burned-out light bulbs in the parking lot won't mean anything if the burglar got in through an unlocked trap door on the roof.

EXAMPLE 1: The manager of Jeff's apartment building gave him a thorough tour of the "highly secure" building before Jeff decided to move in. Jeff was particularly impressed with the security locks on the gates of the high fences at the front and rear of the property. Confident that the interior of the property was accessible only to tenants and their guests, Jeff didn't hesitate to take his kitchen garbage to the dumpsters at the rear of the building late one evening. There he was accosted by an intruder who got in through a rear gate that had a broken lock. Jeff's landlord was held liable because she had failed to maintain the sophisticated, effective locks that had been promised.

EXAMPLE 2: The information packet given to Maria when she moved into her apartment stressed the need to keep careful track of door keys: "If you lose your keys, call the management and the lock will be changed immediately." When Maria lost her purse containing her keys, she immediately called the management company but couldn't reach them because it was after 5 p.m. and there was no after-hours emergency procedure. That evening, Maria was assaulted by someone who got into her apartment by using her lost key. Maria sued the owner and management company on the grounds that they had completely disregarded their own standard (to change the locks promptly) and so were partially responsible (along with the criminal) for the assailant's entry. The jury agreed and awarded Maria a large sum.

Problems With Other Tenants

Sometimes danger lurks within as well as beyond the gate. And your landlord has a duty to take reasonable steps to protect you if another resident on the property (including a roommate) threatens to harm you or your property.

Your landlord should respond to a troublesome tenant in essentially the same way he would respond to a loose stair or broken front-door lock. A landlord who knows about a problem (or should know about it) is expected to take reasonable steps to prevent foreseeable harm to other tenants. If the landlord fails to do that, and you are injured or robbed by another tenant, you may sue and recover damages.

When the Landlord Must Act

The landlord won't be held partially responsible for another tenant's illegal acts unless the problem tenant had done or threatened similar criminal conduct in the recent past, and the landlord knew about it. In short, you'll need to convince an insurance adjuster, judge, or jury that:

- it was reasonable to expect the landlord to know or discover the details of a tenant's past, and
- once known, the landlord could have taken steps to control or evict the troublemaker.

Unless there's a clear history of serious problems with the offending tenant, landlords usually win these cases. On the other hand, tenants sometimes win if they can show that the landlord knew about a resident's tendency towards violence and failed to take reasonable precautions to safeguard the other tenants.

EXAMPLE: Sally complained to her manager that Earl, who lived in another unit, had repeatedly verbally and physically assaulted her. The manager promised to take care of the situation, but did not terminate Earl's tenancy or even warn Earl that he would be evicted if he didn't stop; nor did he place security cameras at the place of the attacks. Earl assaulted Sally again. The judge decided that the management owed Sally a duty to protect her from Earl's foreseeable attack. The jury decided that management breached that duty and that it was the legal cause of Sally's injuries. (Based on *Madhani v. Cooper*, 106 Cal.App.4th 412 (2003).)

TIP

If you fear violence from another tenant, let your landlord know in writing. Not only does this underscore the seriousness of the situation, but it will be irrefutable proof that the landlord was on notice that problems were brewing. When more than one resident complains, the landlord will face more pressure to take action. If there is an altercation later, the landlord cannot plausibly claim ignorance.

CAUTION

Get your facts straight before making accusations. If you believe that certain individuals are breaking the law—or just causing trouble—be certain that you have the facts straight before telling others about them. Otherwise, you might find yourself on the wrong end of a libel or slander lawsuit.

What Your Landlord Must Do

A landlord who knows about the potential for danger from another tenant must do something about the problem tenant, such as warn other tenants or evict the troublemaker.

For example, suppose your neighbor bangs on the walls every time you practice the violin during the afternoon—and the pounding is getting louder. If you've tried to talk things out and been greeted with a raised fist, it's time to alert the landlord. You can reasonably expect the landlord to intervene and attempt to broker a solution—perhaps an adjustment of your practice schedule or some heavy-duty earplugs for the neighbor. If the

circumstances are more threatening—for example, your neighbor brandishes a gun—your landlord might be legally expected to call the police, post a security guard, and warn other tenants pending the speedy eviction of the dangerous tenant.

Intervention and eviction of the troublemaker are the usual ways that landlords meet their duty to take care that residents don't harm other residents. But the law doesn't require your landlord to have a crystal ball.

Termination Rights for Domestic Violence, Stalking, and Sexual Assault

Victims of domestic violence, stalking, or sexual assault have special termination rights. They may, within 60 days of such an incident, lawfully terminate a lease on 30 days' written notice. You must attach to your termination notice a copy of a court-issued restraining order against the perpetrator, a police-issued "emergency protective order," or a police report documenting the incident. (CC § 1946.7.) Only the victim and family members (but not nonfamily roommates) may avoid liability for the rent for the balance of the lease term. If the perpetrator of the incident remains behind, the landlord can evict him or her using a "nuisance" theory, starting with a 3-day notice to quit.

EXAMPLE: Abbot and his mother rented a duplex from Xavier, who knew that Abbot was emotionally disabled and took regular medication to control his behavior. Unknown to his mother or Xavier, Abbot began skipping his medication and eventually attacked Larry, the other tenant in the duplex, with a baseball bat. Xavier was not held liable, since it would have been illegal to refuse to rent to Abbot, a disabled person, under the Federal Fair Housing Amendments Act. Xavier did not know that Abbot had discontinued his medication, nor would it have been reasonable to expect Xavier to monitor Abbot's dosages.

If Xavier had known that Abbot was off his medication, however, he would have been duty-bound to speak to Abbot and his mother, and possibly warn the other resident.

Getting a Restraining Order

If another tenant seriously threatens you and won't leave you alone, and your landlord either won't evict the aggressor or the eviction is taking some time, consider obtaining a court restraining order.

A judge will sign these orders after you demonstrate that you really are in danger—for example, the aggressor has made repeated verbal threats to harm you or your family. The order directs the person to stay away from you. Its principal value is that the police will react faster and more firmly than they might otherwise. To obtain a restraining order, call your local courthouse for information.

If you obtain a restraining order, make a copy and give it to your landlord and to the manager, if any. Ask the landlord to alert other on-site personnel, such as security guards and maintenance personnel, of the existence and meaning of the order. A wise landlord will usually consider a restraining order as ample grounds for a swift termination and eviction. If the aggressor returns after he is evicted, request that the landlord order him off the property and call the police.

If you get no cooperation from your landlord and are still fearful, move. Your safety is worth far more than your right to live in a particular rental space. Your landlord may feel that you have broken the lease and may try to keep your security deposit to cover unpaid rent for the balance of the lease or rental agreement, but if you go to court to contest this, your chances of winning are good. You can argue that by failing to evict the troublemaker, the landlord breached the covenants of habitability and quiet enjoyment, which justified your moving out. (See Chapter 6 for information on the warranty of habitability.)

Illegal Activity on the Property and Nearby

Illegal activities on the premises create problems for law-abiding tenants and enormous financial risks and penalties for landlords. Law-abiding tenants move out, and may also sue if they are hurt or annoyed by drug dealers or other criminals. Landlords face trouble from other quarters—they can be fined for tolerating a legal nuisance, face criminal charges, and even lose their property.

Nice Properties Are Not Immune

If you live in a safe neighborhood, you may think that drug crime is largely a problem in seedy neighborhoods. Think again. Illegal drug use is spread widely throughout American society—the notion that it is a ghetto phenomenon is just plain wrong. A study by the Crime Control Institute, a nonprofit group in Washington, DC, found that drug dealers prefer smaller apartment complexes with some measure of security over large, unprotected housing units. The reason may surprise you: A drug dealer, like a law-abiding tenant, is interested in a safe, controlled environment. But a drug dealer who's smart enough to choose a nice property isn't always smart enough not to hassle the other tenants.

Government Lawsuits Against the Landlord

The legal meaning of "nuisance" bears only a little resemblance to its meaning in everyday life. A legal nuisance is a pervasive, continuing, and serious condition—like a pile of stinking garbage or a group of drug dealers—that threatens public health, safety, or morals.

California has vigorous nuisance abatement laws, which allow the government, and sometimes the neighbors, to sue to stop these sorts of problems. (CC §§ 3479, 3491.) Using public nuisance abatement laws against crime-tolerant landlords is increasingly common in large cities with pervasive drug problems. In extreme cases, where the conduct giving rise to the nuisance complaint is illegal (drug dealing or prostitution, for example), landlords themselves face civil fines or criminal punishment for tolerating the behavior.

Seizure of the Landlord's Property

It's rare, but the government sometimes seizes property because of the illegal activities of one or more tenants. A successful forfeiture proceeding is absolutely devastating from the landlord's point of view. The landlord loses not only the property, but also all the rent money that the landlord received from the drug-dealing tenants.

Few tenants want to live in government-run housing that starts off as a drug den. But a landlord who hears the word "forfeiture" will probably be highly motivated to get rid of the offending tenants. If your building is plagued by drug dealing or other illegal activities, start by involving your local district attorney.

Small Claims Lawsuits Filed by Neighbors

Overworked and understaffed police and health departments are often unable to make a real dent in problem-plagued neighborhoods.

Determined tenants and neighbors have stepped into the breach, bringing their own lawsuits seeking the elimination of the offensive behavior. Basically, tenants and neighbors sue a landlord for failing to take steps to clean up the property, and seek:

- monetary compensation for each of them for having put up with the situation. Each neighbor generally sues for the maximum allowed in state small claims court ($7,500), and the landlord often pays the maximum to *each* one, and
- an order from the judge directing the landlord to evict the troublemakers, install security, and repair the premises.

Small (But Sometimes Mighty) Claims Court

The private enforcement of public nuisance laws has been creatively and successfully pursued in small claims courts in California, where groups of affected neighbors have brought multiple lawsuits targeted at drug houses. This approach makes sense whenever a landlord is confronted by a large group of tenants all suing for the small claims maximum dollar amount, thus motivating the landlord to clean up the property.

In one case in Berkeley, California, after failing to get the police and city council to close down a crack house, neighbors sought damages stemming from the noxious activities associated with a crack house. Each of the 18 plaintiffs collected the maximum amount allowed in small claims court ($3,500 at the time), avoided the expense of hiring counsel, and sent the landlord a very clear and expensive message. The problem was solved within a few weeks.

Getting Results From the Landlord

Here are some suggestions on how to encourage your landlord to fulfill the responsibility to provide a safe place to live.

Evaluate the Situation

Before approaching your landlord with requests for improved security, collect hard evidence concerning the building's vulnerability to crime. The best way to evaluate the safety of your rented home is to conduct a security inspection of the rental property. Your goal is to answer two questions:

- If I (or a family member, roommate, or guest) were here alone at night, would I feel safe?
- If I were an assailant or a thief, how difficult would it be to get into the building or individual rental unit?

Involve Other Tenants

If you are a renter in a multiunit building, chances are that you aren't the only one concerned with safety. Working with other tenants on this issue (or others) has definite advantages:

- **Landlords respond to armies more readily than to individuals.** Once you get other tenants involved, your chances of getting the landlord to implement anticrime measures greatly increase. The consequences of rent withholding, complaints to the police, or small claims actions are much greater if done by a group than by a sole tenant. (These tactics are discussed below.)

- **Involving others reduces the chances of retaliation.** You are protected against landlord retaliation (such as terminations, rent hikes, and withdrawal of services) for exercising your rights to voice your opinions to the landlord, complain to enforcement agencies, and organize collectively. (See Chapter 14 for a thorough explanation of antiretaliation laws.) But if your landlord does retaliate, you'll have to fight it, which will involve time and effort. Acting as a group may make it less tempting for your landlord to retaliate—few landlords want instantly empty buildings or, worse, buildings full of angry residents.

- **You'll learn more about security problems.** For example, maybe the upstairs neighbor, who is home during the day, can tell you that the 24-hour security guard really lounges in the manager's office all afternoon, watching the soaps.

- **Involving others increases your safety.** Once you and your neighbors realize that you are all in the same boat, it is more likely that you will look out for each other.

Resources: Organize Against Drug Dealers

Contact your local police department to find out if they have a "Safe Streets Now!" program in place. This approach to public nuisances (targeting everything from drug dealing to abandoned, unhealthy buildings) empowers neighbors to deal with the problem without directly confronting dealers or even the property's owner. Here's how it works:

Under the auspices of the local police department, neighbors, police, city staff, and community-based organization representatives come together to put pressure on the landlord who is hosting the nuisance. The program consists of these steps:

- The neighbors identify the property creating the public nuisance.

- Neighbors take notes on what's happening, recording their findings in a log and gathering other evidence (such as photos).

- Neighbors phone in or otherwise relay each incidence to the police.

- Neighbors write a "demand letter" to the property owner, demanding that the owner rid the property of the problem and promising to take the owner to small claims court if the nuisance isn't corrected promptly. Each neighbor will sue for $7,500 in damages (the maximum allowed in small claims court). landlords quickly get the picture: Suddenly they're facing many thousands of dollars in damages. This usually gets their attention.

In the majority of cases, landlords voluntarily remove the problem tenants or loiterers from their properties after receiving the demand letter, and the cases never make it to court.

Safe Streets Now! programs are already set up in several California cities. If your town doesn't have one, there's no reason it can't start one—contact another city that has one for guidance (type "Safe Streets Now" into your Internet search engine and scan the results for California cities).

Analyze the Building

Start by circulating a letter to other residents, explaining your concerns and suggestions for improved security on the property, and solicit their comments. Call a meeting to discuss the results and plan your next moves.

You'll learn the most about your building's vulnerability if several tenants walk or drive around the rental property at different times of the day and night—you might see something at 11 p.m. that you wouldn't notice at 11 a.m. A reasonably safe and secure single-family home, duplex, or multiunit rental will have strong locks on windows and doors, good interior and exterior lighting, and other features that will hinder unwanted intrusions. To see how your rental unit, building, and grounds measure up, consult the list of Important Security Features, below.

You may also want to get a security evaluation and advice from your renter's insurance agent. Because insurance companies are potentially liable for large settlements or awards, they are concerned with reducing crime on rental property. So talk to your insurance company and, even more important, encourage your landlord to talk to hers about equipment and safety systems that can prevent break-ins and assaults.

Consider the Neighborhood

The extent of your vulnerability depends on not only the security systems in your building, but also the surrounding neighborhood. If there has been little or no crime in your area, you have less to worry about and less legal reason to expect your landlord to equip the property with extensive security devices. On the other hand, if crime is a problem where you live, gather information on local crime from people in the neighborhood and the police department. Then, armed with what you have learned, you are in a good position to suggest ways both your landlord and other tenants can keep the rental property safe.

Request Improvements

Once you and other tenants have gathered information about your vulnerability to crime and what can be done to reduce your risk, you'll be ready to take specific steps to make your lives safer.

It's quite likely that you know more about the security needs of the rental units and building (and landlords' legal responsibilities) than the owner, especially if the owner is an absentee landlord. To improve security in your rental, you may first have to educate your landlord about:

- **Statutory security requirements.** Since state and often local ordinances or laws require specific security devices, such as deadbolts, peepholes, or window locks, start by asking your landlord to comply with the law. Put your request in writing. (Of course, keep copies of all correspondence.) Attach a copy of the ordinance or statute to your request. If you get no response, submit a second request. Then, if there is still no compliance, consider your options, which include the right to install the locks using the repair and deduct or rent withholding remedies. (See "Protecting Yourself," below.)

- **Promised security measures that are missing or malfunctioning.** If the landlord has promised security beyond the basics dictated by law—such as an advertisement promising garage parking or security personnel—you have a legal right to expect that the landlord deliver; see above. Send a written reminder to the landlord and attach a copy of the advertisement or lease provision that backs up your request.

- **Security required by the surroundings and circumstances.** Your own assessment of the property and the neighborhood may lead you to conclude that the landlord is shirking his duty to protect tenants. But if you do not have a clear-cut ordinance or statute to point to, you will have to do some extra work motivating the landlord. Use the information you've gathered to convince the landlord that, given the area's crime problems, more effective security measures are required—and that if security isn't improved, the landlord could be legally liable for injuries that result.

Oral requests sometimes get results, but more often they are ignored. Putting security requests in writing and having them signed by as many tenants as possible is a far better way to get results. Even the most dim-witted landlord understands that if tenants have a written record of their complaints about personal safety issues—especially when the landlord has not kept promises to provide security systems—and nothing is done, the chances of a successful lawsuit go way up.

So write a letter even if you think it's hopeless, even if your landlord is notoriously stingy or impossibly stubborn. By creating a paper trail, you have provided the landlord with a considerably increased incentive to take action. Your letter should:

- remind the landlord that he or she has control of the problem
- set out the foreseeable consequence (an assault) of not dealing with the property's obvious lack of security
- propose that the solution is relatively easy, and
- suggest that the consequences—a burglary or assault—are serious.

A sample letter alerting the landlord to dangerous conditions is shown below.

Meet With the Landlord

If your written requests don't produce results, invite your landlord to meet with you (and other tenants, if possible) to discuss your concerns. You may want to involve a local mediation service, which has the advantage of giving you a skillful and neutral moderator. You'll be especially glad for the presence of the mediator if your landlord arrives with an attorney. If you or other tenants end up in court over your landlord's failure to keep the premises

---

Sample Letter Alerting the Landlord to Dangerous Conditions

789 Westmoreland Avenue, #5
Central City, CA 00000
555-123-4567

January 3, 20xx

Mr. Wesley Smith, Landlord
123 East Street
Central City, CA 00000

Dear Mr. Smith:

As tenants of the Westmoreland Avenue building, we are concerned that there is a dangerous condition on the property that deserves your prompt attention.

As you know, the large sliding doors on the bottom floor (in the lobby) are secured by turn locks that can be easily forced open. On occasion we have seen a dowel placed in the track to prevent the doors from being opened, but lately the dowels have often been missing. Several times, the doors have even been left open all night.

We are worried that an intruder will have an easy time of getting into the building. There have been several burglaries in the neighborhood within the past two months. The situation would be greatly helped if you could send a glass repairperson to replace the locks with much stronger ones. Needless to say, a burglary or assault is a worrisome prospect.

Thank you for your prompt consideration of this matter.

[signed by *as many tenants as possible*]

Important Security Features

- Exterior lighting directed at entrance ways and walkways that is activated by motion or a timer, and not dependent on the memory of managers or tenants to turn it on. Many security experts regard the absence or failure of exterior lights as the single most common failing that facilitates break-ins and crime.
- Good, strong interior lights in hallways, stairwells, doorways, and parking garages.
- Sturdy deadbolt door locks on individual rental units and solid window and patio door locks, as well as peepholes (with a wide-angle lens for viewing) at the front door of each unit (see above for the locks required by law). Lobby doors should have deadbolt locks. Solid metal window bars or grills over ground-floor windows are often a good idea in higher-crime neighborhoods, but landlords may not be able to install them due to restrictions of local fire codes. All grills or bars should have a release mechanism allowing the tenant to open them from inside (local codes frequently require these grills to open from the inside).
- Intercom and buzzer systems that allow you to control the opening of the front door from the safety of your apartment.
- Neat and compact landscaping that does not obscure entryways or afford easy hiding places adjacent to doorways or windows.
- In some areas, a 24-hour doorman is essential and may do more to reduce crime outside the building than anything else.
- Driveways, garages, and underground parking that are well-lit and secure from unauthorized entries. Fences and automatic gates may be a virtual necessity in some areas.
- Elevators that require a passkey for entry. If this won't solve the problem, you may even want to request the landlord to install closed circuit monitoring. Obviously this is expensive, since it requires someone to watch the monitor, but it may be worth suggesting if your building has fairly high rents or is in a particularly crime-prone area.

safe, the refusal to discuss the situation with you will hardly help the landlord's case. (Chapter 17 gives suggestions on finding and working with a mediator.)

Get Help From the Government

If gentle (or even concerted) persuasion fails to get desired security improvements, call in the reinforcements. Depending on what the exact problem is and where you live, contact either building or health inspectors or local law enforcement agencies, who have the power to order the landlord to comply with the law. For example, if the landlord refuses to oust drug-dealing tenants, contact the local district attorney (and ask about a Safe Streets Now! program—see "Resources: Organize Against Drug Dealers," above). This alone may result in the landlord taking the desired actions.

Withhold Rent

If your rented home becomes truly dangerous, it may be legally considered uninhabitable—which means that you might be justified in withholding rent. And if you're dealing with broken or missing locks, in violation of state law, withholding is definitely an option. (Chapter 6 explains rent withholding in detail.)

Because this is a relatively drastic step, we suggest you consider it carefully—if you withhold rent and trigger an eviction lawsuit for nonpayment of rent, you stand to lose your rental if you lose. Here are some guidelines that must be met by any claim that a unit is uninhabitable because of high crime danger.

- **Make sure the problem is truly serious now, not merely annoying or a potential problem.** For example, having to walk past dope dealers on your way through the front hall is unavoidable, frightening, and loaded with potential for violence. On the other hand, unverified stories regarding prostitution in your neighborhood or even in your building are less compelling.

- **Don't act until you've given the landlord notice of the problem and time to respond.** In general, as discussed in Chapter 6, you must tell the landlord about it and allow time to respond, either by fixing the problem or approaching the legal authorities (police or district attorney), who are better equipped to deal with it. For example, if drug dealers have moved in next door, you must alert the landlord and allow time to begin eviction procedures; if gangs have invaded your neighborhood, you must complain to the landlord and give the police time to act.

Break the Lease

If your rented home is legally considered uninhabitable, you might be justified in moving out, for the same reasons you may be able to withhold rent.

You may also be justified in breaking the lease and moving out if the promised security was an important factor in your decision to rent your place, and the landlord failed to follow through on that promise. This remedy is explained in Chapter 6 in connection with repairs or maintenance that have been promised but not delivered.

> **EXAMPLE:** Wendy, a flight attendant, rented her apartment in Safe Harbor after reading its advertisement in the local newspaper that promised "Security personnel on duty at all times." When she was shown around the property, Wendy told the manager that she often came home late at night. She was assured that there was a 24-hour guard service. However, after coming home several nights in the early morning hours and discovering that there were no security guards on duty, Wendy confronted the management and was told that financial constraints had made it necessary to cut back on the guards' hours. Wendy wrote the landlord a letter asking that the guard service be restored. When it wasn't, she promptly moved out.

Safe Harbor kept Wendy's entire security deposit (one month's rent), claiming that her departure violated the lease and that management had been unable to find a replacement tenant for four weeks. Wendy sued Safe Harbor for the return of her entire deposit, arguing that in fact it was Safe Harbor who had broken the lease by failing to provide security as promised. The judge decided that the promise of 24-hour security was an important part of Safe Harbor's obligations and that its failure to deliver constituted a breach of the lease, which excused Wendy from her obligation to stay and pay rent. And the judge ordered Safe Harbor to refund Wendy a portion of the rent she had already paid, on the grounds that she had paid for an apartment with a guard but had not received it.

You may be able to break a lease and move with little or no financial consequence. Your landlord will have a duty to make reasonable efforts to rerent your unit and apply the new rent to what you owe on the balance of your lease. (This duty is discussed in detail in Chapter 12.) If the rental market is tight and your rental is reasonably attractive and competitively priced, your landlord may have little excuse for not rerenting quickly. Of course, if the dangerous conditions that prompted your early departure are noticed by prospective tenants (who reject the rental for that reason), the landlord may have a hard time rerenting. Fortunately for you, the harder it is for the landlord to rerent, the stronger your case that the rental was unacceptably unsafe, justifying your breaking the lease. In short, you win either way.

Sue in Small Claims Court

Your most effective response to inadequate security or dangerous surroundings might be aggressive action in small claims court. Interestingly, small claims court can be an appropriate tool to deal both with simple problems like the installation of a deadbolt and complex ones like ridding the building of drug-dealing tenants.

If you're lucky, the difference between a secure apartment and an unsecured one might be the simple addition of a better set of outdoor lights, trimming some bushes, or replacing burned-out light bulbs in the garage or hall. If your repeated requests for action have fallen on closed ears, and local inspectors can't or won't come to your aid, what should you do?

Small claims court might be the answer. Simply perform the work yourself (preferably with other tenants) and then sue the landlord for the cost. This route may, however, put you at risk, especially if your lease or rental agreement says "no improvements or alterations without the landlord's consent." Your risk of eviction for violating a lease clause will probably be less if the job you do is required by local law, such as a code-required deadbolt, rather than a modification like trimming the bushes that you have concluded is required for your safety. In short, if it's something clearly required of the landlord, he'll have a hard time laying blame on you for doing his job, and your lease clause violation will appear almost necessary.

Protecting Yourself

Faced with an unsafe living situation, your only option may be to pursue self-help remedies such as installing your own security protections or moving out.

Use Good Judgment

If you live in a dangerous building or high-crime neighborhood, your first thought must be to watch out for yourself. Just as defensive driving techniques may do more to keep you safe than confronting dangerous drivers or equipping your car with every imaginable safety device, you'll want to rely primarily on your own good judgment and willingness to change your habits.

If you have identified vulnerable aspects of your building or rental unit, chances are that others have, too. If you were a burglar or mugger, how would you strike? Avoid dangerous situations—for example:

- Don't use an isolated parking lot late at night.
- Consider curtailing your evening's activities. No late-night movie is worth the risk of an assault.
- Use a fan for air circulation instead of opening easily accessible windows at night.

Install Your Own Security Protections

In some situations, you may be able to take matters into your own hands, at least as regards your own rented space. Although your lease may prohibit you from making alterations or repairs without the landlord's permission (see Chapter 8), you can use self-help methods of rent withholding and repair and deduct if you need to supply the door and window locks mandated by state law (CC § 1941.3). Be sure to follow the steps described in Chapter 8 for notifying the landlord first, and document your costs. And because your landlord has the right to enter in an emergency, you have to give the landlord keys to any locks you install.

You may be able to install effective security devices that do not require permanent installation and thus won't risk violating your landlord's ban on alterations. For example, consider using a motion-activated alarm that you hang from a door. Your local hardware store will have other items.

Consider Moving

Sad to say, often your most effective response to a dangerous rental situation is to move. Many tenants on a tight budget believe they can't afford any better alternatives. While understandable, this view is often wrong. Look around your area for places where low rents don't mean high crime. Although sometimes well-kept secrets, these neighborhoods often exist. Or consider the possibility of getting a roommate or sharing a house so you can afford to live in a better part of town.

If you have a month-to-month rental agreement, you can usually move out with 30 days' notice. Breaking a lease may be a little more difficult, unless you're moving out because your rental is uninhabitable or your landlord failed to follow through with promised security measures, as discussed in "Getting Results From the Landlord," above.

Breaking a Lease, Subleasing, and Other Leasing Problems

What Happens When the Lease Runs Out

Often a tenant wishes to stay in a dwelling after a lease term expires. If you are in this situation, read your lease carefully, as it may have a provision covering what happens at the end of the lease term. In the absence of a lease provision, state law provides that if a lease runs out and the landlord thereafter accepts rent, the tenant becomes a month-to-month tenant under the same terms outlined in the old lease. (CC § 1945.) All the terms of the original lease, with the exception of the period-of-occupancy clause, are still binding and become, in effect, an oral month-to-month agreement. This means that in the case of an expired one-year lease that becomes month to month, the landlord can terminate the tenancy with a 60-day notice, and the tenant can terminate with a 30-day notice. The rent can be increased after a 30- or 60-day notice, depending on how high the increase is.

Sometimes a lease will contain a provision calling for automatic renewal if the tenant stays beyond the end of the lease term. This would mean that if a tenant held over one day after a one-year lease expired, he would have renewed the lease for another year. This provision is legal only if the renewal or extension provision is printed in at least eight point boldface type, immediately above the place where the tenant signs the lease. If a renewal provision is not set forth in this way, the tenant may legally disregard it. (CC § 1945.5.)

Subleases and Assignments

A subtenant is a person to whom a tenant subleases all or part of the property. This can occur where the tenant moves out temporarily—for example, for a couple of months in the summer—and rents the entire dwelling to someone else, or where the tenant rents one or more rooms while continuing to live there. (See Chapter 2 for a discussion of adding a roommate.)

Typically, a subtenant does not have a separate agreement with the landlord. The subtenant's right of occupancy depends on:

- the continuing existence of the tenancy between the landlord and the tenant, and
- whatever implied, oral, or written rental agreement the subtenant has with the tenant, who functions as the subtenant's landlord.

But what about the tenant who has no intention of returning, such as a tenant with a year lease who stays six months and sublets to someone else for the remaining six months of the lease term? Technically, this is not a sublet, but an "assignment," under which the tenant has legally transferred all rights to the property to someone else. We distinguish the term "assignment" from "sublet" in part because lawyers often do, and to explain why many lease and rental agreement forms forbid both assignments and sublets without the owner's consent.

There is one important technical difference between an assignment and sublease: Where an assignment is involved, the new tenant (the "assignee") is responsible to the landlord for everything the original tenant was liable for—even without an agreement between that person and the landlord. (CC § 822.) (The previous occupant (assignor) remains liable to the landlord also, unless the landlord agrees otherwise in writing.) This is different from the situation in which a tenant sublets to a second tenant who is responsible to the first tenant, not the landlord.

Tenants normally face the need to sublease or assign their tenancies in the following situations:

- You have a lease or a rental agreement and want to leave for some set period of time and then return and get your home back (see "Subleasing and Returning Later," below).
- You have a lease and want to leave permanently before it ends (see "How to Break a Lease," below).
- You want to bring in a roommate (see Chapter 2).

Subleasing and Returning Later

Technically speaking, you are entitled to sublease only when you have a lease yourself in the first place. In addition, most leases and rental agreements require the landlord's consent in advance for subletting. If you sublet without it, the sublease is probably invalid, but your landlord can't unreasonably withhold consent if you do ask beforehand. (*Kendall v. Pestana*, 40 Cal.3d 488 (1986).)

If a tenant sublets on the sly when a lease or rental agreement prohibits it, the landlord can evict both the original tenant and the subtenant. In addition, you can't sublease what you don't have a right to. So if you have a month-to-month tenancy, you can sublet on that basis, but you can't give someone a one-year sublease. If you have a one-year lease, you can't sublease beyond that period—though in practice many landlords continue to accept monthly rent after a fixed-term lease expires. Legally, that converts the fixed-term tenancy to a month-to-month one.

Whenever you let anyone move into your place for a while, it is important to have a written agreement, incorporating your lease or rental agreement, which sets out all the terms of the arrangement. We include here an example of a possible sublease arrangement, with the warning that it will have to be modified to suit your individual circumstances. Also, your landlord may require your subtenant to sign a separate rental agreement, giving the new person all the rights and responsibilities of a tenant.

How to Break a Lease

If you want to move out before your lease expires, you may not have too much of a problem. In areas of California that are popular, the same shortage of housing that gives the landlord an advantage at the time of the original rental also makes it possible for a tenant to get out of a lease fairly easily.

Sample Sublease Agreement

Sublease Agreement

This is an agreement between Leon Hernandez of 1500 Acorn Street #4, Cloverdale, California, and Joan Ehrman, now residing at 77 Wheat Avenue, Berkeley, California.

1. In consideration of $300 per month payable on the first day of each month, Leon Hernandez agrees to sublease apartment #4 at 1500 Acorn Street, Cloverdale, California, to Joan Ehrman from August 1, 20xx to December 30, 20xx.

2. Leon Hernandez hereby acknowledges receipt of $1,200, which represents payment of the first and last months' rent and a $600 security deposit. The security deposit will be returned to Joan Ehrman on December 30, 20xx if the premises are completely clean and have suffered no damage.

3. A copy of the agreement between Smith Realty and Leon Hernandez is stapled to this agreement and is incorporated as if set out in full. Joan Ehrman specifically covenants and agrees to adhere to all the rules and regulations set out in Sections 1-10 of this lease.

Leon Hernandez   9/30/20xx
Leon Hernandez   Date

Joan Ehrman   9/30/xx
Joan Ehrman   Date

General Rules

When you sign a lease, you promise to pay rent for certain premises for a certain time. Simply moving out does not get you off the hook as far as paying for the whole lease term is concerned. You have made a contract and are legally bound to fulfill it. This means that you are obligated to pay rent for the full lease term, whether or not you continue to occupy the dwelling. (CC § 1951.2.) If you do not pay, your landlord can sue you, get a judgment, and try to collect the money by doing such things as attaching your wages.

But the law requires landlords to take all reasonable steps to keep losses to a minimum—a concept known as mitigation of damages. (CC § 1951.2.) This means that when a tenant leaves in the middle of the lease term, the landlord must take reasonable efforts to rent the premises to another tenant as soon as reasonably possible.

If the landlord rerents the property quickly and doesn't lose any rent, the former tenant doesn't owe the landlord anything. However, in areas where the market is soft, the tenant could end up paying for several months. The tenant could also end up paying for the difference between the old, high rent and the new, lower market rate rent.

> **EXAMPLE:** Susan Wong rented an apartment from Stephan Leness in January for a term of one year, at the monthly rent of $1,000. Everything went well until September, when Susan had to move to be closer to her invalid mother. Under the general rule, Susan is theoretically liable to Stephan for $3,000—the rent for October, November, and December. However, if Stephan mitigated these damages by taking out an ad and rerenting on October 15, Susan would owe much less. If the new tenant paid $500 for the last half of October and $1,000 in November and December, Stephan must credit the total $2,500 he got from the new tenant against Susan's $3,000 liability. This leaves Susan liable for only $500, plus Stephan's advertising costs of $20, for a total of $520.

To summarize, a fixed-term tenant who leaves before the end of the lease is responsible for:

- the remaining rent due under the lease, plus any reasonable advertising expenses incurred in finding a new tenant, minus
- any rent the landlord can collect from a new tenant between the time the original tenant leaves and the end of the lease term.

CAUTION

If your lease contains a liquidated damages clause—requiring you to pay the landlord a certain amount of money as damages for breaking the lease—a court probably won't make you pay it if the amount of liquidated damages far exceeds the amount the landlord actually lost. You will have to compensate the landlord only for his actual losses. (See "Liquidated Damages Provision" in Chapter 1 for more on liquidated damages clauses.)

CAUTION

Your lease may include a clause stating that the landlord will not unreasonably withhold consent to a proposed sublet or assignment, and that the landlord intends to use the "lock-in provision" provided by state law. If so, and you break the lease and move out without coming up with an acceptable substitute, the landlord can choose not to rerent and mitigate your damages. Instead, the landlord can simply secure the premises and sue you for the unpaid rent when the lease expires. (CC § 1951.4.)

Self-Protection When Breaking a Lease

Notify your landlord in writing as soon as you know that you are going to move out before the end of a lease term. The more notice you give the landlord, the better your chances are that he will find another tenant.

After sending the landlord your written notice, it is wise to stop by and have a talk. The landlord may have another tenant ready to move in and not be concerned by your moving out. In some cases, the landlord may demand an amount of money to compensate him for rerenting the place. If the amount is small, it may be easier to agree to pay rather than to become involved in a dispute. If your landlord has a deposit, you might even offer a part of it (or all of it) in full settlement of all possible damage claims arising from your leaving in the middle of the lease term. As noted above, since the landlord has a duty to try and rerent the place (mitigate damages), and since this is often reasonably easy to do, you should not agree to pay much in the way of damages. Get any agreement you make in writing. A sample agreement is shown below.

Sample Agreement

Agreement

This agreement is between Leon Hernandez of 1500 Acorn Street #4, Cloverdale, California, and Smith Realty Co., of 10 Jones Street, Cloverdale, California, and by its owner, B. R. Smith.

In consideration of the amount of $75, Smith Realty Co. hereby agrees to cancel the lease of Leon Hernandez on Apt. #4 at 1500 Acorn Street, Cloverdale, California, as of October 31, 20xx. The $75 payment is hereby acknowledged to be made this date by subtracting it from Leon Hernandez's $600 security deposit.

B. R. Smith	*9/30/20xx*
B. R. Smith	Date
Leon Hernandez	*9/30/xx*
Leon Hernandez	Date

If it is not possible to deal rationally with your landlord, or if you can't get a written release, you should take steps to protect yourself. Don't let your landlord scare you into paying a lot of money. Simply put an advertisement in your local paper to lease your dwelling at the same rent that you are paying. When people call, show them the place, but tell them that any lease arrangement must be worked out with your landlord. Also request that the potential tenants contact the landlord directly. To protect yourself, keep a list of all tenants who appear suitable and who express an interest in moving in. Include information on your list that shows that the potential tenants are responsible— for example, include something about their job or family. Write a letter to your landlord with a list

of the names, and keep a copy for your file. The landlord has a right to approve or disapprove of whomever you suggest as a tenant, but may not be unreasonable about it; landlords must keep their losses to a minimum (mitigate damages) as discussed above. Also, when you move out, be sure the unit is clean and ready to rent to the next tenant, so that your landlord has no basis to claim that it was not in rentable condition and that you are responsible for rent during the time it took to get it cleaned.

Sample Letter to Landlord Suggesting Potential Tenants

1500 Acorn Street #4
Cloverdale, California
October 1, 20xx

Smith Realty Co.
10 Jones Street
Cloverdale, California

As I told you on September 15, 20xx, I plan to move out of this apartment on October 31, 20xx. Because I wish to keep damages to a minimum, I am giving you the names, addresses, and phone numbers of four people who have expressed an interest in renting this apartment on or about November 1, 20xx at the same rent that I pay. I assume that you will find one of these potential tenants to be suitable, unless of course you have already arranged to rent the apartment.

(include list of names, addresses, and phone numbers)

Very truly yours,

Leon Hernandez
Leon Hernandez

Possible Legal Action

If you move out and break a lease, the landlord may keep your deposit or sue you for the lost rent and the expense of getting a new tenant. This is not likely if the landlord has gotten a new tenant to move in almost immediately after you've moved out, because in such a situation there would be little or no damages. However, occasionally it takes the landlord a little time or expense (for advertising) to get a new tenant. This is especially likely in a resort area (off season) or near a university in the summer. In this case, a landlord may pocket the deposit or sue in small claims or superior court.

If you are sued, you will receive legal documents setting out the landlord's claim. Read them carefully to see if the amount the landlord asks for is fair. As explained above, if you take the proper steps to protect yourself, the landlord should be entitled to little or nothing. In unusual situations, however, the landlord may be entitled to some recovery. For example, if a tenant with a year's lease at a $600 per month rental moved out in midyear and no new tenant could be found who would pay more than $575 per month, then the landlord would likely recover damages. In this case, the old tenant would be liable for the $25 a month difference between what he paid and what the new tenant paid, multiplied by the number of months left on the lease at the time he moved out. A tenant might also be liable for damages if it took the landlord some period of time, such as a month, to find a new tenant. In this case, the first tenant would be liable for the month's rent (if the landlord had made diligent efforts to find a new tenant).

Landlords often simply keep the entire deposit— it's a lot easier than going to court. In that event, you'll have to go to small claims court to sue to get it back. Use the same approach you'd adopt if the landlord had gone to court first.

If you are sued in small claims court for an amount that seems excessive, simply tell the judge your side of the case and bring with you any witnesses and written documentation that would help tell your story. If you are sued in superior court, you may want to see a lawyer, especially if there is a lot of money involved. (See Chapter 17.)

Belongings You Leave Behind

If you leave belongings on the premises when you move out, you must ask the landlord for them, in writing, within 18 days. Your request must describe the property and must give the landlord your mailing address. Within five days of receiving your request, the landlord may demand, in writing, that you pay reasonable costs for storage. You must pay the charges and pick up the property within 72 hours of receiving the landlord's demand.

If the landlord doesn't comply with your request, you can sue for your actual damages and, if the landlord acted in bad faith, for another $250 in damages. (CC § 1965.)

The landlord may notify you, in writing, that the property is still there. The notice should describe the property and tell you where the property can be claimed, how long you have to claim it, and that you may have to pay reasonable costs for storage. The landlord must give you at least 15 days (18 days, if the notice is mailed) to claim the property.

If the property is worth less than $300, the landlord is free to dispose of it. If it is worth more than that, the landlord must sell it at a public sale, subtract costs of sale and storage, and turn the rest over to the county. You have a year to claim the net profit from the sale. (CC §§ 1983, 1988.)

Security Deposits and Last Month's Rent

Almost all landlords require their tenants to put up some money before moving in. This payment might be called a "security deposit," "cleaning fee," "last month's rent," or something else.

Security deposits can add up to a lot of money—often several thousands of dollars. Landlords usually want to get as much as they can so they won't have to go chasing after you for unpaid rent or any costs of repairing or cleaning the premises after you leave. The tenant, who usually wants to fork over as little as possible, often finds that it's very difficult to talk a landlord into reducing a deposit. Unfortunately, there is little we can say that will help you to get a potential landlord to be reasonable in this regard, assuming the deposit is within the statutory maximum discussed below. However, because security deposits constitute a big investment on your part, and because deposits have historically been a major source of friction between landlord and tenant, it is essential that you understand the legal rules in this area.

Amount of Deposit

State law provides that the total of all deposits and fees required by the landlord—for security, cleaning, last month's rent, and so on—may not exceed an amount equal to two months' rent, if the premises are unfurnished. If the premises are furnished, the limit is an amount equal to three months' rent. If you have a waterbed, the maximum allowed deposit increases by half a month's rent—to 2.5 times the monthly rent for unfurnished property and 3.5 times the monthly rent for furnished property. (CC § 1950.5(c), 1950-5(g).)

Suppose the landlord supplies the stove and refrigerator, but no other "furniture." Does this make the place "furnished"? We don't think so—though the statute is not clear on this. If the landlord provides basic furniture (beds, tables, and so on), obviously it is furnished and the landlord is legitimately entitled to a higher deposit because the potential for damage is high. But, in our opinion,

owners are not exposed to that much risk of loss when they provide only the stove and refrigerator, and therefore should be allowed to require a deposit of only up to two months' rent. Also, in the rental business, "furnished" is usually taken to mean the inclusion of all basic furniture.

State law also says: "This subdivision does not preclude a landlord and a tenant from entering into a mutual agreement for the landlord, at the request of the tenant and for a specified fee or charge, to make structural, decorative, furnishing, or other similar alterations, if the alterations are other than cleaning or repairing for which the landlord may charge the previous tenant as provided by subdivision (e)." (CC § 1950.5(c).) The intent of this provision is clearly to allow the landlord to require compensation for strange or unusual alterations requested by the tenant. This, of course, is reasonable. However, there is a danger that some landlords may improperly try to reintroduce all sorts of extra or nonrefundable fees under this exception to the basic deposit rules. Be awake to this possibility!

If the landlord is forced to use some of the security deposit during your tenancy (for example, because you broke something and didn't fix it or pay for it), the landlord may require you to replenish the security deposit.

> **EXAMPLE:** Millie pays her landlord, Maury, a $700 security deposit. Millie goes on vacation, leaving the water running. By the time Maury is notified, the overflow has damaged the paint on the ceiling below. Maury repaints the ceiling at a cost of $350, taking the money out of the security deposit. Maury is entitled to ask Millie to replace that money.

Nonrefundable Deposits

No lease or rental agreement may call any deposit "nonrefundable." Nor may a landlord escape this rule by demanding a "cleaning" or "security" or "pet" fee instead of using the word "deposit."

Under the law, the security deposit rules we discuss here apply to any "payment, fee, deposit or charge" that's intended to cover damage and unpaid rent. (CC § 1950.5.)

Be sure to understand that landlords may impose a fee, up to $30, (which may increase yearly, according to the Consumer Price Index) to cover expenses associated with a credit check. (CC § 1950.6.) Landlords may not charge initiation fees—these are considered part of the security deposit. (CC § 1950.5(b).)

What the Deposits May Be Used For

State law says that the deposit may be used by the landlord "in only those amounts as may be reasonably necessary" to do the following four things *only*:

1. to remedy defaults in payment of rent
2. to repair damage to the premises caused by the tenant (except for "ordinary wear and tear")
3. to clean the premises, if necessary, when the tenant leaves, and
4. if the rental agreement allows it, to pay for the tenant's failure to restore or replace personal property. (CC § 1950.5(e).)

One of the biggest sources of tenant-landlord dispute centers around cleaning. For example, how clean must the tenant leave the premises when the tenant vacates? The Legislature provided the answer, but only for tenancies that begin on or after January 1, 2003: The tenant must return the unit to the same level of cleanliness it was in at the beginning of the tenancy. (CC § 1950.5(b).) For tenants whose tenancies began before that date, there is no clear answer (one reason the Legislature enacted this provision).

If you are stuck with a pre-January 1, 2003 rental agreement or lease that has unclear language and you want to be sure to get your deposit back, we advise that you do two things:

- Clean the place thoroughly. This doesn't normally mean you have to shampoo rugs, dryclean the drapes, or wash the ceiling. A good thorough cleaning, including the refrigerator, stove, bathroom fixtures, and so on, should be adequate.
- Carefully document your cleaning work through pictures, witnesses, and so on. (See "Avoiding Deposit Problems," below.)

Another area of tenant-landlord disputes over the return of deposits has to do with damages to the premises. Some landlords try to charge tenants for everything from a worn spot on a hall rug to faded paint to missing light bulbs. The tenant is not responsible for any damage or wear and tear done to the premises by an earlier tenant. (CC § 1950.5(e).)

Landlord's Duty to Return Deposits

Within three weeks after you move out—whether voluntarily, by abandonment, or by eviction—the landlord must do one of two things:

1. return all of your deposit, or
2. give you personally or by first-class mail an "itemized statement" in writing saying why the landlord is retaining part or all of the deposit, including receipts for work done and items purchased, if the amount is $125 or more, and return any remaining part to you.

Tenants whose tenancies began on or after January 1, 2003 have the right to a pre-move-out inspection of their rental, when they can learn of intended deductions for damage or uncleanliness. (Tenants whose tenancies are terminated or who are evicted because of misconduct do not have this right.) You'll have an opportunity to remedy the problems before the final inspection. Here's how this works: Within a reasonable time after either you or the landlord notify the other of the end of your tenancy, the landlord must tell you in writing of your right to be present at an initial inspection, which must take place (if you request it) no sooner than two weeks before the end of the tenancy. You and the landlord should schedule the inspection at a mutually convenient time, and the landlord must give you 48 hours' notice of the inspection if you haven't agreed upon a time but you still want the inspection. (The two of you can forgo the 48 hours' notice if you both agree.)

Based upon the inspection, the landlord must give you an itemized statement of intended deductions, plus a copy of Civil Code §§ 1950.5(b)(1) through 1950.5(b)(4) and 1950.5(d). If you're not present at the inspection, the landlord should leave the list in the unit. You can remedy the problems as long as you don't violate any "no alterations" clause in your lease or rental agreement—for example, you can certainly do more cleaning, but if there's a deduction for damage that will require major work (such as repairing sheetrock or electrical items), you may need to ask permission first.

The landlord will reinspect when you leave, and must give you another itemized statement of deductions within three weeks after you've vacated. The landlord must also include copies of receipts for work (labor and materials) to clean the rental unit or replace or repair damaged items if the total charges exceed $125. If the landlord or an employee of the landlord did the work, the statement must include the time spent and the reasonable hourly rate charged. Landlords who cannot complete the work within the three-week period, or who do not have the necessary receipts, may deduct a good faith estimate of the charges, but must supply the receipts within 14 days of receiving them. You can waive your rights under these new provisions in writing, but you may rescind (take back) that waiver if you do so within 14 days after receiving the itemized statement of deductions. (CC § 1950.5(g).) If your efforts to fix or clean don't measure up, the landlord can still charge you. If you disagree, you'll be in the same position as anyone fighting a security deposit deduction—you'll argue that it's "clean enough" and the landlord will argue otherwise. The landlord can also charge you for damage or uncleanliness that crops up after the initial inspection. (CC § 1950.5.)

If a landlord fails to return your security deposit within the three weeks or doesn't otherwise follow the legal steps for itemization and return, you won't necessarily get the entire deposit back. That's because a landlord can argue in court that, despite his failure to follow correct procedures, you do owe back rent or have damaged the premises. He can ask the judge to "set off" these amounts against the security deposit. To defeat the landlord's claim of set-off, you'll have to convince the judge that the landlord waited too long to bring these charges up, or that it would be fundamentally unfair to allow him a "second chance" to dip into your security deposit. (*Granberry v. Islay Investments,* 38 Cal. Rptr.2d 650, 9 Cal.4th 738 (1995).)

If the landlord's illegal use or tardy return of your deposit was done in "bad faith," however, a judge may not only not disallow a set-off, but may impose a penalty of up to twice the security deposit as well (you get the penalty). "Bad faith" is hard to pin down, but it involves at least more than simple carelessness or ignorance of the law. Landlords who knowingly break the law, especially those who do so repeatedly, come much closer to acting in "bad faith."

When two or more cotenants rent under the same rental agreement or lease, the landlord does not have to return or account for any of the deposit until all of the tenants leave. If you move out early, however, your landlord might voluntarily work out an appropriate agreement and return your share of the security deposit. If not, you should try to work things out with the remaining tenants (or a new roommate, if there is one).

Effect of Sale of Premises on Security Deposits

A landlord who sells the building is supposed to do one of two things: return the deposit to the tenant, or transfer it to the new owner. (CC § 1950.5(i).)

It's been known to happen, however, that the landlord does neither and simply walks off with the money. The tenant often never knows of this. In fact, the tenant usually doesn't even know the building was sold until sometime later. But the new owner cannot require the tenant to replace any security deposit kept by the old landlord. (CC § 1950.5(j).)

The law requires the new owner to get all security deposits from the old landlord. Whether the new owner does so or not, that person becomes responsible for returning the security deposit to the tenant at the end of the tenancy, just as if the new owner were the old landlord. (CC § 1950.5(j).)

Effect of Foreclosure on Security Deposits

The wave of foreclosures that began in 2007 affected many tenants' homes. Until federal law changed things (on May 20, 2008), most lease-holding tenants lost their leases. Now, if the new owner is the bank, it must honor the lease. If the buyer at the foreclosure sale is a person who intends to occupy the home, lease-holding tenants are entitled to 90 days' notice. Month-to-month tenants are also entitled to 90 days' notice.

Unfortunately, the defaulting owners often disappeared without returning the security deposit. And banks, often eager to get remaining tenants off the property so that they can sell vacant homes, offered tenants "cash for keys" to leave peaceably— but the cash being offered seldom provided for the additional return of the deposit.

Legally, the new owner, bank or otherwise, is subject to the same deposit rules as described just above, when the rental property is voluntarily sold (these rules apply when rental property is sold "whether by sale, assignment, death, appointment of receiver *or otherwise*." (CC § 1950.5(h), italics added.) If your rental was foreclosed and is now owned by a bank or an investor, these new owners must account for and return the deposit as required

by law, regardless of whether the defaulting owner turned the deposit over to the deed or mortgage holder before the foreclosure. If they fail to do so, your recourse is to go to small claims court, as described later in this chapter.

May the Landlord Increase the Security Deposit?

Tenants often ask if it's legal for a landlord to raise their security deposits after they move in. The answer is that it depends on the situation:

- If you have a fixed-term lease (for example, a lease for a year) and the deposit is currently less than the legal limit, the landlord may not raise the security deposit during that year unless the lease allows this.
- If you have a rental agreement and the security deposit and other fees already add up to twice the monthly rent (if the place is unfurnished) or three times the monthly rent (if the place is furnished), the security deposit may not be increased.
- If neither of these two situations describes you and you are a month-to-month tenant, then the landlord may force you to pay more into the security deposit—if she does it right. To legally raise a deposit, she must give you at least 30 days' written notice of the increase, and she must have it properly "served" on you. This means that she must try to have it handed to you at your residence or place of work; a notice served by mail alone is not legal unless you voluntarily go along with it. (CC § 827; CCP § 1162.) See "Rent Increase Notices" in Chapter 3 regarding the law on how the landlord may change terms of a tenancy.

Avoiding Deposit Problems

Problems involving security deposits often arise like this:

- The tenant moves out.
- The landlord keeps all or part of the deposit on the grounds of damage or lack of cleaning.
- The tenant says that the place was left in good condition.

If tenant and landlord can't reach a compromise, the tenant will probably sue the landlord for the money withheld, leaving it up to the judge to decide who is telling the truth. For both sides, this is a pretty risky, messy, and time-consuming way of handling things.

The best way to try to prevent this from happening is to arrange to meet with the landlord or manager before you've moved your belongings out and after you've cleaned up. Be sure to take advantage of your right to a pre-move-out inspection, as explained above. Tour the apartment together and check for any damage, dirt, and so on. Then remedy any uncleanliness or repairs that the landlord has noted.

Your landlord should schedule a final inspection. Assuming you made out a list of damage already there when you moved in (see "The Landlord-Tenant Checklist" in Chapter 1), pull it out now and check it against the present condition of the place. Hopefully any cleaning or repairs you've done since the pre-move-out inspection will be acknowledged. Try to work out any disputes on the spot and ask the landlord to give you the security deposit before you leave. Be reasonable, and be willing to compromise. It is better to give up a few dollars for some questionable damage than to have to sue for the whole deposit later.

If you cannot get the landlord to meet with you when you leave, then make your own tour. Bring at least one witness (a person who helped clean often would make a very convincing witness), take some photos, and keep all your receipts for cleaning and repair materials, so you will be ready to prove your case if you later have to sue in small claims court in order to get your deposit back. (Remember, after you're out, it is usually too late to come back to take pictures.)

When the Landlord Won't Return Your Deposit

Let's assume that three weeks have passed since the day you moved out and you have received neither your deposit nor an itemization of what it was used for. It's time to take action. We suggest the following step-by-step approach.

Step 1. Make a Formal Demand

If you feel that your landlord has improperly kept your deposit, the first thing you should do is ask for it in writing. Here is a sample demand letter.

Sample Letter Demanding Security Deposit

1504 Oak Street #2
Cloverdale, CA
November 21, 20xx

Smith Realty Co.
10 Jones Street
Cloverdale, CA

As you know, until October 31, 20xx, I resided in Apartment #4 at 1500 Acorn Street and regularly paid my rent to your office. When I moved out, I left the unit cleaner than it was when I moved in.

As of today, I have received neither my $600 security deposit nor any accounting from you for that money. Please be aware that I know about my rights under California Civil Code Sec. 1950.5, and that if I do not receive my money within the next week, I will regard the retention of these deposits as showing bad faith on your part and shall sue you not only for the $600 in deposits, but also for twice that amount, as allowed by Sec. 1950.5 of the Civil Code.

May I hear from you promptly.

Very truly yours,

Leon Hernandez

Leon Hernandez

Step 2. Consider Compromise

If the landlord offers to meet you or offers a compromise settlement, try to meet the landlord half way, but don't go overboard. After all, a law requiring that your deposits be returned if you leave a rental property in the same level of cleanliness it had when you moved in and undamaged but for reasonable wear and tear is there to protect you. You might suggest that the dispute be mediated.

Many cities, counties, and nonprofit organizations such as San Francisco's Community Boards, offer tenant-landlord mediation services designed to help you and the landlord arrive at a mutually satisfactory settlement.

Step 3. Sue in Small Claims Court

If the formal demand doesn't work and there is no reasonable prospect of compromise, consider suing the landlord in small claims court. If you rent under a lease or rental agreement that provides for the landlord's attorney fees, then you, too, are entitled to attorney fees if you win your lawsuit and obtain a judgment against the landlord. (CC § 1717. You do not get attorney's fees, however, if you settle or the case is dismissed—even if the outcome is favorable to you.) In such situations, though you cannot bring a lawyer to small claims court, you might ask an attorney to help you prepare the case.

The rules governing small claims proceedings are contained in the Code of Civil Procedure, beginning with Section 116. The cost for filing papers and serving the landlord will be modest. The best source of information on how to prepare and present a small claims court case and collect money if you win is *Everybody's Guide to Small Claims Court in California,* by Ralph Warner (Nolo), which devotes a chapter to tenant-landlord cases, including how to prepare and present a deposit case.

To sue your landlord in small claims court, go to your local courthouse (there may be more than one, so call first to make sure you go to the right place) and find the clerk of the small claims court. The clerk is required by law to help you fill out the papers necessary to sue your landlord.

On the court form, state how much you are claiming the landlord owes you. This amount cannot exceed $7,500. You figure the amount you want to claim by asking for the total deposit, less anything that should reasonably be withheld for unpaid rent, damage, or dirty conditions. Add up to twice the amount of the deposit in "punitive damages" if you believe the landlord's failure to return your deposit (or reasonably itemize expenses) constitutes bad faith. If this adds up to more than $7,500, then you either have to waive the excess over $7,500 or else not use the small claims court. If you have to decide between suing in small claims court or in regular court (for an amount more than $7,500), consider that you may not easily win the full punitive damages.

If your rental agreement is oral, you must file your lawsuit against the landlord within two years after the three weeks (for the landlord to return your deposit) run out. (CCP § 339.5.) If you have a written lease, you have four years in which to file. (CCP §§ 337(1), 337.2, 343.) However, whether the agreement is written or oral, we advise you not to wait, but to file promptly. Judges are just not very sympathetic to old disputes.

After you file the form with the small claims clerk, the clerk will normally send a copy of it to the landlord by certified mail, with an order to appear in court for a trial on the suit at a certain date and time. To find out that date and time, ask the clerk. That date must be not less than 20 nor more than 70 days after the date of the order to appear. (CCP § 116.330.) If the landlord does not sign for the certified mail notice, you will have to arrange for a new court date and arrange to have the papers served by personal service.

Small claims court trials are very informal. No lawyers are present, and there are no formal rules of evidence. There is no jury. When you come to court for your hearing, bring the file or envelope with your records. All papers or pictures that you believe help your case should be included, such as a copy of your lease or rental agreement. Also bring with you all witnesses who have first-hand information about the facts in dispute, especially any people who helped in the cleanup. If you do not have any experience with a court, you can go down a day or two before and watch a few cases. You will see that it is a very simple procedure.

TIP

If you cannot speak English and cannot find a volunteer interpreter or afford to hire an interpreter, the court will probably be able to arrange for a volunteer for you. Have a friend call the clerk about this in advance.

On the day your case is to be heard, get to the court a little early and check for your courtroom (referred to as a "department"). Tell the clerk or bailiff that you are present and sit down and wait until your case is called. When your turn comes, stand at the large table at the front of the room and tell the judge clearly what is in dispute. Remember, the judge hears many cases every day, and she will not be particularly excited by yours. If you are long-winded, she may stop listening and start thinking about what she is going to eat for lunch.

Start your presentation with the problem (for example, "Lester Landlord has failed to return to me $500 in security deposits in the six weeks since I moved out of his house at 222 Spring Street"), and then present the directly relevant facts that explain why you should win (for example, "The house was clean and undamaged, and my rent was paid in full"). Again, be brief and to the point—don't ramble. You may show pictures and documents to the judge. When you are done with your oral presentation, tell the judge you have witnesses who want to testify.

The landlord will also have a chance to tell his side. You can expect it to be very different from yours, but stay cool! When he is done, you may ask him questions if you feel that he has not told the truth or if he has left some things out. But often asking the landlord a lot of vague questions just gives him more opportunity to tell his side of the case. It is especially important not to argue with the landlord or any of his witnesses—just get your facts out and back them up with convincing evidence.

In a case where a landlord has not returned your cleaning deposit after you have moved out and asked for it, you might present your case something like this:

"Good morning, Your Honor. My name is Susan Smit and I now live at 2330 Jones Street. From January 1, 2000 until July 1, 2006, I lived at 1500 Williams Street in a building owned by the Jefferson Realty Company. When I moved out, the Realty Company refused to refund my $700 cleaning deposit even though I left the place spotless. I carefully cleaned the rugs, washed and waxed the kitchen and bathroom floors, washed the inside of the cupboards, and washed the windows. Your Honor, I want to show you some pictures that were taken of my apartment the day I moved out. *(If you completed a checklist of the condition of the premises, you will want to show it to the judge at this time.)* These were taken by Mrs. Edna Jackson, who is here today and will testify. Your Honor, I don't have much else to say, except that in addition to the amount of my deposit, I am asking for the full $600 in statutory damages allowed by law. I am entitled to these damages because I don't believe the landlord had any reason at all to withhold my deposits."

If your landlord failed to alert you to your right to a pre-move-out inspection and is now deducting for cleanliness issues or damages, you will be at an advantage if you can plausibly argue that, had you been afforded the opportunity to remedy these issues, you could (and would) have done so. For example, suppose you're being charged for failing to wax the kitchen floor (which was otherwise clean). You can argue that, had you known of this requirement, it would have been easy for you to comply, and that the landlord should not be allowed to charge you for a task you would have done.

In most courts, your witnesses do not take the witness stand, but remain at the table in front of the judge and simply explain what they know about the dispute. Typical testimony might go like this:

"Good morning, Your Honor. My name is Mrs. Edna Jackson and I live at 1498 Williams Street. On July 1, 2006, when the plaintiff moved out, I helped her move and clean up. The place was very clean when we finished. And just to show how clean it was, I took the pictures that you were just shown. I'm sure those are the pictures I took because I signed and dated them on the back after they were developed."

Step 4. Call the District Attorney

If your landlord has a habit of refusing to return security deposits to tenants, your local district attorney might bring a criminal action for fines and an injunction requiring the landlord to return the deposit. (CC § 1950.5(m).)

Rent Withholding as a Way to Get Deposits Back in Advance

Suppose, after you move in, you learn from other tenants that your landlord has a tendency to cheat tenants out of their security deposits—perhaps by inventing or exaggerating a need for repairs or cleaning after they move out. When you decide to leave, you fear the same sort of trouble and you'd rather not deal with the risk and hassle of suing the landlord in small claims court.

There is a way to handle this problem that many tenants use: A month or two before you leave, tell the landlord that you are not making your usual rent payment, and that she should keep your deposit and apply it to the rent.

Your letter might look like the sample below.

Sample Letter Requesting Landlord to Apply Deposit to Last Month's Rent

1500 Acorn Street #4
Cloverdale, CA
September 15, 20xx

Smith Realty Co.
10 Jones Street
Cloverdale, CA

Dear Sirs:

As you know, I occupy Apartment #4 at 1500 Acorn Street and regularly pay rent to your office once a month.

Please take note that this is a formal written notice of my intention to vacate Apartment #4 on October 31, 20xx.

In speaking to other tenants in this area, I have learned that from time to time the return of cleaning deposits has been the subject of dispute between you and your tenants. Accordingly, I have decided on the following course of action: Instead of sending you the normal $600 rent payment today, I am sending you $200 and ask that you apply the $400 cleaning deposit to my last month's rent.

I will leave the apartment spotless and undamaged so that you will suffer no damage whatsoever. If you should doubt this or want to discuss the matter further, please give me a call and come over. I think that you will be satisfied that I am dealing with you honestly and in good faith and that the apartment, which is clean and in perfect repair now, will be in the same condition when I leave.

Very truly yours,

Leon Hernandez
Leon Hernandez

This type of "rent withholding" is not legal. You have no legal right to compel the landlord to apply your deposit to unpaid rent, and if you do not pay your rent on time, the landlord can serve you with a three-day notice (ordering you to pay the rent or get out in three days). If you do not comply with such a notice, however, it is very unlikely that the landlord will follow it up with a suit to evict you for nonpayment of rent. (The landlord cannot simply lock you out.) It would probably take at least a few weeks to bring a case to trial, and the landlord knows you plan to leave soon, anyway.

Nevertheless, we do not recommend that you use this rent withholding device against a landlord unless you are pretty sure that you're dealing with someone who cheats on security deposits. The fair landlord has a legitimate right and need to get the rent on time and to keep the security deposit until it's clear that the tenant has left the place in good shape. And if you need a good reference from a landlord who's been manipulated by you, forget it.

Interest on Security Deposits

As a matter of fairness, the landlord should pay you interest on your security deposit. It is your money—not his—and he is merely holding it for you. He should put it into some type of interest-bearing account and pay the interest to you. Unfortunately, no state law says that landlords must pay interest on security deposits.

None of the form leases and rental agreements customarily used by landlords require them to pay interest on your security deposit. In fact, the only forms we know of that suggest this are the Davis model lease.

A few local ordinances, including those of East Palo Alto, Hayward, Los Angeles, San Francisco, Santa Monica, and Santa Cruz, require payment of interest on security deposits. Most of these are also rent control cities. (See Chapter 3 for details on these local ordinances.)

Last Month's Rent

Many landlords require some payment for "last month's rent." The legal effect of such a

requirement should depend largely upon the exact language used in the lease or rental agreement.

If the lease or rental agreement says "security for last month's rent," or has a heading called "Security" and then lists "last month's rent" as one of the items on the list, then you have not actually paid the last month's rent, but just provided security for it. So, if the landlord legally raises the rent before you move out, you must pay the difference between the final rent and your security for last month's rent. For example, suppose when you moved in the monthly rent was $400, and the rental agreement said, "Security: … last month's rent: $400." After two years, the rent has been raised to $500, and the tenant leaves. The tenant owes the landlord the $100 difference for the last month's rent.

If, however, the lease or rental agreement does not say that the payment is for security, but simply says "last month's rent: $400," then, in our opinion, the tenant has paid the last month's rent—well in advance of the last month. This money is not a security payment—it's an advance payment of the last month's rent. The landlord does not hold it as a trustee for the tenant, and a rent increase later on will not affect the amount of the last month's rent, which the tenant has already paid. So, in the above example, the tenant would not owe an additional $100 to the landlord.

Despite this commonsense approach, some judges are inclined to rule that the tenant must pay the extra $100. If the rental agreement is unclear as to whether this payment is intended as security, point out to the judge that since the landlord provided the form agreement, by law any ambiguities should be resolved against the writer (the landlord). (CC § 1654.)

When Your Landlord Demands More Money

If your landlord claims, after you have moved out, that your security deposit is not sufficient to cover cleaning or repair costs or unpaid rent, your landlord may:

- negotiate with you directly to collect the amount in dispute
- hire a collection agency to try to collect from you, or
- sue you in small claims court.

Negotiating

Your landlord will likely send you an itemized statement with a balance due at the bottom within three weeks after you move out. If you believe your landlord has a legitimate beef, you might want to negotiate at this point. You may be able to negotiate a payment arrangement that is agreeable to you and to your landlord if you are having financial difficulties. If you wait until your landlord has expended more time and energy trying to collect from you, your landlord may not be as willing to accommodate your needs.

Hiring a Collection Agency

Your landlord may hire a collection agency to try to collect from you. If you are contacted by a collection agency, don't panic. You still have rights despite the seriousness of the debt or what the collection agency tells you in its effort to intimidate you. For a detailed discussion of what to do when the bill collector calls, see *Solve Your Money Troubles: Get Debt Collectors Off Your Back & Regain Financial Freedom,* by Robin Leonard and Margaret Reiter (Nolo).

Small Claims Court

Finally, your landlord may try to sue you in small claims court.

If that happens, you will first receive a copy of the landlord's Claim of Plaintiff form, which sets forth the reasons your former landlord is suing you and for how much. The form should also specify a hearing date. You are entitled to receive service of the Claim of Plaintiff form at least 15 days before the date of the court hearing if you are served within the county in which the courthouse is located. If you are served in a county other than the one where the hearing is to take place, you must be served at least 20 days before the hearing date. (CCP § 116.340(b).)

You do not need to file any papers to defend a case in small claims court. You just show up on the date and at the time indicated, ready to tell your side of the story. Take as many of the following items of evidence as possible:

- Two copies of the Landlord-Tenant Checklist, which you should have filled out with the landlord when you first moved in and again when you moved out. (See Chapter 1.) This evidence is especially important if the Checklist shows that the premises were dirty or damaged when you moved in or that the premises were clean and undamaged when you moved out.
- Photos or a video of the premises before you moved in.
- Photos or videos or notes of the condition of the unit at the pre-move-out inspection.
- Photos or a video of the premises on the day that you moved out, which show that they were clean and undamaged.
- Receipts for professional cleaning of items such as carpets or drapes, or for any repairs that you paid for before moving out.
- One or two witnesses who were familiar with your residence and are willing to testify that the place was clean and undamaged when you moved out. People who helped you clean up or move out are particularly helpful.

Evictions

Many tenants become terrified when they receive a Three-Day Notice to Pay Rent or Quit from the landlord. They believe that if they do not pay or get out in three days, they will be thrown out onto the street on the fourth day. The law simply does not allow this. The landlord must first file a lawsuit in court and notify you of it so that you have an opportunity to defend yourself. If you are going to fight the eviction, you must respond quickly—within five to 15 days from the time you are notified of the lawsuit, depending on the circumstances—or risk losing the suit.

Even if you lose the lawsuit, the court must still issue an order authorizing a law enforcement officer to remove you from the premises. All of this takes time, between about two and six weeks after the termination notice (a three-day, 30-, 60-, or 90-day notice) has expired. After the notice has expired, it will take the landlord about two weeks to get you evicted if you do nothing to contest the lawsuit, and up to six weeks if you do. "Timeline for Eviction," below, will give you an idea of how long different types of eviction cases normally take.

This chapter will help you go to court and defend yourself if you choose to do so. It will also help you understand what your lawyer is doing, if you choose to hire one.

The material set out here is by no means a complete summary of every defense or litigation device available to a tenant. To give you that would make this volume look like a metropolitan phone book. Instead, we concentrate on the basic and most commonly used tools suitable for use in defending against most straightforward eviction proceedings.

RESOURCE

You can supplement this information by consulting the *California Eviction Defense Manual*, and *California Landlord-Tenant Practice*, both of which are published by Continuing Education of the Bar (CEB) in Berkeley, California. The *California Eviction Defense Manual* is the source most often used by lawyers when defending unlawful detainer cases. Unlike many law

books, it is not difficult to use. You should be able to find both books in your county law library. Be sure you consult the latest supplements to these books, which contain the most recent cases and statutes.

Illegal Self-Help Evictions

The most basic thing a tenant should know is that California law clearly states that when landlords wish to evict a tenant, they must first go to court, giving the tenant prior notice of the court proceedings. They cannot legally take the law into their own hands by locking the tenant out, taking the tenant's belongings, removing doors and windows, cutting off the utilities, or harassing the tenant in any other way.

Utility Cut-Offs

Any landlord who causes any utility service (including water, heat, light, electricity, gas, telephone, elevator, or refrigeration) to be cut off with intent to terminate a tenant's occupancy is liable to the tenant for certain damages. (CC § 789.3.) This law applies whether the utilities are paid for by the landlord or the tenant, and whether the landlord cuts off the utilities directly or indirectly—for example, by not paying the utility bill.

The tenant may sue the landlord and recover the following amounts:

- actual (out-of-pocket) losses, including such things as meat spoiling in the refrigerator after the electricity is turned off or motel bills if the tenant has to find a temporary place to live
- punitive damages of up to $100 for each day or part thereof that a utility was turned off (but not less than $250 in punitive damages for each separate violation)
- a reasonable attorney fee, and
- a court order compelling the landlord to turn on the utilities.

You can bring your suit in small claims court (for up to $7,500) or sue in superior court, if you want to sue for more money.

Tenants can also sue for mental anguish if the landlord's acts were especially outrageous. For example, a jury awarded 23 tenants of a San Francisco residential hotel $1.48 million from their landlord. The landlord had cut off water, entered tenants' rooms without notice, and threatened the tenants, most of whom were elderly or disabled. (*Balmoral Hotel Tenants Association v. Lee,* 226 Cal. App.3d 686, 276 Cal.Rptr. 640 (1990).)

Lock-Outs

If the landlord locks you out, removes outside doors or windows, or removes your personal property from your home with the intention of terminating your tenancy, the landlord is in violation of state law. (CC § 789.3.) The damages are the same as set out above for utility cut-offs. You can sue for damages in small claims court, but if you want quick action to get back into your home, see a lawyer, because this law allows you to collect attorney fees. The lawyer might also sue the landlord for "forcible entry and detainer." (CCP § 1159; *Jordan v. Talbot,* 55 Cal.2d 597 (1961).)

You might also call the police or district attorney, because these acts are crimes (forcible entry, malicious mischief, and unauthorized entry). Even if the police won't arrest the landlord, they might persuade the landlord to let you in. Ask the police to write a report on the incident; it might help you in a later lawsuit against the landlord.

Tenants who live in residential hotels (apartment buildings that are called hotels) for more than 30 days are also protected against lock-outs. (CCP § 1159; CC § 1940.)

Illegal Retaliatory Evictions

It is illegal for a landlord to retaliate against a tenant "for having exercised any right under the law." Retaliation includes reducing services, giving a 30-day or 60-day rent increase or termination notice, or even threatening to do so. In recent years, the courts have prevented evictions brought to punish tenants who:

- complain to health authorities or exercise statutory rights, such as the right to repair and deduct (see Chapter 7)
- exercise rights under rent control ordinances (see Chapter 3)
- exercise any other statutory or constitutional right, such as the right to be free of discriminatory treatment based on factors such as race or religion (see Chapter 4) and the right to privacy (see Chapter 5).

Retaliation for Complaints to Government Agencies

If a tenant whose rent is paid up complains to a government agency about defects in the premises, and if the landlord subsequently raises rent, decreases services, or evicts the tenant within 180 days, retaliation is presumed. If the tenant goes to court, the landlord must prove that the action was not retaliatory. (CC § 1942.5(a).) After 180 days, the tenant can still sue, but retaliation is no longer presumed.

Aside from limitations in any applicable rent control ordinance, a landlord can legally raise the rent or terminate the tenancy at any time, if there is a legitimate nonretaliatory reason. But if challenged, the landlord will have to prove that the response was not retaliatory.

Retaliation for Other Acts

If the tenant asserts any other legal right—that is, other than complaining to a government agency about defects in the premises—the tenant must prove retaliation is the motive for any rent increase, decrease in services, or eviction that follows. Under both statutory and common law, the tenant may raise the defense of retaliation or sue the landlord for retaliatory eviction at any time, and it doesn't matter whether the tenant is paid up in rent. (CC § 1942.5(c). Also, see *Glaser v. Meyers,* 137 Cal. App.3d 770 (1982).) (Even so, as time goes on, it becomes harder for the tenant to establish that the landlord still has a retaliatory motive.)

A landlord's conduct can be proof of his motive. In deciding whether a landlord acted with a retaliatory motive, judges look at such things as:

- how soon the landlord raised the rent or terminated the tenancy after the tenant exercised a legal right
- how the landlord treated the complaining tenant as compared to other tenants, and
- whether the landlord appears to have had a legitimate reason for the actions.

Overview of Eviction Procedure

The rest of this chapter, which deals with how you can defend against a formal unlawful detainer (eviction) procedure, is pretty technical and complicated. For this reason, we believe it will help you to carefully read this overview of the eviction process first. In addition, if you live in a rent control or other city listed in Chapter 3 that requires "just cause" for eviction, it is essential that you get a copy of your local ordinance and regulations from your rent control board and study it. Although we will remind you of the many special rights that residents in cities covered by rent control or other eviction protection ordinances enjoy when it comes to defending against eviction, it is impossible for us to deal with each city's ordinance in detail.

The Notice to Quit

A landlord who wants to get you out must properly deliver a termination notice to you. (The method of delivery is required by law and called "service.") To terminate a month-to-month tenancy, the notice need not state a reason, but must give you 30 days to vacate if any occupant has lived in the property less than a year, and 60 days if all occupants have lived there a year or more. Also, if you live in a rent-controlled or other city that requires just cause for eviction, the reason for termination should be stated in the notice. For certain government-subsidized tenancies, the notice must give 90 days and the reason for termination. (CC § 1954.535.) The landlord must then wait until the notice period expires before filing an eviction lawsuit. But if you have a fixed-term lease that has expired—and the landlord has not continued to accept rent for any period following expiration—no notice is required unless the lease itself provides for it. If the landlord has accepted rent after expiration of a fixed-term lease, the tenancy continues on a month-to-month basis, and then must be terminated by notice. (See CC § 1945.)

For an eviction based on an alleged breach of your lease or rental agreement, the notice may give you three days to perform—for example, to pay the rent or get rid of the dog. To terminate a month-to-month tenancy when the landlord does not allege a breach of the rental agreement, the notice need not state a reason but must give you 30 or 60 days to vacate (90 days for government-subsidized tenancies), unless you live in an area that requires a just cause for eviction, in which case the just cause must also be stated. Some local rent control ordinances also require landlords to include other things—for example, the phone number of the Rent Board—in the notice, and some cities' ordinances require longer notice periods. "Tenancy Termination Notices," below, describes the specific notice requirements.

The Summons and Complaint

If you have not met the landlord's demand when the notice period runs out, the landlord may file a Complaint against you in court. Filing a Complaint begins a lawsuit. The landlord will then have a copy of the Complaint served on you, together with another document called a Summons. The Summons will tell you to respond to the court in writing, usually within five days. "The Eviction Lawsuit," below, provides details.

Your Response

If you don't respond to the court, in proper written form and within the time allowed, the landlord may ask the court for a default judgment against you. That means you lose without a trial. (See "After the Lawsuit—Eviction by the Sheriff or Marshal," below, for details on eviction by the sheriff or marshal.)

If you choose to respond, you have several options:

- If the Summons was not properly served on you, or for certain other technical reasons, file a Motion to Quash Service of Summons (see "The Motion to Quash").
- If the Complaint is not in proper technical form or does not properly allege the landlord's right to evict you, file a Demurrer (see "The Demurrer," below).
- If you want to deny statements in the Complaint or allege facts showing why you should win, file an Answer (see "The Answer," below).

These responses (called "responsive pleadings") are not mutually exclusive. So your response may be a Motion to Quash Service of Summons, then a Demurrer, and then an Answer, depending on the court's rulings. Or, you may simply file an Answer as your response. "The Eviction Lawsuit," below, will help you choose the appropriate response.

Trial

After you file your Answer, the case will go to trial. However, it could be decided by a judge (without taking evidence or hearing live witnesses) if the landlord makes a "summary judgment" motion (see "Summary Judgment," below). If the landlord doesn't file this kind of motion and the case doesn't settle, the trial will be heard by a judge without a jury unless either side demands a jury ahead of time, in writing (see "The Trial," below).

Actual Eviction

If you lose the trial, the judge may, in rare circumstances, allow you to stay on if you pay everything you owe the landlord (see "Stopping an Eviction," below). Otherwise, the landlord will get a "Writ of Possession" that the sheriff (or marshal) will serve on you. This will give you five days to leave. If you are not out on the fifth day, the sheriff or marshal will physically throw you out, unless a court grants a temporary stay of the eviction to give you a few extra days to move. (See "Postponing an Eviction" and "After the Lawsuit—Eviction by the Sheriff or Marshal," below.)

You may also appeal the trial court's ruling, on the theory that the court made some error of law. ("Appeal From an Eviction," below, shows you how to do this.) Your eviction will not be delayed (stayed) during the appeal unless you can convince the judge of three things: (1) that the appeal has some merit, (2) that evicting you while the appeal is pending will cause hardship to you, and (3) that delaying the eviction will not harm the landlord. This final requirement means that during the appeal, you will have to pay reasonable rent to the landlord. If you can't or won't do so, the judge won't stay the eviction judgment.

Stopping an Eviction by Filing for Bankruptcy

If you file for bankruptcy before the landlord files his eviction lawsuit, the landlord cannot legally file an eviction lawsuit unless he first goes to the Bankruptcy Court and asks for permission to proceed. If the landlord has started an eviction lawsuit but hasn't gotten a judgment for possession of the property, he must stop it once you file for bankruptcy, and can proceed only after getting permission from the Bankruptcy Court to go ahead. (11 U.S.C. § 362.) But don't get your hopes up —bankruptcy judges usually grant these requests, and it takes only a week or so if the landlord or the landlord's attorney acts quickly.

If you file for bankruptcy after the landlord has completed the eviction lawsuit and obtained a judgment for possession, but before the sheriff arrives, you are out of luck—the sheriff can go ahead and do his job. However, under very narrow circumstances, you may be able to stop an eviction based on nonpayment of rent when the landlord obtained a judgment before you declared bankruptcy. You'll be able to stop the eviction only if, within 30 days of filing bankruptcy, you (1) file a paper with the Bankruptcy Court certifying that California has a law—CCP § 1179—allowing tenants to avoid eviction by paying unpaid rent (plus court costs and any attorney's fees awarded the landlord); (2) deposit that sum with the Bankruptcy Court clerk, plus any rent due 30 days from the date you filed for bankruptcy; and (3) certify to the Bankruptcy Court that you have paid these amounts, serving the landlord (or landlord's attorney) with this certification.

Landlords can sometimes avoid the automatic bankruptcy stay (proceed with an eviction without asking the court for permission), when the reason for the eviction is the tenant's alleged drug use or damage to the property. In these situations, the landlord files a certification to that effect with the Bankruptcy Court.

Some nonlawyer eviction defense organizations (primarily in the Los Angeles area) routinely help tenants file for bankruptcy as a means of buying a little more time to find new premises. While the extra time may seem like a minor miracle at the time, we recommend against filing for bankruptcy solely to stave off an eviction. It can hurt your credit rating and may cause you to lose property you wanted to hang on to. However, if other reasons justify filing for bankruptcy, stopping an eviction temporarily may be a beneficial side effect.

RESOURCE

For more information, see *How to File for Chapter 7 Bankruptcy*, by Stephen Elias, Albin Renauer, and Robin Leonard (Nolo).

Timeline for Eviction

How long does the entire eviction process take? Of course, it varies from case to case. Every lawyer who has defended a lot of eviction cases has a story about how great lawyering brilliantly created a paper blizzard and staved off an eviction for many months. On the other hand, an eviction can occur in a blindingly short period of time if the landlord does everything right and you do nothing.

Nevertheless, the time estimates we set out here (two to three months) should prove broadly accurate, assuming the following facts:

- You have received a 30- or 60-day notice.
- The Summons and Complaint are personally served on you.
- You contest the action by filing written responses with the court.
- All papers (after the Summons and Complaint) are served by mail where this is permitted (the usual practice).
- The landlord (or landlord's attorney) stays on top of the case and files all papers as fast as possible.

Eviction may occur earlier if the landlord:

- personally serves all papers on you instead of mailing them, or
- wins a "summary judgment" and doesn't have to go to trial.

The timeline will be longer if the landlord lets time slip by between any of the procedural steps necessary to move an eviction case along.

It is rare that a landlord's case marches along without one snag or another, many of them caused either by the landlord's attorney's schedule, by courthouse delays, or by the sheriff's backload of papers to serve. Practically speaking, if you added two (and sometimes as many as four) weeks to the timeline, you would have a better picture of how long the typical contested eviction takes. On the other hand, if you fail to take one of the steps indicated in the timeline, or you lose on your Motion to Quash or Demurrer, you should deduct the appropriate number of days.

Tenancy Termination Notices

Now that you have an overview of the eviction process, it's time to deal with the specifics. We start with the paper the landlord uses to notify you that your tenancy is being terminated. This will be either a three-day, 30-day, 60-day, or 90-day (for government-subsidized tenancies) notice.

One very important principle applies to all notice requirements in eviction cases: Because the landlord is trying to evict you from your home, and because the law gives the landlord special privileges in eviction cases (a quicker lawsuit), the landlord must strictly comply with all of the law's notice requirements. (*Kwok v. Bergren,* 130 Cal.App.3d 596, 599 (1982).) If the landlord makes even a small mistake in a required notice, and/or doesn't serve it properly, the eviction itself might be invalid and the landlord may have to start the process over.

Notice to End a Fixed-Term Lease

When a fixed-term lease expires, you are supposed to move out right away, unless your city has a rent control ordinance that requires the landlord to have just cause to evict you. If you don't move, the landlord may file an eviction lawsuit immediately, without first serving any notice on you.

If you live in a city with a rent control or other ordinance requiring just cause for eviction, expiration of the lease does not by itself justify an eviction. You are entitled to remain unless you are evicted for one of the reasons listed in the ordinance.

If the landlord wants to evict you during the term of your lease for your breach of the lease (such as nonpayment of rent), the landlord will have to serve a notice on you before suing to evict. The notice is normally a three-day notice.

The Three-Day Notice Because of a Tenant's Violation

The landlord can serve you with a three-day notice if you or another tenant have violated the terms of your lease or rental agreement.

Kinds of Three-Day Notices

There are basically three types of three-day notices.

Three-Day Notice to Pay Rent or Quit: If you fail to pay your rent on time, the landlord must serve a three-day notice on you before suing to evict you on that ground. The notice must tell you to pay the rent or move in three days. The notice must state the amount of rent you must pay to avoid eviction, and this amount may not be more than what you actually owe in rent. (The three-day notice can ask for less than what you owe, but not more.) It must not, for example, include late charges, check-bounce, or other fees of any kind, or interest or utility charges. The landlord can deduct these amounts from the security deposit or sue for them in small claims court.

Some judges also require landlords to include the dates for which the rent is due. Because rent is almost always due at the beginning of a month (or other rent period), the landlord is entitled to request the total rent for the period for which rent is late, less any partial payments you have made. Thus, if your $850 rent is due on the first of the month, the landlord has the right to ask you in a three-day notice for the entire $850 on the second day of the month. (CCP § 1161(2); *Werner v. Sargeant,* 121 Cal.App.2d 833 (1953).)

If you pay the amount stated in the three-day notice (the landlord does not have to accept partial payments) before the end of the three days, the notice is canceled, and you don't have to leave. (CCP § 1161(3).) After three days, the landlord may refuse your money and proceed with the eviction. A landlord who accepts the rent after the three-day period, however, waives the right to evict for the late payment. (*EDC Associates Ltd. v. Gutierrez,* 153 Cal.App.3d 169 (1984).) When a landlord accepts partial payments but still wants to evict you for not paying the whole rent, the landlord must prepare a new three-day notice stating the now-lower, past-due rent amount.

Three-Day Notice to Perform Covenant (Correct Violation) or Quit: If you are accused of violating some other provision of your lease or rental agreement, the three-day notice must tell you to stop the conduct if it's curable. For example, suppose the landlord believes that you have a dog in violation of a lease provision that prohibits pets. The notice must say in effect, "Either get rid of the dog in three days or move out in three days." In all cases, the violation of the lease or rental agreement must be substantial, not minor, in order to justify evicting you from your home. (*McNeece v. Wood*, 204 Cal.280, 285; CCP § 1161(3) (1928).)

Unconditional Three-Day Notice to Quit: A landlord can serve you with a three-day notice to vacate if the landlord believes that you are committing "waste" (that is, wrecking the place), creating a "nuisance" on the premises (for example, dumping garbage in the backyard or seriously and repeatedly disturbing other tenants or neighbors), or using it for an illegal purpose (such as to sell illegal drugs). In this situation, however, the notice need not give you the alternative of stopping your misbehavior. (CCP § 1161(4).) The landlord can also give you this kind of three-day notice if you sublet the premises, contrary to a lease or rental agreement provision prohibiting sublets.

How a Three-Day Notice Must Be Served on You

To be effective, the three-day notice must be properly served on you. (If there is more than one tenant on a written lease or rental agreement, it is legally sufficient for a landlord to serve just one. *University of Southern California v. Weiss*, 208 Cal. App.2d 759, 769, 25 Cal.Rptr. 475 (1962).) First, the landlord (or landlord's agent) must try to find you and hand it to you. If the server tries to find you at home and at work but can't, the server may hand it to "a person of suitable age and discretion" at your home or work and also mail a copy to you. If there's no one suitable at your home or work to leave it with, then—and only then—may the server serve it on you by the "nail and mail" method. This involves posting a copy in a conspicuous place on your premises, such as the front door, and mailing another to you. (CCP § 1162.)

Who Signed Your Three-Day Pay or Quit Notice?

Take a look at the signature on your three-day notice for late rent. If it is signed by a lawyer hired by your landlord to handle an eviction, or by a management company who manages the property, you may be able to sue on the grounds that the demand violates the federal Fair Debt Collection Practices Act (15 U.S.C. § 1692 and following).

The Fair Debt Collection Practices Act governs debt collectors and requires, among other things, that debtors be given 30 days in which to respond to a demand for payment. A federal appellate court in New York has ruled that when a New York attorney signs a pay or quit notice, the lawyer is acting as a debt collector. Consequently, the tenant must have 30 days to pay or quit, regardless of the state's three-day provision. (*Romea v. Heiberger*, 163 F.3d 111 (2d Cir. 1998).)

Although this ruling governs New York, Connecticut, and Vermont landlords only, there is no reason why tenants in other states could not urge the same reasoning when they are presented with three-day notices signed by a landlord's lawyer. To raise this issue, a tenant would have to file a separate lawsuit, apart from the eviction proceeding, alleging a violation of the federal law. Filing a lawsuit of this nature will not stop the eviction, however. We know of no case law, or even the ruling of a single California judge, that lets a tenant raise this issue as a defense in an eviction lawsuit.

Landlords are often sloppy about following these procedures. It is common, for example, for a landlord to make one attempt to find the tenant at home, and no attempt to find the tenant at work, and then simply nail the notice to the tenant's door and mail a copy. This is not proper service.

Sloppy landlords often fall back on a legal doctrine that states that if the tenant actually receives the notice, it doesn't matter that it wasn't served properly. The theory is that actual receipt of the notice "cures" any defect in service. (*University of Southern California v. Weiss,* 208 Cal.App.2d 759 (1962).) If the case later goes to court, the landlord can prove you received the notice by calling you to the witness stand and asking you. For this reason, it is usually unwise for a tenant who actually received the notice to rely on a landlord's faulty service of notice as a defense.

Counting the Three Days After Service

You have three full days to comply with the demands in a three-day notice. If you do comply, then the landlord may not sue to evict you—unless it's an Unconditional Three-Day Notice to Quit, where your compliance or change in behavior won't make a difference.

If you receive an unconditional notice or don't comply with a three-day notice to pay rent or correct some other violation, the landlord may file a lawsuit on the fourth day (or later).

The date of service is the date you were handed the notice, if you were personally served. If the landlord left the notice with someone else at your home (or office), or posted a copy on the premises and mailed another copy, the date of service is the date the landlord took that action. It doesn't matter that you didn't actually receive the notice until later. (*Walters v. Meyers,* 226 Cal.App.3d. Supp 15 (1990).)

To count the three days, do the following:

- Ignore the date of service and start counting on the next day.
- If you were served personally, count three days.
- If you were served by "nail and mail," count three days. (There used to be some confusion about whether to add an additional five days to account for time in the mail. It is now clear that you are not entitled to the additional five days. (*Losornio v. Motta,* 67 Cal.App.4th 110 (1998).)
- If the third day falls on a Saturday, Sunday, or holiday, ignore that day and move on to the next business day.

EXAMPLE 1: You are served with a three-day notice on Wednesday. To count the three days, do not count Wednesday; begin with Thursday. This makes Saturday the third day. But Saturday is a holiday, and so is Sunday. So the third day is Monday. Therefore, you have until the end of Monday to comply. If the landlord files an eviction lawsuit before Tuesday, it should be thrown out of court if you raise the issue. (See *LaManna v. Vognar,* 17 Cal.App.4th Supp. 1 (1993).) Tenants should raise this issue by filing a Demurrer—see the Demurrer section, below.

EXAMPLE 2: You're served on Friday. Saturday is the first day, Sunday is the second day, and Monday is the third day. Neither of the weekend days extends the three-day period.

After the Three Days

If the three-day notice does not say that your tenancy will be "forfeited" if you don't pay the rent or correct a violation in three days, then you may avoid eviction by offering to pay the rent or comply with your rental agreement or lease after the three days runs out—so long as you do so before the landlord files an eviction lawsuit. (*Briggs v. Electronic Memories & Magnetics Corp.,* 53 Cal. App.3d 900 (1975).) (Obviously, you won't have this choice with unconditional notices.)

EXAMPLE: On May 5, the landlord serves you with a three-day notice to pay $1,000 rent or vacate. It does not say anything about your tenancy being "forfeited" if you fail to comply with the notice. The three days run out on May 8. On May 10, you try to give the $1,000 to the landlord, but she returns it. On May 15, she files a lawsuit to evict you. If you can convince the judge in your Answer (see below) and by arguing the point at trial that you tried to pay the rent on the 10th, you should win the case.

The 30-, 60-, or 90-Day Notice to Terminate a Month-to-Month Tenancy

To terminate a month-to-month tenancy (for reasons other than nonpayment of rent or breach of a rental agreement or lease term), the landlord must normally serve you with a notice that simply says that you are to get out in 30 or 60 days (or more). (Tenants who have resided continuously in the rental for a year or more are entitled to 60 days' notice; others get 30 days.) The notice need not state why the landlord wants you out, unless a rent control ordinance requires that the notice state just cause to evict (discussed below).

If your landlord receives rent or other payments from the Department of Housing & Urban Development (HUD) or a local or state program (most of which operate as "housing authorities") on your behalf, you are entitled to 90 days' notice, not 30 or 60 (CC § 1954.535; *Wasatch Property Management. v. DeGrate,* 35 Cal.4th 111 (2005).) In addition, the landlord must state the reason for termination on the 90-day notice. And if you are a Section 8 tenant, your landlord cannot give you a 90-day notice until your initial rental term has elapsed. During the 90-day period prior to termination, the landlord cannot increase the rent or otherwise require any subsidized tenant to pay more than he or she paid under the subsidy.

A 30- or 60-day notice is not required if the landlord does not want to renew a tenant's lease. (However, in a rent control or other city that requires "just cause" to evict, mere expiration of a lease is not one of the reasons allowed for eviction. The landlord may evict only if the tenant refuses to sign a similar lease or extension whose terms, including rent, are legal under local and state law.) The tenant is entitled to stay until the end of the lease term, but no longer. However, many landlords use a 30- or 60-day notice near the end of a lease term as a practical way to remind the tenant that the lease is about to expire and will not be renewed.

You may also get a 30-day notice from a bank if your landlord's mortgage has been foreclosed upon and the lender who has obtained title to the property wants you out in order to sell it. (In a rent control city requiring just cause for eviction, the 30-day notice may not be used for this purpose unless the ordinance lists it as one of the reasons for eviction. *Gross v. Superior Court,* 171 Cal. App.3d 265 (1985).) The bank (or other buyer) may do this even in the middle of a fixed-term lease.

How a 30- or 60-, or 90-Day Notice Must Be Served on You

Here are some key points about 30-, 60-, or 90-day notices:

- A 30-, 60-, or 90-day notice may be served on any day of the month. It need not be served on the first day, the "rent day," or any other day—unless the rental agreement requires it to be served on a certain day.
- It may be served in the same manner as the three-day notice (see above), *or* by certified or registered mail. (CC § 1946.)
- When you count the 30 or 35 days, if the last day falls on a Saturday, Sunday, or holiday, you have all day Monday to move if you want it.

CAUTION

Don't rely on an extra five days if you were served by certified mail or "nail and mail." There is some authority for this theory—under CCP § 1013, litigants get an additional five days when they're served by non-personal service with papers in an ongoing lawsuit. But terminating a tenancy is not part of a lawsuit—the lawsuit (the unlawful detainer case) begins later, and only if the tenant doesn't comply. (*Lorsonio v. Motta,* 67 Cal. App.4th 110 (1998).) So don't rely on this theory.

EXAMPLE: You have a month-to-month tenancy, pay rent on the first, and have lived there for six months. If your landlord serves you with a 30-day notice on July 15, you are supposed to vacate on August 15. But if it falls on a weekend or holiday, the next business day is "moving day."

Withdrawal of a 30-, 60-, or 90-Day Notice

Now and then a landlord will accept rent covering a period beyond the 30, 60, or 90 days. When this happens, the legal effect is the withdrawal of the termination. (*Highland Plastics, Inc. v. Enders,* 109 Cal.App.3d Supp. 1 (1980).)

> **EXAMPLE:** The landlord serves you with a 30-day notice on June 10, requiring you to move on July 10. Your rent is $500 a month, due on the first. On July 1, you pay the usual $500 rent. If the landlord accepts it, she has accepted rent for the whole month of July, including the part beyond July 10. By doing so, she has probably impliedly withdrawn the notice.

The 30-, 60-, or 90-Day Notice in Rent Control Cities With Just Cause Requirements

Many local rent control ordinances (including those of Los Angeles, San Francisco, Oakland, Hayward, Berkeley, Beverly Hills, East Palo Alto, Palm Springs, Thousand Oaks, West Hollywood, and Santa Monica) limit the landlord's right to evict. (See Chapter 3 for more on rent control.) San Diego has its own just cause eviction ordinance, without rent control, for tenants who have lived in their rental units two years or more. The City of Glendale has just cause eviction requirements, also in the absence of rent control provisions. These ordinances require the landlord to have a good faith "just cause" or "good cause" reason to evict, and they specify a list of acceptable reasons. It does not matter whether the tenant has a month-to-month tenancy or had a fixed-term lease that has expired.

Typically, the causes that these ordinances consider "just" fall into three classes:

- Wrongdoing by the tenant—such as nonpayment of rent or creating a legal nuisance. As discussed above, a three-day notice is typically used in this situation.

Under the ordinances of some cities, including Berkeley, Santa Monica, Los Angeles, and San Francisco, the landlord must first notify the tenant of certain types of lease or rental agreement violations—for example, moving in too many people, damaging the premises, or making too much noise—and give the tenant a chance to correct it before serving the termination notice. In other types of situations—such as using the premises to sell illegal drugs—the landlord need not give the tenant the alternative of stopping the misbehavior.

- Tenant refuses to sign a new lease or extension—in cities with just cause eviction requirements, a landlord cannot evict merely because the tenant's lease has expired, unless the tenant refuses to sign a new lease with similar (and legal) terms at a legal rent.

- Landlord needs to make major repairs or do large-scale remodeling on the premises. Under the terms of many ordinances, however, a tenant has the right to move back in after the remodeling is completed, at the original rent plus an extra "pass-through" increase that allows the landlord to recover part of the cost of the improvements.

- Convenience of the landlord, such as to move in a parent or other family member. Most just cause ordinances allow landlords to evict in order to move in themselves or have certain close relatives move in, if the landlord has no other comparable vacant units.

- "Ellis Act" evictions, when the landlord simply plans to take the rental unit off the market, permanently. Some cities require even more notice than is required under state law, such as 120 days, to terminate a month-to-month tenancy for this reason. Check your local rent control or just cause eviction ordinance or regulations.

Cities define differently which relatives are eligible to evict a tenant. All include parents and children of the landlord, and some also include the landlord's brothers, sisters, and grandparents. In many cities, a landlord must own at least half of the property to qualify to move relatives in. In Los Angeles, a particular relative of a landlord may justify evicting a tenant only once, and the landlord must pay the evicted tenant's costs of finding another place to live and moving. Check your local ordinance on all of these details.

CAUTION
Some landlords have abused the move-in provision by falsely telling the tenant that the landlord or a relative is going to move in. Later—after the tenant moves out—they rent the place out at a higher rent. By state law, all cities with rent control have "vacancy decontrol," which allows the landlord to raise the rent whenever the place becomes vacant after a voluntary vacancy or an eviction following some tenant wrongdoing. But this ruse is illegal. If this is your situation, or your landlord has similarly acted in bad faith—for example, he seeks to evict you because he needs to make major repairs, but never obtained permits—you might have a good reason to contest the eviction. See discussion of affirmative defenses in "The Answer," Item 3, below.

Your Rights if Your Landlord Suffers Foreclosure

This section deals with the rights of a tenant whose landlord has suffered a foreclosure, and the property in which you live is now owned by a bank, other lender, or other person or entity that has purchased the property at the foreclosure sale. The information in this section does *not* apply to owners who have suffered foreclosure. It applies only to *tenants* of landlords whose properties were foreclosed by their mortgage lender.

The Effect of Foreclosure

When an owner defaults on a mortgage, the mortgage holder, usually a bank, arranges for the property to be sold at a foreclosure sale. At such sales, that mortgage holder usually winds up owning the property, though sometimes a third party investor outbids the mortgage holder and winds up with the property. Before May 20, 2009, most renters lost their leases upon foreclosure. The rule was that if the mortgage was recorded with the county Recorder's Office before the lease was signed, a foreclosure wiped out the lease. Leases signed before the mortgage was recorded survived (and continue to survive) the foreclosure.

Because most leases last no longer than a year, it was all too common for the mortgage to predate the lease and destroy it upon foreclosure. After foreclosure, the new owner could terminate the tenancy on 60 days' written notice, and the tenant would have to leave unless the new owner accepted rent so as to create at least an implied month-to-month tenancy—which itself could later be terminated by 30-day or 60-day notice.

These harsh consequences for leases signed after the mortgage was recorded changed dramatically in 2009 (leases signed before the mortgage was recorded continued to enjoy their survival). Effective May 20, 2009, the federal "Protecting Tenants at Foreclosure Act of 2009" provides that when a "federally related" mortgage loan is foreclosed upon (that's virtually all bank loans, but excluding private loans, such as those between family members), and *when the bank takes over as owner*, post-mortgage leases now survive a foreclosure—meaning the tenant can stay at least until the end of the lease. Month-to-month tenants are entitled to 90 days' notice before having to move out. This notice period is even longer than the normal 30-day or 60-day notice required to terminate a month-to-month tenancy.

So much for the rules when the bank takes over as owner. If the property is bought at the fore-closure sale by a purchaser who intends to live on the property, that individual may terminate a lease with 90 days' notice (again, remember that leases signed pre-mortgage remain in effect, regardless of the intentions of the new owner). But there are some important qualifications for tenants who want to take advantage of this new right to 90 days' notice. They must be "bona fide" tenants, which means:

- the tenant isn't the spouse, child, or parent of the owner,
- the leasing transaction was conducted in an "arms' length," and
- the rent isn't "substantially below" fair market value.

This ability of a new owner to oust a tenant on 90 days' notice applies *only* where the individual wanting to live in the property is the purchaser *at the foreclosure sale*, not where the bank becomes the owner and then later sells to an individual. In that case, the buyer must honor the lease because the bank was required to do so, and he or she bought the property subject to that lease.

The new law also means that a new owner, whether a bank or an individual who bought as an investor, can insist the tenant comply with the lease or rental agreement the tenant entered into with the old owner. This means that on the first rent due date after the property changes hands, you must pay the same rent to the new owner. If you don't pay, the new owner can give you a 3-day notice to pay rent or quit if necessary.

If you receive notice that the property in which you live has been foreclosed (that is, a "trustee's sale" has been held), you should stop paying rent to the now-former owner and pay it to the new owner. If you don't know who that is, set aside your rent payment each month, so that you can pay it to the new owner once you find out who that is. If you receive a 3-day notice to pay rent or quit from the new owner, you might want to confirm with your county's Recorder's Office—usually located at the county seat—that the person or entity giving you the notice is truly the new owner.

In sum, for post-mortgage leases, when the new owner is the bank (or another federally-insured lending institution) that foreclosed on the property, that bank becomes your landlord and must honor your lease. In the case of a month-to-month tenancy, it must give 90 days' notice of termination

of tenancy. These protections apply to Section 8 tenants, too. Individual buyers who intend to live on the property can terminate your lease with 90 days' notice.

Tenants who live in cities with "just cause" eviction protection are also protected from terminations at the hands of an acquiring bank or new owner. These tenants can rely on their city's ordinance's list of allowable reasons for termination. Because a change of ownership, without more, does not justify a termination under the cities' lists of allowable reasons to evict, the fact that the change occurred through foreclosure will not justify a termination. However, a new owner who wants to do an "owner move-in" eviction may do so, as long as the owner complies with the ordinance's procedures.

Cash for Keys

To encourage tenants to leave quickly and save on the court costs associated with an eviction, banks offer tenants a cash payout in exchange for their rapid departure. Thinking that they have little choice, many tenants—even protected Section-8 and rent-control tenants—take the deal. To make matters worse, real estate agents who claim to be working for the banks try to pressure tenants to leave, implying such tenants have no rights. Do not be intimidated by real estate agents or banks or their attorneys. Know your rights and stand your ground, unless, of course, a financial offer to move quickly seems like a good deal. Keep in mind that it will cost the bank one to two thousand dollars to evict you and that the process, if you contest the case, could take well over a month.

Responding to Termination Notices: Month-to-Month Tenants

Month-to-month tenants have always known that their tenancies could be terminated upon 30 or 60 days' notice, depending on the longevity of their tenancy. The 2009 federal legislation changed the rules a bit, depending on whether the tenant is "bona fide" or not (see the explanation just above):

- Bona fide tenants. You are entitled to 90 days' notice, no matter who purchases the property upon foreclosure.
- Non-bona fide tenants. You are entitled to 30 or 60 days' notice, depending on whether your tenancy is over two years old.

Responding to Termination Notices: Tenants With Leases

If the property you rent changes ownership due to a foreclosure, you may receive any one of several different kinds of termination notices (you may even receive two at once). Whether the notice is legally valid, and your proper response to the notice, will depend on a number of factors. You'll need to know, first, whether the mortgage was signed before the lease, or after; then, whether the mortgage was federally-related or between private parties who didn't involve a bank. You'll also need to determine whether you meet the qualifications for a "bona fide" tenant. Consult the flow chart below. After following it out to the description that fits you, go to the numbered paragraph that describes your rights and gives you advice on how to proceed.

(1) **Your rights:** Because your lease was signed before the date the mortgage was recorded, it's preserved. (You'll probably need to take a trip to the county Recorder's Office to confirm when the deed of trust was recorded.)

Your response: Inform the new owner that your lease predates the mortgage. Present a copy of your written lease. If you are nonetheless named in an eviction lawsuit, you should defend on this basis. In Item 4.k of the Answer, type "Plaintiff is not entitled to possession of the subject property, as defendants' lease was signed on _____ , 20___ , prior to the recording

of the deed of trust foreclosed upon, by which plaintiff became owner. Therefore, plaintiff became owner subject to defendant's leasehold."

(2) **Your rights:** Unfortunately, you cannot take advantage of the new federal legislation, because the mortgage was a private loan. Your lease was extinguished when the property was sold, because it was signed after the date the loan or mortgage was recorded. Although your lease is now over, a 3- or 30-day notice is improper; you are entitled to 60 days' notice. (C.C.P. Sec. 1161b(a).)

Your response: Inform the new owner that you are entitled to 60 days' notice to move. If the owner does not give you 60 days' notice and files an unlawful detainer against you, Item 5/k of your Answer should read, "Defendants, as lawful tenants in possession of the subject property when foreclosure took place, were entitled to 60 days' notice of termination, per C.C.P. Section 1161b, and such notice was not given. Therefore, defendants' tenancy was not lawfully terminated."

(3) **Your rights:** Your lease was extinguished when the property was sold, because it was signed after the date the loan or mortgage was recorded, and you cannot take advantage of the new federal legislation because the mortgage did not involve a bank.

Your response: The new owner properly gave you 60 days' notice (some will mistakenly give you 90 days, which obviously suffices). (C.C.P. § 1161b(a)). You must move within 60 or 90 days.

(4) **Your rights:** As a bona fide tenant, you are entitled to the benefit of the new federal legislation, which requires the bank to honor your lease.

Your response: If you receive any termination notice, inform the bank or their attorney, preferably in writing, that you are a "bona fide tenant." Show them a copy of your written

Termination Notices Post-Foreclosure (Tenants With Leases)

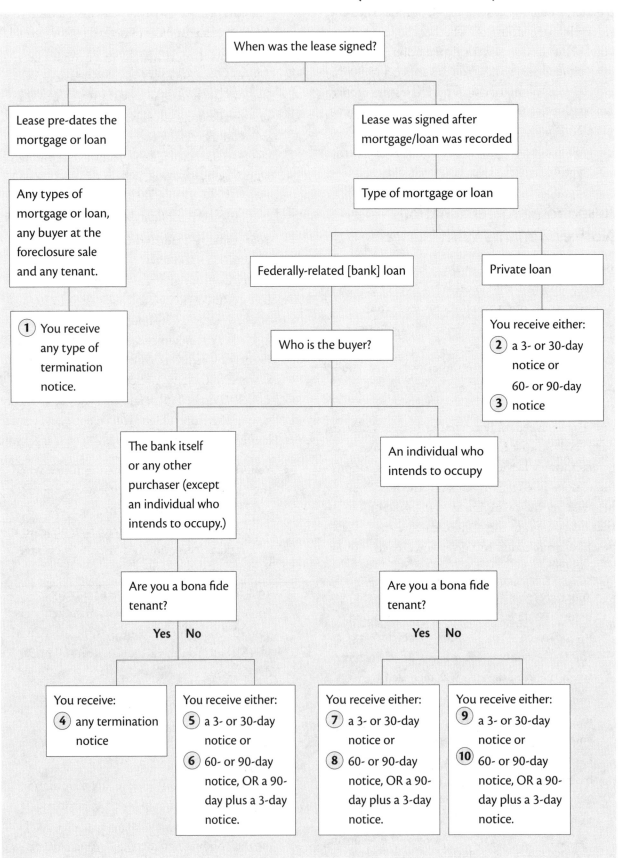

lease, or summarize the terms of any verbal agreement. You should also pay the bank the rent that you paid to the former owner.

Why a 3-Day and a 90-Day Notice?

Some banks send tenants both a 3-day and a 90-day notice, particularly in the case of single-family properties. Here's why: When owners *who also live on the property* default, they can properly be told to move with a 3-day notice. Many banks don't know, however, whether the residents are tenants or former owners. To cover each possibility, they send two notices. But you're a tenant, not an owner, so the 3-day notice is inappropriate. See the text below for advice on how to respond to a 3-day notice.

(5) **Your rights:** Because you are not a bona fide tenant, you don't enjoy the benefit of the new federal law. Your lease was wiped out at foreclosure because it was signed after the mortgage was recorded. You are, however, entitled to 60 days' notice under state law, not 30 days and certainly not 3 days.

Your response: Contact the bank and explain that under state law, C.C.P. § 1161b(a), you are entitled to 60 days. If the bank doesn't correct its notice (or send you a new one), and serves you with an eviction Complaint, Item 4k of your Answer should read, "Defendants, as lawful tenants in possession of the subject property when foreclosure took place, were entitled to 60 days' notice of termination, per C.C.P. § 1161b (a), and such notice was not given. Therefore, defendants' tenancy was not lawfully terminated."

(6) **Your rights:** Because you are not a bona fide tenant, you don't enjoy the benefit of the new federal law. Your lease was wiped out at foreclosure because it was signed after the mortgage was recorded. You are, however, entitled to 60 days' notice under state law.

Your response: If you got a 60 day notice, you have 60 days to move. If you've mistakenly been given a 90 day notice, you have 90 days. If you got a 90-day notice plus a 3-day notice, contact the bank and explain that you are not the former owner, but a tenant, and that the 3-day period does not apply to you (see "Why a 3-Day and a 90-Day Notice?" above). If you don't do that and the new owner files an eviction lawsuit without naming you as a defendant, you will have to act quickly by filing a Claim of Right to Possession once the Sheriff arrives with a 5-day notice to move, directed to the former owner. (See "The Complaint and Summons," above).

(7) **Your rights:** As a bona fide tenant, you are entitled to 90 days' notice when an individual who intends to occupy buys at the foreclosure sale.

Your response: Contact the individual or their attorney and explain that 3, 30, or even 60 days is not sufficient, in light of the new federal law. If they won't budge and serve you with eviction papers, you can defend against it by raising your right to 90 days' notice in your court-filed Answer. See "Filling out the form Answer," below.

(8) **Your rights:** As a bona fide tenant, you are entitled to 90 days' notice when an individual who intends to occupy buys at the foreclosure sale.

Your response: You have 90 days to move. If you are served with a 3-day notice as well, contact the owner and explain that you are a tenant, not an owner, which means that the 3-day period does not apply to you. If you don't do that and the new owner files an eviction lawsuit without naming you as a defendant, you will have to act quickly by filing a Claim of Right to Possession (see "The Complaint and Summons," above).

(9) **Your rights:** Because you're not a bona fide tenant, you don't enjoy the benefit of the new

federal law—your lease was wiped out upon foreclosure. However, you are entitled to 60 days' notice (not 30 and not 3) under state law.

Your response: If the new owner brings an unlawful detainer action, you should defend on that basis, and your first step would be to fill out Item 4.k in the Answer as follows: "Plaintiff has not properly terminated defendants' tenancy with the 60-day notice required by C.C.P. § 1161b, having used a _____-day notice instead."

(10) **Your rights:** Because you are not a bona fide tenant, you don't enjoy the benefit of the new federal law. Your lease was wiped out at foreclosure because it was signed after the mortgage was recorded. You are, however, entitled to 60 days' notice under state law.

Your response: If you received a 60- or 90-day notice, you have that amount of time in which to move. If you also received a 3-day notice, contact the individual owner and explain that you are not the former owner, but a tenant, and that the 3-day period does not apply to you.

Your Options After a Three-Day or 30-, 60-, or 90-Day Notice Is Served

If you get a three-day, 30-day, 60-day, or 90-day notice, sit down and think things over. Don't worry—you won't be thrown out on the fourth, 31st, 61st, or 91st day, as the case may be. As we mentioned, the landlord must first sue to evict you, and you must be notified of the lawsuit. Only if you lose the lawsuit can you be evicted, and then only by the sheriff or marshal. Usually, it will take the landlord over a month to finish the lawsuit (longer if you contest it) and, if the landlord wins, get the sheriff or marshal to give you an eviction order.

You have several choices:

- Comply with the notice—for example, pay the rent, get rid of the dog, or simply move out. If the landlord is in the right and you are able to comply, this may be the best course. In the majority of eviction cases (except possibly in some rent control areas), the tenant ultimately ends up moving.

- Negotiate a solution with the landlord, either by yourself, through a neighborhood or city-sponsored mediation program, or through a lawyer. (See Chapter 17 for a discussion of mediation services.) It will cost the landlord time and money to file an eviction lawsuit, which gives the landlord some incentive to work out a fair deal with you.

- Let the landlord file an eviction lawsuit—and then fight like hell to win. The discussion in this chapter should help you decide your chance of winning. You may also want to get some advice from a tenants' organization or an experienced tenants' lawyer.

If you decide to fight the eviction, you can represent yourself or hire a lawyer. If your lease or rental agreement requires the loser to pay the winner's attorney fees—and your chances of winning look pretty good—you may well want to do the latter.

If you decide to represent yourself, prepare carefully. The key is to do your homework—both on the law and on the facts. Get your witnesses, receipts, photos, and other evidence lined up, and learn the procedural rules set out in this chapter.

The Eviction Lawsuit

Landlords may not use small claims court to evict a tenant. Eviction lawsuits must be brought in superior court. (CCP §§ 86, 116.220.) An eviction lawsuit is technically called an "unlawful detainer" lawsuit. We use both terms interchangeably, but courts and lawyers almost always use the term "unlawful detainer."

One very important rule cuts across all other rules in an eviction case: The landlord must strictly comply with all legal requirements. (*Vasey v. California Dance Co.*, 70 Cal.App.3d 742 (1977).) This is the price the landlord pays for a special, quick procedure, and reflects the seriousness of the matter, which seeks to deprive you of your home.

Where the Lawsuit Is Filed

A few years ago, California had two levels of civil trial courts: municipal courts, which heard cases involving less than $25,000, and superior courts, which handled cases over that amount. Because all residential evictions for nonpayment of rent involved much less than $25,000, they were heard in municipal court.

Now, California has only one type of court in which trials are held: superior court. More populous counties have "divisions" or "branches." The eviction case filed by your landlord will normally be heard in the court or its division nearest the rental property.

The Complaint and Summons

The Complaint is the paper the landlord files in court to get the case going. It states the basic facts that justify eviction and asks the court to order you out and to enter a judgment against you for unpaid rent, court costs, and sometimes attorney fees.

Before you can be evicted, you must receive proper notice of an unlawful detainer suit against you by being named in the Complaint and served with a Summons. The Summons is a notice from the court telling you that you must file a written response (Answer, Demurrer, or Motion to Quash) with the court within five days or lose the lawsuit. The Summons also tells you whether you should give your response to the landlord's attorney or to the landlord. If the Summons and Complaint aren't served on you according to law, you can ask the court to dismiss the lawsuit.

If you are living in the property but are not named as a defendant in the Complaint, and the person named in the Complaint was not served with a document called a "Prejudgment Claim of Right to Possession," you may protect yourself against eviction for a while by filing a Claim of Right to Possession. Here's how this process works: If, on filing the unlawful detainer lawsuit, the landlord believes that there are adults other than the tenant listed on the lease or rental agreement living in the property, and if the landlord does not know their names, the landlord can reach those known-but-unnamed occupants by having a sheriff, marshal, or registered process server serve a Prejudgment Claim of Right to Possession on the defendant and these other occupants of the property. When this happens, any unnamed occupants must fill out the Prejudgment Claim of Right to Possession within ten days, to protect their rights. If an unnamed-but-served adult occupant doesn't do this, the occupant will not be able to stop the eviction later on by filing the Claim of Right to Possession after judgment.

On the other hand, if the landlord does not take the step of serving a Prejudgment Claim of Right to Possession at the outset, a person who is not named in the judgment (and hence not named in the writ of possession) may stop the eviction by filing the Claim of Right to Possession. The appendix contains a blank Prejudgment Claim of Right to Possession form, as well as a regular Claim of Right to Possession form.

Responding to the Summons

Your first response to the Summons can be one of three documents, each of which is discussed below:

- Motion to Quash—if the Summons was not properly served on you or if there was a defect in the summons itself
- Demurrer—if the Complaint is not in proper technical form or does not properly allege the landlord's right to evict you, and
- Answer—if you want to deny statements in the Complaint or allege new facts.

! CAUTION

Always file an Answer, even if you've moved out! Even if you have moved out, you should file a written response (usually an Answer) unless the landlord or landlord's attorney has assured you, preferably in writing, that the eviction will not proceed against you because you have moved out. Ideally, you'll want them to file a dismissal with the court, which will clearly end the case. If you move out but don't file a written response, and the landlord goes ahead and obtains a default judgment, you'll wind up having a judgment for rent that you perhaps do not owe, and for court costs. (You might also owe attorney fees, if your lease or rental agreement has a fees clause.)

Be sure to check your lease or rental agreement for an attorney's fees clause even if you get the landlord to file a dismissal. You could still be liable for the landlord's attorney's fees unless the dismissal also specifies that you do not owe fees and costs. You'll want the dismissal to specify that there is no "prevailing party" in the lawsuit.

You have five days to file your written response. You must count Saturdays and Sundays, but not other judicial holidays, in the five days. However, if the fifth day is a Saturday or Sunday, you can file your response the next day court is open.

> **EXAMPLE 1:** Teresa is served with a Summons on Tuesday. She counts Wednesday as day 1, Thursday as 2, Friday as 3, Saturday as 4, and Sunday as 5. Because court isn't open on Sunday, she can file her response on Monday.'

> **EXAMPLE 2:** Joe is served with a Summons on Wednesday. His five days are over on Monday, too.

> **EXAMPLE 3:** Laura is served with a Summons on Thursday. The next Monday is a court holiday. She counts Friday as day 1, Saturday as 2, Sunday as 3, Tuesday as 4, and Wednesday as 5. Wednesday is her last day to file a response.

If this is your first responsive pleading, you will have to pay a filing fee. The amount depends on how many defendants there are. It will probably be between $180 and $195 per defendant. Call the court clerk (civil division) for information on filing fees in your county. If you win—but not if you settle or the case is dismissed—you will get a judgment for your filing fee against the landlord as "costs."

If you are unable to pay the filing fees, you may apply to have them waived on the basis that your income is low, by filing an Application for Waiver of Court Fees and Costs form. If you receive certain governmental aid (SSI/SSP, CalWORKS, Food Stamps, and/or county general assistance), or if your gross monthly household income is under a certain level ($1,020.83 as of February 29, 2006, plus $354.16 for each additional household member), you are entitled to have your fees waived if you file an application asking that they be waived. (The dollar amounts are raised approximately every six months, and published on another court form called Information Sheet on Waiver of Court Fees and Costs.) If you don't receive such aid, and your income is higher than this, the court does not have to waive your fees, but might still do so if you show hardship.

An Application for Waiver of Court Fees and Costs, and a blank Order on Application for Waiver of Court Fees and Costs, is included in the appendix in the back of this book. If you fill these forms out correctly—the clerk is required to assist you—and present them to the clerk, the clerk must file any other documents you present at the same time, without your having to pay the fee right then. (Rule 985(b), California Rules of Court.) Later, if the court denies your application, you'll have to pay the filing fee within ten days of being notified. If you don't pay up, the papers you filed will be "unfiled," and a default judgment will be entered against you.

The Motion to Quash

Once you become aware that the landlord has filed an unlawful detainer action against you, your first step is to decide whether the landlord has complied with the strict requirements for how the Summons must be served on you. If the landlord didn't follow the rules exactly, you are entitled to file a paper called a "Motion to Quash Service of Summons," asking the court to rule that service of the Summons was improper. (CCP § 418.10.) You can also file a Motion to Quash based on a defect in the Summons itself—for example, that it lists the wrong court or judicial district. If this ruling is in your favor, the landlord has to start all over again.

How the Summons Must Be Served

The landlord cannot get sloppy about service of the Summons and Complaint. Whether or not you actually receive these documents, the landlord's failure to strictly abide by the rules governing their service means that the court has no authority (jurisdiction) to hear the case.

There are two allowable ways to serve a Summons and Complaint: personal service and substituted service.

Personal Service: The landlord must first attempt personal service of the Summons and Complaint. Someone over the age of 18 who is not a named party to the lawsuit—someone other than the landlord—must personally hand you the papers. (CCP §§ 414.10 and 415.10.) Even if you don't accept the papers, service has properly been made as long as you are personally presented with them. It is a common practice, when people realize they are about to be served, to slam the door in the server's face. Forget it. The server can deposit the papers outside the door (after you slam it) and you will be considered served.

Substituted Service: If several unsuccessful attempts are made to personally serve you (three is the general rule), the server may make substituted service by:

- leaving a copy of the Summons and Complaint with a competent person in your house (this can be someone less than 18 years of age), or with a person over 18 at your business

- explaining the nature of the papers to the person with whom they are left, and
- mailing a copy of the papers to the address where the papers were left. (CCP § 415.20(b).)

If this method of service is used, your time to respond is extended from five to 15 days.

"Posting and Mailing" Service: In limited situations, state law allows the landlord's process server to post copies of the Summons and Complaint on your front door and mail a second set of copies. (CCP § 415.45.) Before a landlord can use posting and mailing, the landlord must get written permission from a judge after showing that the process server made several unsuccessful attempts to serve the papers at reasonable times. If this method of service is used, your time to respond is extended from five to 15 days.

When to File a Motion to Quash Service of Summons

If you file a Motion to Quash, make sure you have a valid reason. Courts do not allow you to file motions solely for the purpose of delay. If there are adequate legal grounds for a motion, the request will be heard and possibly granted, and the judge will not inquire into your motives.

Typical grounds for a tenant's Motion to Quash based on defective service are:

- the Summons was served on one defendant but not the other
- the wrong person was served
- no one was served
- the process server used substituted service without first trying personal service, or
- the landlord himself served the Summons.

There is another ground for a Motion to Quash, which we describe here but don't enthusiastically recommend. If the complaint fails as an unlawful detainer complaint (perhaps because it doesn't allege a defective or improperly served three-day or other notice), the complaint may still survive as a regular civil complaint, one in which the landlord is suing over a broken contract (your lease or rental agreement is the contract). Now, a regular civil complaint must be served by a 30-day summons; but since this complaint used a five-day summons, it's defective. To attack it, you can use a Motion to Quash. (*Delta Imports v. Municipal Court,* 146 Cal.App.3d 1033 (1983).) But you can also use another kind of motion, called a Demurrer, which we recommend. (Demurrers are covered below.) A Demurrer will get you a delay of 27 days (a Motion to Quash results in only five to seven days' delay).

Overview of Motion to Quash

There are three parts to a Motion to Quash.

The Notice of Motion and Motion to Quash: This notifies the other side (the landlord or the landlord's attorney) that you are making the motion and have scheduled a court hearing on a certain day.

Memorandum of Points and Authorities: This is a short statement of the legal authority for your position.

Your Declaration: This is a written statement, made under penalty of perjury, stating the facts supporting your conclusion that service of the Summons was improper.

If you want to file a Motion to Quash, you must do so within your five-day period to respond.

Preparing the Motion to Quash

Step 1: Make several copies of the blank numbered legal paper with the superior court heading and the blank numbered legal paper in the appendix. You can also buy blank numbered legal paper at a stationery store. Most commonly used word processing software, like Microsoft *Word*, or Corel's *WordPerfect*, allow you to generate such line-numbered documents.

Step 2: Take a piece of numbered paper with the superior court heading and put your name, address, and telephone number in the same location (and on approximately the same lines) as is shown in the sample. Don't go crazy about trying to line up your text exactly with the numbers. Just do the best you can.

Step 3: Put the county where you are being sued, the court division or branches, as applicable, and the case number in the spaces as indicated on the sample. Get this information from the Summons and Complaint that were served on you.

Step 4: Call the court clerk and ask when and in what department or division motions are heard. In large cities, this tends to be every morning. In less populous areas, motions may be heard only once or twice a week.

Step 5: Once you find out which dates and times are available and which department hears motions, immediately fill in the blanks as follows:

(1) Pick a date that is no less than 8 and no more than 12 days from the date you plan to file the motion. (C.C.P. § 1167 specifies a 3-to-7-day period or window, but Rule 3.1327(a), Calif. Rules of Court, references C.C.P. § 1013, which adds five more days, for an 8-to-12-day window, where the papers are mailed to the landlord or her attorney.)

(2) Fill in the time the court hears motions.

(3) Fill in the department where motions are heard.

(4) Fill in the address of the court.

Step 6: Prepare your Points and Authorities.

Skip a couple of lines after the last line of your Notice of Motion and Motion to Quash, type the words POINTS AND AUTHORITIES in capitals, and then begin typing your points and authorities. You can copy the first sentence directly from the sample. You also need to explain:

- what the landlord did wrong, and
- the specific statute the landlord violated.

If the Summons and Complaint weren't served by someone over 18 or if they were served by someone who was a party to the action, the landlord violated CCP § 414.10. If the server used substituted service without first unsuccessfully attempting personal service, the landlord violated CCP § 415.20(b). If some other requirement for

Sample Motion to Quash

1   TOM TENANT
        1234 Apartment St.
2   Berkeley, CA 94710
        510-123-4567
3

4   Defendant in Pro Per

5

6

7

8   SUPERIOR COURT OF THE STATE OF CALIFORNIA, COUNTY OF ALAMEDA

9   BERKELEY-ALBANY DIVISION/BRANCH

10   )

      LENNY LANDLORD ,   )   Case No. 5-0258

11   )

             Plaintiff(s),   )   DEFENDANT'S NOTICE OF MOTION TO

12   )

      v.   )   QUASH SERVICE OF SUMMONS; POINTS AND

13   )

      TOM TENANT ,   )   AUTHORITIES; DEFENDANT'S DECLARATION

14   )

             Defendant(s).   )   IN SUPPORT THEREOF

15   _____)

16

17   To: LENNY LANDLORD, plaintiff, and to LAURA LAWYER, his attorney;

18   PLEASE TAKE NOTICE THAT on _____(1)_____ , 20___ , at ___(2)___ in Department No.

19 ___(3)___ of the above-entitled court, located at _____(4)_____ ,

20 defendant will appear specially pursuant to Code of Civil Procedure Section 418.10 and will move the court for

21 an order quashing the service of Summons herein on the ground(s) that the Summons and Complaint in this

22 case was personally served on him by Lenny Landlord, plaintiff in this case, in violation of Code of Civil Prodedure

23 Section 414.10, which requires service of the Summons and Complaint to be served by one not a party to the

24 action.

25   ////

26   ////

27   ////

28   ////

Sample Motion to Quash (cont'd)

1   The motion shall be based upon this notice, the memorandum of points and authorities in support there of,

2 the files and records of this case, and the declaration of Tom Tenant, attached hereto.

3 Dated: February 10 , 20 xx   *Tom Tenant*

                                        TOM TENANT

4   Defendant in Pro Per

5

6   POINTS AND AUTHORITIES

7   I. DEFENDANT'S MOTION IS PROPERLY NOTICED.

8   Code of Civil Procedure Section 1167.4 specifies a 3-to-7-day period for noticing unlawful detainer motions

9 to quash. However, Rule 3.1327(a), California Rules of Court, requires motions to quash to be noticed "in

10 compliance with [C.C.P.] sections 1013 and 1167.4." Therefore, when the defendant serves the moving papers by

11 mail, five days' additional notice is required under section 1013, and the 3-to-7-day period for notice is extended

12 to an 8-to-12-day period.

13   II. DEFENDANT'S MOTION TO QUASH SHOULD BE GRANTED.

14   A defendant in an unlawful detainer action is entitled to file a Motion to Quash Service of Summons when

15 service has not been validly completed. Code of Civil Procedure Sec. 418.10.

16   In this action, service of the Summons and Complaint was made personally by the plaintiff, Lenny Landlord.

17   Service by a party to the action violates Code of Civil Procedure Sec. 414.10, which requires that service of a

18 Summons and Complaint must be made by a person over 18 who is not a party to the action.

19   Respectfully submitted,

20   *Tom Tenant*

                            TOM TENANT

21   Defendant in Pro Per

22

23

24

25

26

27

28

Declaration

DECLARATION

TOM TENANT declares and says:

1. I am a tenant at 1234 Apartment St., Berkeley, CA 94710.

2. On January 8, 20xx, I was served with the Summons and Complaint in this case by my landlord, Lenny Landlord. I have not been served with those papers in any other manner or by another person.

3. I declare under penalty of perjury under the laws of the State of California that the foregoing is true and correct.

Dated: February , 20 xx

Tom Tenant
_____
TOM TENANT
Defendant in Pro Per

substituted service was missed, Section 415.20(b) was violated.

If the landlord erred for some other reason, you will need to find a legal basis for your conclusion and put it in the Points and Authorities. Talk to a tenants' group or lawyer, or research the law yourself.

RESOURCE
See *Legal Research: How to Find & Understand the Law,* by Stephen Elias and the Editors of Nolo (Nolo).

Step 7: Prepare a Declaration.

Skip a couple of lines after the last line of your Points and Authorities, type the word DECLARATION in capitals, and type your statement, as shown in the sample. Number each paragraph. The judge will use your declaration in place of oral testimony as a basis for deciding whether to grant your motion. So use simple sentences, and don't argue. ("Just the facts, ma'am.") Review your information to make sure it accurately and clearly tells the court what the landlord did wrong.

Note: The sample Notice of Motion and Motion to Quash, Declaration, and Memorandum of Points and Authorities is based on the scenario that your landlord handed the Summons and Complaint to you (a no-no) rather than having another person serve it. The papers will, of course, have to be modified appropriately if you bring your motion on another ground.

Preparing the Proof of Service by First-Class Mail—Civil

After you have served your motion on the landlord (which must be done by someone other than you, who is not a party to the lawsuit), you'll need to file a document with the court that shows that you complied with legal service requirements. The form you'll use is the Proof of Service by First-Class Mail—Civil, shown below and included in this

book's Appendix. Follow these instructions to prepare the document (after your server has served the landlord, that person will finish it and sign it, but you can begin it now). Note that the Judicial Council has also written a set of instructions, which you'll find in the Appendix, right after the form.

Top of the form: Put your name in the top box (after the words, "Attorney or party without an attorney"). Add your address, phone number, and email (optional). After "Attorney for (name)" write "in pro per." Enter your name in the third box, under the line, "Respondent/Defendant." Add the landlord's name under "Petitioner/Plaintiff." In the third box, enter the county and the name and address of the court, which will be the same as the information you entered on the papers that will be served. Leave the tall box on the right blank, but add the case number (again, it's on the papers being served) to the box at the lower right.

Item 1: This statement declares that the person serving the papers is over 18 years of age and either lives in or is employed in the county where the papers are being mailed. You don't need to add anything to this item.

Item 2: The server should print his or her home or business address.

Item 3: Provide the name of each document that the server will mail. Leave the date and "city and state" lines blank for now; your server will fill this information in after he or she actually places the documents in the mail.

Item 4: Your server will check either box a or box b, depending on how the server mailed the documents. Box a is for servers who personally deposit the envelope in a mail box. Box b is for those who mail from their business, as long as the business has an established procedure for collecting mail and mailing it on the same day it's placed in their "out" box.

Item 5: Provide the name and address of the person to whom the server will mail the documents. If the documents are going to be mailed to more than one person, you'll need to use and attach another form, "Attachment to Proof of Service by

First-Class Mail—Civil (Persons Served)." This form, POS-030(P), is in the Appendix, but not shown here. To fill it out, enter the name of the case at the top, as it appears on the Complaint, and the case number. Provide the names and addresses of any additional persons served.

At the bottom, after your server has mailed the documents, he or she will fill in the date he or she signed the form, print his or her name, and sign the document. Your server is now stating, under penalty of perjury, that the information provided on the form is true and correct.

RESOURCE
For more information on Motions to Quash, consult the *California Eviction Defense Manual* (CEB), available in most law libraries.

How to Serve the Motion to Quash

After you have prepared your Motion to Quash, you must have a copy of it served on the landlord promptly, to give her enough time to respond before the hearing date. As a defendant, you cannot serve your own legal papers, but you can have a friend or relative do it. The server must be a person over 18 and not a party to the action—that is, not named in the Complaint as a plaintiff or defendant.

Step 1: Complete the document called Proof of Service by Mail, following the instructions in the box below. You will find a blank tear-out form in the appendix; make several copies before using it, as you may need more later.

Step 2: Make two copies of your Notice of Motion and Motion, Points and Authorities, and Declaration, and the filled-in but unsigned Proof of Service by First-Class Mail—Civil. Refer back to "Preparing the Proof of Service by First-Class Mail—Civil" to make sure that the Proof of Service is complete and correct (enter any missing information now).

Step 3: Attach a copy of the unsigned Proof of Service to each set of your motion papers.

Step 4: Have your server mail one set of copies (the motion papers and the Proof of Service) to the landlord's attorney (listed on the Summons) or the landlord if there is no attorney. The papers must be mailed on the day indicated on the Proof of Service.

Step 5: Now have your server fill in the blanks in the last paragraph of the Proof of Service and sign the document. Attach it to the original motion.

Step 6: Take the original motion papers and one set of copies to the court clerk. Give the original set of papers to the clerk, who will stamp (or have you stamp) your copies with a "filed" message. This is your proof that you filed the originals with the clerk. The clerk will ask you to pay the filing fee.

Step 7: The clerk will note the date you indicated for the hearing on the Notice of Motion and enter it on the court calendar after you leave.

Step 8: Rule 3.1327, California Rules of Court, says that the landlord may oppose the motion orally, at the hearing, or file a written opposition and serve it on you one court day before the hearing.

Step 9: Judges sometimes make a tentative decision solely on the basis of the papers filed. If so, this tentative decision may be posted outside the courtroom on the date of the hearing. Some courts even have specific telephone lines connected to answering machines that list tentative rulings. Increasingly, tentative rulings are posted on the court's own website. (See "Tentative Rulings on the Web," below, for instructions on how to access your court's website.) If the decision is for the landlord, some courts require you to call the landlord before the hearing if you want to argue your side.

Step 10: The day of the hearing, go a little early and check with the clerk's office to make sure your case is on the calendar. If it isn't, find out why. If it is, go to the courtroom indicated.

CAUTION
Don't file by mail. Though it is legal to file papers by mail, we don't recommend it. The time limits are so tight in unlawful detainer cases (three to seven

Proof of Service By First-Class Mail

POS-030

ATTORNEY OR PARTY WITHOUT ATTORNEY *(Name, State Bar number, and address):*	FOR COURT USE ONLY

TELEPHONE NO.:

E-MAIL ADDRESS *(Optional):*   FAX NO. *(Optional):*

ATTORNEY FOR *(Name):*

SUPERIOR COURT OF CALIFORNIA, COUNTY OF

STREET ADDRESS:

MAILING ADDRESS:

CITY AND ZIP CODE:

BRANCH NAME:

PETITIONER/PLAINTIFF:

RESPONDENT/DEFENDANT:

PROOF OF SERVICE BY FIRST-CLASS MAIL—CIVIL	CASE NUMBER:

(Do not use this Proof of Service to show service of a Summons and Complaint.)

1. I am over 18 years of age and **not a party to this action.** I am a resident of or employed in the county where the mailing took place.

2. My residence or business address is:

3. On *(date):*   I mailed from *(city and state):*
  the following **documents** *(specify):*

  ☐ The documents are listed in the *Attachment to Proof of Service by First-Class Mail—Civil (Documents Served)* (form POS-030(D)).

4. I served the documents by enclosing them in an envelope and *(check one):*
  a. ☐ **depositing** the sealed envelope with the United States Postal Service with the postage fully prepaid.
  b. ☐ **placing** the envelope for collection and mailing following our ordinary business practices. I am readily familiar with this business's practice for collecting and processing correspondence for mailing. On the same day that correspondence is placed for collection and mailing, it is deposited in the ordinary course of business with the United States Postal Service in a sealed envelope with postage fully prepaid.

5. The envelope was addressed and mailed as follows:
  a. **Name** of person served:
  b. **Address** of person served:

  ☐ The name and address of each person to whom I mailed the documents is listed in the *Attachment to Proof of Service by First-Class Mail—Civil (Persons Served)* (POS-030(P)).

I declare under penalty of perjury under the laws of the State of California that the foregoing is true and correct.

Date:

▶

_____   _____
(TYPE OR PRINT NAME OF PERSON COMPLETING THIS FORM)   (SIGNATURE OF PERSON COMPLETING THIS FORM)

Form Approved for Optional Use Judicial Council of California POS-030 [New January 1, 2005]	**PROOF OF SERVICE BY FIRST-CLASS MAIL—CIVIL** **(Proof of Service)**	Code of Civil Procedure, §§ 1013, 1013a *www.courtinfo.ca.gov*

days) that a postal foul-up or a mishandling in the clerk's office can cause you no end of grief.

Tentative Rulings on the Web

Your court may use its website to announce tentative rulings. To find your court's site, go first to the Judicial Council website at www.courtinfo.ca.gov. Choose the Courts link at the top, then the Superior Courts link on the next page. Find your county on the alphabetical list of California counties, and click the word "website." Look for a link to tentative rulings.

The Court Hearing on a Motion to Quash

The evening before the hearing, you should sit down, relax, and go over the points stated in your motion papers to familiarize yourself with them. On the day of the hearing, dress conservatively, though you don't have to wear a business suit. Try to get to the courtroom a little early.

When your case is called, step forward. Some judges begin by asking questions, but others prefer that the person bringing the motion (you) talk first. In any case, don't start talking until the judge asks you to begin. Your argument should be straightforward and based on the facts and issues set forth in your declaration and motion papers and the landlord's responses to your papers.

Don't refer to any facts not contained in the declarations, or state your opinion of the landlord, or argue the merits of your situation beyond what you have raised in your motion papers.

After the landlord or landlord's lawyer has had a chance to argue their side, you can respond. The judge will either rule on the motion or take the matter "under submission" and decide later.

If the judge denies the motion, you will have some time to file your next response (or whatever other action is required at that time). If you win, the landlord may have another Summons ready to serve on you right there, and you start all over again.

The Demurrer

Once the landlord has properly served you with a Summons and Complaint, you are entitled to file an Answer to the Complaint or a Demurrer. (CCP § 1170.) You must either answer or demur within five days from the date the Summons and Complaint were properly served—or after any Motion to Quash that you made was denied. If the fifth day falls on a holiday, the last day for your response is extended to the next business day.

When you file a Demurrer, what you are really saying is, "Assuming, only for the purpose of argument, that everything the landlord says in the Complaint is true, it still doesn't provide legal justification for the court to order me evicted."

Note that when you file a Demurrer, you assume that the facts as stated by the landlord in the Complaint are true only for the purpose of this particular pleading. You are not conceding the truth of anything in the Complaint. Once the court rules on your Demurrer, you will still have a chance to file a written Answer, in which you may deny any factual allegations in the Complaint that you believe are false or don't actually know to be true.

When to File a Demurrer

Here are some of the principal legal grounds on which you may properly demur to a Complaint:

- **The three-day notice wasn't in the alternative.** All three-day notices—including those based on nonpayment of rent—must be in the alternative, unless the landlord is alleging violation of a lease provision that is not curable within that time (Unconditional Three-Day Notice to Quit). For example, if you receive a Three-Day Notice to Quit because you have a dog (or failed to pay the rent) and the notice fails to say that you have the alternative of getting rid of the dog (or paying the rent) in three days, it is defective. See above for details on three-day notices.

- **The three-day notice failed to tell the tenant where, or during what days or hours, the**

rent could be paid. If the notice omits this information, it's defective. (CCP § 1161(2).)

- **The Complaint was filed too soon.** The date the Complaint was filed will be stamped on the first page of the Complaint. Look at this date. If it is before the three days or the 30, 60, or 90 days given by the notice, you can demur. (See *LaManna v. Vognar,* 17 Cal.App.4th Supp. 1 (1993).)

- **The complaint fails to state a cause of action in unlawful detainer, is instead a civil complaint alleging a contractual dispute, and is defective because the landlord used the wrong time period for a civil Summons (five days instead of 30).** As noted above, you could also file a motion to quash. Indeed, one case (*Delta Imports v. Municipal Court,* 146 Cal.App.3d 1033 (1983)) suggests that a Motion to Quash is the tenant's exclusive remedy. There are, however, many cases holding that a Demurrer is the proper pleading in this situation. (See, for example, *Hinman v. Wagnon,* 172 Cal. App.2d 24 (1959).)

Overview of the Demurrer

You need to prepare three documents to file a Demurrer:

- The Demurrer
- Notice of Hearing
- Memorandum of Points and Authorities.

Don't use a declaration to support your Demurrer. In a Demurrer, the only question is whether the allegations in the landlord's Complaint (assuming they are true only for the purpose of the hearing), are sufficient to state a case. Since that is purely a question of law, any facts you might submit by declaration would be irrelevant to your Demurrer.

Filling Out the Demurrer

A blank Demurrer form is in the appendix. For instructions on how to complete the Demurrer, refer to Steps 1-3 for preparing the Motion to Quash set out above.

The list of legal grounds for a Demurrer are discussed just above.

If the first reason for filing applies to your situation, type in: "The three-day notice attached to the Complaint simply ordered me to vacate, without giving me the alternative of stopping any alleged breach of the rental agreement."

If the second reason for filing applies to you, type: "The three-day notice failed to state the days/ times/place where rent could be paid."

If the third ground fits your situation, type in: "The Complaint was filed prematurely, before the time set in the notice expired."

Sign and date the Demurrer.

Filling Out the Memorandum of Points and Authorities

There is a blank Points and Authorities form in the appendix with the caption "Points and Authorities in Support of Demurrer." To complete the top portion of this form, refer to Steps 1-3 for preparing the Motion to Quash, above. For the bottom portion of the form, repeat each ground for your Demurrer in the numbered paragraphs provided. (See the sample.) This time, however, you should follow each ground by an appropriate legal reference. For the first ground, this is: CCP § 1161(3); *Feder v. Wreden Packing and Provision Co.,* 89 Cal.App. 671 (1928). For the second ground, put CCP § 1161(2). For the third ground, put CCP § 1161(2).

Attach your Points and Authorities to your Demurrer.

Filling Out the Notice of Hearing on Demurrer

A blank tear-out form for the Notice of Hearing is in the appendix, and a sample is shown here. Turn back to "The Eviction Lawsuit/Responding to the Summons" in this chapter and locate the instructions accompanying the Notice of Motion to Quash. Follow them for the Notice of Hearing on Demurrer, with the following exceptions:

Sample Demurrer

1	TOM TENANT
	1234 Apartment St.
2	Berkeley, CA 94710
	510-123-4567
3	
4	Defendant in Pro Per
5	
6	
7	
8	SUPERIOR COURT OF THE STATE OF CALIFORNIA, COUNTY OF __ALAMEDA__
9	_____BERKELEY/ALBANY_____ DIVISION/BRANCH
10	)
11	LENNY LANDLORD _____ ,) Case No. ____5-0258____
	)
12	_____ ,) DEMURRER OF
	Plaintiff(s),)
13	v.) TOM TENANT
	)
14	TOM TENANT _____ ,)
15	) TO THE COMPLAINT OF
	_____ ,)
16	Defendant(s).) LENNY LANDLORD
	)
17	Defendant(s) demur to the Complaint on the following ground(s):
18	1. The three-day notice attached to the Complaint simply ordered me to vacate, without
19	giving me the alternative of stopping any alleged breach of the rental agreement.
20	_____
21	2. _____
22	_____
23	_____
24	3. _____
25	_____
26	_____
27	
28	Dated: _____ *Tom Tenant*
	Tom Tenant

Demurrer   Page 1 of 1

Sample Points and Authorities

1   TOM TENANT
    1234 Apartment St.
2   Berkeley, CA 94710
    510-123-4567
3

4   Defendant in Pro Per

5

6

7

8   SUPERIOR COURT OF THE STATE OF CALIFORNIA, COUNTY OF ___ALAMEDA___

9   _____BERKELEY/ALBANY_____ DIVISION/BRANCH

10   )
)
11 LENNY LANDLORD _____ ,) Case No. ____5-0258____
)
12 _____ ,) POINTS AND AUTHORITIES
)
13 v.   ) IN SUPPORT OF DEMURRER
)
14 _____ ,)
) (CCP § 430.10)
15 TOM TENANT _____ ,)
          Defendant(s).   )
16 _____)

17

18   I. DEFENDANT'S DEMURRER IS PROPERLY BEFORE THE COURT

19   A defendant in an unlawful detainer action may demur. C.C.P. § 1170. Although dicta in Delta Imports v.

20 Municipal Court, 146 Cal.App.3d 1033 (1983), suggests that a motion to quash is the remedy where a complaint

21 fails to state a cause of action in unlawful detainer, Delta did not overrule prior cases. See Hinman v. Wagnon, 172

22 Cal.App.2d 24 (1959), where the court held that a demurrer was proper where the incorporated 3-day notice was

23 defective on its face. The court sustained a dismissal following sustaining the demurrer without leave to amend.

24   The periods for noticing hearing on a demurrer are not stated in the unlawful detainer statutes, so C.C.P.

25 Section 1177 incorporates the regular provisions of the Code of Civil Procedure, such as C.C.P. Section 1005

26 requiring that motions be noticed on 16 court days' notice, plus five calendar days for mailing. Rule 325(b),

27 California Rules of Court, specifies that demurrers shall be heard in accordance with Section 1005.

28   ////

Sample Points and Authorities (cont'd)

1	II. ARGUMENT
2	The three-day notice attached to the complaint simply ordered me to vacate, without giving me the
3	alternative of stopping any alleged breach of the rental agreement. Code of Civil Procedure Section 1161(3);
4	Feder v. Wreden Packing and Provision Co., 39 Cal. App. 671 (1928).
5	
6	
7	
8	
9	
10	
11	
12	
13	
14	
15	
16	
17	
18	
19	
20	
21	
22	
23	
24	
25	
26	
27	Dated: _____ *Tom Tenant*
	Tom Tenant
28	

Notice of Hearing on Demurrer

1 | TOM TENANT
1234 Apartment St.
2 | Berkeley, CA 94710
510-123-4567
3

4 | Defendant in Pro Per

5

6

7

8 | SUPERIOR COURT OF THE STATE OF CALIFORNIA, COUNTY OF ___ALAMEDA___

9 | ___BERKELEY/ALBANY___ DIVISION/BRANCH

10
| LENNY LANDLORD |) |
11 | |) Case No. ___5-0258___ |
| |) |
12 | Plaintiff(s), |) NOTICE OF HEARING ON DEMURRER OF |
| |) |
13 | v. |) ___TOM TENANT___ |
| |) |
14 | TOM TENANT |) |
| |) TO THE COMPLAINT OF |
15 | |) |
| Defendant(s). |) ___LENNY LANDLORD___ |
16 | |) |

17

18 | To: _____

19 | PLEASE TAKE NOTICE THAT on _____, _____, at

20 | _____ in Department No._____ of the above entitled court, located at _____

21 | _____,

22 | a hearing will be held on Defendant's demurrer to the Complaint, a copy of which is served with this notice.

23

24 | Dated: _____   *Tom Tenant*
_____
Tom Tenant

25

26

27

28

- Call the court clerk and ask when Demurrers (rather than motions) are heard by the court.
- Unless the court clerk says otherwise (some courts insist that Demurrers in unlawful detainer cases be heard on short notice), select a hearing date that is at least 16 court (not calendar) days—don't count Saturdays, Sundays, or holidays—after the date you plan to file your Demurrer, plus five calendar days (add them because the copy of the demurrer and other papers will be mailed to the landlord or landlord's attorney).

Filing and Serving the Demurrer

After you have prepared your Demurrer, here's how to file and serve it.

Step 1: Complete the document called Proof of Service by First-Class Mail—Civil, following the instructions found in the discussion of Motion to Quash, above. You will find a tear-out form in the appendix; make several copies before using it, as you may need more later. The server must be a person over 18 and not a party to the action—that is, not named in the Complaint as a plaintiff or defendant. As a defendant, you cannot serve your own legal papers.

Step 2: Make two copies of your Demurrer papers (Notice of Hearing, Demurrer, and Points and Authorities) and the Proof of Service. Print the server's name on the last line of both copies of the Proof of Service.

Step 3: Attach one copy of the Proof of Service by First-Class Mail—Civil, to each set of copies of your Demurrer papers.

Step 4: Have your server mail one set of copies (your Demurrer papers and an unsigned Proof of Service) to the landlord's attorney (listed on the Summons) or the landlord if there is no attorney.

Step 5: Now have your server fill in the blanks in the last paragraph of the Proof of Service and sign it, stating that the mailing has occurred. Attach this original to your original Demurrer papers.

Step 6: Take the original Demurrer papers and one set of copies to the court clerk. Give the original set of papers to the clerk, who will stamp (or have you stamp) your copy with a "filed" notation, in the upper-right corner. This is your proof that you filed the originals with the clerk.

Step 7: The clerk will note the date you indicated for the hearing on the Demurrer and enter it on the court calendar.

If the landlord desires to respond to your Demurrer, he or she must file a response at least nine court days before the hearing. If you wish to make a written response to those papers, you must do so at least five court days before the hearing. (CCP § 1005.)

Step 8: Courts sometimes make a tentative decision solely on the basis of the papers filed. (See "Tentative Rulings on the Web," above.) If you want to argue your side even if the tentative decision is against you, some courts require you to call the landlord (or landlord's attorney) and say you're still going to argue.

Step 9: On the day of the hearing, check to see that your case is on the calendar. If it isn't, ask the clerk why and get it rescheduled.

> **CAUTION**
>
> **Don't file by mail.** Though it is legal to file papers by mail, we don't recommend it. The time limits are so tight in unlawful detainer cases that a postal foul-up or a mishandling in the clerk's office could result in your papers not being filed on time and a default being entered against you.

At the Hearing

See the discussion on hearings on a Motion to Quash, above.

Other Procedures

Other motions may be appropriate at this stage of the proceedings. For instance, a "motion to strike" might be appropriate if the landlord's Complaint requests relief that is not justified by the allegations. For more on this, consult the *California*

Eviction Defense Manual, published by Continuing Education of the Bar (CEB).

The Answer

The Answer is where you tell your version of what happened. You must file it with the court within five days of receiving the Summons and Complaint (15 days if substituted service was used), unless you file a Motion to Quash or Demurrer instead. If you miss the deadline, the landlord can take a default judgment against you. Defaults are discussed just below.

Even if you first file a Demurrer or Motion to Quash, you will have to file an Answer sooner or later, unless the landlord drops the case.

If your Demurrer is upheld by the court, the landlord will have to amend the Complaint. Then you can demur again, if you have grounds, or file an Answer. If, on the other hand, your Demurrer is overruled, you will have to file an Answer within five days after the date of the notice of the court order overruling the Demurrer.

Filling Out the Form Answer

Fortunately, a form Answer has been developed by the California Judicial Council specifically for unlawful detainer cases. A blank tear-out copy is located in the appendix, and you may obtain additional copies from the court or from the Judicial Council's website. (See "Get the Form From the Net," below.) A sample is included here.

Top of the Form: This is self-explanatory. Put your name in both the top box—"Attorney or Party Without Attorney"—and the one marked "Defendant." You will find the name and address of the court and the case number on the Complaint.

Item 1: Fill in your name.

Item 2: If the Complaint expressly asks for more than $1,000 in rent, check Box b. If it does not, check Box a.

If you checked Box b (as our sample Answer does), you have a little more work to do before going to Item 3. Follow these directions and you should have no trouble.

Carefully read the Complaint, paragraph by paragraph. As you do, take the following actions for each paragraph:

a. If you agree with *everything* in the paragraph, go on to the next one.

b. If you disagree with *any* statement in a paragraph, enter the paragraph number in the space on the Answer form after 2.b(1). You may very well disagree with more than one paragraph. If so, enter the numbers of all such paragraphs. If you don't have enough space to list all the paragraphs, check the box labeled "Continued on Attachment 2.b(1)" and type up an attachment on a separate piece of paper. Use 8½" x 11" paper (numbered legal paper is not required) and clearly label each attachment with the number of the paragraph on the printed form answer to which it refers. Each attachment should be on one side of a separate sheet and should be stapled to the Answer.

c. If you don't have enough information to agree or disagree with a statement in a paragraph, enter the paragraph number in the space on the Answer form labeled 2.b(2). Again, if you need more room, check the box labeled "Continued on Attachment 2.b(2)" and prepare an attachment page.

Do a careful job of reading each paragraph of the Complaint. The court will accept as true any of the landlord's statements in any paragraph that isn't listed on your Answer form. For example, suppose a landlord's Complaint alleges, in Paragraph 8.a, that the tenant was served with a three-day notice to pay rent or quit on January 7th. If the tenant doesn't list "8.a" as one of the denied paragraphs in Item 2.a(2) of the Answer, the tenant has admitted that he or she was served the notice. At trial, the judge will not permit the tenant to say otherwise. Any paragraph that isn't listed after Box 2.b(1) or 2.b(2) will be accepted as true by the court.

Item 3. Affirmative Defenses: An affirmative defense is any defense that involves a set of facts different from those raised in the Complaint. Another way of saying this is that an affirmative defense consists of new facts that constitute a legal excuse or justification. For example, the fact that you did not pay the landlord the rent is justified by the additional fact, or affirmative defense, that he failed, despite your request, to fix a leaky roof, overflowing toilet, or nonworking heating system. The Answer lists common affirmative defenses; check any that you plan to raise if your eviction goes to trial.

Here's another example. Suppose the landlord seeks to evict you because you didn't pay your full rent. If your defense is that you didn't pay the rent because you properly used the repair and deduct remedy to address a serious problem, as discussed in Chapter 6, it is based on different facts from those found in the Complaint and is therefore an affirmative defense—in this case, Item 3.b.

Another example is an eviction that was supposedly based on just cause—such as a landlord in a rent control city evicting a tenant on the grounds that the owner needs to make major repairs. If this eviction was made in bad faith—for example, the tenant checked with the city and found out that the landlord had not taken out the necessary building permits—the tenant would have an affirmative defense to the eviction. In this case, the tenant should check Item 3.g and list the name of this city's rent control or just cause eviction ordinance and the date of its enactment (see the rent control chart in Chapter 3 for this information).

In Item 3.j, state the facts on which you base your affirmative defense. See the examples below. Generally, the fewer words you use to describe your defense, the better. If your entire statement fits in the space under 3.j., check Box (1) of Item 3.j. However, even if you try to be brief, the room provided will probably not be enough. If you need more space, check Box (2) of Item 3.j. Then take a sheet of 8½" x 11" paper, label it "Attachment to Item 3.j. of Answer" at the top, and explain the facts regarding each affirmative defense.

Affirmative Defenses in Rent Control Cities: If you live in a rent control city, it is possible that you have been charged more rent than the ordinance allows. (See Chapter 3.) If this is the case, the landlord's claim that you failed to pay rent can be defeated on the ground that the rent demanded in the three-day notice was higher than it should have been. Although this defense is technically raised by a simple denial in Item 2 of the Answer, it is also a good idea to describe your position in an affirmative defense—in this case, Item 3.g.

State law says that landlords in rent control cities that require registration of rents (Berkeley, Santa Monica, East Palo Alto, Los Angeles, and West Hollywood) can't be penalized for good faith mistakes in the amount of rent they charge. (CC § 1947.7.) Landlords may argue that the statute also protects them from having a three-day notice thrown out because it demanded the wrong rent. Your response should be that dismissal of a Complaint because of a deficient three-day notice is not one of the penalties covered by the statute.

If you receive a 30- or 60-day notice of eviction because the landlord or the landlord's relative plans to move in (a just cause for eviction in many rent control cities), do a little checking before you decide to leave. If the landlord says he is moving in himself, find out where he lives now. If he lives in a fancy neighborhood and you live in a not-so-fancy one, it would seem very unusual for him to really plan to move in. If your rent is among the lowest rents in the building, the landlord may want you out pretty badly, because he can make the greatest profit by evicting you and charging a higher rent to a new tenant. In either case, see if he owns other vacant apartments he could move into instead. If he does, most ordinances require that he occupy one of these.

If a landlord claims that a relative is moving in, try to find out if the relative really exists, and if it would make sense for the relative to want to live there. For example, if the landlord's daughter is going to college in another city, it is not likely that she would want to move into your place in the middle of the semester.

If you do move out because the landlord says that she or a relative is moving in, go back and check up on whether the person moved in and, if so, how long he or she stayed. If it turns out that this was merely a scheme to take advantage of vacancy decontrol, you might be able to file a profitable lawsuit.

State law requires that in rent controlled cities that require landlords to register their properties with the rent board, landlords who evict tenants to move a relative (or the landlord) into the property must have the relative actually live there for six continuous months. If this doesn't happen, the tenant can sue the landlord. (CC § 1947.10.) Individual ordinances may require a longer stay (San Francisco requires 36 months).

If a court determines that the landlord or relative never intended to stay in the unit, the tenant can move back in. The court can also award the tenant three times the increase in rent the tenant paid while living somewhere else, and three times the cost of moving back in. If the tenant decides not to move back into the old unit, the court can award three times the amount of one month's rent of the old unit and three times the costs incurred moving out of it. The tenant can also recover attorney fees and costs. In one case, the court awarded a tenant $200,000 for a wrongful eviction based on a phony-relative ploy. (*Beeman v. Burling*, 216 Cal. App.3d 1586, 265 Cal.Rptr. 719 (1990).)

Here are some brief examples of affirmative defenses, with references to sections in this book where these issues are discussed in greater detail.

Item 3.a. Breach of Warranty of Habitability: If you are being evicted for nonpayment of rent and the landlord had reason to know that there are deficiencies in your apartment affecting its habitability, you should check Box 3.a. and put the details in 3.j. and any attachments. (See Chapter 6.)

Sample Statement of Details:

> On December 25, 20xx, I notified my landlord (the plaintiff in this action) that the heating unit in my apartment was broken and asked that it be fixed. This was not done." Or, "On March 19, 20xx, I notified my landlord that the roof was seriously leaking in three places. The roof has never been fixed.

Item 3.b. Use of Repair and Deduct Remedy: If you used the repair and deduct remedy, and the landlord failed to give you credit in the three-day notice for the amount you deducted from your rent (see Chapter 6), check this box and put the details in 3.j.

Answer—Unlawful Detainer

UD-105

ATTORNEY OR PARTY WITHOUT ATTORNEY *(Name and Address):*	TELEPHONE NO:	

TOM TENANT
1234 Apartment Street
Berkeley, CA 94710

ATTORNEY FOR *(Name):* Defendant in Pro Per

NAME OF COURT: Alameda County Superior Court
STREET ADDRESS: Berkeley—Albany Judicial Division
MAILING ADDRESS: 2000 Center St.
CITY AND ZIP CODE: Berkeley, CA 94704
BRANCH NAME:

PLAINTIFF: LENNY LANDLORD

DEFENDANT: TOM TENANT

ANSWER—Unlawful Detainer	CASE NUMBER: 5-0258

1. Defendant *(names):*

    TOM TENANT

    answers the complaint as follows:

2. ***Check ONLY ONE of the next two boxes:***
    a. ☐ Defendant generally denies each statement of the complaint. *(Do not check this box if the complaint demands more than $1,000.*
    b. ☑ Defendant admits that all of the statements of the complaint are true EXCEPT
        (1) Defendant claims the following statements of the complaint are false *(use paragraph numbers from the complaint or explain):*
            5.d., 6.a.(1), 6.b.(1), 7.a.(1), 9

            ☑ Continued on Attachment 2b (1).
        (2) Defendant has no information or belief that the following statements of the complaint are true, so defendant denies them *(use paragraph numbers from the complaint or explain):*

            ☐ Continued on Attachment 2b (2).

3. AFFIRMATIVE DEFENSES   (***NOTE:*** *For each box checked, you must state brief facts to support it in the space provided at the top of page two (item 3j)).*
    a. ☑ *(nonpayment of rent only)* Plaintiff has breached the warranty to provide habitable premises.
    b. ☐ *(nonpayment of rent only)* Defendant made needed repairs and properly deducted the cost from the rent, and plaintiff did not give proper credit.
    c. ☐ *(nonpayment of rent only)* On *(date):*   before the notice to pay or quit expired, defendant offered the rent due but plaintiff would not accept it.
    d. ☐ Plaintiff waived, changed, or canceled the notice to quit.
    e. ☐ Plaintiff served defendant with the notice to quit or filed the complaint to retaliate against defendant.
    f. ☐ By serving defendant with the notice to quit or filing the complaint, plaintiff is arbitrarily discriminating against the defendant in violation of the Constitution or laws of the United States or California.
    g. ☐ Plaintiff's demand for possession violates the local rent control or eviction control ordinance of *(city or county, title of ordinance, and date of passage):*

        (Also, briefly state the facts showing violation of the ordinance in item 3j.)
    h. ☐ Plaintiff accepted rent from defendant to cover a period of time after the date the notice to quit expired.
    i. ☐ Other affirmative defenses are stated in item 3j.

Page 1 of 2

Form Approved by the Judicial Council of California
UD-105 [Rev. January 1, 2007]

ANSWER—Unlawful Detainer

Civil Code, §1940 et seq.;
Code of Civil Procedure, § 425.12
www.courtinfo.ca.gov

Answer—Unlawful Detainer (continued)

		UD-105
PLAINTIFF *(Name):* LENNY LANDLORD	CASE NUMBER:	
DEFENDANT *(Name):* TOM TENANT	A-12345-B	

3. **AFFIRMATIVE DEFENSES** (cont'd)
    j. Facts supporting affirmative defenses checked above *(identify each item separately by its letter from page one):*

      3.a. I did not pay rent because the landlord did not fix the broken heater in my apartment, despite my repeated requests.

    (1) ☐ All the facts are stated in Attachment 3j.   (2) ☑ Facts are continued in Attachment 3j.

4. **OTHER STATEMENTS**
    a. ☐ Defendant vacated the premises on *(date):*
    b. ☐ The fair rental value of the premises alleged in the complaint is excessive *(explain):*

    c. ☐ Other *(specify):*

5. **DEFENDANT REQUESTS**
    a. that plaintiff take nothing requested in the complaint.
    b. costs incurred in this proceeding.
    c. ☐ reasonable attorney fees.
    d. ☑ that plaintiff be ordered to (1) make repairs and correct the conditions that constitute a breach of the warranty to provide habitable premises and (2) reduce the monthly rent to a reasonable rental value until the conditions are corrected.
    e. ☐ Other *(specify):*

6. ☑ Number of pages attached *(specify):*

UNLAWFUL DETAINER ASSISTANT (Business and Professions Code sections 6400- 6415)

7. *(Must be completed in all cases)* An **unlawful detainer assistant** ☐ did not ☐ did for compensation give advice or assistance with this form. *(If defendant has received **any** help or advice for pay from an unlawful detainer assistant, state:*
    a. Assistant's name: b. Telephone No.:
    c. Street address, city, and ZIP:
    d. County of registration: e. Registration No.:   f. Expires on (date):

TOM TENANT	▶ *Tom Tenant*
(TYPE OR PRINT NAME)	(SIGNATURE OF DEFENDANT OR ATTORNEY)

	▶
(TYPE OR PRINT NAME)	(SIGNATURE OF DEFENDANT OR ATTORNEY)

(Each defendant for whom this answer is filed must be named in item 1 and must sign this answer unless his or her attorney signs.)

VERIFICATION
(Use a different verification form if the verification is by an attorney or for a corporation or partnership.)
I am the defendant in this proceeding and have read this answer. I declare under penalty of perjury under the laws of the State of California that the foregoing is true and correct. Date:

TOM TENANT	▶ *Tom Tenant*
(TYPE OR PRINT NAME)	(SIGNATURE OF DEFENDANT)

UD-105 [Rev. January 1, 2007]   **ANSWER—Unlawful Detainer**   Page 2 of 2

Item 3.c. Landlord's Refusal to Accept Rent: If you tried to pay the rent during the time allowed you by a three-day notice but the landlord refused to accept it, check this box. If you tried to pay the rent after the three days (but before the lawsuit was filed) and the notice did not mention "forfeiture" of your tenancy, check this box. (See the discussion of three-day notices above.)

Item 3.d. Cancellation of Notice: Sometimes, after a three-day or 30-, 60-, or 90-day notice is served, the landlord (or the landlord's agent) says something to indicate that he didn't mean it, that you can have more time, or something else inconsistent with the notice. If this happens, he may have implicitly waived or canceled the notice, so check Item 3.d.

Sample Statement of Details

> After I received the notice, Plaintiff's resident manager told me that she had served the notice on me only to scare me, and as long as I paid by the end of the month, no eviction lawsuit would be filed.

Item 3.e. Retaliatory Eviction: Retaliatory eviction is a very common defense. If you believe that your landlord is illegally retaliating against you (see above), check Item 3.e. and put the details in 3.j.

Sample Statement of Details

> After Plaintiff twice refused to respond to our request that he fix the toilet, we complained to the city health department. Forty-five days later, we received a 30-Day Notice to Quit. We believe that we are being evicted in retaliation for our complaint to the health department.

Item 3.f. Discrimination: The landlord may not evict you because of your race, religion, sex, sexual preference, or job; because you have children; or for any reason based on your personal characteristic or trait. (See Chapter 4.)

Sample Statement of Details

> Plaintiff served me with the 30-day notice because he doesn't want African-American people living in his rental units.

Item 3.g. Just Cause for Eviction Ordinances: If you live in a city with a rent control ordinance that requires just cause for eviction, and you dispute the just cause alleged in the Complaint, simply deny that allegation of the Complaint (by putting the paragraph number in Item 2.b(1)). If, however, the landlord committed some violation of the just cause ordinance that you cannot raise by a denial, then check Item 3.g. (See Chapter 3 and "Tenancy Termination Notices" in this chapter.)

Sample Statements of Details

> The rent control ordinance of the City of Santa Monica says that a three-day notice must tell me of my right to call the rent board for advice. The notice served on me by Plaintiff did not say this, so it is invalid.

> The rent control ordinance of the City of San Jose requires a 90-day notice of termination of tenancy, not a 60-day notice, when the tenant has lived in the property for a year or more.

> The rent control ordinance of the City of San Francisco requires that the 30-day notice state a just cause to evict. The 30-day notice served on me by the landlord did not do this.

> Landlord has sued to evict me because she wants her mother to live in the unit. This is not a just cause to evict because under the rent control ordinance of the City of San Francisco, landlord must first establish that there are no other vacant units that her mother can live in. In fact, at the time she served me with the 30-day notice, she had two equivalent vacancies.

Item 3.h. Acceptance of Rent Beyond Notice Period: If the landlord served a 30-, 60-, or 90-day notice and then accepted rent covering a period beyond the 30, 60, or 90 days, he has implicitly withdrawn the notice, so check this box. (*Highland Plastics v. Enders,* 109 Cal.App.3d Supp. 1 (1980).)

Item 3.i. Other Affirmative Defenses: Sometimes landlords orally allow tenants to get behind on their rent or to make certain repairs to their premises in exchange for free rent, or they make other agreements on which the tenant relies because of a good relationship with the landlord. Then, when a falling-out occurs, the landlord will attempt an eviction on the basis of a particular tenant default and deny that any oral agreement was made. In such a case, you have an affirmative defense based on the agreement and should check this box and place the details on 3.j.

Item 3i.: Eviction following Foreclosure: As explained in "Your Rights if Your Landlord Suffers Foreclosure," above, banks or third-party foreclosure-sale buyers must generally honor existing leases, and must in any event give 90 days' notice of termination of where allowed in the case of a buyer who wants to live in the property, or to terminate a month-to-month tenancy. If the new owner has brought an unlawful detainer case against you and failed to comply with the law, you should check this box and place the details on 3.j, starting with, "Plaintiff has failed to comply with the federal "Protecting Tenants at Foreclosure Act of 2009" as follows: Then state the specifics, including what type of tenancy you had and why any notice provided was incorrect.

Item 4. Other Statements:

Item 4.a.: If you have moved out by the time you get around to filing this Answer, check this box. Remember, even though you've moved, the landlord may still be seeking a judgment against you for rent or post-termination daily "holdover damages." It is important to file this Answer to have your day in court if you still owe the landlord money.

Item 4.b.: Although the landlord may not accept rent after the expiration of the notice to quit, the court will award the landlord the fair market rental value of the premises for the time between the expiration of the notice and the day the judgment is entered. This is normally computed by dividing the total rent amount by 30 to arrive at a daily rental, and then multiplying this amount by the number of days. If you believe that the "fair rental value" stated in the Complaint is too high, check this box. Then explain any habitability problems on the premises, any change in the neighborhood that might have affected rental value, or any other reason you think the landlord's estimate is excessive. If the action against you is based on nonpayment of rent, and you are defending the lawsuit on the basis that the landlord breached the implied warranty to provide habitable premises, you should have checked Box 3.a and explained why the premises are not worth what the landlord says they are. In this case, simply type "See item 3.a" in this space.

Item 4.c.: This box gives you a chance to say anything relevant and not covered by the other boxes.

Item 5. Defendant Requests:

Item 5.a.: This item is self-explanatory. You don't want the court to meet any of the landlord's requests made in the Complaint, such as past due rent for damages. You indicate your specific requests for costs in the rest of Item 5. If your affirmative defense was the landlord's breach of the warranty of habitability (Item 3.a) or you believe the "fair rental value" stated in the Complaint is excessive, check Item 5.d. If you are going to hire an attorney, check Item 5.c, "reasonable attorney fees." You are entitled to reasonable attorney fees if you win with a court judgment and your rental agreement or lease provides for landlord's attorney fees. (See Chapter 17 for a discussion of attorney fees.) Obviously, you cannot get attorney fees if you did not have an attorney. If you believe you are entitled to some other remedy, provide details in Item 5.e.

Item 6. Attachments: If you have prepared any attachments, check the box here and list the number and name of each attachment.

Signing and Verifying Your Answer

Here are the rules:

- The Answer must be signed by all of the named defendants.
- The verification at the bottom of the Answer (the statement under penalty of perjury that the statements in the Answer are true) need be signed only by any one defendant.

Filing and Serving Your Answer

After you've prepared your Answer, here's how to file and serve it.

Step 1: Complete the document called Proof of Service by First Class Mail—Civil, following the instructions found in the box in "The Eviction Lawsuit," above. You will find a blank tear-out form in the appendix. You can use this form or the optional Judicial Council form called Proof of Service—Civil. (We prefer our form because it is simpler and easier to use.) Make several copies before using either form, as you may need more later. The server must be a person over 18 and not a party to the action—that is, not named in the Complaint as a plaintiff or defendant. As a defendant, you cannot serve your own legal papers.

Step 2: Make two copies of your Answer and the unsigned but filled-in Proof of Service by Mail. Print the server's name on the last line of both copies of the Proof of Service.

Step 3: Attach one copy of the Proof of Service to each copy of your Answer.

Step 4: Have your server mail one copy of the Answer and attached unsigned Proof of Service to the landlord's attorney (listed on the Summons), or the landlord if there is no attorney. The papers must be mailed on the day indicated on the Proof of Service.

Step 5: Now have your server fill in the blanks in the last paragraph of the Proof of Service and sign it, stating that the mailing has occurred. Attach this original to your original Answer.

Step 6: Take the original Answer and Proof of Service and a copy to the court clerk. (It is possible to file papers by mail, but this is not advised. A postal service or clerk's office foul-up could cause grave problems given the short time limits in these kinds of cases.) Give the original set of papers to the clerk, who will stamp (or have you stamp) your copy package with a "filed" notation in the upper right-hand corner. This is your proof that you filed the originals with the clerk.

> **! CAUTION**
>
> **Make sure your Answer is filed within five days of the day the Complaint was served (or your Motion to Quash or Demurrer was overruled).** If you miss this deadline, you may find yourself having to dig yourself out from under a default judgment obtained by the landlord. See "The Complaint and Summons," above, for how to compute the five-day period.

Setting Aside a Default Judgment

If you miss the deadline for responding to the landlord's Complaint, the landlord may ask the court for a default judgment against you. That means you lose without a trial and the landlord has the legal right to evict you. If this happens, you may file a motion asking the court to set aside the default judgment. If the motion is granted, you may then file your Answer and have your trial.

To persuade the judge to grant your motion to set aside a default, you must show all of the following:

- That you have a pretty good excuse (such as illness) for your failure to respond to the Summons in five days. "I didn't know how to respond, and it took me a few days to get hold of a copy of *California Tenants' Rights*" might work, but don't count on it.
- That you did not unnecessarily delay too long in filing your motion to set aside the default.

There is no set period of time for which a delay is or is not excusable. It depends on the facts of each case.

- That you have a defense to the lawsuit.

In addition, be sure to ask for a stay (postponement) of the eviction until the court rules on your motion to set aside the default.

Moving to set aside a default can be tricky. We recommend that you try to get a lawyer or tenants' rights advocate to help you with it. If you still want to do it yourself, the necessary forms and procedures are contained in the *California Eviction Defense Manual,* published by Continuing Education of the Bar (CEB), and available in most county law libraries.

Discovery: Learning About the Landlord's Case

"Discovery" is the process of finding out what evidence the other side has before the trial begins, so you can prepare your own case to meet it. Discovery is conducted in two basic ways.

One is to question the other party face to face in a proceeding called a deposition (discussed below).

The second is to send the other party a written document that specifies what is being sought. This document typically consists of:

- questions (interrogatories)
- a request that certain documents be produced for inspection
- a request that a physical inspection of the premises be allowed
- a request that certain facts be admitted as true, or
- all of the above.

You can make any of these requests following the instructions below. The law provides a set period of time within which a party must respond to discovery requests. The response must be given within five days, or within ten days if the request was served on you by mail (CCP §§ 1013, 2030.260(a), 2031.260, 2033.250).

Request for Inspection

Use a Request to Inspect to make the other side let you see and copy any documents or other things before trial. You may want to see copies of leases, building inspector's reports, or checks.

The landlord must respond to your request within five days. (CCP § 2031.260.) Add five days to each of these periods if you mailed the request for inspection to the landlord (or to the landlord's attorney), instead of personally serving them. (CCP § 1013.) If the landlord refuses to respond adequately to your discovery request within that time, you may ask the court to impose sanctions on the landlord, which include paying your costs or preventing the landlord from using certain evidence. (CCP § 2031.310.)

Take a look at our sample Request to Inspect. You will find a blank tear-out copy in the appendix. You'll need to fill in your name, address, and telehone number; the county where you are being sued; the court district and the case documents you are requesting; and where and when you want to see and copy these documents. If you want to inspect or photograph the rental premises, you'll also need to specify the location, date, and time you wish to do this.

After you've prepared your Request to Inspect, you must file and serve it.

Step 1: Make one copy of your Request to Inspect.

Step 2: Complete the document called Proof of Service by Mail, following the instructions found in the box in "The Motion to Quash," above. You will find a blank tear-out form in the appendix; make several copies before using it, as you may need more later. The server must be a person over 18 and not a party to the action—that is, not named in the Complaint as a plaintiff or defendant. As a defendant, you cannot serve your own legal papers.

Step 3: Make a copy of the Proof of Service by Mail, print your server's name on the last line of the copy, and attach it to the copy of your Request to Inspect.

Sample Request for Inspection

1 TOM TENANT
    1234 Apartment St.
2 Berkeley, CA 94710
    510-123-4567
3

4 Defendant in Pro Per

5

6

7

8 SUPERIOR COURT OF THE STATE OF CALIFORNIA, COUNTY OF __ALAMEDA__

9 _____BERKELEY/ALBANY_____ DIVISION/BRANCH

10 LENNY LANDLORD_____ ,) Case No. ____5-0258____
)
11 _____ ,)
)
12   Plaintiff(s),   ) REQUEST TO INSPECT AND FOR
)
13 v.   ) PRODUCTION OF DOCUMENTS
)
14 TOM TENANT_____ ,)
)
15 _____ ,)
)
16   Defendant(s).   ) (Code of Civil Procedure Sec. 2031.101–2031.510)
)

17

18 To: _____ , Plaintiff,

19 and _____ , Plaintiff's attorney:

20   Defendant requests that you produce and permit the copying of the following documents: _____

21 [describe documents]_____ .

22   Defendant requests that you produce these documents at the following address: ____ [your address or

23 or any other location]_____ , at the following date and time: __ [within 5 days, plus 5 days,

24 if this request is served by mail] .

25   Defendant further requests permission to enter, inspect, and photograph the premises located at _____

26 [address of premises you wish to inspect, otherwise leave blank]_____

27 at the following date and time: [within 5 days, plus 5 days, if this request is served by mail] .

28 Dated: _____   *Tom Tenant*
                                           Tom Tenant

Request to Inspect and for Production of Documents   Page 1 of 1

Step 4: Have your server place these papers in the mail with first-class postage attached.

Step 5: Now have your server fill in the blanks in the last paragraph of the Proof of Service and sign it.

Step 6: Keep the originals of your Proof of Service by Mail and Request to Inspect in your records. You need not file these papers with the court clerk unless a dispute arises over your request.

Interrogatories

The discovery devices most often used in unlawful detainer cases are written interrogatories. These are questions you pose that the other side must answer. Of course, the other side may pose their own set of questions to you, too. You can use a set of Form Interrogatories designed for eviction cases (see CCP § 2030.010-2030.410). These are set out in the appendix. Here is how to use them:

- **Read the interrogatories.** If any is relevant to the issues in your case, check off the number of that interrogatory in the proper box of the blank tear-out "Form Interrogatories—Unlawful Detainer."

- **Do not simply check off every box in the Form Interrogatories.** If you do, the landlord may take you to court and get sanctions against you (usually a fine) based on the claim that you are using the interrogatories for purposes of harassment and delay. Make sure that the interrogatory pertains to some denial or affirmative defense you raised—for example, in your Answer—and that the landlord's answer might help you know what to expect at trial.

- **Tear out the Interrogatories and follow these instructions:**

Step 1: Complete the document called Proof of Service by First Class Mail—Civil, following the instructions in "The Motion to Quash," above. You will find a blank tear-out form in the appendix; make several copies before using it, as you may need more later. The server must be a person over 18 and not a party to the action—that is, not named in the Complaint as a plaintiff or defendant. As a defendant, you cannot serve your own legal papers.

Step 2: Make one copy of your Interrogatories and the Proof of Service by Mail. Fill in the server's name on the last line of the copy of the Proof of Service.

Step 3: Attach the copy of the Proof of Service to the copy of your Interrogatories.

Step 4: Have your server mail the copy package (the Interrogatories and the Proof of Service) to the landlord's attorney (listed on the Summons) or the landlord, if there is no attorney. The package must be mailed on the day indicated on the Proof of Service. You may also include a full set of the Interrogatories themselves if you wish.

Step 5: Now have your server fill in the blanks in the last paragraph of the Proof of Service and sign it. Attach this original to your original Interrogatories. Place these documents in your file. You don't have to file them with the court unless a dispute arises.

The landlord or landlord's attorney must respond to your interrogatories within five days. (CCP § 2030.260(a)), plus five days if you served them by mail. If the landlord (or landlord's attorney) refuses to respond adequately within that time, you may ask the court to impose sanctions on the other side. (CCP §§ 2030.290-2030.300.)

The Deposition

Depositions are oral statements made under oath. The other party must sit down with you in your lawyer's office or another site and answer questions. You must arrange (and pay for) a court reporter to take down the questions and answers. The transcript can be used against the person if he tries to change his story at trial.

Explaining how to set up and conduct a deposition is beyond the scope of this book. More to the point is what happens if the landlord's attorney serves a notice of deposition on you, telling you to appear somewhere at a certain time for a deposition. All you have to do is appear and answer the questions. However, you may be tricked into giving an answer that later comes back to haunt you. For this reason, if possible, it is often a good idea to have a lawyer there to help you avoid the traps set by the landlord's attorney.

RESOURCE

For more information on how to prepare for a deposition and how to give one, see *Nolo's Deposition Handbook*, by Paul Bergman and Albert Moore (Nolo).

The Request to Admit

You can find out just what you and the landlord agree and disagree about by requesting the landlord to admit certain statements that you believe to be true. If they are admitted, it saves you the trouble of having to prove them in court. If, on the other hand, the landlord denies a statement, and you later prove it to be true, the landlord can be required to reimburse you for the cost of the proof. We don't provide you the forms for this discovery device, but if you are interested in using it, consult *Civil Discovery Practice in California,* published by Continuing Education of the Bar (CEB) and available in most law libraries.

Negotiating a Settlement

At any point in a dispute, you may negotiate a settlement with the landlord. The keys to any settlement are (1) that each side has something the other wants, and (2) that each side is willing to talk to the other in a reasonable manner.

The landlord usually wants you to get out, pay back rent, or both. The owner wants minimum expense and hassle. You have the power to cause the landlord expense and trouble by your use of the defenses and procedural tools described in this chapter. Therefore, the landlord may be willing (reluctantly) to give you more time to get out, reduce the claim for back rent, or even pay your moving expenses if you are willing to give up your defenses and procedural tools and agree to get out on a specific, mutually agreeable day. If you are

planning to move anyway, this sort of compromise may make excellent sense.

Of course, depending on the facts of your situation, you might instead want to hang tough, go to trial, and win everything. But you always run the risk of losing. The landlord is often in the same boat. What this amounts to is that, commonly, it may be in both of your interests to lessen your risks by negotiating a settlement both of you can live with.

EXAMPLE: When Tom fails to pay his rent of $800 on May 1, his landlord, Lenny, serves a three-day notice on him, and when that runs out without Tom paying the rent, Lenny sues Tom for an eviction order and a judgment for the $800. Tom's Answer says that Lenny breached the implied warranty of habitability by not getting rid of cockroaches. Lenny tells Tom that at trial Lenny will try to prove that the cockroaches were caused by Tom's poor housekeeping. Lenny thinks he will win the trial, and Tom thinks that he will win. Each of them is sensible enough to know, however, that they might lose—and that it is certain that a trial will take up a lot of time and energy (and maybe some costs and attorney fees). So they get together and hammer out a settlement agreement: Tom agrees to get out by July 1, and Lenny agrees to drop his lawsuit and any claim for back rent.

Here are a few pointers about negotiation:
- It is common for the tenant to receive forgiveness of past rent (or some of it) plus, in some instances, moving expenses. Sometimes tenants bargain for even some financial help with a new security deposit, as a condition of moving out without a court fight.
- Be courteous, but don't be weak. If you have a good defense, let the landlord know that you have the resources and evidence to fight and win if the landlord won't agree to a reasonable settlement.
- If you are in a rent control city and your defense is that the landlord breached rent

Sample Settlement of Unlawful Detainer Action

SETTLEMENT AGREEMENT

1. Tom Tenant ("tenant")

resides at the following premises: 1234 Apartment Street, Berkeley, CA 94710

("premises").

2. Lenny Landlord ("landlord")

is the owner of the premises.

3. On January 8 , 20 xx landlord caused a Summons and Complaint

in unlawful detainer to be served on tenant. The complaint was filed in the Superior Court for the County of

Alameda , Berkeley-Albany District, and carries

the following civil number: 5-0258 .

4. Landlord and tenant agree that tenant shall vacate the premises on or before March 1 ,

20 xx . In exchange for this agreement, and upon full performance by tenant, landlord agrees to file a voluntary

dismissal with prejudice of the Complaint specified in clause #3.

5. Also in exchange for tenant's agreement to vacate the premises on or before the date specified in clause

#4, landlord agrees to:

(*Choose one or more of the following*)

☑ Forgive all past due rent

☐ Forgive past due rent in the following amount: $_____

☐ Pay the tenant $_____ to cover tenant's moving expenses, new deposit requirements and

other incidentals related to the tenant moving out.

6. Any sum specified in clause #5 to be paid by the landlord shall be paid as follows:

(*Choose one or more of the following*)

☑ Upon tenant surrendering the keys to the premises

☐ Upon the signing of this agreement

☐ $_____ upon the signing of this agreement and $_____ upon

tenant surrendering the keys

☐ in the following manner:

Sample Settlement of Unlawful Detainer Action (con'td)

1

2

3

4

5

6

7

8

9

10

11

12

13

14

15

16

17

18

19

20

21

22

23

24

25

26

27

28

7. The tenant's security deposit being held by landlord shall be handled as follows:

☐ Upon the signing of this agreement

☐ restored in full to the tenant upon surrender of the keys

☑ treated according to law

☐ other:

8. Tenant and landlord also agree:

a) to waive all claims and demands that each may have against the other for any transaction directly or indirectly arising from their Landlord-Tenant relationship

b) that this settlement agreement not be construed as reflecting on the merits of the dispute and

c) that landlord shall not make any negative representations to any credit reporting agency or to any other person or entity seeking information about whether tenant was a good or bad tenant.

9. Time is of the essence in this agreement. If tenant fails to timely comply with this agreement, landlord may immediately rescind this agreement in writing and proceed with his or her legal and equitable remedies.

10. This agreement was executed on _____ January _____ , 20 __XX__ at _____ Berkeley, California _____ .

Signed: _____ *Tom Tenant* _____
Tom Tenant

Signed: _____ *Lenny Landlord* _____
Lenny Landlord

control rules, consult the staff at your local rent board. They may be able to help.

- Put the settlement agreement in writing. If you can (and you may not be able to), try to avoid agreeing to a "stipulated judgment," which enables the landlord to get you out very quickly if he thinks you are not abiding by the settlement agreement. Also, credit reporting agencies get records of judgments, so a stipulated judgment may hurt your credit rating.

- If your lease or rental agreement has an attorney's fees clause, you'll want to avoid having to pay the landlord's fees (and court costs), which may be considerable even though the case hasn't proceeded very far. Include a statement in your settlement agreement that there is no "prevailing party" and that neither side owes the other for fees and costs.

The sample form settlement agreement shown previously may be used with appropriate modification. A blank tear-out copy is in the appendix.

Summary Judgment

Although the landlord is entitled to a trial date within three weeks after you file your Answer, landlords don't have to wait that long to obtain a judgment if they can convince the court that there is no substantial disagreement over the facts. For instance, if you both agree that you have been conducting a mail order business from your apartment, but disagree as to whether this is a breach of the lease, which limits the use of the premises to residential use, the court can decide the case without holding a full trial. This speedy procedure is termed a "summary judgment."

If the landlord files a Motion for Summary Judgment, you will be served with the Notice of Motion and an accompanying Declaration setting out the landlord's version of the facts. Under C.C.P. §§ 1170.7 and 1013, and Rule 3.1351(a), Cal. Rules of Court, the landlord must personally serve the motion papers on you no later than five days in advance of the hearing, or ten days if

they're served by mail. If you wish to contest the motion, you should file and serve a statement of your own, called a "Declaration in Opposition to Motion for Summary Judgment," setting forth your version of the facts. Your statement must respond specifically to the facts that the landlord, in his declaration, states were undisputed. If you don't contradict the landlord's statements, the judge will consider them undisputed. You can support your statement with declarations (from you or others), or references to other documents such as the Complaint. If your statement contradicts the landlord's facts in important particulars, and the difference in facts is important to the case, the judge should deny the motion and require the landlord to proceed to trial.

Refer to the instructions for completing the Declaration accompanying the Motion to Quash for the required format. If the landlord or landlord's attorney personally serves the motion on you, you're entitled to only five days notice. This does not allow you much time to respond. Though the law does not say how soon before the hearing your opposing declaration needs to be filed, get it filed as soon as you can. Filing it the day before court, or worse, bringing it with you to court on the day of the hearing, may result in your losing the case. Serve it according to the method described for serving the Answer. For additional information, consult the *California Eviction Defense Manual*, published by Continuing Education of the Bar (CEB), available in most law libraries.

Although technically you can oppose the motion orally, we advise against it. California Rule of Court 3.1351(b) does provide, "Any opposition to the motion and any reply to an opposition may be made orally at the time of hearing." In theory, this means that you should be able to go to the hearing and ask the judge to place you under oath to refute any statement made in the landlord's written declaration. However, we think it is imperative that you file a written declaration under penalty of perjury, and serve it on the other party (or their attorney), at least the day before the hearing, as allowed under subdivision (c) of this rule. We say this because this rule is very new, many judges will not be acquainted with it, and they may be strongly inclined to rule against you if you simply show up without filing a written opposition. Remember, you must personally or otherwise serve your opposition papers on the landlord or his attorney in time to be received at least one court day before the hearing.

The Trial

After you file your Answer, the landlord may ask the court clerk to set the case for trial by filing a "Request to Set Case for Trial" with the court clerk. Having received this memo from the landlord, the clerk is supposed to set the case for trial within 20 days. (CCP § 1170.5(a).) You may file a motion to have this date extended, and it might be granted if you can show the judge that, for example, a key witness (such as you) must be out of town that day. Consult the *California Eviction Defense Manual* (CEB), which is available at law libraries, for how to file and serve this motion.

When you receive a copy of the landlord's Request to Set Case for Trial, check to see whether the landlord has requested a jury trial (landlords rarely ask for jury trials). If so, you needn't make a request of your own. If the landlord doesn't want a jury trial, and if you do, you will need to tell the court. Your right to demand a jury trial is secured by state law. (CCP § 1171.) You probably should demand a jury if you will have a lawyer representing you at trial. Requesting a jury trial often prompts the judge to try to get you and the landlord to settle the case before trial, which can be helpful to you. In the experience of most landlord-tenant lawyers, 12 ordinary people tend to be more sympathetic to tenants than one crusty old (or even young) judge. If, however, you will be representing yourself at trial, you might be better off having a judge decide the case. Judge trials are much more simple and informal than jury trials, which are usually too complicated for most nonlawyers to comfortably handle by themselves.

RESOURCE

If you decide to represent yourself at trial before a judge or a jury, consult *Win Your Lawsuit*, by Judge Roderic Duncan (Nolo), for information on how to present your case.

You will find a blank tear-out Demand for Jury Trial form in the appendix. Here are instructions for completing, filing, and serving the Demand.

CAUTION

Jury trials aren't free. If you request a jury trial, you will have to post about $150 with the court to pay for the jurors for one day of trial. If you win, you can recover these fees from the landlord. If the landlord posted the jury fees and wins, the landlord can recover these from you. You must pay the fee at least five days before trial, or you will lose the right to a jury trial. (CCP § 631(b).) (If you cannot afford the fee, you can ask the court to waive it by filling out a fee waiver form called "Application for Waiver of Additional Court Fees and Costs." Go to the Judicial Council website (www.courtinfo.ca.gov/forms) to download the form (see downloading instructions in "Get the Form From the Net," above). You cannot use the Application for Waiver of Court Fees and Costs (described earlier), because this form covers only filing fees, not jury fees.

Step 1: Complete the document called Proof of Service by Mail, following the instructions above. You will find a blank tear-out form in the appendix; make several copies before using it, as you may need more later. The server must be a person over 18 and not a party to the action—that is, not named in the Complaint as a plaintiff or defendant. As a defendant, you cannot serve your own legal papers.

Step 2: Make copies of Demand for Jury Trial and Proof of Service forms.

Step 3: Attach a copy of the unsigned Proof of Service to a copy of the Demand for Jury Trial.

Step 4: Have your server mail one copy package to the landlord or the landlord's attorney, then fill in the last paragraph of the original Proof of Service and sign it.

Sample Demand for Jury Trial

1 | TOM TENANT
1234 Apartment St.
2 | Berkeley, CA 94710
510-123-4567
3

4 | Defendant in Pro Per

5

6

7

8 | SUPERIOR COURT OF THE STATE OF CALIFORNIA, COUNTY OF ___ALAMEDA___

9 | _____BERKELEY/ALBANY_____ DIVISION/BRANCH

10 | LENNY LANDLORD _____,) Case No. _____5-0258_____
11 | _____ ,)
12 | Plaintiff(s),) DEMAND FOR JURY TRIAL
13 | v.)
14 | TOM TENANT _____,)
15 | _____ ,)
16 | Defendant(s).)

17

18 | To the clerk of the above-entitled court:

19 | Defendant(s) hereby demand a jury trial in this action.

20

21

22 | Dated: _____   *Tom Tenant*_____
Tom Tenant
23

24

25

26

27

28

Step 5: File the original Demand and original signed Proof of Service with the court. Have the court clerk stamp the second copy package for your files.

If you learn before trial which judge will hear the case, and you have reason to believe that this judge may not be fair to you, you may file a motion to disqualify the judge. (CCP § 170.6.) This is called a "peremptory challenge" and is described in the *California Eviction Defense Manual* (CEB). File the motion at least five days before trial, together with a statement that you believe the judge will be prejudiced against you. You need not prove that the judge is prejudiced or even state detailed reasons for your belief—the disqualification is automatic. You may do this only once in any case. If you do it, you cannot be sure which judge will replace the one you disqualified—the next one might even be worse! So don't use your challenge lightly.

Before the trial, carefully organize your witnesses, documents, and photographs; and any other evidence you think is important. Ask yourself what it would take to convince a neutral person that you are right, and then organize that evidence for the judge.

At trial, be courteous and respectful to everyone. The purpose of a trial is to resolve disputes in a civilized manner; it's not a forum for yelling, sarcasm, and the like. Address yourself to the judge and the witnesses only, not the other party or the opposing attorney. It's advantageous to be forceful and to stand up for your rights, and a serious mistake to be rude or unnecessarily hostile. The most important thing is to present your side of the case clearly and with as few complications as possible. Try not to be repetitive. If you confuse, bore, or annoy the judge, you lessen your chance of winning.

TIP

Watch and learn. If you are worried about representing yourself, watch several contested unlawful detainer trials before your court date. You'll learn what to do and, equally important, what to avoid.

The Judgment

If you win, the landlord cannot evict you, and you can get a judgment for your court costs—mainly your filing fee and jury fees, if you paid them. If your lease or rental agreement provides for attorney fees for the prevailing party—or just for the landlord—you can recover them, too, if you hired an attorney. (CCP § 1717.)

If the landlord wins, the judgment will award possession of the premises. It may also award money for unpaid rent (if the action was based on nonpayment of rent), prorated hold-over charges, costs, and attorney fees (if provided by the lease or rental agreement).

If you asserted a habitability defense in your Answer, and the judge finds the landlord substantially breached the habitability requirements, you will be required to pay into the court, within five days, the amount the judge determines is the reasonable rental value of the premises (in their "untenantable state") up to the time of the trial. If you don't make the payment on time, you will not be the "prevailing party" for purposes of awarding attorney fees and costs, and the court must award possession of the property to the landlord. (CCP § 1174.2.) The landlord may then try to collect the money part of the judgment—including court costs and applicable attorney's fees—and the court must award possession of the property to the landlord. For this reason, it's very important to pay any reduced rent the judge ordered you to pay. Not doing so can convert a partial win into a big loss—snatching defeat from the jaws of victory.

If you do make your payment on time and you are the "prevailing party," the court can order the landlord to make repairs and to charge only the reasonable rental value of the premises until the repairs are made. The court can maintain continuing supervision over the landlord until the repairs are completed. (CCP § 1174.2.)

Stopping an Eviction

In rare cases, even if you lose an eviction lawsuit, the judge may give you "relief from forfeiture" of your tenancy—that is, save you from eviction. For example, suppose you didn't pay your rent because you felt the rental unit was uninhabitable, and the judge, while agreeing that there were problems, was not convinced that the rental unit was not habitable and therefore ruled against you. The judge may nonetheless stop the eviction. (CCP §§ 1179 and 1174(c).)

To persuade the judge to do this, you will probably have to show two things:

- that the eviction would cause a severe hardship on you or your family—for example, because your kids are in school, or you cannot find other housing, or you would have to move away from your job, or you are elderly or handicapped, and
- that you are willing and able to pay both the money you owe the landlord (for back rent and costs and fees, if there is a costs and fees clause in your lease or rental agreement), and the rent in the future.

You will find a blank tear-out Application and Declaration for Relief From Eviction form in the appendix, plus a proposed order. Here are the instructions for completing them.

Step 1: Complete the document called Proof of Service by Mail (see the instructions in "The Motion to Quash," above). You will find a blank tear-out form in the appendix; make several copies before using it, as you may need more later. The server must be a person over 18 and not a party to the action—that is, not named in the Complaint as a plaintiff or defendant. As a defendant, you cannot serve your own legal papers.

Step 2: Make copies of the Application and Declaration for Relief From Eviction and Proof of Service forms.

Step 3: Attach a copy of the unsigned Proof of Service to a copy of the Application and Declaration for Relief From Eviction.

Step 4: Have your server mail one copy package to the landlord or his attorney, then fill in the last paragraph of the original Proof of Service and sign it.

Step 5: File the original Application and Declaration for Relief From Eviction, the proposed Order (the judge will complete it), and the original signed Proof of Service with the court. Have the court clerk stamp the second copy package for your files.

Postponing an Eviction

Even if the judge will not stop the eviction, the judge may postpone (stay) it for a limited time, for a good reason—for example, to give you more time to find another place—or to let you stay where you are during your appeal. If you need time to find another place, explain how difficult it is to locate available housing in your city and ask for a stay of about 30 days. File an application for a stay as soon as possible after you receive notice of the judgment.

If you seek a stay during an appeal, you must show the court that (1) you will suffer "extreme hardship" if you are evicted, and (2) that the landlord will not be hurt by the stay. The judge will condition the stay on your paying rent into court as it comes due. The court may also impose other conditions on the stay. If the trial court denies a stay during appeal, you may ask the appellate court to grant a stay. (CCP § 1176.) You will probably need a lawyer's help to accomplish this.

You will find a blank tear-out Application and Declaration for Stay of Eviction form plus a proposed Order in the appendix. Here are the instructions for completing them.

Step 1: Complete the document called Proof of Service by Mail, following the instructions found in "The Motion to Quash," above. You will find a blank tear-out form in the appendix; make several copies before using it, as you may need more later. The server must be a person over 18 and not a party to the action—that is, not named in the Complaint as a plaintiff or defendant. As a defendant, you cannot serve your own legal papers.

Sample Application for Stay of Eviction

1 TOM TENANT
   1234 Apartment St.
2 Berkeley, CA 94710
   510-123-4567
3

4 Defendant in Pro Per

5

6

7

8 SUPERIOR COURT OF THE STATE OF CALIFORNIA, COUNTY OF ___ALAMEDA___

9 _____BERKELEY/ALBANY_____ DIVISION/BRANCH

10 LENNY LANDLORD_____ ,) Case No. ____5-0258____

11 _____)
                            ,)
12   Plaintiff(s),   ) APPLICATION AND DECLARATION
)
13 v.   ) FOR STAY OF EVICTION
)
14 TOM TENANT_____ ,)
)
15 _____ ,)
         Defendant(s).   )
16 _____)

17

18 Defendant(s) _____

19 _____ hereby apply

20 for stay of execution from any writ of restitution or possession in this case, for the following period of time:

21 _____ .

22   Such a stay is appropriate in this case for the following reason(s): _____

23 _____

24 _____ .

25   I declare under penalty of perjury that the above statements are true and correct to the best of my

26 knowledge.

27 Dated: _____   *Tom Tenant*_____
                                  Tom Tenant
28

Application and Declaration for Stay of Eviction   Page 1 of 1

Step 2: Make copies of the Application and Declaration for Stay of Eviction and Proof of Service forms.

Step 3: Attach a copy of the unsigned Proof of Service to a copy of the Application for Relief From Eviction.

Step 4: Have your server mail one copy package to the landlord or the landlord's attorney, then fill in the last paragraph of the original Proof of Service and sign it.

Step 5: File the original Application and Declaration for Stay of Eviction, the proposed Order (the judge will complete it) and the original signed Proof of Service with the court. Have the court clerk stamp the second copy package for your files.

Appeal From an Eviction

To appeal a court's eviction order, you must file a paper called "Notice of Appeal" with the clerk of the court. You must file it within 30 days of receiving notice that judgment was entered against you. The appeal is to the Appellate Division of the Superior Court.

On appeal, you may argue only issues of law, not fact. This means that you may argue that the trial court erred by ruling that, for example, there can be no breach of the implied warranty of habitability if the lease says that the tenant waives his rights under this doctrine—an issue of law. But you may not argue that the judge was wrong in believing the landlord's testimony rather than yours, because that is an issue of fact. After you file your Notice of Appeal, the Appellate Division will tell you when your brief (the document in which you argue points of law) must be filed in that court.

Appeals are pretty technical, and we recommend that you get a lawyer if possible.

> ! **CAUTION**
>
> **Filing a Notice of Appeal does not auto-matically stop the sheriff or marshal from carrying out an eviction.** To do that, you must seek a stay of the eviction from the trial court judge, as discussed in the preceding section. If you plan to appeal and feel you have a good argument that the trial court misinterpreted the law, include these facts in your application for the stay.

You will find a blank tear-out Notice of Appeal form in the appendix. Here are the instructions for completing it.

Step 1: Complete the document called Proof of Service by Mail. You will find a blank tear-out form in the appendix; make several copies before using it, as you may need more later. The server must be a person over 18 and not a party to the action—that is, not named in the Complaint as a plaintiff or defendant. As a defendant, you cannot serve your own legal papers.

Step 2: Make copies of the Notice of Appeal and Proof of Service forms.

Step 3: Attach a copy of the unsigned Proof of Service to a copy of the Notice of Appeal.

Step 4: Have your server mail one copy package to the landlord or the landlord's attorney, then fill in the last paragraph of the original Proof of Service and sign it.

Step 5: File the original Notice of Appeal and original signed Proof of Service with the court. Have the court clerk stamp the second copy package for your files.

After the Lawsuit—Eviction by the Sheriff or Marshal

If the landlord wins the eviction case in court (or by default, because you never responded in writing to the landlord's lawsuit within the time allowed), the judge will sign a "writ of possession." The landlord will give this writ to the sheriff's or marshal's department and pay a fee, which will be added to the judgment against you. A deputy sheriff will serve the writ on you, along with an order that you vacate within five days. It might take the sheriff a few days to serve you with the writ. Some sheriffs serve these writs only on certain days of the week.

Notice of Appeal

1 TOM TENANT
   1234 Apartment St.
2 Berkeley, CA 94710
   510-123-4567
3

4 Defendant in Pro Per

5

6

7

8   SUPERIOR COURT OF THE STATE OF CALIFORNIA, COUNTY OF ___ALAMEDA___

9   ____BERKELEY/ALBANY____   DIVISION/BRANCH
)
10 LENNY LANDLORD_____ ,) Case No. ____5-0258____
)
11 _____ ,)
            Plaintiff(s),   ) NOTICE OF APPEAL AND NOTICE
12   )
    v.   ) TO PREPARE CLERK'S TRANSCRIPT
13 TOM TENANT_____)
                                    ,)
14 _____)
                                    ,)
15   Defendant(s).   )
)
16

17   Defendant(s) _____

18 _____ hereby appeal to the Appellate Department

19 of the Superior Court.

20   Defendant(s) hereby request that a Clerk's Transcript be prepared, and that this transcript include all

21 documents filed in this action and all minute orders and other rulings and judgments issued by the court in this

22 action.

23

24 Dated: _____   **Tom Tenant**_____
                                    Tom Tenant
25

26

27

28

If you are served with the writ and are not out in five days, the sheriff or marshal will return and physically evict you and your family. That official is not allowed to throw your belongings out with you. Neither is the landlord, who must store them. (You may have to pay storage fees to get them back. See Chapter 12.)

If you are served with a five-day notice to vacate by the sheriff, it's time to move. It is much better to manage your own moving than be thrown out by the sheriff.

What if you occupied the premises on or before the date the eviction action was filed, but you are not named in the writ of possession or were not served with a Prejudgment Claim of Right to Possession? If you're in this situation, you can delay your eviction by filing a form called a "Claim of Right to Possession and Notice of Hearing" after the sheriff serves the writ of possession on you or other tenants. (CCP § 1174.3.) The sheriff or marshal who serves the writ of possession is required by statute to serve a copy of the form at the same time. We have included a copy here.

The sheriff should have filled in the case number on the front of the form.

Here's how to make a claim:

Step 1: Fill out the Claim of Right to Possession and Notice of Hearing form.

Step 2: Give the form to the sheriff or marshal. Submitting the Claim form will stop the eviction. You can give the sheriff the form any time until and including when the sheriff comes back to evict you. You do not have to take it to the sheriff's office, although you may; you can just hand it to the sheriff.

Step 3: Send the court the filing fee (or a form requesting waiver of the fee) within two court days, as explained on the Claim of Right to Possession

and Notice of Hearing form. If you submit 15 days' rent with your filing fee, the hearing will be held within five to 15 days. If you don't submit 15 days' rent with your filing fee, the hearing will be held in five days. (See sample letter to court.)

When the court holds its hearing, it will determine the validity of your claim. If the court rules in your favor, the Complaint will be deemed to have been served on you at the hearing, and you will be able to respond to it in any of the ways discussed above. If the court rules against you, it will order the sheriff to proceed with the eviction.

Sample Letter to Court Regarding Claim of Right to Possession

(Date)

Superior Court of California
County of _____ ,
_____ Judicial Diivision/Branch

Re: Unlawful Detainer Action, Case No. _____

Enclosed is a check for $_____ as payment of the fee for filing a Claim of Right to Possession. I filed a Claim of Right to Possession to the premises at _____
_____ on _____ ,
20____ , by giving the Claim to the sheriff/marshal of _____ County.

I have also enclosed a check for $_____ , an amount equal to 15 days' rent of the premises.

Sincerely,

Tom Tenant

Tom Tenant

Claim of Right of Possession and Notice of Hearing Form

CLAIMANT OR CLAIMANT'S ATTORNEY *(Name and Address)*:	TELEPHONE NO.:	*FOR COURT USE ONLY*

ATTORNEY FOR *(Name)*:

NAME OF COURT:
STREET ADDRESS:
MAILING ADDRESS:
CITY AND ZIP CODE:
BRANCH NAME:
PLAINTIFF:

DEFENDANT:

CLAIM OF RIGHT TO POSSESSION AND NOTICE OF HEARING	CASE NUMBER:

Complete this form only if ALL of these statements are true:

1. You are NOT named in the accompanying form called Writ of Possession.
2. You occupied the premises on or before the date the unlawful detainer (eviction) action was filed. *(The date is in the accompanying Writ of Possession.)*
3. You still occupy the premises.
4. A Prejudgment Claim of Right to Possession form was NOT served with the Summons and Complaint.

NOTICE TO LEVYING OFFICER:
☐ Claim granted   ☐ Claim denied

Clerk, by _____

(For levying officer use only)
Completed form was received on

Date: _____ Time: _____

By: _____

I DECLARE THE FOLLOWING UNDER PENALTY OF PERJURY:

1. My name is *(specify)*:

2. I reside at *(street address, unit No., city and ZIP code)*:

3. The address of "the premises" subject to this claim is *(address)*:

4. On *(insert date)*: [_____], the landlord or the landlord's authorized agent filed a complaint to recover possession of the premises. *(This date is in the accompanying Writ of Possession.)*

5. I occupied the premises on the date the complaint was filed *(the date in item 4)*. I have continued to occupy the premises ever since.

6. I was at least 18 years of age on the date the complaint was filed *(the date in item 4)*.

7. I claim a right to possession of the premises because I occupied the premises on the date the complaint was filed *(the date in item 4)*.

8. I was not named in the Writ of Possession.

9. I understand that if I make this claim of possession, a COURT HEARING will be held to decide whether my claim will be granted.

10. *(Filing fee)* To obtain a court hearing on my claim, I understand that after I present this form to the levying officer I must go to the court and pay a filing fee of $_____ or file with the court the form "Application for Waiver of Court Fees and Costs." I understand that if I don't pay the filing fee or file the form for waiver of court fees *within two court days,* the court will immediately deny my claim.

11. *(Immediate court hearing unless you deposit 15 days' rent)* To obtain a court hearing on my claim, I understand I must also deliver to the court a copy of this completed claim form or a receipt from the levying officer. I also understand the date of my hearing will be set immediately if I don't deliver to the court an amount equal to 15 days' rent.

(Continued on reverse)

CP10 [Rev. January 1, 1991]   **CLAIM OF RIGHT TO POSSESSION AND NOTICE OF HEARING**   Code of Civil Procedure, §§ 715.010, 715.020, 1174.3

Claim of Right of Possession and Notice of Hearing Form

PLAINTIFF *(Name)*:	CASE NUMBER:
DEFENDANT *(Name)*:	

12. I am filing my claim in the following manner *(check the box that shows how you are filing your claim. Note that you must deliver to the court a copy of the claim form or a levying officer's receipt)*:

   a. ☐ *(With 15 days' rent payment)* I presented this claim form to the sheriff, marshal, or other levying officer, AND within two court days I shall deliver to the court the following: (1) a copy of this completed claim form or a receipt, (2) the court filing fee or form for proceeding in forma pauperis, and (3) an amount equal to 15 days' rent. — OR —

   b. ☐ *(Without 15 days' rent payment)* I presented this claim form to the sheriff, marshal, or other levying officer, AND within two court days I shall deliver to the court the following: (1) a copy of this completed claim form or a receipt, and (2) the court filing fee or form for proceeding in forma pauperis.

IMPORTANT: Do not take a copy of this claim form to the court unless you have first given the form to the sheriff, marshal, or other levying officer.

(To be completed by the court)
Date of hearing: Time: Dept. or Div.:   Room:
Address of court:

> NOTICE: If you fail to appear at this hearing you will be evicted without further hearing.

13. **Rental agreement.** I have *(check all that apply to you)*:

   a. ☐ an oral rental agreement with the landlord.
   b. ☐ a written rental agreement with the landlord.
   c. ☐ an oral rental agreement with a person other than the landlord.
   d. ☐ a written rental agreement with a person other than the landlord.
   e. ☐ other *(explain)*:

I declare under penalty of perjury under the laws of the State of California that the foregoing is true and correct.

> WARNING: Perjury is a felony punishable by imprisonment in the state prison.

Date:

▶

....   _____
(TYPE OR PRINT NAME)   (SIGNATURE OF CLAIMANT)

> NOTICE: If your claim to possession is found to be valid, the unlawful detainer (eviction) action against you will be determined at trial. At trial, you may be found liable for rent, costs, and, in some cases, treble damages.

—NOTICE TO OCCUPANTS—

YOU MUST ACT AT ONCE if all the following are true:

1. **You are NOT named in the accompanying form called Writ of Possession.**
2. **You occupied the premises on or before the date the unlawful detainer (eviction) action was filed.** *(The date is in the accompanying Writ of Possession.)*
3. **You still occupy the premises.**
4. **A Prejudgment Claim of Right to Possession form was NOT served with the Summons and Complaint.**

You can complete and SUBMIT THIS CLAIM FORM *(in person with identification)*
   (1) before the date of eviction at the sheriff's or marshal's office located at *(address)*:

   (2) OR at the premises at the time of the eviction. *(Give this form to the officer who comes to evict you.)*

If you do not complete and submit this form (and pay a filing fee or file the form for proceeding in forma pauperis if you cannot pay the fee), YOU WILL BE EVICTED along with the parties named in the writ.

After this form is properly filed, A HEARING WILL BE HELD to decide your claim. If you do not appear at the hearing, you will be evicted without a further hearing.

CP10 [Rev. January 1, 1991]   **CLAIM OF RIGHT TO POSSESSION**   Page two
                                  AND NOTICE OF HEARING

Renter's Insurance

Attitudes towards insurance vary—some people wouldn't be without it, while others consider it a giant rip-off. Our job is not to argue this question one way or the other, but to tell you how renter's insurance works.

Renter's insurance is a package of several types of insurance designed to cover tenants for more than one risk. Each insurance company's package will be slightly different—types of coverage offered, the dollar amounts specified for coverage, and the deductible will vary. There is nothing we can tell you here that will substitute for your shopping around and comparing policies and prices. It's a good idea to talk to friends and see if they are happy with their insurance—but realize that prices for renter's insurance can be very different depending upon where you live.

The average renter's policy covers you against losses to your belongings occurring as a result of fire and theft, up to the amount stated on the face of the policy, which is often $15,000 or $25,000. As thefts have become more common, most policies have included deductible amounts of $250, or even $500. This means that if your apartment is burglarized, you collect from the insurance company only for the amount of your loss over and above the deductible amount.

Many renter's policies completely exclude certain property from theft coverage, including cash, credit cards, and pets. Others limit the amount of cash covered to $100, jewelry and furs to $500. The value of home computers and equipment may be included as part of the contents coverage amount, or they may be separately scheduled on the policy. If you live in a flood- or earthquake-prone area, you'll have to pay extra for coverage. Earthquake policies, for example, typically run from $2 to $4

for each $1,000 of coverage, with a deductible of 10% to 15% of total coverage. Make sure your policy covers what you think it does. If it doesn't, check out the policies of other companies. As a general rule, you can get whatever coverage you want if you are willing to pay for it.

If you do take out insurance on valuable items, you should inventory them: Note down their values and take photos or make videotapes. Include the estimated value of each item, backed up with information on the model number and date of purchase. Keep the inventory and photos at work or some place other than your apartment, so that if there is a disaster, your inventory won't suffer the same fate as your belongings.

In addition to fire and theft coverage, most renter's policies give you (and your family living with you) personal liability coverage to an amount stated in the policy ($100,000 is typical). This means that if you injure someone (for example, you accidentally hit a guest on the head with a golf ball), a guest is injured through your negligence on the rental property that you occupy (for example, he slips on a broken front step), or you damage his belongings (for example, your garden hose floods the neighbor's cactus garden), you are covered. There are a lot of exclusions to personal liability coverage. Any damage you do with a motor vehicle, with a boat, or through your business won't be covered.

CAUTION

Your landlord's homeowner's insurance won't cover you. Even if you live in a duplex with your landlord and the landlord has a homeowner's policy, this policy won't protect your belongings if there is a fire or theft. Of course, if you suffer a loss as a result of your landlord's negligence, you may have a valid claim against her. Most landlords have insurance specifically to protect against this sort of risk.

If you have a loss, be sure your insurance company treats you fairly. You are entitled to the present fair market value (what the property would sell for, not the replacement cost) of anything stolen or destroyed by fire or any other hazard covered by the policy after the deductible amount of the policy is subtracted, unless your policy specifies "replacement value." If the company won't pay you a fair amount, consider taking the dispute to small claims court if it is for $7,500 or less. If the loss is a major one, you might consider seeing a lawyer, but agree to pay the lawyer only a percentage of what he or she can recover over and above what the insurance company offers you without the lawyer's help.

Recently, many landlords have begun inserting a clause into their leases or rental agreements requiring that the tenant purchase renter's insurance. This is legal under California law. The landlord's motive for doing so is threefold:

- If the tenant's property is damaged in any way that is not the landlord's legal responsibility and the damage is covered by the renter's policy, the landlord won't have to rely on his or her own insurance policy.
- Anyone who suffers a personal injury on the property in a situation where the tenant is at fault is less likely to also sue the landlord.
- A number of landlords believe that tenants who are willing to buy insurance are more responsible than other tenants.

Finding Earthquake Insurance Can Be Difficult

The occurrence and risk of earthquakes in California has made it increasingly difficult for tenants to obtain renter's insurance. Insurance Code § 10083 requires insurance companies to offer earthquake coverage with every homeowner's policy (renter's insurance is considered a form of homeowner's insurance), but most large companies are limiting the number of policies and type of coverage they issue as a result of the 1994 Northridge earthquake, which cost the insurance industry billions of dollars. Smaller companies are, however, continuing to offer policies, sometimes only for specified, earthquake-safe buildings. Independent brokers are usually the best sources for available and affordable policies.

Condominium Conversion

Converting buildings from rental properties into condominiums was unusual several years ago. Now, however, the general shortage of new homes, coupled with favorable tax laws, has created a condominium boom.

Condominium ownership as an abstract idea can make great sense. People have a basic need to own their own spaces, and with the high cost of land and construction, condominiums are often the only way this need can find expression. But many tenants of existing rental properties are unable or unwilling to pay large sums of money to purchase their units.

Here is a little story about what this could mean to you.

One day the mail carrier delivers an identical letter to all the tenants in a multiunit building. The owner, it seems, has decided to convert the building from rental units to owner-occupied condominiums. Everyone will either have to buy their apartments and a share of the common space (such as halls and grounds) or move out. Those with leases must leave when they run out, and those with month-to-month tenancies under a written rental agreement must leave in 30 or 60 days. The letter concludes politely that the owners hope that they have caused no inconvenience and are sure that many tenants will welcome this opportunity to buy their units at the rock bottom price of $200,000 each.

Is there anything tenants can do if they want neither to move nor to buy their units? Yes.

Legal Protection for Tenants

Converting rental units to a condominium constitutes a "subdivision" under California law. This means that the project must comply with the statewide Subdivision Map Act, and that the landowner must apply for and receive approval of a "plan," or project, from the county agency in charge of reviewing the applications. (GC § 66427.1.) In addition, many cities, including Berkeley, Los Angeles, Oakland, San Francisco, San Jose, Santa Monica, and West Hollywood, have enacted their own ordinances, which impose additional requirements.

Statewide Application and Notice Requirements

A landowner who wishes to convert rental property to condominiums, or who intends to demolish existing rental property and replace it with new condos, must follow the procedures outlined in the Subdivision Map Act (if a local ordinance applies, the procedures outlined there must be followed, too). The state law specifies that the landowner must:

- apply for tentative tract map approval with the county or, if there is a local ordinance, with the city.
- participate in the public hearing held by the planning agency, which will recommend approval or disapproval of the project. The agency can also attach conditions to its approval. The landowner may appeal the decision to the agency's governing body (the board of supervisors or the city council, if there is a local ordinance involved).
- receive a public report from the State Department of Real Estate, which is granted only when the landowner has complied with all the conditions of the tentative tract map issued by the planning agency. At this point, the application process ends.

According to state law, tenants who will be evicted because of a planned condo conversion must be given notice of all the steps outlined above. These notice periods are as follows:

- Sixty days before the filing of a tentative tract map application, you must be told of the owner's intent to convert. (GC §§ 66427.1(a), 7060.4(b).) Tenants who are 62 years of age or older, or who are disabled, and who have lived in the unit for at least one year are entitled to one year's notice.

- Ten days before the application for a public report, you must be told of the owner's intention to ask the Department of Real Estate to issue the final report. (GC § 66427.1(a).)
- Ten days before the county or city approves the final map, you must be told of its readiness. (GC § 66427.1(b).)
- One hundred and eighty days before eviction, you must be given notice of the owner's intent to convert to condominiums. (GC § 66427.1(c).)
- Ten days before *any* hearing regarding the proposed conversion, you must be informed of the hearing, where you have the right to appear and speak. (GC §§ 66451.3, 65090, and 65091.)

Local ordinances may impose stricter notice requirements.

The Tenants' Right to Purchase

Once the subdivision tract map has received final approval by way of the State Department of Real Estate's public report, you must be given the chance to purchase your apartment before anyone else. The selling price and terms must be as good as or better than those that will be offered to the public at large, and you have 90 days following the issuance of the final report in which to exercise your option. (GC § 66427.1(d).)

Conversions That Don't Comply With Proper Notice to the Tenants

A landowner's failure to abide by the notice requirements imposed by state law will not necessarily defeat his bid to have his conversion project approved by the county agency reviewing the project. State law provides that a tentative or final map may not be disapproved solely because the tenants were not given the full amount of notice. There must be other reasons for disapproval besides the lack of notice to the tenants. (GC § 66451.4.)

Renting After Conversion Has Been Approved

Landlords who have received condo conversion approval will typically continue to rent the units in the building during the time that it takes to sell all the units. Tenants who have been residents since before the approval are, of course, aware of the tenuousness of their position and should have the benefit of the 90 days "right of first refusal" when their unit is put up for sale (see the discussion above). But what about the tenant who begins a tenancy *after* the final conversion approval?

State law insists that a landowner explicitly explain the situation to a new renter. (GC § 66459(a).) If you enter into a lease or rental agreement *after* the final approval of a subdivision map for that property, and if the project consists of five or more units, your landlord must include a clause in the lease that reads (in bold, 14-point type) as follows:

THE UNIT YOU MAY RENT HAS BEEN APPROVED FOR SALE TO THE PUBLIC AS A CONDOMINIUM PROJECT, COMMUNITY APARTMENT PROJECT OR STOCK COOPERATIVE PROJECT (WHICHEVER APPLIES). THE RENTAL UNIT MAY BE SOLD TO THE PUBLIC AND, IF IT IS OFFERED FOR SALE, YOUR LEASE MAY BE TERMINATED. YOU WILL BE NOTIFIED AT LEAST 90 DAYS PRIOR TO ANY OFFERING TO SELL. IF YOU STILL LAWFULLY RESIDE IN THE UNIT, YOU WILL BE GIVEN A RIGHT OF FIRST REFUSAL TO PURCHASE THE UNIT.

As a further precaution, the landlord is not even allowed to refer to his property as an "apartment" in a lease or rental agreement once the final approval for his conversion project has come through. (GC § 66459(b).) Unfortunately, however, these notice provisions lack any real "teeth," since the landlord's failure to comply will not invalidate a sale. (GC § 66459(e).)

Your Right to Assistance After Conversion

Although state law does not require the landlord to assist tenants in the selection and cost of replacement housing, many local ordinances do. These ordinances typically provide for assistance to elderly, disabled, or low-income tenants, and to families with minor children. Some ordinances direct the landlord to offer lifetime leases to elderly tenants. Often, moving costs must be covered by the landlord. If you live in Los Angeles, San Francisco, Oakland, San Diego, San Jose, or Santa Monica and you are evicted due to the sale of your apartment, check your local code to find out whether you qualify for assistance.

Changing the Law

Tenants can also band together to get the local government to pass an ordinance allowing condominium conversions only if a number of conditions have been met. A good condominium conversion ordinance should require most, if not all, of the following conditions, before a conversion can take place:

- Fifty percent of the current tenants approve of the conversion.
- All tenants over 65 or disabled are allowed to continue as tenants for life if they wish.
- No conversions are allowed where the landlord has evicted large groups of tenants or greatly raised rents to get rid of tenants just before the conversion.
- No conversions of any kind are allowed when the rental vacancy rate in a city is below 5%,

unless new rental units are being built at least fast enough to replace those converted.

- Special scrutiny is given to conversion of units rented to people with low and moderate incomes, to see that the units are priced at a level that the existing tenants can afford.
- The landlord provides adequate relocation assistance.

To stop a proposed condominium conversion, it is essential that tenants act together and that they create political alliances with sympathetic groups in the city. You will want to start by checking out your landlord carefully. Look for facts about the landlord that would tend to make local government agencies unsympathetic to the conversion. Among the best are the following:

- The landlord is from out of town and has recently bought your building (and perhaps others) as a speculation.
- The landlord has a long history of violating housing codes and generally is known as a bad landlord.
- The landlord raised rents excessively, terminated tenancies for no reason, and did other things to clear out the building before the conversion was announced.
- The building is occupied by many older people (or others on fixed incomes) who have no place to go, and the landlord has made little or no effort to either allow them to stay on at terms they can afford or find them a decent place to live.
- The landlord is making an excellent return on his money as rental units, and conversion to condominiums would result in huge profits.

Lawyers, Legal Research, and Mediation

Most of the time, you'll be able to learn of your rights, and hopefully communicate them to your landlord and enforce them, without the need to look at the law itself or consult an attorney. But sometimes you'll need to do one or both—for example, you may want to make sure that the steps you're taking to withhold rent are the current, legally-required steps; and you may want to consult with an attorney before taking on your landlord by yourself in an eviction lawsuit. This chapter gives you some suggestions on how to find and understand the law (statutes and cases), and how to find a good lawyer. If gentle persuasion fails and you appear headed for a formal conflict with your lawyer, almost always you'll want to first try mediation, an efficient, low-cost alternative to court. This chapter gives you the information you need on that score, too.

Lawyers

This book is not designed to replace an attorney. It is meant to give you a clear understanding of your rights and obligations, and help you decide whether you need a lawyer.

Lawyers, like most of the rest of us, are in business to make money. Most charge from $200 to $300 an hour. Clearly, when you have a dispute with your landlord that involves a few hundred dollars, it does not make good sense to pay someone as much (or more) than that to try to vindicate your position. In addition, if your lease has an "attorney fees" clause, there is the danger that you will lose and end up paying both your landlord and your attorney, too.

When Do You Need a Lawyer?

There is no simple answer to the question of when you need a lawyer. This is because there are many possible areas of dispute between landlord and tenant, and many levels of tenant ability to deal with problems. Throughout this book, we suggest

times when the advice or other services of an attorney would be useful, but here are a few general pointers:

- If you believe that you have been discriminated against in a significant way, especially if there are others who have suffered a similar experience, consider seeing an attorney (but read about discrimination in Chapter 4 first).
- If your landlord sues you for a lot of money, or if you suffer a significant physical or emotional injury because of action or inaction by the landlord or manager, see an attorney.
- If you have any problem that you can't understand or solve by reading this book, you should do some legal research yourself or get some professional advice.
- If you're being evicted and have concluded that you may have trouble conducting your defense, consider at least consulting with an attorney.

What Lawyers Can Do for You

There are three basic ways a lawyer can help with the problems a tenant commonly faces.

Consultation and Advice

The lawyer can listen to the details of your situation, analyze it for you, and advise you on your position and best plan of action. Ideally, the lawyer will give you more than just conclusions—an attorney can educate you about your whole situation and tell you all the various alternatives available. Then you can make your own choices. Or, you may just want a lawyer to look over the papers you have prepared, to be sure they are correct. This kind of service is the least expensive, as it involves only an office call and a little time. Find out the fee before you go in.

Negotiation

The lawyer has special talents, knowledge, and experience that will help you negotiate with the landlord. In case of serious problems, a lawyer can probably do this more successfully than you, especially if you are at odds with the landlord, or if your landlord has an attorney. Without spending much time, the attorney can often accomplish a lot through a letter or phone call. Receiving a message on an attorney's letterhead is, in itself, often very sobering to a landlord. Also, if bad turns to worse, a lawyer can convincingly threaten legal action. You can then decide at a later time whether to actually pursue it.

Lawsuits

In some instances, your case may merit going into court with a lawsuit. Having your lawyer go into court can be expensive and is only rarely warranted. If the landlord sues you first, it is more likely that you will end up in court, and very likely that you will need a lawyer's help.

Finding a Lawyer

Finding a lawyer who charges reasonable prices and whom you feel can be trusted is not always an easy task. There is always the danger that by just picking a name out of the telephone book you may get someone unsympathetic (perhaps an attorney who specializes in representing landlords) or an attorney who will charge too much. Here are some suggestions.

Legal Aid

If you are very poor, you may qualify for free help from your Legal Aid (often called Legal Services) office. Check your phone directory for their location, or ask your County Clerk. Legal Aid personnel may not be able to represent tenants in court, but may offer self-help materials.

Tenants' Rights Organizations

In a number of California communities, tenants have gotten together and established tenants advocacy organizations. Many of these groups provide free or low-cost tenant counseling, provided by paralegals, and sometimes by volunteer lawyers.

Counseling involves helping tenants understand their rights and sometimes extends to helping them prepare paperwork necessary to file or defend a lawsuit. Local bar associations also sometimes provide clinics for low-income tenants.

"Tenants Together" is a relatively recent, statewide tenants' rights organization (www.tenantstogether. org). A nonprofit organization funded by grants and private donations, the organization educates, organizes, and advocates on behalf of tenants. Their website has excellent information, and they provide a foreclosure hotline.

Personal Referrals

If you're looking for a lawyer on your own, this is the best approach. If you know someone who has consulted a lawyer on a landlord-tenant matter and was pleased with the lawyer, call that lawyer first.

Prepaid Legal Plans

Many unions, employers, private companies, and consumer groups now offer membership in prepaid legal plans.

The services provided by the plans vary widely. Some give legal services at reduced fees; some offer free advice. If a plan offers extensive free advice, your initial membership fee may be worth the consultation you receive, even if you use it only once. Most plans have renewal fees; it's common to join a plan for a specific service and then not renew.

There's no guarantee that the lawyers available through these plans are any good. Check out the plan, and if possible its lawyers, in advance. And when using any of these prepaid plans, remember this: The lawyer is typically paid very little by the prepaid plan for dealing with you. Some lawyers sign up in the hope they can talk you into buying extra services not covered by your monthly premium. The best plans are those that do not permit the consulting lawyers to "self-refer." This means that the person you're talking to cannot attempt to persuade you to become his or her client.

Private Law Clinics

To market their services, some law firms advertise on TV, over the Internet, and on radio, offering low initial consultation fees. This generally means that a basic consultation is cheap (often less than $50), but anything after that isn't. If you consult a law clinic, the trick is to quickly extract what information you need and to resist any attempt to make you think you need further services.

Lawyer Referral Panels

Most county bar associations maintain lawyer referral services. Usually, you can get a referral to an attorney who specializes in landlord-tenant law, and an initial consultation for free or for a low fee. But some of the panels don't really screen the listed attorneys, and some of the attorneys participating may not have much experience or ability. If you contact an attorney this way, be sure to ask about experience with tenant problems, and make sure the lawyer is sympathetic to tenants' rights.

Yellow Pages

If all else fails, every Yellow Pages has an extensive list of lawyers (under "attorneys") both by specialty and in alphabetical order. Many of the ads quote initial consultation rates. Look for a lawyer who specializes in landlord-tenant law, especially one who represents only tenants.

Shop around by calling different law offices and stating your problem. Ask to talk to a lawyer personally; if the law firm won't allow it, this should give you an idea of how accessible the lawyer is. Ask some specific questions. Do you get clear, concise answers? If not, try someone else. If the lawyer says little except to suggest that he handle the problem (with a substantial fee, of course), watch out. You are talking with someone who either doesn't know the answer and won't admit it (common), or someone who pulls rank on the basis of professional standing. Don't be a passive client or deal with a lawyer who wants you to be one.

Keep in mind that lawyers learn mostly from experience and special training, not from law school. Because you're already well informed (you've read this book), you should be in a good position to evaluate a lawyer's preparedness to handle your problem.

Remember, lawyers whose offices and lifestyles are reasonably simple are more likely to help you for less money than lawyers who feel naked unless wearing a $2,000 suit. You should be able to find an attorney willing to represent you for either a flat rate or an hourly rate of between $200 and $300, depending on where the lawyer's office is located (big city lawyers tend to be pricier) and how complex your case is.

Nolo's Lawyer Directory

You may also want to consider Nolo's Lawyer Directory (choose the Lawyer Directory link on the home page, www.nolo.com). Lawyers are listed by category (you'll want the Real Estate group). These attorneys are paid advertisers, whom Nolo has not screened beyond ascertaining, at the time the ad was sold, that the lawyer is in good standing with the State Bar. Every lawyer has written a profile, consisting of answers to questions concerning the types of cases they handle, their qualifications, work history, personality and philosophy (regarding their practice), and fees. Assuming these lawyers have correctly and candidly answered the profile questions (Nolo did not confirm the answers), you'll get an idea of whether an attorney is likely to be a good fit. Be sure to follow-up with your own questions (and ask for a list of references or current or former clients whom you can call) when you contact a lawyer from this listing.

Typing Services

What if you don't want to hire a lawyer but don't want to do all your legal paperwork yourself? There's a middle ground. A number of businesses, known as "legal typing services" or "independent paralegals," assist people doing their own legal work in filling out the forms. Most typing services concentrate on family law or bankruptcy, but some handle landlord-tenant matters, too.

Typing services aren't lawyers. They can't give legal advice and can't represent you in court—only lawyers can. You must decide what steps to take in your case, and the information to put in any needed forms. Typing services can, however:

- provide written instructions and legal information needed to handle your own case
- provide the appropriate forms, and
- type your papers so they'll be accepted by the court.

Typing services commonly charge far less than attorneys, because typing service customers do much of the work and make the basic decisions. Also, most typing services handle only routine cases.

If you're looking for a typing service, go online and search for "legal document preparation [your county]." For example, a search for "legal document preparation San Francisco" resulted in four hits, and more outside the county. Or, check classified sections of newspapers under Referral Services, usually immediately following Attorneys. Also check the Yellow Pages under "Divorce Assistance" or "Legal Clinics." A local legal aid office may provide a reference, as will the occasional court clerk. Many offices have display ads in local throwaway papers like the *Classified Flea Market*.

Occasionally, a typing service has taken money from a customer and then failed to deliver the services as promised. As with any other business rip-off, you, as a consumer, can sue in small claims or regular court, and report the matter to your local district attorney's consumer fraud division. But legal remedies are often ineffective. The best precaution is to select a reliable typing service at the beginning. As with finding a lawyer, a recommendation from a satisfied customer is

best. Also, as a general matter, the longer a typing service has been in business, the better.

Paralegals who handle eviction matters, whether for the tenant or landlord, must be registered and bonded as an "unlawful detainer assistant." (B&P §§ 6400-6415.) If the service isn't registered, don't use it. The court forms that an eviction service prepares, such as the Answer (discussed in Chapter 14), require you to state under penalty of perjury whether an "unlawful detainer assistant" helped you. If you hired an unlawful detainer assistant, you must give the eviction service's name, address, and registration number on the form.

Legal Research

We don't have space here to show you how to do your own legal research in anything approaching a comprehensive fashion. *Legal Research: How to Find & Understand the Law,* by Stephen Elias and the Editors of Nolo (Nolo), is an excellent resource if you wish to learn basic legal research skills, something we highly recommend. (See order information at the back of this book.) Our goal here is only to tell you how to find the basic laws that control your residential tenancy. In addition, we show you how to locate the important judicial decisions (most of which are mentioned in this book) that interpret these laws.

Statutes and Ordinances

Landlord-tenant laws and legal procedure are principally contained in two parts of California law—the Civil Code (CC) and the Code of Civil Procedure (CCP), both of which are available online at all law libraries and most public libraries. The Civil Code is divided into numerous sections, dealing generally with people's legal rights and responsibilities to each other. Most of California's substantive landlord-tenant law is contained in Sections 1940 through 1991 of this code, with laws governing minimum building standards, payment of rent, change and termination of tenancy, privacy, and security deposits, to name a few. The Code of Civil Procedure is a set of laws that tells how people enforce legal rights in civil lawsuits. Eviction lawsuit procedures are contained in Sections 1161 through 1179 of the Code of Civil Procedure. Also of interest are the small claims court procedures mentioned in Sections 116.110 through 116.950.

RESOURCE

You can read California statutes online by going to Nolo's website at www.nolo.com, choosing the Legal Research link under Free Legal Information, then State Law Resources. Clicking the California link will take you to the state website, with all of the codes. Incidentally, while on Nolo's site, take advantage of the short and helpful articles on how to understand statutes and cases.

In this book, we make frequent references to statutes found in sources like the California Code of Civil Procedure and California Civil Code. We use standard abbreviations like CCP and CC to make future references to these sources easier. For your convenience, there is a list of standard abbreviations used in this book located on the last page of the "Your Legal Companion," at the beginning of this book.

Cases

Although codes contain the text of applicable laws passed each year by the legislature, they don't contain the text of any of the appellate court decisions that determine what those laws mean. Sometimes these cases are extremely important. For example, the case of *Green v. Superior Court* adopted a "common law" rule allowing tenants in substandard housing to withhold rent—without paying to make repairs themselves. To gain access to the printed reports of important court decisions, you have to go to a law library, either "real" or "virtual."

The best way to learn of the existence of written court decisions that interpret a particular law is to first look in an "annotated code." An annotated code is a set of volumes of a particular code, such as the Civil Code or Code of Civil Procedure mentioned above, that contains not only all the laws (as do the regular codes), but also a brief summary of many of the court decisions interpreting each law. These annotated codes—published by West Publishing Company (West's Annotated California Codes—blue volumes) and by Bancroft-Whitney (Deering's California Codes—brown volumes)—can be found in some public libraries and any county law library or law school library in the state. (Unfortunately, they aren't available for free online.) They have comprehensive indexes by topic, and are kept up to date each year with paperback supplements ("pocket parts") located in a pocket in the back cover of each volume. Don't forget to look through these pocket parts for the latest law changes or case decisions since the hardcover volume was printed.

Each brief summary of a court decision is followed by the title of the case, the year of the decision, and the "citation." The citation is a sort of shorthand identification for the set of books, volume, and page where the case can be found. The "official" volumes of cases are published by the California Supreme Court as the Official Reports of the California Supreme Court (abbreviated "Cal.," "Cal.2d," "Cal.3d," or "Cal.4th," respectively, representing the first, second, third, and fourth "series" of volumes) and by the California Courts of Appeal as Official Reports of the California Courts of Appeal (similarly abbreviated "Cal.App.," "Cal.App.2d," "Cal.App.3d," and "Cal.App.4th"). The same cases are also published in "unofficial volumes" by the West Publishing Company. These are California Reporter (abbreviated "Cal.Rptr." and "Cal. Rptr.2d") and Pacific Reporter (abbreviated "P." or "P.2d," respectively, for the first and second series). The case is the same whether you read it in the official or unofficial reporter.

Below are examples of case citations which should take some of the mystery out of legal

Examples of Case Citations

Green v. Superior Court (1974) 10 Cal. 3d 616 11 Cal. Rptr. 704, 517 P.2d 1168

- case name
- year of decision
- volume number
- 3rd series of Official Reports of the California Supreme court
- page number
- volume number
- the case also appears in California Reporter, the unofficial reports
- page number
- volume number
- the case is also listed in 2nd series of Pacific Reporter
- page number

Glaser v. Myers (1982) 137 Cal. App. 3d 770, 187 Cal. Rptr. 242

- case name
- year of decision
- 3rd series of Official Reports of the California Courts of Appeal, volume 137, page 700
- the case is also listed in the California Reporter, the unofficial reports, volume 187, page 242

Lee v. Vignoli (1979) 98 Cal. App. Supp. 24, 160 Cal. Rptr. 79

- case name
- year of decision
- 3rd series of Official Reports of the California Courts of Appeal, volume 98, page 24 of the supplement in the back of the volume
- the case is also appears in volume 160, page 79 of the California Reporter

Lindsey v. Normet (1972) 405 U.S. 56, 92 S.Ct. 862, 187 Cal. Rptr. 242

- case name
- year of decision
- volume 45, page 56 of the Official Reports of the United States Supreme Court
- also published in volume 92, page 862 of the Supreme Court Reporter, an unofficial source
- also published in the 2nd series of "Lawyers Edition" of the U.S. Supreme Court Reports volume 31, page 36

research. If, in the course of your research, you still have questions, again we recommend *Legal Research: How to Find & Understand the Law,* by Stephen Elias and The Editors of Nolo (Nolo).

Where to Find Statutes, Ordinances, and Cases

Every California county maintains a law library that is open to the public. All have the California statutes (including annotated versions), written court opinions, and expert commentary. You can find and read any statute or case we've referred to at the law library by looking it up according to its citation. For most of you, the fastest and most convenient way to read codes is on the Internet, as explained above.

Instead, you may want to start your research with a good background resource. We mention several of these (The *California Eviction Defense Manual,* for example) throughout the book. Another good resource, usually kept behind the desk at the reference counter of most libraries, is a loose-leaf two-volume set published by The Rutter Group entitled *California Practice Guide: Landlord-Tenant.*

If you are interested in reading local ordinances, you stand a good chance of finding those online, too. Go to www.statelocalgov.net/state-ca.htm and look to see if your city is listed. Those of you covered by rent control will find the law in your city's ordinances. Look at Chapter 3, "Rent Control Laws," where we list websites that contain local rent control laws and information.

You can also read cases on the Internet. Our favorite site is VersusLaw, at www.versuslaw.com. For the modest sum of $13.95 per month, you'll have unlimited access to VersusLaw's extensive collection, including Supreme Court cases and cases from the California appellate and Supreme courts.

Mediation

Mediation involves bringing in a neutral third party to help disputants settle differences. The mediator normally has no power to impose a solution if the parties can't agree. Generally, mediation works well in situations where the parties want to settle their disputes in order to work together in the future. In a landlord-tenant context, mediation can be extremely helpful in a number of areas, such as disputes about noise, the necessity for repairs, a tenant's decision to withhold rent because defects have not been repaired, rent increases, privacy, and many more. Many tenants and especially groups of tenants with a list of grievances find that mediating disputes with a landlord is a better approach to problem solving than is withholding rent, filing a lawsuit, and so on.

Mediators do not impose a decision on the parties, but use their skills to facilitate a compromise. Mediation is most effective when procedures are established in advance. Typically, the tenant or landlord with a problem contacts some respected neutral organization, such as a city or county landlord-tenant mediation project (not every area has one, but many do); the American Arbitration Association; or a neighborhood dispute resolution center, such as San Francisco's Community Board Program, and arranges for this group to mediate a landlord-tenant dispute. There are a great number of mediation programs in California, and if you ask your District Attorney's office or county clerk, you should find one.

At the mediation session, each side gets to state their position. Just doing this often cools people off considerably and frequently results in a compromise. If the dispute is not taken care of easily, however, the mediator may suggest several ways to resolve the problem, or may even keep everyone talking long enough to realize that the problem goes deeper than the one being mediated. For example, a landlord who thinks she runs a tight ship may learn that the real problem from the tenant's point of view is that her manager is lazy and slow to make repairs. This, of course, may lead to the further discovery that the manager is angry at several tenants for letting their kids pull up his tulips.

Because mediation lets both sides air their grievances, it often works well to improve the climate of stormy landlord-tenant relationships. And if it doesn't, you haven't lost much, especially if you make sure mediation occurs promptly and you use it only in situations where your landlord has some arguably legitimate position. If mediation fails, you can still fight it out in court.

Small claims court judges often use mediation as a required first step. Parties are required to attend a mediation session and to attempt to settle their differences before the case will be heard in court.

Tear-Out Forms

* Be sure that the back of the forms you submit to the court are printed upside-down, as they are appendix forms.

Get the Form Online

Several of the court forms used in this book are written by the Judicial Council, California's official forms publisher. The forms in this book were the most recent available when this book went to press, but the Council revises them from time to time.

You can use the Internet to confirm that you're using the most current form, and you can download and print any form (hardware and software permitting). The Judicial Council's website is www.courtinfo.ca.gov/forms.

To make sure that the form in this book's appendix is the most current form, check the form's title, number, and revision date (printed in the lower left-hand corner). On the Judicial Council's website, use the pull-down menu and select the "All forms listed by Number" category. When you find your form, check the "date revised" date. If that date is later than the date on the form in the appendix, use the newer form. To print a form, you'll need software (such as Adobe Acrobat). You can download this application from the site. The quality of your printed form will vary according to the quality of your printer. You can also fill in the form online, but you won't be able to save the file to your computer.

Landlord/Tenant Checklist
General Condition of Rental Unit and Premises

Street Address _____ Unit Number _____ City _____

	Condition on Arrival	Condition on Initial Move-Out Inspection	Condition on Departure	Actual or Estimated Cost of Cleaning, Repair/Replacement
Living Room				
Floors & Floor Coverings				
Drapes & Window Coverings				
Walls & Ceilings				
Light Fixtures				
Windows, Screens, & Doors				
Front Door & Locks				
Smoke Detector				
Fireplace				
Other				
Kitchen				
Floors & Floor Coverings				
Walls & Ceilings				
Light Fixtures				
Cabinets				
Counters				
Stove/Oven				
Refrigerator				
Dishwasher				
Garbage Disposal				
Sink & Plumbing				
Smoke Detector				
Other				

© nolo

	Condition on Arrival	Condition on Initial Move-Out Inspection	Condition on Departure	Actual or Estimated Cost of Cleaning, Repair/Replacement
Dining Room				
Floors & Floor Coverings				
Walls & Ceilings				
Light Fixtures				
Windows, Screens, & Doors				
Smoke Detector				
Other				
Bathroom				
Floors & Floor Coverings				
Walls & Ceilings				
Windows, Screens, & Doors				
Light Fixtures				
Bathtub/Shower				
Sinks & Counters				
Toilet				
Other				
Other				
Bedroom				
Floors & Floor Coverings				
Windows, Screens, & Doors				
Walls & Ceilings				
Light Fixtures				
Smoke Detector				
Other				
Other				
Other				

Other Areas	Condition on Arrival	Condition on Initial Move-Out Inspection	Condition on Departure	Actual or Estimated Cost of Cleaning, Repair/Replacement
Heating System				
Air Conditioning				
Lawn/Garden				
Stairs & Hallway				
Patio, Terrace, Deck, etc.				
Basement				
Parking Area				
Other				
Other				
Other				
Other				
Other				

☐ Tenants acknowledge that all smoke detectors and fire extinguishers were tested in their presence and found to be in working order, and that the testing procedure was explained to them. Tenants agree to test all detectors at least once a month and to report any problems to Landlord/Manager in writing. Tenants agree to replace all smoke detector batteries as necessary.

Notes:

Furnished Property

	Condition on Arrival	Condition on Initial Move-Out Inspection	Condition on Departure	Actual or Estimated Cost of Cleaning, Repair/Replacement
Living Room				
Coffee Table				
End Tables				
Lamps				
Chairs				
Sofa				
Other				
Other				
Kitchen				
Broiler Pan				
Ice Trays				
Other				
Other				
Dining Area				
Chairs				
Stools				
Table				
Other				
Other				
Bathroom				
Mirrors				
Shower Curtain				
Hamper				
Other				

	Condition on Arrival	Condition on Initial Move-Out Inspection	Condition on Departure	Actual or Estimated Cost of Cleaning, Repair/Replacement
Bedroom				
Beds (single)				
Beds (double)				
Chairs				
Chests				
Dressing Tables				
Lamps				
Mirrors				
Night Tables				
Other				
Other				
Other Area				
Bookcases				
Desks				
Pictures				
Other				
Other				

Use this space to provide any additional explanation:

Landlord/Tenant Checklist completed on moving in on _____, 20_____.

_____ and _____

Landlord/Manager

_____
Tenant

_____
Tenant

_____
Tenant

Landlord/Tenant Checklist completed at Initial Move-Out Inspection on _____, 20_____.

_____ and _____

Landlord/Manager

_____
Tenant

_____
Tenant

_____
Tenant

Landlord/Tenant Checklist completed on moving out on _____, 20_____.

_____ and _____

Landlord/Manager

_____
Tenant

_____
Tenant

_____
Tenant

Fixed-Term Residential Lease

1. **Identification of Landlord and Tenants.** This Agreement is made and entered into on _____ , 20____ , between _____ ("Tenants") and _____ ("Landlord"). Each Tenant is jointly and severally liable for the payment of rent and performance of all other terms of this Agreement.

2. **Identification of Premises and Occupants.** Subject to the terms and conditions set forth in this Agreement, Landlord rents to Tenants, and Tenants rent from Landlord, for residential purposes only, the premises located at _____ _____ , California ("the premises"). The premises will be occupied by the undersigned Tenants and the following minor children: _____ _____ .

3. **Limits on Use and Occupancy.** The premises are to be used only as a private residence for Tenants and any minors listed in Clause 2 of this Agreement, and for no other purpose without Landlord's prior written consent. Occupancy by guests for more than ten days in any six-month period is prohibited without Landlord's written consent and will be considered a breach of this Agreement.

4. **Defining the Term of the Tenancy.** The term of the rental will begin on _____ , 20____ and will expire on _____ , 20____ . Should Tenants vacate before expiration of the term, Tenants will be liable for the balance of the rent for the remainder of the term, less any rent Landlord collects or could have collected from a replacement tenant by reasonably attempting to rerent. Tenants who vacate before expiration of the term are also responsible for Landlord's costs of advertising for a replacement tenant.

5. **Amount and Schedule for the Payment of Rent.** Tenants will pay to Landlord a monthly rent of $ _____ , payable in advance on the _____ day of each month, except when that day falls on a weekend or legal holiday, in which case rent is due on the next business day. Rent will be paid to _____ at _____ _____ , or at such other place as Landlord may designate.

    a. The form of payment will be ☐ cash ☐ personal check ☐ certified funds or money order ☐ credit card ☐ automatic credit card debit ☐ bank debit

    ☐ b. [*Check if rent will be accepted personally, not by mail.*] Rent is accepted during the following days and hours: _____ _____

    ☐ c. [*Check if rent will be paid by electronic funds transfer.*] Rent may be paid by electronic funds transfer to account number_____ in the name of _____ (*Account holder*) at _____ (*Institution*), _____ (*Branch*), a financial institution located at _____ _____ (*Address*) and _____ (*Telephone number*) .

    ☐ d. [*Prorated rent.*] On signing this agreement, Tenants will pay to Landlord for the period of _____ , 20____ , through _____ , 20____ , the sum of $_____ as rent, payable in advance.

6. **Late Charges.** Because Landlord and Tenants agree that actual damages for late rent payments are very difficult or impossible to determine, Landlord and Tenants agree to the following stated late charge as liquidated damages. Tenants will pay Landlord a late charge if Tenants fail to pay the rent in full within _____ days after the date it is due. The late charge will be $ _____ , plus $ _____ for each additional day that the rent continues to be unpaid. The total late charge for any one month will not exceed $ _____ . Landlord does not waive the right to insist on payment of the rent in full on the date it is due.

7. **Returned Check and Other Bank Charges.** In the event any check offered by Tenants to Landlord in payment of rent or any other amount due under this Agreement is returned for lack of sufficient funds, a "stop payment," or any other reason, Tenants will pay Landlord a returned check charge in the amount of $_____ .

8. **Amount and Payment of Deposits.** On signing this Agreement, Tenants will pay to Landlord the sum of $_____ as a security deposit. Tenants may not, without Landlord's prior written consent, apply this security deposit to the last month's rent or to any other sum due under this Agreement. Within three weeks after Tenants have vacated the premises, Landlord will furnish Tenants with an itemized written statement of the reasons for, and the dollar amount of, any of the security deposit retained by the Landlord, receipts for work done or items purchased, if available, along with a check for any deposit balance. Under Section 1950.5 of the California Civil Code, Landlord may withhold only that portion of Tenants' security deposit necessary to: (1) remedy any default by Tenants in the payment of rent; (2) repair damages to the premises exclusive of ordinary wear and tear; (3) clean the premises if necessary to restore it to the same level of cleanliness it was in at the beginning of the tenancy; and (4) remedy any default by Tenants, under this Agreement, to restore, replace, or return any of Landlord's personal property mentioned in this Agreement, including but not limited to the property referred to in Clause 11.

    Landlord will pay Tenants interest on all security deposits as follows:

    ☐ a. Per state law, no interest payments are required.

    ☐ b. Local law requires that interest be paid or credited, or Landlord has decided voluntarily to do so, which will occur as follows: _____
    _____

9. **Utilities.** Tenants will be responsible for payment of all utility charges, except for the following, which shall be paid by Landlord: _____
    _____

    ☐ Tenants' gas or electric meter serves area(s) outside of their premises, and there are not separate gas and electric meters for Tenants' unit and the area(s) outside their unit. Tenants and Landlord agree as follows: _____
    _____
    _____

10. **Prohibition of Assignment and Subletting.** Tenants will not sublet any part of the premises or assign this Agreement without the prior written consent of Landlord.

11. **Condition of the Premises.** Tenants agree to: (1) keep the premises clean and sanitary and in good repair and, upon termination of the tenancy, to return the premises to Landlord in a condition identical to that which existed when Tenants took occupancy, except for ordinary wear and tear; (2) immediately notify Landlord of any defects or dangerous conditions in and about the premises of which they become aware; and (3) reimburse Landlord, on demand by Landlord, for the cost of any repairs to the premises, including Landlord's personal property therein, damaged by Tenants or their guests or invitees through misuse or neglect.

    Tenants acknowledge that they have examined the premises, including appliances, fixtures, carpets, drapes, and paint, and have found them to be in good, safe, and clean condition and repair, except as noted here: _____
    _____
    _____
    _____
    _____
    _____
    _____
    _____
    _____

12. **Possession of the Premises.** If, after signing this Agreement, Tenants fail to take possession of the premises, they will still be responsible for paying rent and complying with all other terms of this Agreement. In the event Landlord is unable to deliver possession of the premises to Tenants for any reason not within Landlord's control, including, but not limited to, failure of prior occupants to vacate or partial or complete destruction of the premises, Tenants will have the right to terminate this Agreement. In such event, Landlord's liability to Tenants will be limited to the return of all sums previously paid by Tenants to Landlord.

13. **Pets.** No animal, bird, or other pet may be kept on the premises without Landlord's prior written consent, except properly trained dogs needed by blind, deaf, or disabled persons and:

   ☐ a. None.

   ☐ b. _____ , under the following conditions:

      _____

14. **Landlord's Access for Inspection and Emergency.** Landlord or Landlord's agents may enter the premises in the event of an emergency or to make repairs or improvements, supply agreed services, show the premises to prospective buyers or tenants, and conduct an initial move-out inspection requested by tenants. Except in cases of emergency, Tenants' abandonment of the premises, or court order, Landlord will give Tenants reasonable notice of intent to enter and will enter only during regular business hours of Monday through Friday from 9:00 a.m. to 6:00 p.m. and Saturday from 10:00 a.m. to 1:00 p.m. The notice will include the purpose, date, and approximate time of entry.

15. **Extended Absences by Tenants.** Tenants agree to notify Landlord in the event that they will be away from the premises for _____ consecutive days or more. During such absence, Landlord may enter the premises at times reasonably necessary to maintain the property and inspect for damage and needed repairs.

16. **Prohibitions Against Violating Laws and Causing Disturbances.** Tenants are entitled to quiet enjoyment of the premises. Tenants and their guests or invitees will not use the premises or adjacent areas in such a way as to: (1) violate any law or ordinance, including laws prohibiting the use, possession, or sale of illegal drugs; (2) commit waste or nuisance; or (3) annoy, disturb, inconvenience, or interfere with the quiet enjoyment and peace and quiet of any other tenant or nearby resident.

17. **Repairs and Alterations**

   a. Tenants will not, without Landlord's prior written consent, alter, rekey, or install any locks to the premises or install or alter any burglar alarm system. Tenants will provide Landlord with a key or keys capable of unlocking all such rekeyed or new locks as well as instructions on how to disarm any altered or new burglar alarm system.

   b. Except as provided by law or as authorized by the prior written consent of Landlord, Tenants will not make any repairs or alterations to the premises. Landlord will not unreasonably withhold consent for such repairs, but will not authorize repairs that require advanced skill or workmanship or that would be dangerous to undertake. Landlord will not authorize repairs unless such repairs are likely to return the item or element of the rental to its predamaged state of usefulness and attractiveness.

18. **Damage to the Premises.** In the event the premises are partially or totally damaged or destroyed by fire or other cause, the following will apply:

   a. If the premises are totally damaged and destroyed, Landlord will have the option to: (1) repair such damage and restore the premises, with this Agreement continuing in full force and effect, except that Tenants' rent will be abated while repairs are being made; or (2) give written notice to Tenants terminating this Agreement at any time within thirty (30) days after such damage, and specifying the termination date; in the event that Landlord gives such notice, this Agreement will expire and all of Tenants' rights pursuant to this Agreement will cease.

   b. Landlord will have the option to determine that the premises are only partially damaged by fire or other cause. In that event, Landlord will attempt to repair such damage and restore the premises within thirty (30) days after such damage. If only part of the premises cannot be used, Tenants must pay rent only for the usable part, to be determined solely by Landlord. If Landlord is unable to complete repairs within thirty (30) days, this Agreement will expire and all of Tenants' rights pursuant to this Agreement will terminate at the option of either party.

c. In the event that Tenants, or their guests or invitees, in any way caused or contributed to the damage of the premises, Landlord will have the right to terminate this Agreement at any time, and Tenants will be responsible for all losses, including, but not limited to, damage and repair costs as well as loss of rental income.

d. Landlord will not be required to repair or replace any property brought onto the premises by Tenants.

19. **Tenants' Financial Responsibility and Renters' Insurance.** Tenants agree to accept financial responsibility for any loss or damage to personal property belonging to Tenants and their guests and invitees caused by theft, fire, or any other cause. Landlord assumes no liability for any such loss. Landlord recommends that Tenants obtain a renters' insurance policy from a recognized insurance firm to cover Tenants' liability, personal property damage, and damage to the premises.

20. **Waterbeds.** No waterbed or other item of water-filled furniture may be kept on the premises without Landlord's written consent.

☐ Landlord grants Tenants permission to keep water-filled furniture on the premises. Attachment _____ : Agreement Regarding Use of Waterbed is attached to and incorporated into this Agreement by reference.

21. **Tenant Rules and Regulations**

☐ Tenants acknowledge receipt of, and have read a copy of, tenant rules and regulations, which are labeled Attachment _____ and attached to and incorporated into this Agreement by reference. Landlord may change the rules and regulations without notice.

22. **Payment of Attorney Fees in a Lawsuit.** In any action or legal proceeding to enforce any part of this Agreement, the prevailing party ☐ will not ☐ will recover reasonable attorney fees and court costs.

23. **Authority to Receive Legal Papers.** Any person managing the premises, the Landlord, and anyone designated by the Landlord are authorized to accept service of process and receive other notices and demands, which may be delivered to:

☐ a. the manager, at the following address and telephone number: _____
_____
_____

☐ b. the Landlord, at the following address and telephone number: _____
_____
_____

☐ c. the following: _____
_____
_____

24. **Cash-Only Rent.** Tenants will pay rent in the form specified above in Clause 5a. Tenants understand that if Tenants pay rent with a check that is not honored due to insufficient funds, or with a money order or cashier's check whose issuer has been instructed to stop payment, Landlord has the legal right to demand that rent be paid only in cash for up to three months after Tenants have received proper notice. (California Civil Code § 1947.3.) In that event, Landlord will give Tenants the legally required notice, and Tenants agree to abide by this change in the terms of this tenancy.

25. **Additional Provisions**

☐ a. None

☐ b. Additional provisions are as follows: _____
_____
_____
_____
_____
_____
_____

26. **State Database Disclosure.** Notice: Pursuant to Section 290.46 of the Penal Code, information about specified registered sex offenders is made available to the public via an Internet website maintained by the Department of Justice at www.meganslaw. ca.gov. Depending on an offender's criminal history, this information will include either the address at which the offender resides or the community of residence and ZIP Code in which he or she resides.

27. **Grounds for Termination of Tenancy.** The failure of Tenants or Tenants' guests or invitees to comply with any term of this Agreement, or the misrepresentation of any material fact on Tenants' Rental Application, is grounds for termination of the tenancy, with appropriate notice to Tenants and procedures as required by law.

28. **Entire Agreement.** This document constitutes the entire Agreement between the parties, and no promises or representations, other than those contained here and those implied by law, have been made by Landlord or Tenants. Any modifications to this Agreement must be in writing signed by Landlord and Tenants.

_____   _____
Landlord/Manager   Date

_____
Landlord/Manager's Street Address, City, State, & Zip

_____

_____

_____   _____
Tenant   Date

_____   _____
Tenant   Date

_____   _____
Tenant   Date

Month-to-Month Residential Rental Agreement

1. Identification of Landlord and Tenants. This Agreement is made and entered into on _____ , 20_____ , between _____ ("Tenants") and _____ ("Landlord"). Each Tenant is jointly and severally liable for the payment of rent and performance of all other terms of this Agreement.

2. **Identification of Premises and Occupants.** Subject to the terms and conditions set forth in this Agreement, Landlord rents to Tenants, and Tenants rent from Landlord, for residential purposes only, the premises located at _____ _____ , California ("the premises"). The premises will be occupied by the undersigned Tenants and the following minor children: _____ _____ .

3. **Limits on Use and Occupancy.** The premises are to be used only as a private residence for Tenants and any minors listed in Clause 2 of this Agreement, and for no other purpose without Landlord's prior written consent. Occupancy by guests for more than ten days in any six-month period is prohibited without Landlord's written consent and will be considered a breach of this Agreement.

4. **Defining the Term of the Tenancy.** The rental will begin on _____ , 20_____ and will continue on a month-to-month basis. This tenancy may be terminated by Landlord or Tenants and may be modified by Landlord, by giving 30 days' written notice to the other, or 60 days' notice by Landlord to Tenant, in accordance with Civil Code Section 827 or 1946.1 (subject to any local rent control ordinances that may apply).

5. **Amount and Schedule for the Payment of Rent.** Tenants will pay to Landlord a monthly rent of $ _____ , payable in advance on the _____ day of each month, except when that day falls on a weekend or legal holiday, in which case rent is due on the next business day. Rent will be paid to _____ _____ at _____ _____ , or at such other place as Landlord may designate.

   a. The form of payment will be ☐ cash ☐ personal check ☐ certified funds or money order ☐ credit card ☐ automatic credit card debit ☐ bank debit

   ☐ b. [*Check if rent will be accepted personally, not by mail.*] Rent is accepted during the following days and hours: _____ _____ _____

   ☐ c. [*Check if rent will be paid by electronic funds transfer.*] Rent may be paid by electronic funds transfer to account number_____ in the name of _____ (*Account holder*) at _____ (*Institution*), _____ (*Branch*), a financial institution located at _____ _____ (*Address*) and _____ (*Telephone number*) .

   ☐ d. [*Prorated rent.*] On signing this agreement, Tenants will pay to Landlord for the period of _____ , 20_____ , through _____ , 20_____ , the sum of $_____ as rent, payable in advance.

6. **Late Charges.** Because Landlord and Tenants agree that actual damages for late rent payments are very difficult or impossible to determine, Landlord and Tenants agree to the following stated late charge as liquidated damages. Tenants will pay Landlord a late charge if Tenants fail to pay the rent in full within _____ days after the date it is due. The late charge will be $ _____ , plus $ _____ for each additional day that the rent continues to be unpaid. The total late charge for any one month will not exceed $ _____ . Landlord does not waive the right to insist on payment of the rent in full on the date it is due.

7. **Returned Check and Other Bank Charges.** In the event any check offered by Tenants to Landlord in payment of rent or any other amount due under this Agreement is returned for lack of sufficient funds, a "stop payment," or any other reason, Tenants will pay Landlord a returned check charge in the amount of $_____ .

8. **Amount and Payment of Deposits.** On signing this Agreement, Tenants will pay to Landlord the sum of $_____ as a security deposit. Tenants may not, without Landlord's prior written consent, apply this security deposit to the last month's rent or to any other sum due under this Agreement. Within three weeks after Tenants have vacated the premises, Landlord will furnish Tenants with an itemized written statement of the reasons for, and the dollar amount of, any of the security deposit retained by the Landlord, receipts for work done or items purchased, if available, along with a check for any deposit balance. Under Section 1950.5 of the California Civil Code, Landlord may withhold only that portion of Tenants' security deposit necessary to: (1) remedy any default by Tenants in the payment of rent; (2) repair damages to the premises exclusive of ordinary wear and tear; (3) clean the premises if necessary to restore it to the same level of cleanliness it was in at the beginning of the tenancy; and (4) remedy any default by Tenants, under this Agreement, to restore, replace, or return any of Landlord's personal property mentioned in this Agreement, including but not limited to the property referred to in Clause 11.

   Landlord will pay Tenants interest on all security deposits as follows:

   ☐ a. Per state law, no interest payments are required.

   ☐ b. Local law requires that interest be paid or credited, or Landlord has decided voluntarily to do so, which will occur as follows: _____

   _____

9. **Utilities.** Tenants will be responsible for payment of all utility charges, except for the following, which shall be paid by Landlord: _____

   _____

   ☐ Tenants' gas or electric meter serves area(s) outside of their premises, and there are not separate gas and electric meters for Tenants' unit and the area(s) outside their unit. Tenants and Landlord agree as follows: _____

   _____

   _____

10. **Prohibition of Assignment and Subletting.** Tenants will not sublet any part of the premises or assign this Agreement without the prior written consent of Landlord.

11. **Condition of the Premises.** Tenants agree to: (1) keep the premises clean and sanitary and in good repair and, upon termination of the tenancy, to return the premises to Landlord in a condition identical to that which existed when Tenants took occupancy, except for ordinary wear and tear; (2) immediately notify Landlord of any defects or dangerous conditions in and about the premises of which they become aware; and (3) reimburse Landlord, on demand by Landlord, for the cost of any repairs to the premises, including Landlord's personal property therein, damaged by Tenants or their guests or invitees through misuse or neglect.

   Tenants acknowledge that they have examined the premises, including appliances, fixtures, carpets, drapes, and paint, and have found them to be in good, safe, and clean condition and repair, except as noted here: _____

   _____

   _____

   _____

   _____

   _____

   _____

   _____

   _____

12. **Possession of the Premises.** If, after signing this Agreement, Tenants fail to take possession of the premises, they will still be responsible for paying rent and complying with all other terms of this Agreement. In the event Landlord is unable to deliver possession of the premises to Tenants for any reason not within Landlord's control, including, but not limited to, failure of prior occupants to vacate or partial or complete destruction of the premises, Tenants will have the right to terminate this Agreement. In such event, Landlord's liability to Tenants will be limited to the return of all sums previously paid by Tenants to Landlord.

13. **Pets.** No animal, bird, or other pet may be kept on the premises without Landlord's prior written consent, except properly trained dogs needed by blind, deaf, or disabled persons and:

☐ a. None.

☐ b. _____ , under the following conditions:

_____

14. **Landlord's Access for Inspection and Emergency.** Landlord or Landlord's agents may enter the premises in the event of an emergency or to make repairs or improvements, supply agreed services, show the premises to prospective buyers or tenants, and conduct an initial move-out inspection requested by tenants. Except in cases of emergency, Tenants' abandonment of the premises, or court order, Landlord will give Tenants reasonable notice of intent to enter and will enter only during regular business hours of Monday through Friday from 9:00 a.m. to 6:00 p.m. and Saturday from 10:00 a.m. to 1:00 p.m. The notice will include the purpose, date, and approximate time of entry.

15. **Extended Absences by Tenants.** Tenants agree to notify Landlord in the event that they will be away from the premises for _____ consecutive days or more. During such absence, Landlord may enter the premises at times reasonably necessary to maintain the property and inspect for damage and needed repairs.

16. **Prohibitions Against Violating Laws and Causing Disturbances.** Tenants are entitled to quiet enjoyment of the premises. Tenants and their guests or invitees will not use the premises or adjacent areas in such a way as to: (1) violate any law or ordinance, including laws prohibiting the use, possession, or sale of illegal drugs; (2) commit waste or nuisance; or (3) annoy, disturb, inconvenience, or interfere with the quiet enjoyment and peace and quiet of any other tenant or nearby resident.

17. **Repairs and Alterations**

a. Tenants will not, without Landlord's prior written consent, alter, rekey, or install any locks to the premises or install or alter any burglar alarm system. Tenants will provide Landlord with a key or keys capable of unlocking all such rekeyed or new locks as well as instructions on how to disarm any altered or new burglar alarm system.

b. Except as provided by law or as authorized by the prior written consent of Landlord, Tenants will not make any repairs or alterations to the premises. Landlord will not unreasonably withhold consent for such repairs, but will not authorize repairs that require advanced skill or workmanship or that would be dangerous to undertake. Landlord will not authorize repairs unless such repairs are likely to return the item or element of the rental to its predamaged state of usefulness and attractiveness.

18. **Damage to the Premises.** In the event the premises are partially or totally damaged or destroyed by fire or other cause, the following will apply:

a. If the premises are totally damaged and destroyed, Landlord will have the option to: (1) repair such damage and restore the premises, with this Agreement continuing in full force and effect, except that Tenants' rent will be abated while repairs are being made; or (2) give written notice to Tenants terminating this Agreement at any time within thirty (30) days after such damage, and specifying the termination date; in the event that Landlord gives such notice, this Agreement will expire and all of Tenants' rights pursuant to this Agreement will cease.

b. Landlord will have the option to determine that the premises are only partially damaged by fire or other cause. In that event, Landlord will attempt to repair such damage and restore the premises within thirty (30) days after such damage. If only part of the premises cannot be used, Tenants must pay rent only for the usable part, to be determined solely by Landlord. If Landlord is unable to complete repairs within thirty (30) days, this Agreement will expire and all of Tenants' rights pursuant to this Agreement will terminate at the option of either party.

c. In the event that Tenants, or their guests or invitees, in any way caused or contributed to the damage of the premises, Landlord will have the right to terminate this Agreement at any time, and Tenants will be responsible for all losses, including, but not limited to, damage and repair costs as well as loss of rental income.

d. Landlord will not be required to repair or replace any property brought onto the premises by Tenants.

19. **Tenants' Financial Responsibility and Renters' Insurance.** Tenants agree to accept financial responsibility for any loss or damage to personal property belonging to Tenants and their guests and invitees caused by theft, fire, or any other cause. Landlord assumes no liability for any such loss. Landlord recommends that Tenants obtain a renters' insurance policy from a recognized insurance firm to cover Tenants' liability, personal property damage, and damage to the premises.

20. **Waterbeds.** No waterbed or other item of water-filled furniture may be kept on the premises without Landlord's written consent.

☐ Landlord grants Tenants permission to keep water-filled furniture on the premises. Attachment _____ : Agreement Regarding Use of Waterbed is attached to and incorporated into this Agreement by reference.

21. **Tenant Rules and Regulations**

☐ Tenants acknowledge receipt of, and have read a copy of, tenant rules and regulations, which are labeled Attachment _____ and attached to and incorporated into this Agreement by reference. Landlord may change the rules and regulations without notice.

22. **Payment of Attorney Fees in a Lawsuit.** In any action or legal proceeding to enforce any part of this Agreement, the prevailing party ☐ will not ☐ will recover reasonable attorney fees and court costs.

23. **Authority to Receive Legal Papers.** Any person managing the premises, the Landlord, and anyone designated by the Landlord are authorized to accept service of process and receive other notices and demands, which may be delivered to:

☐ a. the manager, at the following address and telephone number: _____
_____
_____

☐ b. the Landlord, at the following address and telephone number: _____
_____
_____

☐ c. the following: _____
_____
_____

24. **Cash-Only Rent.** Tenants will pay rent in the form specified above in Clause 5a. Tenants understand that if Tenants pay rent with a check that is not honored due to insufficient funds, or with a money order or cashier's check whose issuer has been instructed to stop payment, Landlord has the legal right to demand that rent be paid only in cash for up to three months after Tenants have received proper notice. (California Civil Code § 1947.3.) In that event, Landlord will give Tenants the legally required notice, and Tenants agree to abide by this change in the terms of this tenancy.

25. **Additional Provisions**

☐ a. None

☐ b. Additional provisions are as follows: _____
_____
_____
_____
_____
_____

26. **State Database Disclosure.** Notice: Pursuant to Section 290.46 of the Penal Code, information about specified registered sex offenders is made available to the public via an Internet website maintained by the Department of Justice at www.meganslaw.ca.gov. Depending on an offender's criminal history, this information will include either the address at which the offender resides or the community of residence and ZIP Code in which he or she resides.

27. **Grounds for Termination of Tenancy.** The failure of Tenants or Tenants' guests or invitees to comply with any term of this Agreement, or the misrepresentation of any material fact on Tenants' Rental Application, is grounds for termination of the tenancy, with appropriate notice to Tenants and procedures as required by law.

28. **Entire Agreement.** This document constitutes the entire Agreement between the parties, and no promises or representations, other than those contained here and those implied by law, have been made by Landlord or Tenants. Any modifications to this Agreement must be in writing signed by Landlord and Tenants.

_____   _____
Landlord/Manager   Date

_____
Landlord/Manager's Street Address, City, State, & Zip

_____

_____   _____
Tenant   Date

_____   _____
Tenant   Date

_____   _____
Tenant   Date

Notice to Repair

To _____ ,

Landlord of the premises located at _____

_____ .

    NOTICE IS HEREBY GIVEN that unless certain defects on the premises are repaired within a reasonable time, the undersigned tenant shall exercise any and all rights accruing to him pursuant to law, including those granted by California Civil Code Sections 1941–1942.

    The defects are the following _____

_____

_____

_____

_____

_____

_____

_____

_____

_____ :

_____   _____

Signature of Tenant   Date

Notice of Rent Withholding

To _____ ,

Landlord of the premises located at _____

_____ .

    NOTICE IS HEREBY GIVEN that because of your failure to comply with your implied warranty of habitability by refusing to repair defects on the premises, as previously demanded of you, the undersigned tenant has elected to withhold this month's rent in accordance with California law. Rent payments will be resumed in the future, as they become due, only after said defects have been properly repaired.

_____   _____

Signature of Tenant   Date

Authority: *Green v. Superior Court,* 10 Cal.3d 616 (1974).

Agreement Regarding Tenant Alterations to Rental Unit

_____ (Landlord)

and _____ (Tenant)

agree as follows:

1. Tenant may make the following alterations to the rental unit at: _____

    _____

2. Tenant will accomplish the work described in Paragraph 1 by using the following materials and procedures: _____

    _____

    _____ .

3. Tenant will do only the work outlined in Paragraph 1 using only the materials and procedures outlined in Paragraph 2.

4. The alterations carried out by Tenant (check either a or b):

    ☐ will become Landlord's property and are not to be removed by Tenant during or at the end of the tenancy

    ☐ will be considered Tenant's personal property, and as such may be removed by Tenant at any time up to the end of the tenancy. Tenant promises to return the premises to their original condition upon removing the improvement.

5. Landlord will reimburse Tenant only for the costs checked below:

    ☐ the cost of materials listed in Paragraph 2

    ☐ labor costs at the rate of $ _____ per hour for work done in a workmanlike manner acceptable to Landlord up to _____ hours.

6. After receiving appropriate documentation of the cost of materials and labor, Landlord shall make any payment called for under Paragraph 5 by:

    ☐ lump sum payment, within _____ days of receiving documentation of costs, or

    ☐ by reducing Tenant's rent by $ _____ per month for the number of months necessary to cover the total amounts under the terms of this agreement.

7. If under Paragraph 4 of this contract the alterations are Tenant's personal property, Tenant must return the premises to their original condition upon removing the alterations. If Tenant fails to do this, Landlord will deduct the cost to restore the premises to their original condition from Tenant's security deposit. If the security deposit is insufficient to cover the costs of restoration, Landlord may take legal action, if necessary, to collect the balance.

8. If Tenant fails to remove an improvement that is his or her personal property on or before the end of the tenancy, it will be considered the property of Landlord, who may choose to keep the improvement (with no financial liability to Tenant), or remove it and charge Tenant for the costs of removal and restoration. Landlord may deduct any costs of removal and restoration from Tenant's security deposit. If the security deposit is insufficient to cover the costs of removal and restoration, Landlord may take legal action, if necessary, to collect the balance.

9. If Tenant removes an item that is Landlord's property, Tenant will owe Landlord the fair market value of the item removed plus any costs incurred by Landlord to restore the premises to their original condition.

10. If Landlord and Tenant are involved in any legal proceeding arising out of this agreement, the prevailing party shall recover reasonable attorney fees, court costs and any costs reasonably necessary to collect a judgment.

_____   _____
Signature of Landlord   Date

_____   _____
Signature of Tenant   Date

If you are getting public benefits, are a low-income person, or do not have enough income to pay for household's basic needs and your court fees, you may use this form to ask the court to waive all or part of your court fees. The court may order you to answer questions about your finances. If the court waives the fees, you may still have to pay later if:

- You cannot give the court proof of your eligibility,
- Your financial situation improves during this case, or
- You settle your civil case for **$10,000** or more. The trial court that waives your fees will have a lien on any such settlement in the amount of the waived fees and costs. The court may also charge you any collection costs.

Clerk stamps date here when form is filed.

Fill in court name and street address:

① **Your Information** *(person asking the court to waive the fees):*

Name: _____

Street or mailing address: _____

City: _____ State: _____ Zip: _____

Phone number: _____

② **Your Job,** if you have one *(job title):* _____

Name of employer: _____

Employer's address: _____

Fill in case number and name:

Case Number:

Case Name:

③ **Your lawyer,** if you have one *(name, firm or affiliation, address, phone number, and State Bar number):*

_____

_____

a. The lawyer has agreed to advance all or a portion of your fees or costs *(check one):* Yes ☐ No ☐

b. *(If yes, your lawyer must sign here)* Lawyer's signature: _____

If your lawyer is not providing legal-aid type services based on your low income, you may have to go to a hearing to explain why you are asking the court to waive the fees.

④ **What court's fees or costs are you asking to be waived?**

☐ Superior Court (See *Information Sheet on Waiver of Superior Court Fees and Costs* (form FW-001-INFO).)

☐ Supreme Court, Court of Appeal, or Appellate Division of Superior Court (See *Information Sheet on Waiver of Appellate Court Fees and Costs* (form APP-015/FW-015-INFO).)

⑤ **Why are you asking the court to waive your court fees?**

a. ☐ I receive *(check all that apply):* ☐ Medi-Cal ☐ Food Stamps ☐ SSI ☐ SSP ☐ County Relief/General Assistance ☐ IHSS (In-Home Supportive Services) ☐ CalWORKS or Tribal TANF (Tribal Temporary Assistance for Needy Families) ☐ CAPI (Cash Assistance Program for Aged, Blind and Disabled)

b. ☐ My gross monthly household income (before deductions for taxes) is less than the amount listed below. *(If you check 5b you must fill out 7, 8 and 9 on page 2 of this form.)*

Family Size	Family Income	Family Size	Family Income	Family Size	Family Income	
1	$1,128.13	3	$1,907.30	5	$2,686.46	*If more than 6 people at home, add $389.59 for each extra person.*
2	$1,517.71	4	$2,296.88	6	$3,076.05	

c. ☐ I do not have enough income to pay for my household's basic needs *and* the court fees. I ask the court to *(check one):* ☐ waive all court fees ☐ waive some of the court fees ☐ let me make payments over time *(Explain):* _____ *(If you check 5c, you must fill out page 2.)*

⑥ ☐ Check here if you asked the court to waive your court fees for this case in the last six months.

(If your previous request is reasonably available, please attach it to this form and check here: ☐ *)*

I declare under penalty of perjury under the laws of the State of California that the information I have provided on this form and all attachments is true and correct.

Date: _____

_____   ▶   _____
Print your name here   *Sign here*

Judicial Council of California, *www.courtinfo.ca.gov*
Revised July 2, 2009, Mandatory Form
Government Code, § 68633
Cal. Rules of Court, rules 3.51, 8.26, and 8.818

Request to Waive Court Fees

FW-001, Page 1 of 2

If you checked 5a on page 1, do not fill out below. If you checked 5b, fill out questions 7, 8, and 9 only. If you checked 5c, you **must** *fill out this entire page. If you need more space, attach form MC-025 or attach a sheet of paper and write Financial Information and your name and case number at the top.*

(7) ☐ Check here if your income changes a lot from month to month. Fill out below based on your average income for the past 12 months.

(8) **Your Monthly Income**

a. Gross monthly income *(before deductions):* $ _____
   List each payroll deduction and amount below:
   (1) _____ $ _____
   (2) _____ $ _____
   (3) _____ $ _____
   (4) _____ $ _____

b. Total deductions *(add 8a (1)-(4) above):* $ _____

c. Total monthly take-home pay *(8a minus 8b):* $ _____

d. List the source and amount of *any* other income you get each month, including: spousal/child support, retirement, social security, disability, unemployment, military basic allowance for quarters (BAQ), veterans payments, dividends, interest, trust income, annuities, net business or rental income, reimbursement for job-related expenses, gambling or lottery winnings, etc.
   (1) _____ $ _____
   (2) _____ $ _____
   (3) _____ $ _____
   (4) _____ $ _____

e. **Your total monthly income is** *(8c plus 8d):* $ _____

(9) **Household Income**

a. List all other persons living in your home and their income; include only your spouse and all individuals who depend in whole or in part on you for support, or on whom you depend in whole or in part for support.

Name	Age	Relationship	Gross Monthly Income
(1)			$
(2)			$
(3)			$
(4)			$

b. **Total monthly income of persons above:** $ _____

Total monthly income *and* household income *(8e plus 9b):* $ _____

To list any other facts you want the court to know, such as unusual medical expenses, family emergencies, etc., attach form MC-025. Or attach a sheet of paper, and write Financial Information and your name and case number at the top. Check here if you attach another page. ☐

Important! **If your financial situation or ability to pay court fees improves, you must notify the court within five days on form FW-010.**

(10) **Your Money and Property**

a. Cash - $ _____

b. All financial accounts *(List bank name and amount):*
   (1) _____ $ _____
   (2) _____ $ _____
   (3) _____ $ _____
   (4) _____ $ _____

c. Cars, boats, and other vehicles

Make / Year	Fair Market Value	How Much You Still Owe
(1)	$	$
(2)	$	$
(3)	$	$

d. Real estate

Address	Fair Market Value	How Much You Still Owe
(1)	$	$
(2)	$	$
(3)	$	$

e. Other personal property (jewelry, furniture, furs, stocks, bonds, etc.):

Describe	Fair Market Value	How Much You Still Owe
(1)	$	$
(2)	$	$
(3)	$	$

(11) **Your Monthly Expenses**
(Do not include payroll deductions you already listed in 8b.)

a. Rent or house payment & maintenance $ _____
b. Food and household supplies $ _____
c. Utilities and telephone $ _____
d. Clothing $ _____
e. Laundry and cleaning $ _____
f. Medical and dental expenses $ _____
g. Insurance (life, health, accident, etc.) $ _____
h. School, child care $ _____
i. Child, spousal support (another marriage) $ _____
j. Transportation, gas, auto repair and insurance $ _____
k. Installment payments (list each below):
   Paid to:
   (1) _____ $ _____
   (2) _____ $ _____
   (3) _____ $ _____
l. Wages/earnings withheld by court order $ _____
m. Any other monthly expenses *(list each below).* $ _____
   Paid to: How Much?
   (1) _____ $ _____
   (2) _____ $ _____
   (3) _____ $ _____

Total monthly expenses *(add 11a –11m above):* $ _____

INFORMATION SHEET ON WAIVER OF SUPERIOR COURT FEES AND COSTS

If you have been sued or if you wish to sue someone, or if you are filing or have received a family law petition, and if you cannot afford to pay court fees and costs, you may not have to pay them in order to go to court. If you are getting public benefits, are a low-income person, or do not have enough income to pay for your household's basic needs *and* your court fees, you may ask the court to waive all or part of your court fees.

1. To make a request to the court to waive your fees in superior court, complete the *Request to Waive Court Fees* (form FW-001). If you qualify, the court will waive all or part of its fees for the following:

    • Filing papers in superior court (other than for an appeal in a case with a value of over $25,000)
    • Making and certifying copies   • Giving notice and certificates
    • Sheriff's fee to give notice   • Sending papers to another court department
    • Court fees for telephone hearings   • Having a court-appointed interpreter in small claims court
    • Reporter's daily fee *(for up to 60 days after the grant of the fee waiver, at the court-approved daily rate)*
    • Preparing, certifying, copying, and sending the clerk's transcript on appeal.

2. You may ask the court to waive other court fees during your case in superior court as well. To do that, complete a *Request to Waive Additional Court Fees (Superior Court)* (form FW-002). The court will consider waiving fees for items such as the following, or other court services you need for your case:

    • Jury fees and expenses   • Fees for a peace officer to testify in court
    • Fees for court-appointed experts   • Court-appointed interpreter fees for a witness
    • Reporter's daily fees (*beyond the 60-day*   • Other necessary court fees
    period after the grant of the fee waiver, at the court-approved daily rate)

3. If you want the Appellate Division of Superior Court or the Court of Appeal to review an order or judgment against you and you want the court fees waived, ask for and follow the instructions on *Information Sheet on Waiver of Appellate Court Fees, Supreme Court, Court of Appeal, Appellate Division* (form APP-015/FW-015-INFO).

IMPORTANT INFORMATION!

• **You are signing your request under penalty of perjury. Please answer truthfully, accurately, and completely.**

• **The court may ask you for information and evidence.** You may be ordered to go to court to answer questions about your ability to pay court fees and costs and to provide proof of eligibility. Any initial fee waiver you are granted may be ended if you do not go to court when asked. You may be ordered to repay amounts that were waived if the court finds you were not eligible for the fee waiver.

• **If you receive a fee waiver, you must tell the court if there is a change in your finances.** You must tell the court within five days if your finances improve or if you become able to pay court fees or costs during this case. (File *Notice to Court of Improved Financial Situation or Settlement* (form FW-010) with the court.) You may be ordered to repay any amounts that were waived after your eligibility came to an end.

• **If you receive a judgment or support order in a family law matter:** You may be ordered to pay all or part of your waived fees and costs if the court finds your circumstances have changed so that you can afford to pay. You will have the opportunity to ask the court for a hearing if the court makes such a decision.

• **If you win your case in the trial court:** In most circumstances the other side will be ordered to pay your waived fees and costs to the court. The court will not enter a satisfaction of judgment until the court is paid. (This does not apply in unlawful detainer cases. Special rules apply in family law cases. (Government Code, section 68637(d), (e).)

• **If you settle your civil case for $10,000 or more:** Any trial court waived fees and costs must first be paid to the court out of the settlement. **The court will have a lien on the settlement in the amount of the waived fees and costs.** The court may refuse to dismiss the case until the lien is satisfied. A request to dismiss the case (use form CIV-110) must have a declaration under penalty of perjury that the waived fees and costs have been paid. Special rules apply to family law cases.

• **The court can collect fees and costs due to the court.** If waived fees and costs are ordered paid to the trial court, the court can start collection proceedings and add a $25 fee plus any additional costs of collection to the other fees and costs owed to the court.

• **The fee waiver ends.** The fee waiver expires 60 days after the judgment, dismissal, or other final disposition of the case or earlier if a court finds that you are not eligible for a fee waiver.

• **If you are in jail or state prison:** Prisoners may be required to pay the full cost of the filing fee in the trial court but may be allowed to do so over time.

Judicial Council of California, *www.courtinfo.ca.gov*
Revised July 1, 2009
Government Code, §§ 68630–68640
California Rules of Court, rule 3.51

**Information Sheet on Waiver of
Superior Court Fees and Costs**

FW-001-INFO, Page 1 of 1

Order on Court Fee Waiver
(Superior Court)

Clerk stamps date here when form is filed.

(1) Person who asked the court to waive court fees:

Name: _____

Street or mailing address: _____

City: _____ State: _____ Zip: _____

(2) Lawyer, if person in (1) has one *(name, address, phone number,*

e-mail, and State Bar number): _____

_____

_____

_____

(3) A request to waive court fees was filed
on *(date):* _____

☐ The court made a previous fee waiver order in this case
on *(date):* _____

Read this form carefully. All checked boxes ☑ are court orders.

Fill in court name and street address:

Superior Court of California, County of

Fill in case number and case name:

Case Number:

Case Name:

Notice: The court may order you to answer questions about your finances and later order you to pay back the waived fees. If this happens and you do not pay, the court can make you pay the fees and also charge you collection fees. If there is a change in your financial circumstances during this case that increases your ability to pay fees and costs, you must notify the trial court within five days. (Use form FW-010.) If you win your case, the trial court may order the other side to pay the fees. If you settle your civil case for **$10,000** or more, the trial court will have a lien on the settlement in the amount of the waived fees. The trial court may not dismiss the case until the lien is paid.

---

(4) After reviewing your *(check one):* ☐ *Request to Waive Court Fees* ☐ *Request to Waive Additional Court Fees*
the court makes the following orders:

a. ☐ The court **grants** your request, as follows:

(1) ☐ **Fee Waiver.** The court grants your request and waives your court fees and costs listed below. *(Cal. Rules of Court, rule 3.55.)* You do not have to pay the court fees for the following:

- Filing papers in Superior Court
- Making copies and certifying copies
- Sheriff's fee to give notice
- Reporter's daily fee *(for up to 60 days following the fee waiver order at the court-approved daily rate)*
- Preparing and certifying the clerk's transcript on appeal
- Giving notice and certificates
- Sending papers to another court department
- Court-appointed interpreter in small claims court
- Court fees for phone hearings

(2) ☐ **Additional Fee Waiver.** The court grants your request and waives your additional superior court fees and costs that are checked below. *(Cal. Rules of Court, rule 3.56.)* You do not have to pay for the checked items.

☐ Jury fees and expenses
☐ Fees for court-appointed experts
☐ Reporter's daily fees *(beyond the 60-day period following the fee waiver order)*
☐ Other *(specify):* _____

☐ Fees for a peace officer to testify in court
☐ Court-appointed interpreter fees for a witness

(3) ☐ **Fee Waiver for Appeal.** The court grants your request and waives the fees and costs checked below, for your appeal. *(Cal. Rules of Court, rules 3.55, 3.56, 8.26, and 8.818.)* You do not have to pay for the checked items.

☐ Preparing and certifying clerk's transcript for appeal
☐ Other *(specify):* _____

Judicial Council of California, *www.courtinfo.ca.gov*
Revised July 1, 2009, Mandatory Form
Government Code, § 68634(e)
California Rules of Court, rule 3.52

Order on Court Fee Waiver (Superior Court)

FW-003, Page 1 of 2

Your name: _____

b. ☐ The court **denies** your request, as follows:

> **Warning!** If you miss the deadline below, the court cannot process your request for hearing or the court papers you filed with your original request. If the papers were a notice of appeal, the appeal may be dismissed.

(1) ☐ The court **denies** your request because it is incomplete. You have **10 days** after the clerk gives notice of this order (see date below) to:
- Pay your fees and costs, or
- File a new revised request that includes the items listed below (specify incomplete items):

_____

(2) ☐ The court **denies** your request because the information you provided on the request shows that you are not eligible for the fee waiver you requested (specify reasons):

_____

The court has enclosed a blank *Request for Hearing About Court Fee Waiver Order (Superior Court)*, form FW-006. You have **10 days** after the clerk gives notice of this order (see date below) to:
- Pay your fees and costs, or
- Ask for a hearing in order to show the court more information. *(Use form FW-006 to request hearing.)*

c. ☐ The court needs more information to decide whether to grant your request. You must go to court on the date below. The hearing will be about (specify questions regarding eligibility): _____

_____
_____

☐ Bring the following proof to support your request if reasonably available:

_____
_____

Name and address of court if different from page 1:

Hearing Date → Date: _____ Time: _____
Dept.: _____ Rm.: _____

> **Warning!** If item c is checked, and you do not go to court on your hearing date, the judge will deny your request to waive court fees, and you will have 10 days to pay your fees. If you miss that deadline, the court cannot process the court papers you filed with your request. If the papers were a notice of appeal, the appeal may be dismissed.

Date: _____ Signature of (check one): ☐ Judicial Officer ☐ Clerk, Deputy

🦻 **Request for Accommodations.** Assistive listening systems, computer-assisted real-time captioning, or sign language interpreter services are available if you ask at least 5 days before your hearing. Contact the clerk's office for *Request for Accommodation,* Form MC-410. (Civil Code, § 54.8.)

Clerk's Certificate of Service

I certify that I am not involved in this case and *(check one):* ☐ A certificate of mailing is attached.

☐ I handed a copy of this order to the party and attorney, if any, listed in ① and ②, at the court, on the date below.

☐ This order was mailed first class, postage paid, to the party and attorney, if any, at the addresses listed in ① and ②, from *(city):* _____, California on the date below.

Date: _____ Clerk, by _____, Deputy

CLAIMANT OR CLAIMANT'S ATTORNEY *(Name and Address)*:	TELEPHONE NO.:	*FOR COURT USE ONLY*
ATTORNEY FOR *(Name)*:		

NAME OF COURT:

STREET ADDRESS:

MAILING ADDRESS:

CITY AND ZIP CODE:

BRANCH NAME:

PLAINTIFF:

DEFENDANT:

PREJUDGMENT CLAIM OF RIGHT TO POSSESSION	CASE NUMBER:

Complete this form only if ALL of these statements are true: 1. You are NOT named in the accompanying Summons and Complaint. 2. You occupied the premises on or before the date the unlawful detainer (eviction) Complaint was filed. 3. You still occupy the premises.	*(To be completed by the process server)* DATE OF SERVICE: *(Date that this form is served or delivered, and posted, and mailed by the officer or process server)*

I DECLARE THE FOLLOWING UNDER PENALTY OF PERJURY:

1. My name is *(specify)*:

2. I reside at *(street address, unit No., city and ZIP code)*:

3. The address of "the premises" subject to this claim is *(address)*:

4. On *(insert date)*: [   ], the landlord or the landlord's authorized agent filed a complaint to recover possession of the premises. *(This date is the court filing date on the accompanying Summons and Complaint.*

5. I occupied the premises on the date the complaint was filed *(the date in item 4)*. I have continued to occupy the premises ever since.

6. I was at least 18 years of age on the date the complaint was filed *(the date in item 4)*.

7. I claim a right to possession of the premises because I occupied the premises on the date the complaint was filed *(the date in item 4)*.

8. I was not named in the Summons and Complaint.

9. I understand that if I make this claim of right to possession, I will be added as a defendant to the unlawful detainer (eviction) action.

10. *(Filing fee)* I understand that I must go to the court and pay a filing fee of $ or file with the court the form "Application for Waiver of Court Fees and Costs." I understand that if I don't pay the filing fee or file with the court the form for waiver of court fees within 10 days from the date of service on this form (excluding court holidays), I will not be entitled to make a claim of right to possession.

(Continued on reverse)

CP10.5 [New January 1, 1991] Optional Form	**PREJUDGMENT CLAIM OF RIGHT TO POSSESSION**	Code of Civil Procedure §§ 415.46, 715.010, 715.020, 1174.25

PLAINTIFF (Name):	CASE NUMBER:
DEFENDANT (Name):	

NOTICE: If you fail to file this claim, you will be evicted without further hearing.

11. (Response required within five days after you file this form.) I understand that I will have five days (excluding court holidays) to file a response to the Summons and Complaint after I file this Prejudgment Claim of Right to Possession form.

12. **Rental agreement.** I have (check all that apply to you):
  a. ☐ an oral rental agreement with the landlord.
  b. ☐ a written rental agreement with the landlord.
  c. ☐ an oral rental agreement with a person other than the landlord.
  d. ☐ a written rental agreement with a person other than the landlord.
  e. ☐ other (explain):

I declare under penalty of perjury under the laws of the State of California that the foregoing is true and correct.

WARNING: Perjury is a felony punishable by imprisonment in the state prison.

Date:

▶

....   _____
(TYPE OR PRINT NAME)   (SIGNATURE OF CLAIMANT)

NOTICE: If you file this claim of right to possession, the unlawful detainer (eviction) action against you will be determined at trial. At trial, you may be found liable for rent, costs, and, in some cases, treble damages.

— NOTICE TO OCCUPANTS —

YOU MUST ACT AT ONCE if all the following are true:

1. **You are NOT named in the accompanying Summons and Complaint.**
2. **You occupied the premises on or before the date the unlawful detainer (eviction) complaint was filed.** *(The date is the court filing date on the accompanying Summons and Complaint.)*
3. **You still occupy the premises.**

(Where to file this form) You can complete and SUBMIT THIS CLAIM FORM WITHIN 10 DAYS from the date of service (on the reverse of this form) at the court where the unlawful detainer (eviction) complaint was filed.

(What will happen if you do not file this form) If you do not complete and submit this form and pay a filing fee or file the form for proceeding in forma pauperis if you cannot pay the fee), YOU WILL BE EVICTED.

After this form is properly filed, you will be added as a defendant in the unlawful detainer (eviction) action and your right to occupy the premises will be decided by the court. If you do not file this claim, you will be evicted without a hearing.

1

2

3

4

5

6

7

8

9

10

11

12

13

14

15

16

17

18

19

20

21

22

23

24

25

26

27

28

1

2

3

4   Defendant in Pro Per

5

6

7

8   SUPERIOR COURT OF THE STATE OF CALIFORNIA, COUNTY OF _____

9   _____ DIVISION/BRANCH

10   )
)
     _____ ,) Case No._____
11   )
     _____ ,)
12   Plaintiff(s),   )
)
13   v.   )
)
14   _____ ,)
)
15   _____ ,)
                Defendant(s).   )
16   _____)

17

18

19

20

21

22

23

24

25

26

27

28   Dated: _____   _____

ATTORNEY OR PARTY WITHOUT ATTORNEY *(Name, State Bar number, and address)*:	*FOR COURT USE ONLY*
TELEPHONE NO.:	
E-MAIL ADDRESS *(Optional)*: FAX NO. *(Optional)*:	
ATTORNEY FOR *(Name)*:	

SUPERIOR COURT OF CALIFORNIA, COUNTY OF

STREET ADDRESS:

MAILING ADDRESS:

CITY AND ZIP CODE:

BRANCH NAME:

PETITIONER/PLAINTIFF:

RESPONDENT/DEFENDANT:

PROOF OF SERVICE BY FIRST-CLASS MAIL—CIVIL	CASE NUMBER:

(Do not use this Proof of Service to show service of a Summons and Complaint.)

1. I am over 18 years of age and **not a party to this action.** I am a resident of or employed in the county where the mailing took place.

2. My residence or business address is:

3. On *(date):*   I mailed from *(city and state):*
   the following **documents** *(specify):*

   ☐ The documents are listed in the *Attachment to Proof of Service by First-Class Mail—Civil (Documents Served)* (form POS-030(D)).

4. I served the documents by enclosing them in an envelope and *(check one):*
   a. ☐ **depositing** the sealed envelope with the United States Postal Service with the postage fully prepaid.
   b. ☐ **placing** the envelope for collection and mailing following our ordinary business practices. I am readily familiar with this business's practice for collecting and processing correspondence for mailing. On the same day that correspondence is placed for collection and mailing, it is deposited in the ordinary course of business with the United States Postal Service in a sealed envelope with postage fully prepaid.

5. The envelope was addressed and mailed as follows:
   a. **Name** of person served:
   b. **Address** of person served:

   ☐ The name and address of each person to whom I mailed the documents is listed in the *Attachment to Proof of Service by First-Class Mail—Civil (Persons Served)* (POS-030(P)).

I declare under penalty of perjury under the laws of the State of California that the foregoing is true and correct.

Date:

▶

_____   _____
(TYPE OR PRINT NAME OF PERSON COMPLETING THIS FORM)   (SIGNATURE OF PERSON COMPLETING THIS FORM)

Form Approved for Optional Use
Judicial Council of California
POS-030 [New January 1, 2005] **PROOF OF SERVICE BY FIRST-CLASS MAIL—CIVIL**
(Proof of Service) Code of Civil Procedure, §§ 1013, 1013a
www.courtinfo.ca.gov

INFORMATION SHEET FOR PROOF OF SERVICE BY FIRST-CLASS MAIL—CIVIL

(This information sheet is not part of the Proof of Service and does not need to be copied, served, or filed.)

NOTE: This form should **not** be used for proof of service of a summons and complaint. For that purpose, use *Proof of Service of Summons* (form POS-010).

Use these instructions to complete the *Proof of Service by First-Class Mail—Civil* (form POS-030).

A person over 18 years of age must serve the documents. There are two main ways to serve documents: (1) by personal delivery and (2) by mail. Certain documents must be personally served. You must determine whether personal service is required for a document. Use the *Proof of Personal Service–Civil* (form POS-020) if the documents were personally served.

The person who served the documents by mail must complete a proof of service form for the documents served. **You cannot serve documents if you are a party to the action.**

INSTRUCTIONS FOR THE PERSON WHO SERVED THE DOCUMENTS

The proof of service should be printed or typed. If you have Internet access, a fillable version of the Proof of Service form is available at *www.courtinfo.ca.gov/forms*.

Complete the top section of the proof of service form as follows:

First box, left side: In this box print the name, address, and telephone number of the person *for* whom you served the documents.

Second box, left side: Print the name of the county in which the legal action is filed and the court's address in this box. The address for the court should be the same as on the documents that you served.

Third box, left side: Print the names of the Petitioner/Plaintiff and Respondent/Defendant in this box. Use the same names as are on the documents that you served.

First box, top of form, right side: Leave this box blank for the court's use.

Second box, right side: Print the case number in this box. The case number should be the same as the case number on the documents that you served.

Complete items 1–5 as follows:

1. You are stating that you are over the age of 18 and that you are not a party to this action. You are also stating that you either live in or are employed in the county where the mailing took place.

2. Print your home or business address.

3. Provide the date and place of the mailing and list the name of each document that you mailed. If you need more space to list the documents, check the box in item 3, complete the *Attachment to Proof of Service by First-Class Mail—Civil (Documents Served)* (form POS-030(D)), and attach it to form POS-030.

4. For item 4:

    Check box a if you personally put the documents in the regular U.S. mail.
    Check box b if you put the documents in the mail at your place of business.

5. Provide the name and address of each person to whom you mailed the documents. If you mailed the documents to more than one person, check the box in item 5, complete the *Attachment to Proof of Service by First-Class Mail—Civil (Persons Served)* (form POS-030(P)), and attach it to form POS-030.

At the bottom, fill in the date on which you signed the form, print your name, and sign the form. By signing, you are stating under penalty of perjury that all the information you have provided on form POS-030 is true and correct.

PROOF OF SERVICE BY FIRST CLASS MAIL—CIVIL
(Proof of Service)

SHORT TITLE:	CASE NUMBER:

ATTACHMENT TO PROOF OF SERVICE BY FIRST-CLASS MAIL—CIVIL (PERSONS SERVED)

(This Attachment is for use with form POS-030)

NAME AND ADDRESS OF EACH PERSON SERVED BY MAIL:

Name of Person Served	Address *(number, street, city, and zip code)*

Form Approved for Optional Use
Judicial Council of California
POS-030(P) [New January 1, 2005]

**ATTACHMENT TO PROOF OF SERVICE BY FIRST-CLASS MAIL—CIVIL
(PERSONS SERVED)**
(Proof of Service)

Page _____ of _____

4 Defendant in Pro Per

5
6
7

8 SUPERIOR COURT OF THE STATE OF CALIFORNIA, COUNTY OF _____

9 _____ DIVISION/BRANCH

10

11 _____ ,) Case No._____

12 Plaintiff(s),) POINTS AND AUTHORITIES

13 v.) IN SUPPORT OF DEMURRER

14 _____ ,)
) (CCP § 430.10)
15 _____ ,)

16 Defendant(s).)
    _____)

17

I. DEFENDANT'S DEMURRER IS PROPERLY BEFORE THE COURT

A defendant in an unlawful detainer action may demur. C.C.P. § 1170. Although dicta in Delta Imports v. Municipal Court, 146 Cal.App.3d 1033 (1983), suggests that a motion to quash is the remedy where a complaint fails to state a cause of action in unlawful detainer, Delta did not overrule prior cases. See Hinman v. Wagnon, 172 Cal.App.2d 24 (1959), where the court held that a demurrer was proper where the incorporated 3-day notice was defective on its face. The court sustained a dismissal following sustaining the demurrer without leave to amend.

The periods for noticing hearing on a demurrer are not stated in the unlawful detainer statutes, so C.C.P. Section 1177 incorporates the regular provisions of the Code of Civil Procedure, such as C.C.P. Section 1005 requiring that motions be noticed on 16 court days' notice, plus five calendar days for mailing. Rule 325(b), California Rules of Court, specifies that demurrers shall be heard in accordance with Section 1005.

//////

1

2

3

4

5

6

7

8

9

10

11

12

13

14

15

16

17

18

19

20

21

22

23

24

25

26

27 Dated: _____   _____

28

1

2

3

4   Defendant in Pro Per

5

6

7

8   SUPERIOR COURT OF THE STATE OF CALIFORNIA, COUNTY OF _____

9   _____ DIVISION/BRANCH

10   )
)
11   _____ ,)   Case No. _____
)
12   _____ ,)
            Plaintiff(s),   )   NOTICE OF HEARING ON DEMURRER OF
)
13   v.   )   _____
)
14   _____ ,)
)   TO THE COMPLAINT OF
15   _____ ,)
            Defendant(s).   )   _____
16   _____)

17

18   To: _____

19   PLEASE TAKE NOTICE THAT on _____ , _____ , at

20   _____ in Department No. _____ of the above entitled court, located at _____

21   _____ ,

22   a hearing will be held on Defendant's demurrer to the Complaint, a copy of which is served with this notice.

23

24

25

26   Dated: _____   _____

27

28

ATTORNEY OR PARTY WITHOUT ATTORNEY *(Name and Address)*:

TELEPHONE NO:

ATTORNEY FOR *(Name)*:

NAME OF COURT:
STREET ADDRESS:
MAILING ADDRESS:
CITY AND ZIP CODE:
BRANCH NAME:

PLAINTIFF:

DEFENDANT:

CASE NUMBER:

ANSWER—Unlawful Detainer

1. Defendant *(names)*:

answers the complaint as follows:

2. **Check ONLY ONE of the next two boxes:**

   a. ☐ Defendant generally denies each statement of the complaint. *(Do not check this box if the complaint demands more than $1,000.*

   b. ☐ Defendant admits that all of the statements of the complaint are true EXCEPT

      (1) Defendant claims the following statements of the complaint are false *(use paragraph numbers from the complaint or explain)*:

      ☐ Continued on Attachment 2b (1).

      (2) Defendant has no information or belief that the following statements of the complaint are true, so defendant denies them *(use paragraph numbers from the complaint or explain)*:

      ☐ Continued on Attachment 2b (2).

3. AFFIRMATIVE DEFENSES   *(**NOTE:** For each box checked, you must state brief facts to support it in the space provided at the top of page two (item 3j)).*

   a. ☐ *(nonpayment of rent only)* Plaintiff has breached the warranty to provide habitable premises.

   b. ☐ *(nonpayment of rent only)* Defendant made needed repairs and properly deducted the cost from the rent, and plaintiff did not give proper credit.

   c. ☐ *(nonpayment of rent only)* On *(date)*:   before the notice to pay or quit expired, defendant offered the rent due but plaintiff would not accept it.

   d. ☐ Plaintiff waived, changed, or canceled the notice to quit.

   e. ☐ Plaintiff served defendant with the notice to quit or filed the complaint to retaliate against defendant.

   f. ☐ By serving defendant with the notice to quit or filing the complaint, plaintiff is arbitrarily discriminating against the defendant in violation of the Constitution or laws of the United States or California.

   g. ☐ Plaintiff's demand for possession violates the local rent control or eviction control ordinance of *(city or county, title of ordinance, and date of passage)*:

      (Also, briefly state the facts showing violation of the ordinance in item 3j.)

   h. ☐ Plaintiff accepted rent from defendant to cover a period of time after the date the notice to quit expired.

   i. ☐ Other affirmative defenses are stated in item 3j.

Form Approved by the Judicial
Council of California
UD-105 [Rev. January 1, 2007]

ANSWER—Unlawful Detainer

Civil Code, §1940 et seq.;
Code of Civil Procedure, § 425.12
www.courtinfo.ca.gov

PLAINTIFF *(Name)*:	CASE NUMBER:
DEFENDANT *(Name)*:	

3. AFFIRMATIVE DEFENSES (cont'd)
   j. Facts supporting affirmative defenses checked above *(identify each item separately by its letter from page one)*:

   (1) ☐ All the facts are stated in Attachment 3j.   (2) ☐ Facts are continued in Attachment 3j.

4. OTHER STATEMENTS
   a. ☐ Defendant vacated the premises on *(date)*:
   b. ☐ The fair rental value of the premises alleged in the complaint is excessive *(explain)*:

   c. ☐ Other *(specify)*:

5. DEFENDANT REQUESTS
   a. that plaintiff take nothing requested in the complaint.
   b. costs incurred in this proceeding.
   c. ☐ reasonable attorney fees.
   d. ☐ that plaintiff be ordered to (1) make repairs and correct the conditions that constitute a breach of the warranty to provide habitable premises and (2) reduce the monthly rent to a reasonable rental value until the conditions are corrected.
   e. ☐ Other *(specify)*:

6. ☐ Number of pages attached *(specify)*:

UNLAWFUL DETAINER ASSISTANT (Business and Professions Code sections 6400- 6415)

7. *(Must be completed in all cases)* An **unlawful detainer assistant** ☐ did not ☐ did for compensation give advice or assistance with this form. *(If defendant has received **any** help or advice for pay from an unlawful detainer assistant, state:*
   a. Assistant's name: b. Telephone No.:
   c. Street address, city, and ZIP:
   d. County of registration: e. Registration No.:   f. Expires on (date):

▶

_____   _____
(TYPE OR PRINT NAME)   (SIGNATURE OF DEFENDANT OR ATTORNEY)

▶

_____   _____
(TYPE OR PRINT NAME)   (SIGNATURE OF DEFENDANT OR ATTORNEY)

(Each defendant for whom this answer is filed must be named in item 1 and must sign this answer unless his or her attorney signs.)

VERIFICATION
(Use a different verification form if the verification is by an attorney or for a corporation or partnership.)
I am the defendant in this proceeding and have read this answer. I declare under penalty of perjury under the laws of the State of California that the foregoing is true and correct. Date:

▶

_____   _____
(TYPE OR PRINT NAME)   (SIGNATURE OF DEFENDANT)

2

3

4   Defendant in Pro Per

5

6

7

8   SUPERIOR COURT OF THE STATE OF CALIFORNIA, COUNTY OF _____

9   _____ DIVISION/BRANCH

10   )

11   _____ ,)   Case No._____

)

12   _____ ,)   REQUEST TO INSPECT AND FOR
                Plaintiff(s),   )

13   v.   )   PRODUCTION OF DOCUMENTS
)

14   _____ ,)
)

15   _____ ,)
               Defendant(s).   )   (Code of Civil Procedure Sec. 2031.101–2031.510)

16   _____)

17

18   To: _____ , Plaintiff,

19   and _____ , Plaintiff's attorney:

20   Defendant requests that you produce and permit the copying of the following documents: _____

21   _____ .

22   Defendant requests that you produce these documents at the following address: _____

23   _____ , at the following date and time: _____

24   _____ .

25   Defendant further requests permission to enter, inspect, and photograph the premises located at _____

26   _____

27   at the following date and time: _____ .

28   Dated: _____   _____

ATTORNEY OR PARTY WITHOUT ATTORNEY *(Name, State Bar number, and address):*	UNLAWFUL DETAINER ASSISTANT
	(Check one box): An unlawful detainer assistant ☐ did ☐ did not for compensation give advice or assistance with this form. *(If one did, state the following)*:
	ASSISTANT'S NAME:
	ADDRESS:
ATTORNEY FOR *(Name):*	
SUPERIOR COURT OF CALIFORNIA, COUNTY OF:	TEL. NO.:
	COUNTY OF REGISTRATION:
SHORT TITLE:	REGISTRATION NO.:
	EXPIRES *(DATE):*

FORM INTERROGATORIES—UNLAWFUL DETAINER	CASE NUMBER:
Asking Party:	
Answering Party:	
Set No.:	

Sec. 1. Instructions to All Parties

(a) These are general instructions. For time limitations, requirements for service on other parties, and other details, see Code of Civil Procedure sections 2030.010-2030.410 and the cases construing those sections.

(b) These interrogatories do not change existing law relating to interrogatories nor do they affect an answering party's right to assert any privilege or objection.

Sec. 2. Instructions to the Asking Party

(a) These interrogatories are designed for optional use in unlawful detainer proceedings.

(b) There are restrictions that generally limit the number of interrogatories that may be asked and the form and use of the interrogatories. For details, read Code of Civil Procedure sections 2030.030–2030.070.

(c) In determining whether to use these or any interrogatories, you should be aware that abuse can be punished by sanctions, including fines and attorney fees. See Code of Civil Procedure section 128.7.

(d) Check the box next to each interrogatory that you want the answering party to answer. Use care in choosing those interrogatories that are applicable to the case.

(e) Additional interrogatories may be attached.

Sec. 3. Instructions to the Answering Party

(a) An answer or other appropriate response must be given to each interrogatory checked by the asking party. Failure to respond to these interrogatories properly can be punished by sanctions, including contempt proceedings, fine, attorneys fees, and the loss of your case. See Code of Civil Procedure sections 128.7 and 2030.300.

(b) As a general rule, within five days after you are served with these interrogatories, you must serve your responses on the asking party and serve copies of your responses on all other parties to the action who have appeared. See Code of Civil Procedure sections 2030.260–2030.270 for details.

(c) Each answer must be as complete and straightforward as the information reasonably available to you permits. If an interrogatory cannot be answered completely, answer it to the extent possible.

(d) If you do not have enough personal knowledge to fully answer an interrogatory, say so, but make a reasonable and good faith effort to get the information by asking other persons or organizations, unless the information is equally available to the asking party.

(e) Whenever an interrogatory may be answered by referring to a document, the document may be attached as an exhibit to the response and referred to in the response. If the document has more than one page, refer to the page and section where the answer to the interrogatory can be found.

(f) Whenever an address and telephone number for the same person are requested in more than one interrogatory, you are required to furnish them in answering only the first interrogatory asking for that information.

(g) Your answers to these interrogatories must be verified, dated, and signed. You may wish to use the following form *at the end of your answers:*

I declare under penalty of perjury under the laws of the State of California that the foregoing answers are true and correct.

_____   _____
(DATE)   (SIGNATURE)

Sec. 4. Definitions

Words in **BOLDFACE CAPITALS** in these interrogatories are defined as follows:

(a) **PERSON** includes a natural person, firm, association, organization, partnership, business, trust, corporation, or public entity.

(b) **PLAINTIFF** includes any **PERSON** who seeks recovery of the **RENTAL UNIT** whether acting as an individual or on someone else's behalf and includes all such **PERSONS** if more than one.

Form Approved for Optional Use
Judicial Council of California
DISC-003/UD-106 [Rev. January 1, 2007]

FORM INTERROGATORIES–UNLAWFUL DETAINER

Code of Civil Procedure,
§§ 2030.010-2030.410, 2033.710
www.courtinfo.ca.gov

the name, **ADDRESS**, and telephone number of each **PERSON** who has the **DOCUMENT** (see also §71.5);

(e) state each modification not in writing, the date, and the name, **ADDRESS,** and telephone number of the **PERSON** agreeing to the modification, and the date the modification was made (see also §71.5).

(f) identify all **DOCUMENTS** that evidence each modification of the agreement not in writing and for each state the name, **ADDRESS,** and telephone number of each **PERSON** who has the **DOCUMENT** (see also §71.5).

☐ 70.12 Has any **PERSON** acting on the **PLAINTIFF'S** behalf been responsible for any aspect of managing or maintaining the **RENTAL UNIT** or **PROPERTY**? If so, for each **PERSON** state:
(a) the name, **ADDRESS**, and telephone number;
(b) the dates the **PERSON** managed or maintained the **RENTAL UNIT** or **PROPERTY**;
(c) the **PERSON'S** responsibilities.

☐ 70.13 For each **PERSON** who occupies any part of the **RENTAL UNIT** (except occupants named in the complaint and occupants' children under 17) state:
(a) the name, **ADDRESS**, telephone number, and birthdate;
(b) the inclusive dates of occupancy;
(c) a description of the portion of the **RENTAL UNIT** occupied;
(d) the amount paid, the term for which it was paid, and the person to whom it was paid;
(e) the nature of the use of the **RENTAL UNIT**;
(f) the name, **ADDRESS**, and telephone number of the person who authorized occupancy;
(g) how occupancy was authorized, including failure of the **LANDLORD** or **PLAINTIFF** to protest after discovering the occupancy.

☐ 70.14 Have you or anyone acting on your behalf obtained any **DOCUMENT** concerning the tenancy between any occupant of the **RENTAL UNIT** and any **PERSON** with an ownership interest or managerial responsibility for the **RENTAL UNIT**? If so, for each **DOCUMENT** state:

(a) the name, **ADDRESS**, and telephone number of each individual from whom the **DOCUMENT** was obtained;
(b) the name, **ADDRESS**, and telephone number of each individual who obtained the **DOCUMENT**;
(c) the date the **DOCUMENT** was obtained;
(d) the name, **ADDRESS**, and telephone number of each **PERSON** who has the **DOCUMENT** (original or copy).

71.0 Notice

*[If a defense is based on allegations that the 3-day notice or 30- day **NOTICE TO QUIT** is defective in form or content, then either party may ask any applicable question in this section.]*

☐ 71.1 Was the **NOTICE TO QUIT** on which **PLAINTIFF** bases this proceeding attached to the complaint? If not, state the contents of this notice.

☐ 71.2 State all reasons that the **NOTICE TO QUIT** was served and for each reason:
(a) state all facts supporting **PLAINTIFF'S** decision to terminate defendant's tenancy;

(b) state the names, **ADDRESSES**, and telephone numbers of all **PERSONS** who have knowledge of the facts;
(c) identify all **DOCUMENTS** that support the facts and state the name, **ADDRESS**, and telephone number of each **PERSON** who has each **DOCUMENT**.

☐ 71.3 List all rent payments and rent credits made or claimed by or on behalf of defendant beginning 12 months before the **NOTICE TO QUIT** was served. For each payment or credit state:
(a) the amount;
(b) the date received;
(c) the form in which any payment was made;
(d) the services performed or other basis for which a credit is claimed;
(e) the period covered;
(f) the name of each **PERSON** making the payment or earning the credit;
(g) the identity of all **DOCUMENTS** evidencing the payment or credit and for each state the name, **ADDRESS**, and telephone number of each **PERSON** who has the **DOCUMENT**.

☐ 71.4 Did defendant ever fail to pay the rent on time? If so, for each late payment state:
(a) the date;
(b) the amount of any late charge;
(c) the identity of all **DOCUMENTS** recording the payment and for each state the name, **ADDRESS**, and telephone number of each **PERSON** who has the **DOCUMENT**.

☐ 71.5 Since the beginning of defendant's tenancy, has **PLAINTIFF** ever raised the rent? If so, for each rent increase state:
(a) the date the increase became effective;
(b) the amount;
(c) the reasons for the rent increase;
(d) how and when defendant was notified of the increase;
(e) the identity of all **DOCUMENTS** evidencing the increase and for each state the name, **ADDRESS**, and telephone number of each **PERSON** who has the **DOCUMENT**.

[See also section 70.11 (d) - (f).]

☐ 71.6 During the 12 months before the **NOTICE TO QUIT** was served was there a period during which there was no permit or certificate of occupancy for the **RENTAL UNIT**? If so, for each period state:
(a) the inclusive dates;
(b) the reasons.

☐ 71.7 Has any **PERSON** ever reported any nuisance or disturbance at or destruction of the **RENTAL UNIT** or **PROPERTY** caused by defendant or other occupant of the **RENTAL UNIT** or their guests? If so, for each report state;
(a) a description of the disturbance or destruction;
(b) the date of the report;
(c) the name of the **PERSON** who reported;
(d) the name of the **PERSON** to whom the report was made;
(e) what action was taken as a result of the report;
(f) the identity of all **DOCUMENTS** evidencing the report and for each state the name, **ADDRESS**, and telephone number of each **PERSON** who has each **DOCUMENT**.

DISC-003/UD-106

73.0 Malicious Holding Over

[If a defendant denies allegations that defendant's continued possession is malicious, then either party may ask any applicable question in this section. Additional questions in section 75.0 may also be applicable.]

73.1 If any rent called for by the rental agreement is unpaid, state the reasons and the facts upon which the reasons are based.

73.2 Has defendant made attempts to secure other premises since the service of the **NOTICE TO QUIT** or since the service of the summons and complaint? If so, for each attempt:
(a) state all facts indicating the attempt to secure other premises;
(b) state the names, **ADDRESSES,** and telephone numbers of all **PERSONS** who have knowledge of the facts;
(c) identify all **DOCUMENTS** that support the facts and state the name, **ADDRESS,** and telephone number of each **PERSON** who has each **DOCUMENT.**

73.3 State the facts upon which **PLAINTIFF** bases the allegation of malice.

74.0 Rent Control and Eviction Control

74.1 Is there an ordinance or other local law in this jurisdiction which limits the right to evict tenants? If your answer is no, you need not answer sections 74.2 through 74.6.

74.2 For the ordinance or other local law limiting the right to evict tenants, state:
(a) the title or number of the law;
(b) the locality.

74.3 Do you contend that the **RENTAL UNIT** is exempt from the eviction provisions of the ordinance or other local law identified in section 74.2? If so, state the facts upon which you base your contention.

74.4 Is this proceeding based on allegations of a need to recover the **RENTAL UNIT** for use of the **LANDLORD** or the landlord's relative? If so, for each intended occupant state:
(a) the name;
(b) the residence **ADDRESSES** from three years ago to the present;
(c) the relationship to the **LANDLORD;**
(d) all the intended occupant's reasons for occupancy;
(e) all rental units on the **PROPERTY** that were vacated within 60 days before and after the date the **NOTICE TO QUIT** was served.

74.5 Is the proceeding based on an allegation that the **LANDLORD** wishes to remove the **RENTAL UNIT** from residential use temporarily or permanently (for example, to rehabilitate, demolish, renovate, or convert)? If so, state:
(a) each reason for removing the **RENTAL UNIT** from residential use;
(b) what physical changes and renovation will be made to the **RENTAL UNIT;**
(c) the date the work is to begin and end;
(d) the number, date, and type of each permit for the change or work.

71.8 Does the complaint allege violation of a term of a rental agreement or lease (other than nonpayment of rent)? If so, for each covenant:
(a) identify the covenant breached;
(b) state the facts supporting the allegation of a breach;
(c) state the names, **ADDRESSES,** and telephone numbers of all **PERSONS** who have knowledge of the facts;
(d) identify all **DOCUMENTS** that support the facts and state the name, **ADDRESS,** and telephone number of each **PERSON** who has each **DOCUMENT.**

71.9 Does the complaint allege that the defendant has been using the **RENTAL UNIT** for an illegal purpose? If so, for each purpose:
(a) identify the illegal purpose;
(b) state the facts supporting the allegation of illegal use;
(c) state the names, **ADDRESSES,** and telephone numbers of all **PERSONS** who have knowledge of the facts;
(d) identify all **DOCUMENTS** that support the facts and state the name, **ADDRESS,** and telephone number of each **PERSON** who has each **DOCUMENT.**

[Additional interrogatories on this subject may be found in sections 75.0, 78.0, 79.0, and 80.0.]

72.0 Service

*[If a defense is based on allegations that the **NOTICE TO QUIT** was defectively served, then either party may ask any applicable question in this section.]*

72.1 Does defendant contend (or base a defense or make any allegations) that the **NOTICE TO QUIT** was defectively served? If the answer is "no", do not answer interrogatories 72.2 through 72.3.

72.2 Does **PLAINTIFF** contend that the **NOTICE TO QUIT** referred to in the complaint was served? If so, state:
(a) the kind of notice;
(b) the date and time of service;
(c) the manner of service;
(d) the name and **ADDRESS** of the person who served it;
(e) a description of any **DOCUMENT** or conversation between defendant and the person who served the notice.

72.3 Did any person receive the **NOTICE TO QUIT** referred to in the complaint? If so, for each copy of each notice state:
(a) the name of the person who received it;
(b) the kind of notice;
(c) how it was delivered;
(d) the date received;
(e) where it was delivered;
(f) the identity of all **DOCUMENTS** evidencing the notice and for each state the name, **ADDRESS,** and telephone number of each **PERSON** who has the **DOCUMENT.**

(e) the identity of each **DOCUMENT** evidencing the intended activity (for example, blueprints, plans, applications for financing, construction contracts) and the name, **ADDRESS**, and telephone number of each PERSON who has each **DOCUMENT**.

☐ 74.6 Is the proceeding based on any ground other than those stated in sections 74.4 and 74.5? If so, for each:
(a) state each fact supporting or opposing the ground;
(b) state the names, **ADDRESSES**, and telephone numbers of all **PERSONS** who have knowledge of the facts;
(c) identify all **DOCUMENTS** evidencing the facts and state the name, **ADDRESS**, and telephone number of each **PERSON** who has each **DOCUMENT**.

75.0 Breach of Warranty to Provide Habitable Premises

[If plaintiff alleges nonpayment of rent and defendant bases his defense on allegations of implied or express breach of warranty to provide habitable residential premises, then either party may ask any applicable question in this section.]

☐ 75.1 Do you know of any conditions in violation of state or local building codes, housing codes, or health codes, conditions of dilapidation, or other conditions in need of repair in the **RENTAL UNIT** or on the **PROPERTY** that affected the **RENTAL UNIT** at any time defendant has been in possession? If so, state:
(a) the type of condition;
(b) the kind of corrections or repairs needed;
(c) how and when you learned of these conditions;
(d) how these conditions were caused;
(e) the name, **ADDRESS**, and telephone number of each **PERSON** who has caused these conditions.

☐ 75.2 Have any corrections, repairs, or improvements been made to the **RENTAL UNIT** since the **RENTAL UNIT** was rented to defendant? If so, for each correction, repair, or improvement state:
(a) a description giving the nature and location;
(b) the date;
(c) the name, **ADDRESS**, and telephone number of each **PERSON** who made the repairs or improvements;
(d) the cost;
(e) the identity of any **DOCUMENT** evidencing the repairs or improvements;
(f) if a building permit was issued, state the issuing agencies and the permit number of your copy.

☐ 75.3 Did defendant or any other **PERSON** during 36 months before the **NOTICE TO QUIT** was served or during defendant's possession of the **RENTAL UNIT** notify the **LANDLORD** or his agent or employee about the condition of the **RENTAL UNIT** or **PROPERTY**? If so, for each written or oral notice state:
(a) the substance;
(b) who made it;
(c) when and how it was made;
(d) the name and **ADDRESS** of each **PERSON** to whom it was made;
(e) the name and **ADDRESS** of each person who knows about it;
(f) the identity of each **DOCUMENT** evidencing the notice and the name, **ADDRESS**, and telephone number of each **PERSON** who has it;

(g) the response made to the notice;
(h) the efforts made to correct the conditions;
(i) whether the **PERSON** who gave notice was an occupant of the **PROPERTY** at the time of the complaint.

☐ 75.4 During the period beginning 36 months before the **NOTICE TO QUIT** was served to the present, was the **RENTAL UNIT** or **PROPERTY** (including other rental units) inspected for dilapidations or defective conditions by a representative of any governmental agency? If so, for each inspection state:
(a) the date;
(b) the reason;
(c) the name of the governmental agency;
(d) the name, **ADDRESS**, and telephone number of each inspector;
(e) the identity of each **DOCUMENT** evidencing each inspection and the name, **ADDRESS**, and telephone number of each **PERSON** who has it.

☐ 75.5 During the period beginning 36 months before the **NOTICE TO QUIT** was served to the present, did **PLAINTIFF** or **LANDLORD** receive a notice or other communication regarding the condition of the **RENTAL UNIT** or **PROPERTY** (including other rental units) from a governmental agency? If so, for each notice or communication state:
(a) the date received;
(b) the identity of all parties;
(c) the substance of the notice or communication;
(d) the identity of each **DOCUMENT** evidencing the notice or communication and the name, **ADDRESS**, and telephone number of each **PERSON** who has it.

☐ 75.6 Was there any corrective action taken in response to the inspection or notice or communication identified in sections 75.4 and 75.5? If so, for each:
(a) identify the notice or communication;
(b) identify the condition;
(c) describe the corrective action;
(d) identify each **DOCUMENT** evidencing the corrective action and the name, **ADDRESS**, and telephone number of each **PERSON** who has it.

☐ 75.7 Has the **PROPERTY** been appraised for sale or loan during the period beginning 36 months before the **NOTICE TO QUIT** was served to the present? If so, for each appraisal state:
(a) the date;
(b) the name, **ADDRESS**, and telephone number of the appraiser;
(c) the purpose of the appraisal;
(d) the identity of each **DOCUMENT** evidencing the appraisal and the name, **ADDRESS,** and telephone number of each **PERSON** who has it.

☐ 75.8 Was any condition requiring repair or correction at the **PROPERTY** or **RENTAL UNIT** caused by defendent or other occupant of the **RENTAL UNIT** or their guests? If so, state:
(a) the type and location of condition;
(b) the kind of corrections or repairs needed;
(c) how and when you learned of these conditions;
(d) how and when these conditions were caused;
(e) the name, **ADDRESS**, and telephone number of each **PERSON** who caused these conditions;

DISC-003/UD-106

[See also section 71.0 for additional questions.]

76.0 Waiver, Change, Withdrawal, or Cancellation of Notice to Quit

[If a defense is based on waiver, change, withdrawal, or cancellation of the NOTICE TO QUIT, then either party may ask any applicable question in this section.]

☐ 76.1 Did the PLAINTIFF or LANDLORD or anyone acting on his or her behalf do anything which is alleged to have been a waiver, change, withdrawal, or cancellation of the NOTICE TO QUIT? If so:
(a) state the facts supporting this allegation;
(b) state the names, ADDRESSES, and telephone numbers of all PERSONS who have knowledge of these facts;
(c) identify each DOCUMENT that supports the facts;

☐ 76.2 Did the PLAINTIFF or LANDLORD accept rent which covered a period after the date for vacating the RENTAL UNIT as specified in the NOTICE TO QUIT? If so:
(a) state the facts;
(b) state the names, ADDRESSES, and telephone numbers of all PERSONS who have knowledge of the facts;
(c) identify each DOCUMENT that supports the facts and state the name, ADDRESS, and telephone number of each PERSON who has it.

77.0 Retaliation and Arbitrary Discrimination

[If a defense is based on retaliation or arbitrary discrimination, then either party may ask any applicable question in this section.]

☐ 77.1 State all reasons that the NOTICE TO QUIT was served or that defendant's tenancy was not renewed and for each reason
(a) state all facts supporting PLAINTIFF'S decision to terminate or not renew defendant's tenancy;
(b) state the names, ADDRESSES, and telephone numbers of all PERSONS who have knowledge of the facts;
(c) identify all DOCUMENTS that support the facts and state the name, ADDRESS, and telephone number of each PERSON who has it.

78.0 Nonperformance of the Rental Agreement by Landlord

[If a defense is based on nonperformance of the rental agreement by the LANDLORD or someone acting on the LANDLORD'S behalf, then either party may ask any applicable question in this section.]

☐ 78.1 Did the LANDLORD or anyone acting on the LANDLORD'S behalf agree to make repairs, alterations, or improvements at any time or provide services to the PROPERTY or RENTAL UNIT? If so, for each agreement state:
(a) the substance of the agreement;
(b) when it was made;
(c) whether it was written or oral;
(d) by whom and to whom;
(e) the name and ADDRESS of each person who knows about it;
(f) whether all promised repairs, alterations, or improvements were completed or services provided;
(g) the reasons for any failure to perform;
(h) the identity of each DOCUMENT evidencing the agreement or promise and the name ADDRESS, and telephone number of each PERSON who has it.

☐ 78.2 Has PLAINTIFF or LANDLORD or any resident of the PROPERTY ever committed disturbances or interfered with the quiet enjoyment of the RENTAL UNIT (including, for example, noise, acts which threaten the loss of title to the property or loss of financing, etc.)? If so, for each disturbance or interference, state:
(a) a description of each act;
(b) the date of each act;
(c) the name, ADDRESS, and telephone number of each PERSON who acted;
(d) the name, ADDRESS, and telephone number of each PERSON who witnessed each act and any DOCUMENTS evidencing the person's knowledge;
(e) what action was taken by the PLAINTIFF or LANDLORD to end or lessen the disturbance or interference.

79.0 Offer of Rent by Defendant

[If a defense is based on an offer of rent by a defendant which was refused, then either party may ask any applicable question in this section.]

☐ 79.1 Has defendant or anyone acting on the defendant's behalf offered any payments to PLAINTIFF which PLAINTIFF refused to accept? If so, for each offer state:
(a) the amount;
(b) the date;
(c) purpose of offer;
(d) the manner of the offer;
(e) the identity of the person making the offer;
(f) the identity of the person refusing the offer;
(g) the date of the refusal;
(h) the reasons for the refusal.

80.0 Deduction from Rent for Necessary Repairs

[If a defense to payment of rent or damages is based on claim of retaliatory eviction, then either party may ask any applicable question in this section. Additional questions in section 75.0 may also be applicable.]

☐ 80.1 Does defendant claim to have deducted from rent any amount which was withheld to make repairs after communication to the LANDLORD of the need for the repairs? If the answer is "no," do not answer interrogatories 80.2 through 80.6.

☐ 80.2 For each condition in need of repair for which a deduction was made, state:
(a) the nature of the condition;
(b) the location;
(c) the date the condition was discovered by defendant;
(d) the date the condition was first known by LANDLORD or PLAINTIFF.

(e) the dates and methods of each notice to the **LANDLORD** or **PLAINTIFF** of the condition;

(f) the response or action taken by the **LANDLORD** or **PLAINTIFF** to each notification;

(g) the cost to remedy the condition and how the cost was determined;

(h) the identity of any bids obtained for the repairs and any **DOCUMENTS** evidencing the bids.

[ ] 80.3 Did **LANDLORD** or **PLAINTIFF** fail to respond within a reasonable time after receiving a communication of a need for repair? If so, for each communication state:

(a) the date it was made;

(b) how it was made;

(c) the response and date;

(d) why the delay was unreasonable.

[ ] 80.4 Was there an insufficient period specified or actually allowed between the time of notification and the time repairs were begun by defendant to allow **LANDLORD** or **PLAINTIFF** to make the repairs? If so, state all facts on which the claim of insufficiency is based.

[ ] 80.5 Does **PLAINTIFF** contend that any of the items for which rent deductions were taken were not allowable under law? If so, for each item state all reasons and facts on which you base your contention.

[ ] 80.6 Has defendant vacated or does defendant anticipate vacating the **RENTAL UNIT** because repairs were requested and not made within a reasonable time? If so, state all facts on which defendant justifies having vacated the RENTAL UNIT or anticipates vacating the rental unit.

81.0 Fair Market Rental Value

*[If defendant denies **PLAINTIFF** allegation on the fair market rental value of the **RENTAL UNIT**, then either party may ask any applicable question in this section. If defendant claims that the fair market rental value is less because of a breach of warranty to provide habitable premises, then either party may also ask any applicable question in section 75.0.]*

[ ] 81.1 Do you have an opinion on the fair market rental value of the **RENTAL UNIT**? If so, state:

(a) the substance of your opinion;

(b) the factors upon which the fair market rental value is based;

(c) the method used to calculate the fair market rental value.

[ ] 81.2 Has any other **PERSON** ever expressed to you an opinion on the fair market rental value of the **RENTAL UNIT**? If so, for each **PERSON**:

(a) state the name, **ADDRESS**, and telephone number;

(b) state the substance of the **PERSON'S** opinion;

(c) describe the conversation or identify all **DOCUMENTS** in which the **PERSON** expressed an opinion and state the name, **ADDRESS**, and telephone number of each **PERSON** who has each **DOCUMENT**.

[ ] 81.3 Do you know of any current violations of state or local building codes, housing codes, or health codes, conditions of delapidation or other conditions in need of repair in the **RENTAL UNIT** or common areas that have affected the **RENTAL UNIT** at any time defendant has been in possession? If so, state:

(a) the conditions in need of repair;

(b) the kind of repairs needed;

(c) the name, ADDRESS, and telephone number of each PERSON who caused these conditions.

SETTLEMENT AGREEMENT

1. _____ ("tenant")

resides at the following premises: _____

_____ ("premises").

2. _____ ("landlord")

 is the owner of the premises.

3. On _____, 20_____ landlord caused a Summons and Complaint

in unlawful detainer to be served on tenant. The complaint was filed in the Superior Court for the County of

_____, _____ District, and carries

the following civil number:_____ .

4. Landlord and tenant agree that tenant shall vacate the premises on or before _____ ,

20_____ . In exchange for this agreement, and upon full performance by tenant, landlord agrees to file a voluntary

dismissal with prejudice of the Complaint specified in clause #3.

5. Also in exchange for tenant's agreement to vacate the premises on or before the date specified in clause #4,

landlord agrees to:

(*Choose one or more of the following*)

☐ Forgive all past due rent

☐ Forgive past due rent in the following amount: $_____

☐ Pay the tenant $_____ to cover tenant's moving expenses, new deposit requirements and

other incidentals related to the tenant moving out.

6. Any sum specified in clause #5 to be paid by the landlord shall be paid as follows:

(*Choose one or more of the following*)

☐ Upon tenant surrendering the keys to the premises

☐ Upon the signing of this agreement

☐ $_____ upon the signing of this agreement and $_____ upon tenant

surrendering the keys

☐ in the following manner:

1 7. The tenant's security deposit being held by landlord shall be handled as follows:

2   ☐ Upon the signing of this agreement

3   ☐ restored in full to the tenant upon surrender of the keys

4   ☐ treated according to law

5   ☐ other:

6 8. Tenant and landlord also agree:

7   a) to waive all claims and demands that each may have against the other for any transaction directly or

8 indirectly arising from their Landlord-Tenant relationship

9   b) that this settlement agreement not be construed as reflecting on the merits of the dispute and

10   c) that landlord shall not make any negative representations to any credit reporting agency or to any other

11 person or entity seeking information about whether tenant was a good or bad tenant.

12   9. Time is of the essence in this agreement. If tenant fails to timely comply with this agreement, landlord may

13 immediately rescind this agreement in writing and proceed with his or her legal and equitable remedies.

14   10. This agreement was executed on _____ , _____ at

15 _____ .

16

17   Signed: _____

18   _____

19   Signed: _____

20   _____

21

22

23

24

25

26

27

28

1

2

3

4 Defendant in Pro Per

5

6

7

8 SUPERIOR COURT OF THE STATE OF CALIFORNIA, COUNTY OF _____

9 _____ DIVISION/BRANCH

10   )

11 _____ ,)   Case No._____

12 _____ ,)
          Plaintiff(s),   )   DEMAND FOR JURY TRIAL

13 v.   )

14 _____ ,)

15 _____ ,)

16   Defendant(s).   )
_____)

17

18   To the clerk of the above-entitled court:

19   Defendant(s) hereby demand a jury trial in this action.

20

21 Dated: _____   _____

22

23

24

25

26

27

28

1

2

3

4   Defendant in Pro Per

5

6

7

8   SUPERIOR COURT OF THE STATE OF CALIFORNIA, COUNTY OF _____

9   _____ DIVISION/BRANCH

10   )
       _____,) Case No._____
11   )
       _____,)
12   Plaintiff(s),   ) APPLICATION AND DECLARATION
)
13   v.   ) FOR RELIEF FROM EVICTION
)
14   _____,)
)
15   _____,)
            Defendant(s).   ) (Code of Civil Procedure Secs. 1174(c), 1179)
16   _____)

17

18   Defendant(s) _____

19   _____ ,

20   hereby apply for relief from eviction, after judgment for plaintiff in this action.

21   If Defendants are evicted, they will suffer hardship in the following way(s): _____

22   _____

23   _____ .

24   Defendants are willing and able to pay all money they presently owe to Plaintiff, as a condition to this

25   application being granted. Defendants are also willing and able to pay the rent as it comes due in the future.

26   I declare under penalty of perjury that the above statements are true and correct to the best of my

27   knowledge.

28   Dated: _____   _____

©nolo NOLO

1 Name:
   Address:
2
   Phone:
3
4 Defendant in Pro Per
5
6
7
8 SUPERIOR COURT OF THE STATE OF CALIFORNIA, COUNTY OF _____
9 _____ DIVISION/BRANCH
10   )
                                                ,) Case No._____
11 _____   )
                                                ,)
12 _____   )
              Plaintiff(s),   ) ORDER GRANTING RELIEF
)
13 v.   ) FROM EVICTION
)
14 _____   ,)
)
15 _____   ,)
              Defendant(s).   )
16 _____   )

17

18   Defendant's motion for Relief From Eviction came on for hearing in Department _____ of the

19 above-entitled Court on _____ , _____ , said defendant appearing in

20 pro per and Plaintiff(s) appearing by _____ .

21 The matter having been argued and submitted,

22   IT IS HEREBY ORDERED that Defendant's Application for Relief From Eviction is granted at the following date

23 and time: _____ .

24

25 Dated: _____   _____
                                            Judge of the Superior Court
26

27

28

1

2

3

4   Defendant in Pro Per

5

6

7

8   SUPERIOR COURT OF THE STATE OF CALIFORNIA, COUNTY OF _____

9   _____ DIVISION/BRANCH

10   )
)   Case No._____
11   _____ ,)
)
12   _____ ,)
              Plaintiff(s),   )   APPLICATION AND DECLARATION
)
13   v.   )   FOR STAY OF EVICTION
)
14   _____ ,)
)
15   _____ ,)
              Defendant(s).   )
16   _____)

17

18   Defendant(s) _____

19   _____ hereby apply

20   for stay of execution from any writ of restitution or possession in this case, for the following period of time:

21   _____ .

22   Such a stay is appropriate in this case for the following reason(s): _____

23   _____

24   _____ .

25   I declare under penalty of perjury that the above statements are true and correct to the best of my

26   knowledge.

27

28   Dated: _____   _____

Handwritten note (top right): See Exparte for stay of eviction oA Law Library Thumbnail/flash drive

1   Name:
       Address:

2

       Phone:

3

4   Defendant in Pro Per

5

6

7

8   SUPERIOR COURT OF THE STATE OF CALIFORNIA, COUNTY OF _____

9   _____ DIVISION/BRANCH

10   )

   _____,)   Case No._____

11   )

   _____,)

12   Plaintiff(s),   )   ORDER GRANTING STAY OF EVICTION

)

13   v.   )

)

14   _____,)

)

15   _____,)

          Defendant(s).   )

16   _____)

17

18   Defendant's motion for Stay of Eviction came on for hearing in Department _____ of the above-

19   entitled Court on _____ , _____ , said defendant appearing in pro per

20   and Plaintiff(s) appearing by_____.

21   The matter having been argued and submitted,

22   IT IS HEREBY ORDERED that Defendant's Application for Stay of Eviction is Granted.

23

24   Dated: _____   _____

                                                            Judge of the Superior Court

25

26

27

28

1

2

3

4   Defendant in Pro Per

5

6

7

8   SUPERIOR COURT OF THE STATE OF CALIFORNIA, COUNTY OF _____

9   _____ DIVISION/BRANCH

10   )
)
11 _____,) Case No._____
)
12 _____,)
            Plaintiff(s),   ) NOTICE OF APPEAL AND NOTICE
)
13 v.   ) TO PREPARE CLERK'S TRANSCRIPT
)
14 _____,)
)
15 _____,)
            Defendant(s).   )
16 _____)

17

18 Defendant(s) _____

19 _____ hereby appeal to the Appellate Department

20 of the Superior Court.

21   Defendant(s) hereby request that a Clerk's Transcript be prepared, and that this transcript include all

22 documents filed in this action and all minute orders and other rulings and judgments issued by the court in this

23 action.

24

25 Dated: _____   _____

26

27

28

CLAIMANT OR CLAIMANT'S ATTORNEY *(Name and Address)*:	TELEPHONE NO.:	*FOR COURT USE ONLY*

ATTORNEY FOR *(Name)*:

NAME OF COURT:

STREET ADDRESS:

MAILING ADDRESS:

CITY AND ZIP CODE:

BRANCH NAME:

PLAINTIFF:

DEFENDANT:

CLAIM OF RIGHT TO POSSESSION AND NOTICE OF HEARING	CASE NUMBER:

Complete this form only if ALL of these statements are true:

1. **You are NOT named in the accompanying form called Writ of Possession.**
2. **You occupied the premises on or before the date the unlawful detainer (eviction) action was filed.** *(The date is in the accompanying Writ of Possession.)*
3. **You still occupy the premises.**
4. **A Prejudgment Claim of Right to Possession form was NOT served with the Summons and Complaint.**

NOTICE TO LEVYING OFFICER:

☐ Claim granted ☐ Claim denied

Clerk, by _____

(For levying officer use only)

Completed form was received on

Date: _____ Time: _____

By: _____

I DECLARE THE FOLLOWING UNDER PENALTY OF PERJURY:

1. My name is *(specify)*:

2. I reside at *(street address, unit No., city and ZIP code)*:

3. The address of "the premises" subject to this claim is *(address)*:

4. On *(insert date)*: [_____], the landlord or the landlord's authorized agent filed a complaint to recover possession of the premises. *(This date is in the accompanying Writ of Possession.)*

5. I occupied the premises on the date the complaint was filed *(the date in item 4)*. I have continued to occupy the premises ever since.

6. I was at least 18 years of age on the date the complaint was filed *(the date in item 4)*.

7. I claim a right to possession of the premises because I occupied the premises on the date the complaint was filed *(the date in item 4)*.

8. I was not named in the Writ of Possession.

9. I understand that if I make this claim of possession, a COURT HEARING will be held to decide whether my claim will be granted.

10. *(Filing fee)* To obtain a court hearing on my claim, I understand that after I present this form to the levying officer I must go to the court and pay a filing fee of $ _____ or file with the court the form "Application for Waiver of Court Fees and Costs." I understand that if I don't pay the filing fee or file the form for waiver of court fees *within two court days*, the court will immediately deny my claim.

11. *(Immediate court hearing unless you deposit 15 days' rent)* To obtain a court hearing on my claim, I understand I must also deliver to the court a copy of this completed claim form or a receipt from the levying officer. I also understand the date of my hearing will be set immediately if I don't deliver to the court an amount equal to 15 days' rent.

(Continued on reverse)

CLAIM OF RIGHT TO POSSESSION AND NOTICE OF HEARING Code of Civil Procedure, §§ 715.010, 715.020, 1174.3

PLAINTIFF *(Name):*	CASE NUMBER:
DEFENDANT *(Name):*	

12. I am filing my claim in the following manner *(check the box that shows how you are filing your claim. Note that you must deliver to the court a copy of the claim form or a levying officer's receipt):*

a. ☐ *(With 15 days' rent payment)* I presented this claim form to the sheriff, marshal, or other levying officer, AND within two court days I shall deliver to the court the following: (1) a copy of this completed claim form or a receipt, (2) the court filing fee or form for proceeding in forma pauperis, and (3) an amount equal to 15 days' rent. — OR —

b. ☐ *(Without 15 days' rent payment)* I presented this claim form to the sheriff, marshal, or other levying officer, AND within two court days I shall deliver to the court the following: (1) a copy of this completed claim form or a receipt, and (2) the court filing fee or form for proceeding in forma pauperis.

IMPORTANT: Do not take a copy of this claim form to the court unless you have first given the form to the sheriff, marshal, or other levying officer.

(To be completed by the court)			
Date of hearing:	Time:	Dept. or Div.:	Room:
Address of court:			

NOTICE: If you fail to appear at this hearing you will be evicted without further hearing.

13. **Rental agreement.** I have *(check all that apply to you):*

a. ☐ an oral rental agreement with the landlord.

b. ☐ a written rental agreement with the landlord.

c. ☐ an oral rental agreement with a person other than the landlord.

d. ☐ a written rental agreement with a person other than the landlord.

e. ☐ other *(explain):*

I declare under penalty of perjury under the laws of the State of California that the foregoing is true and correct.

WARNING: Perjury is a felony punishable by imprisonment in the state prison.

Date:

▶

. . . .

(TYPE OR PRINT NAME)	(SIGNATURE OF CLAIMANT)

NOTICE: If your claim to possession is found to be valid, the unlawful detainer (eviction) action against you will be determined at trial. At trial, you may be found liable for rent, costs, and, in some cases, treble damages.

—NOTICE TO OCCUPANTS—

YOU MUST ACT AT ONCE if all the following are true:

1. You are NOT named in the accompanying form called Writ of Possession.

2. You occupied the premises on or before the date the unlawful detainer (eviction) action was filed. *(The date is in the accompanying Writ of Possession.)*

3. You still occupy the premises.

4. A Prejudgment Claim of Right to Possession form was NOT served with the Summons and Complaint.

You can complete and SUBMIT THIS CLAIM FORM *(in person with identification)*

(1) before the date of eviction at the sheriff's or marshal's office located at *(address):*

(2) OR at the premises at the time of the eviction. *(Give this form to the officer who comes to evict you.)*

If you do not complete and submit this form (and pay a filing fee or file the form for proceeding in forma pauperis if you cannot pay the fee), YOU WILL BE EVICTED along with the parties named in the writ.

After this form is properly filed, A HEARING WILL BE HELD to decide your claim. If you do not appear at the hearing, you will be evicted without a further hearing.

Index

Exterminators

for bedbugs, 180–182

for insects, vermin, and rodents, 22

Extreme hardship, evictions postponed due to, 272, 274

F

FACT (Fair and Accurate Credit Transaction), Disposal Rule, 20–21

Fair Credit Reporting Act, 20

Fair Debt Collection Practices Act, 227

Fair Employment and Housing Act, 84, 87–88, 91

Families with children

condominium conversion assistance, 284

discrimination against, 84, 86, 88–89

Family day care homes, 14

Federal Communications Commission (FCC)

landlord violations of satellite rules, 139

Over-the-Air Reception Devices Rule, 138–140

website, 141

Federal Fair Housing Act, 84

Federal Telecommunications Act, 137

Federal Trade Commission (FTC), FACT Act, 20–21

Fees

agreement provisions, 9

credit-check and screening, 18–19

finder's, 18

relocation, 67

See also Attorney fees

Fireplaces, State Housing Law, 103

Fire safety inspections/violations, 23–24, 112

Fit and habitable

constructive evictions and, 117–118

court decisions, 106–107

health, safety, or property risks, 105, 152–153

industry/local codes, 105–106, 122, 123

state statutes, 102, 256, 271

Fixed-Term Residential Lease, Appendix A

Fixtures, ownership of, 134

Foreclosures

evictions and, 82, 229, 231–236, 260

security deposits and, 211

Forfeiture of property, criminal activities and, 193

Form Interrogatories—Unlawful Detainer, Appendix A

Forms

from Nolo Press, 8

online, Judicial Council, 254, Appendix A

for rental/lease agreements, 7

tear-out, Appendix A

Fremont

rent control ordinances, 58, 66

vacancy decontrol, 67

Furnished units, security deposits and, 208

Furnishings, agreement provisions, 8

G

Garbage facilities, 22, 23, 103, 107

Glendale

just cause evictions, 53, 67, 230

rent control ordinances, 58, 67

vacancy decontrol, 67

Government-subsidized programs

discrimination against recipients of, 85

eviction notice requirements, 38

just cause evictions and, 73

rent increases, 7, 47

rent withholding procedures, 114

Section 8 housing, 47

termination notices, 229

Ground fault circuit interrupters, 106

Guests

agreement provisions, 11, 14, 41

distinguished from roommates, 41

relationship with landlord, 41

unduly restrictive rules, 14, 100

See also Roommates

"Guidance on the Lead-Based Paint Disclosure Rule" (HUD), 172

H

Habitability standards, implied warranty, 102, 106, 256, 271

See also Fit and habitable

Hayward

interest on security deposits, 216

just cause evictions, 52, 68–69, 230

rent control ordinances, 52, 58, 67–68

vacancy decontrol, 68

Health inspectors

privacy rights and, 98–99

reporting violations to, 112, 222

security assistance, 197

Hearing officers, rent control board, 55–57

overview, 269
  Request to Set Case for Trial, 269
Two-plus-one rule, 88
Typing services, 288–289

U

Uniform Housing Code, fit and habitable statutes, 105–106, 256, 271
United States Code, abbreviations, 2
United States Toxic Mold Safety and Protection Act, 177
Unlawful detainers
  Answer, 254–261, Appendix A
  defined, 236
  Form Interrogatories—Unlawful Detainer, Appendix A
  improper, 248
  landlord complaints, 60
  rent control and, 80
  Settlement of Unlawful Detainer Action, 266–267
  See also Eviction procedures/lawsuits
Unruh Civil Rights Act, 84, 85–86, 87
Untenantable state of premises, 271
U.S. Civil Rights Act, 84
U.S. Department of Housing and Urban Development. *See* HUD
Utilities
  as carbon monoxide source, 174–176
  cut-offs by landlord, 221–222
  fit and habitable statutes, 102, 105
  plumbing inspections, 22
  specified in rental agreements, 9
  telephone jacks, 106
  trash/garbage facilities, 22, 23, 103, 107
  wiring/electricity safety, 22, 23–24

V

Vacancy decontrol
  for apartments, 59
  Berkeley, 60
  Beverly Hills, 62
  Campbell, 64
  East Palo Alto, 64
  Fremont, 67
  Glendale, 67
  Hayward, 68

Los Angeles, 70
  Los Gatos, 71
  Oakland, 72
  overview, 50
  Palm Springs, 72
  San Diego, 74
  San Francisco, 75
  San Jose, 77
  Santa Monica, 77–78
  Thousand Oaks, 79
  West Hollywood, 80
Vacation rentals, 87–88
Ventilation
  mold control role, 177–179
  State Housing Law, 22

W

Wages, lost due to injuries, 155
Waiver of right to appeal, agreement provisions, 13
Waiver of right to jury trial, agreement provisions, 13
Waiver of right to legal notice, agreement provisions, 12
Waivers of self-help repair rights, agreement provisions, 12–14
Warranty of habitability, implied, 102, 106, 256, 271
Water damage, 21, 102, 176–179
Water-filled furniture, 15, 208
Waterproofing/weather protection, 21, 102
Water supply, 22, 102
Wear and tear vs. damage, 107, 209
Weatherproof, defined, 21
West Hollywood
  condominium conversion ordinances, 282
  just cause evictions, 80–82, 230
  rent control ordinances, 53, 59, 80
  vacancy decontrol, 80
Westlake Village, rent control ordinances, 82
Windows, landlord responsibility for, 123
Witnesses
  to condition of unit at move-out, 212, 217
  to injuries on premises, 145–146
Writs of possession, evictions and, 274, 276

Y

Yards, as location priority, 6, 10

Online Legal Forms

Nolo offers a large library of legal solutions and forms, created by Nolo's in-house legal staff. These reliable documents can be prepared in minutes.

Online Legal Solutions

- **Incorporation.** Incorporate your business in any state.
- **LLC Formations.** Gain asset protection and pass-through tax status in any state.
- **Wills.** Nolo has helped people make over 2 million wills. Is it time to make or revise yours?
- **Living Trust (avoid probate).** Plan now to save your family the cost, delays, and hassle of probate.
- **Trademark.** Protect the name of your business or product.
- **Provisional Patent.** Preserve your rights under patent law and claim "patent pending" status.

Online Legal Forms

Nolo.com has hundreds of top quality legal forms available for download—bills of sale, promissory notes, nondisclosure agreements, LLC operating agreements, corporate minutes, commercial lease and sublease, motor vehicle bill of sale, consignment agreements and many, many more.

Review Your Documents

Many lawyers in Nolo's consumer-friendly lawyer directory will review Nolo documents for a very reasonable fee. Check their detailed profiles at **www.nolo.com/lawyers/index.html**.

NOLO® *Law for All*

Find a Tenant's Attorney

- *Qualified lawyers*
- *In-depth profiles*
- *Respectful service*

When you want help to deal with your landlord, you don't want just any lawyer—you want an expert in the field, who can provide up-to-the-minute advice to help you protect your rights. You need a lawyer who has the experience and knowledge to answer your questions about leases, evictions, rent control, security and privacy issues, and all other legal issues that tenants encounter.

Nolo's Lawyer Directory is unique because it provides an extensive profile of every lawyer. You'll learn about not only each lawyer's education, professional history, legal specialties, credentials and fees, but also about their philosophy of practicing law and how they like to work with clients. It's all crucial information when you're looking for someone to trust with an important personal issue.

All lawyers listed in Nolo's directory are in good standing with their state bar association. They all pledge to work diligently and respectfully with clients—communicating regularly, providing a written agreement about how legal matters will be handled, sending clear and detailed bills, and more. And many directory lawyers will review Nolo documents, such as a lease, will, or living trust, for a fixed fee, to help you get the advice you need.

www.lawyers.nolo.com

The attorneys shown above are fictitious. Any resemblance to an actual attorney is purely coincidental.